Iranian Culture in Bahram
Beyzaie's Cinema and Theatre

Iranian Culture in Bahram Beyzaie's Cinema and Theatre

Paradigms of Being and Belonging (1959–79)

Saeed Talajooy

I.B.TAURIS
LONDON · NEW YORK · OXFORD · NEW DELHI · SYDNEY

I.B. TAURIS
Bloomsbury Publishing Plc
50 Bedford Square, London, WC1B 3DP, UK
1385 Broadway, New York, NY 10018, USA
29 Earlsfort Terrace, Dublin 2, Ireland

BLOOMSBURY, I.B. TAURIS and the I.B. Tauris logo are trademarks of
Bloomsbury Publishing Plc

First published in Great Britain 2023
This paperback edition published 2025

Copyright © Saeed Talajooy 2023

Saeed Talajooy has asserted his right under the Copyright, Designs and Patents Act, 1988, to be identified as Author of this work.

For legal purposes the Acknowledgements on p. viii constitute an extension of this copyright page.

Cover design by Adriana Brioso
Cover image: Beyzaie's *The Crow* (1977), photograph by Aziz Saati.

All rights reserved. No part of this publication may be reproduced or transmitted in any form or by any means, electronic or mechanical, including photocopying, recording, or any information storage or retrieval system, without prior permission in writing from the publishers.

Bloomsbury Publishing Plc does not have any control over, or responsibility for, any third-party websites referred to or in this book. All internet addresses given in this book were correct at the time of going to press. The author and publisher regret any inconvenience caused if addresses have changed or sites have ceased to exist, but can accept no responsibility for any such changes.

A catalogue record for this book is available from the British Library.

A catalog record for this book is available from the Library of Congress.

ISBN: HB: 978-0-7556-4866-5
PB: 978-0-7556-4870-2
ePDF: 978-0-7556-4867-2
eBook: 978-0-7556-4868-9

Typeset by Deanta Global Publishing Services, Chennai, India

To find out more about our authors and books visit www.bloomsbury.com and sign up for our newsletters.

Contents

List of illustrations vi
Acknowledgements viii

1 Bahram Beyzaie's contour in time: Analysing the travels and travails of an artist to extract a theory of creativity 1
2 The Puppet Trilogy (1962–3): Deconstruction of the hero/villain binary 37
3 *Uncle Moustache* (1970): Carnivalesque deconstruction of hegemonic masculinity 71
4 *Downpour* (1971–2): The reformist intellectual and the meta-cinematic subversion of hegemonic masculinity 91
5 *The Journey* (1972): A Sisyphean quest for belonging in a world of toxic masculinity, violence and blind obedience 133
6 *Stranger and the Fog* (1974): Rituals of existence: Homecoming, becoming and departing 155
7 *The Crow* (1977): City, home and the pitfalls of Iranian modernity 193
8 Conclusion: In dialogue with time 237

Notes 243
Bibliography 256
Index 269

Illustrations

Tables

1.1	The Political Eras and Their Reflections in Beyzaie's Major Creative Works	28
1.2	The Recurrence of Expressive Moods in Various Eras	31

Figures

2.1	Hero refuses to kill Demon (Hamid Amjad's Collection)	59
2.2	Brochure of Abbas Javanmard's staging of *Sunset* and *Tale* (Hamid Amjad's Collection)	69
3.1	Screenshots from *Uncle Moustache*. Minutes 2′–14′.30″	82
3.2	Screenshots from *Uncle Moustache*. Minutes 14′.30″–19′.30″	85
3.3	Screenshots from *Uncle Moustache*. Minutes 19′.30″–29′	86
4.1	The cycle reflecting how patriarchy reproduces itself	93
4.2	Screenshots from *Downpour*. Minutes 3′–9′	99
4.3	Screenshots from *Downpour*. Minutes 10′–15′	100
4.4	Screenshots from *Downpour*. Minutes 15′.30″–24′.30″	102
4.5	Screenshots from *Downpour*. Minutes 25′–26′.10″	103
4.6	Screenshots from *Downpour*. Minutes 26′.10″–26′.40″	104
4.7	Screenshots from *Downpour*. Minutes 33′.30″–43′.40″	108
4.8	Screenshots from *Downpour*. Minutes 54′.40″–65′.30″	112
4.9	Screenshots from *Downpour*. Minutes 69′.20″–85′.30″	118
4.10	Screenshots from *Downpour*. Minutes 89′.20″–102′.30″	122
4.11	Screenshots from *Downpour*. Minutes 103′.30″–106′.30″	123
4.12	Screenshots from *Downpour*. Minutes 106′.40″–115′.30″	126
4.13	Screenshots from *Downpour*. Minutes 116′.40″–124′.14″	128
5.1	Screenshots from *The Journey*. Minutes 0′.30″–4′.30″	138
5.2	Screenshots from *The Journey*. Minutes 6′.30″–8′.30″	140
5.3	Screenshots from *The Journey*. Minutes 8′.55″–13′.55″	141
5.4	Screenshots from *The Journey*. Minutes 14′.15″–15′.35″	142
5.5	Screenshots from *The Journey*. Minutes 15′.40″–19′.10″	144
5.6	Screenshots from *The Journey*. Minutes 20′.05″–21′.25″	145
5.7	Screenshots from *The Journey*. Minutes 21′.30″–22′.35″	147
5.8	Screenshots from *The Journey*. Minutes 23′.20″–25′.20″	148
5.9	Screenshots from *The Journey*. Minutes 25′.30″–28′.35″	150
5.10	Screenshots from *The Journey*. Minutes 30′.15″–32′.40″	153

6.1	Screenshots from *Stranger and the Fog*. Minutes 1′.40″–13′.55″	161
6.2	Screenshots from *Stranger and the Fog*. Minutes 16′.50″–37′.05″	165
6.3	Screenshots from *Stranger and the Fog*. Minutes 38′.50″–44′.50″	169
6.4	Screenshots from *Stranger and the Fog*. Minutes 45′.00″–55′.30″	172
6.5	Screenshots from *Stranger and the Fog*. Minutes 56′.40″–75′.30″	176
6.6	Screenshots from *Stranger and the Fog*. Minutes 78′.45″–84′.40″	182
6.7	Screenshots from *Stranger and the Fog*. Minutes 85′.30″–112′.40″	185
6.8	Screenshots from *Stranger and the Fog*. Minutes 114′.10″–139′.20″	188
7.1	Screenshots from *The Crow*. Minutes 2′.10″–13′.55″	206
7.2	Screenshots from *The Crow*. Minutes 14′.50″–28′.40″	210
7.3	Screenshots from *The Crow*. Minutes 30′.40″–34′.35″	213
7.4	Screenshots from *The Crow*. Minutes 35′.30″–44′.45″	216
7.5	Screenshots from *The Crow*. Minutes 49′.30″–64′.40″	220
7.6	Screenshots from *The Crow*. Minutes 66′.50″–77′.25″	226
7.7	Screenshots from *The Crow*. Minutes 77′.25″–94′.30″	230
7.8	Screenshots from *The Crow*. Minutes 95′.40″–108′.05″	232

Acknowledgements

First and Foremost, I would like to express my gratitude to Bahram Beyzaie for his patience and exemplary precision in responding to my questions during my research and to Mojdeh Shamsaie for her support whenever my research required an interview with Bahram Beyzaie.

Special mention is also due for the invaluable backing that I received from my friends, colleagues and relatives, Hamid Amjad, Jila Esmailian, Nagmeh Samini, Ali Ansari, Siavush Randjbar-Daemi, Mehdi Talajooy, Shaghayegh Talajooy, Ehsan Omidvar, Amir Hossein Siadat, Parviz Jahed, Yasmin Barghi and Hamed Sarrafi, who supported my vision, provided me with the photos, films, books, interviews and articles that I did not have or helped me identify the best photo options for the cover. Of equal importance were also the contributions of my wife, Parmis Mozafari, who read and commented on some sections of this book, and my daughter, Baran, and son, Bijhan, who provided positive comments and emotional support.

Of special value to my long-term research on Iranian drama and cinema have also been the vibrant research environments of the institutions that I have studied and taught at in the last three decades: Faculty of Foreign Languages at the University of Tehran, Department of English at the University of Allamah Tabatabaei, Workshop Theatre at the University of Leeds (particularly Professor Jane Plastow), the Mellon Programme at University College London, and the Faculty of Asian and Middle Eastern Studies at the University of Cambridge (particularly Professor Charles Melville and Dr Christine von Ruymbeke). The same goes with the multisided research cultures of the School of Modern Languages and the Institute of Iranian Studies at the University of St Andrews, which enabled me to sharpen my analytical tools in literary, dramatic, cinematic, cultural and historical studies.

Some aspects of my research on Iranian theatre and cinema, including Bahram Beyzaie's oeuvre, were also supported by two grants from The Honeyman Foundation and one from The British Institute of Persian Studies, which enabled me to launch a conference on Iranian Cultural Production in 2016 and a Workshop on Bahram Beyzaie's Cinema and Theatre in 2017 when Beyzaie came to St Andrews to receive his honorary doctorate for a lifetime of creative and scholarly contribution to Iranian culture.

Finally, I would also like to thank the reviewers and the editors whose comments contributed to improving the manuscript of this monograph, particularly Professor Nasrin Rahimieh, Dr Saeed Zeydabadi-Nejad, Mr Rory Gormley, Ms Yasmin Garcha and Mr Mohammad Raffi.

1

Bahram Beyzaie's contour in time

Analysing the travels and travails of an artist to extract a theory of creativity

Prologue: Knowing Bahram Beyzaie

Writing about Bahram Beyzaie (1938–), the Iranian playwright, filmmaker and scholar of global performing traditions and mythology, is a daunting task. His multisided character as an artist and scholar and the variety of cultural activities he has engaged in since 1958 have made him a cultural icon for Iranians. He combines analytical and scholarly knowledge of his and several other cultures with a literary genius characterized by the mastery of different registers and expressive tools of the Persian language representative of people from various walks of life in different historical eras and a visual genius that extracts several layers of suggestiveness from dramatic and cinematic situations in which objects, colours and sounds in background or foreground, work with the other elements to establish multi-layered dialogues with the viewers. This has resulted in several filmic masterpieces which have influenced three generations of Iranian filmmakers and dramatic masterworks whose trendsetting influence on modern Persian literature and drama transcends that of any other writers and playwrights. This is important as even now, at the age of 84, with sixty-four years of experience in experimenting with traditional and modern Iranian and non-Iranian forms in plays, films and filmscripts that have inspired many into becoming creative writers, artists or scholars, he is still teaching at Stanford University, while producing plays and publishing works that challenge the dominant discourses of Iranian cinema and theatre as well as political and religious establishments.

I first came to know Beyzaie in the summer of 1981. Two years earlier, my friends and I, a bunch of enthusiastic teenagers with idealistic dreams about the future of our revolution, had decided that we needed a library for our neighbourhood and had set up a library in the garage of the house of my friend, whose brother, a civil engineer, supported our plan. Within four months, we accumulated about 600 books and had more than seventy contributors and subscribers. The first year, from June 1979 to September 1980, was a success, but with our scattering into different senior high schools and Iraq's invasion of Iran in 1980 and the intensification of the conflicts between political parties and the Islamic state in 1981, the physical work involved and the politically charged idea of maintaining a library proved unwise, particularly because the Basiji students of our neighbourhood had started questioning our motives.[1] The library fell into disuse, and we began to dismantle it in the spring of 1981 just before the beginning of the armed struggles between the state and leftist political parties. There among the books that we had collected were a few plays that my friend's cousin, a university student, had given to our library. The generous man had other copies of them and did not want them back. The books would automatically go to our friend, but his father, due to the raids and arrests that had already started, did not want any of the books in his house. Happy to have more books, we, the three originators of the idea of the library, distributed them among ourselves, and I ended up with the oddest books I had ever seen so far, Gholamhossein Sa'edi's *Māh-e Asal* (Honeymoon, 1978) and Beyzaie's *Marg-e Yazdgerd* (Death of Yazdgerd, 1979).

To my 15-year-old mind, which had passed through the most stunning years of Pahlavi modernization (1971–8), the revolution, the raiding of the US embassy, the start of Iran-Iraq war and the early stages of the Islamist purging of dissenting groups, these plays were intriguing depictions of the inanity of living under secular or religious monarchy in a modern world. Yet, Beyzaie's play, with its symbolic ritualizations, dazzling language, role-playing games, uncertain identities, double seductions and ironic incantations, was an enigmatic *Blind Owlish* curiosity that I had to hold onto until I could 'properly' understand. Soon this play became even more intriguing because I found that the author of this say-it-all piece was the person whose films, *Amu Sibilu* (Uncle Moustache, 1970) and *Safar* (*The Journey*, 1972), I had already seen in *Kānun-e Parvaresh-e Fekri-e Kudakān va Nojavānān* (*Centre for the Intellectual Development of Children and Young Adults* (Kānun, 1965–). I began to follow his works closely along those of other Iranian and non-Iranian authors and filmmakers, and by the time I recovered from a seven-year disruption in my education in 1991 to embark on studying English Literature at the University of Tehran, I had seen all the films and read most of the plays he had published until then. He was one among many, but without knowing it, I had been influenced by Beyzaie more than others because most of my interests, literature, drama, cinema, history, psychology and mythology, had been enhanced while trying to comprehend the de-familiarizing, experimental forms he had created.

Time passed, and my immersion in world literatures in English disrupted my attention to the Iranian cultural products, but in 1998 when I was completing my MLitt thesis on Eugene O'Neill and Henrik Ibsen and writing performance reviews for drama journals, I saw his *Kārnāmeh-ye Bondār-e Bidakhsh* (The Account of Bondar the Premier), which ignited in me a new passion for conducting research on Iranian drama. The chance of doing so, however, never occurred until 2003, when I started my PhD on Wole Soyinka (1934–) in Leeds. Just three months into my research, I realized that my research was missing a Beyzaie link. The two masters of ritual drama and culturally charged sociopolitical and existential studies of human life had to be compared. This led to a detailed study of their works, which earned me a PhD. After finishing my PhD, I also published a few articles on Iranian dramatists and edited a *Special Issue of Iranian Studies* on Beyzaie, but I knew that I had a lot more to say about him and, thus, translated some of his plays, collected more sources and taught his works along other authors' works to prepare for this study, which I think has been long due.

I knew that the main challenge in fulfilling such a task was the organization of the book, but my writing gradually evolved to its present form, which combines material from my critical analysis of his works with his interviews and the secondary material about his oeuvre. The result is a two-volume book that despite all its deficiencies may function as a preface to the works of a creative intellectual who has played a unique role in the contemporary history of Iranian culture. Dedicating two volumes to the works of an author may seem excessive to some, but no one else in the history of modern Iranian cultural production has created more than a hundred full-length plays, screenplays and films about different aspects of Iranian culture, history and myths of which thirty can be ranked as masterpieces. This is particularly important as these two volumes are not just about Beyzaie but as much about more than fifty aspects of Iranian culture that Beyzaie has dealt with in his works and no one else has written about in English. Therefore, my intention, in these two volumes, is not to single out the points of power or deficiencies of Beyzaie's works to offer constructive, or non-constructive, reviews, but to analyse his works in the light of contemporary theory and identify their dialogue with various aspects of Iranian culture and detect the aesthetic and thematic contribution of Beyzaie's forms and the original forms and narrative that he has handled to world drama, literature and cinema. Due to the vast number of his works, I have had to limit my direct focus mainly on his film. Thus, after examining three of his 1960s plays in Chapter 2 to demonstrate the rise of his deconstructing emancipatory aesthetics, I dedicate each of my chapters to one of his films. Nevertheless, in each chapter, I also examine the evolution of the film's major forms and discourses in Iranian culture and in his other plays and filmscripts.

In my writing, when I analyse Beyzaie's plays, I use the term 'Beyzaie' as subject when discussing the motifs and 'the play' when analysing the meanings and functions that have been given to his plays in time. However, when analysing his films, due to their audio-visual presence, I use 'Beyzaie' as subject when the vision is clearly Beyzaie's, and 'the film' as subject when discussing an idea that may have evolved due to my own understanding of a motif or a quality that may have been included in the film due to Beyzaie's cooperation with his crew. This is because though writing plays or filmscripts is an individual endeavour and Beyzaie has been Iran's most influential writer in that front, making films or staging plays is a collective act that involves the labours and ideas of actors, set and costume designers, light and sound engineers, musicians and film editors. The importance of such artists is so that Dariush Farhang, a director, actor and costume designer, once stated that in Iranian cinema, 'except for Taqvaei and at a much higher level Beyzaie, no other directors have had the vision or the technical virtuosity required for a director's task', and thus, it has often been the cinematographers and technical crew who decided the required kinds of lighting, costume, camera angles or editing.[2] Though Farhang exaggerates the failures of other directors, his statements along Iraj Raminfar's and others in the field, about Beyzaie's thoroughness and positive impacts on the people with whom he has worked, give a glimpse of what the artists involved in such support technical activities do and what they think about Beyzaie.[3]

When Beyzaie began making films, Iranian cinema had already been evolving for several decades and functioned well as an industry with mainstream and alternative trends.[4] It had also given rise to several leading cinematographers, actors and directors. Farrokh Ghaffary's *South of the City* (1958) and *Night of the Hunchback* (1965), Ebrahim Golestan's *Brick and Mirror* (1965) and Darisuh Mehrjui's *The Cow* (1969) had also already started the cinematic tradition that is now known as the Iranian New Wave. With Beyzaie, however, the missing link of this space of alterity, modern indigenous filmic style, began to evolve. As Dariush Ashoori, the Iranian philosopher and Beyzaie's close high school friend, states, since his teenage years, Beyzaie watched films, often several times, and took notes to analyse how successful Western, Indian or Japanese directors framed their shots, set the angles of or moved their cameras, edited their rushes or made transitions.[5] As Raminfar, who was Beyzaie's set and costume designer for three decades, says, Beyzaie's imagination, memory, precision and technical knowledge were inspiring, and unlike many others, but like most leading directors at international levels, he produced his shooting scripts or staging directions in advance rather than leaving them to the time of shooting or rehearsal. Thus, in 1969, when Beyzaie started making films, his long-term fascination with cinematic expression and experience in writing on theatre and cinema and working with actors had prepared him for the task. Nevertheless, since the beginning of his career, his theatre background gave him the opportunity to work with the best practitioners and technicians of Iranian cinema and a team of dedicated artists who helped him fulfil his surrealistic visions. Indeed, though Beyzaie's film crew often compare working with him with going to university,[6] it is undeniable that the visual worlds of Beyzaie's films owe some of their qualities to such designers as Raminfar, cinematographers as Mehrdad Fakhimi and Asghar Rafi Jam or editors like Shamim Bahar. Thus, in my writing, I also reflect on the contributions of his film colleagues to his work.

Beyzaie as a decoder of neglected aspects of history and culture

Influential cultural products are products and producers of culture, with the mind of the artist working like a catalyst in the webs of intercultural and intracultural systems of signs hovering around producers and consumers living within or on the intersections of multiple axes of the networks of power relations and their corresponding fields of knowledge. Thus, the choices that artists make when dealing with words, images, events, characters, relationships and backgrounds may produce meanings that diverge from their conscious intentions. However, the potential meanings embedded in their signs or given to them by the following generations of spectators or readers are as important as those embodied at the time of production. In my analysis, therefore, though I explore the impacts of personal trauma on Beyzaie's narrative of selfhood, the reflections of this trauma in his characters and how this trauma may have triggered his desire for creativity and the impetus for creativity in his characters, my focus is to act like an ideal reader for the cultural discourses and potential interpretations that can be extracted from the totality of their motifs. I study Beyzaie, the man, and his works as intrinsically linked but separate cultural phenomena in the context of Iran's contemporary history to extract the origins, descents, emergence, forms, thematic structures, cultural functions and receptions of his works. In this context, I may refer to qualities that others have criticized or extoled, but in all cases my purpose is to offer in-depth analyses of his works rather than criticize them for having or not having certain qualities. In short, my purpose is to offer thick interdisciplinary descriptions of Beyzaie's oeuvre in all its functions, but without claiming that his works are the best of their kind or my studies are exhaustive.

In 1977, when Beyzaie had already established himself as one of the most innovative directors and playwrights of the modern indigenous-style Iranian drama, and had directed four successful films, Hagir Daryoush, a filmmaker and literary journalist, asked him about the sources of his inspiration and why he was concerned with reformulating indigenous dramatic forms. His response revealed a perspective that has remained true until now:

> D: I remember that you were also interested in theatre. I think you wrote articles about the roots of our theatre, and some wondered whether your aim was cinema or theatre.
> B: I did not choose theatre; theatre chose me. When it could not find anyone, it placed itself on my path with the bewildering plays of Shakespeare or Greek or Far East playwrights. I was not tricked until one day theatre revealed its beauty to me in a *ta'ziyeh* play that charmed my soul. This was when cinema had turned its back on me. [. . .] I felt I had to rise to its challenge, find the causes of its enchanting beauty and the reasons for my fascination. It made me aware of my paucity, aware of what I was. Suddenly, I became conscious of the abyss behind me, of the baseless grounds under my feet. I realized that my historical wounds cannot be healed or beautified with cosmetic borrowings from others and that my ancestral treasure had been hidden from me. I studied history and found myself heir to an immense world of atrocity and fear. Yet I gradually began to hear the voice of people, the voice of those who have not been mentioned in history. For four years I wrote exegeses on Iranian theatre tradition. Until that strange day when I realized that I myself had to create [. . .]. I sat down and wrote. It is now twenty years that I have been looking for my lost dreams.[7]

Beyzaie had noticed that the dominant tendency in artistic and theatre establishments, which were obsessed with the Western definitions of theatre, was to deny that Iran had a performing tradition. Thus, he dedicated the first decade of his work to reviving indigenous Iranian forms and introducing Asian theatre traditions to Iranian practitioners. Nevertheless, these lines also signify the foremost sources of his critical probing and thematic and formal creativity: myth, ritual performance, reformulating Iranian forms at aesthetic and thematic levels for a modern audience, anti-colonial and anti-mimicry creativity and creating alternative histories of marginalized people. In this context, the terms, 'anti-colonial' and 'anti-mimicry' need unpacking. Whereas up to the modern times, Iran had always been either a colonizer or a colonized country, in the modern era, it was never formally colonized. However, during the nineteenth and twentieth centuries, it suffered extreme forms of economic exploitation and lost some of its arable lands to the Russian and British empires. These issues triggered several anti-colonial discourses with positive and negative outcomes. The positive ones led to the reformist movements which initiated Iran's path towards modernity in the 1800s, but the negative ones became obsessed with blaming others for the failures of Iran at two fronts: (1) nationalists blaming the Greeks, Arabs, Turks and Mongols without analysing the internal failures that led to Iran's colonization by these invaders and (2) Islamists accusing the West and Westernized reformists without noticing how their obsession with religion had led to Iran's failures at several fronts. Beyzaie's works reflect one of the best approaches to these discourses because while remaining cosmopolitan in his eclectic inspection and reshaping of artistic techniques, he has been mainly concerned with modernizing Iranian artistic forms rather than imitating forms imported from the West. The same is true at their thematic levels because rather than blaming others for the failures of Iranian culture, he has been more concerned with identifying the failures that expose Iranians to internal tyrants and external invaders. In other words, instead of shouting at others or rejecting change, he has worked with several other artists to patiently recreate the artistic traditions of his own culture. This is important as the cultural arena of 1960s and 1970s Iran was inundated by those who were alienated from the realities of the culture due to their obsessions with Western, communist or Islamist discourses. The negative aspects of Iranian anti-colonial discourses had taken over and taking Iran headlong towards a revolution that brought Islamists to power.

Beyzaie's research on Iranian forms can also be linked to his concerns about the absence of a history of people, which he most recently reiterated in an interview with Hamid Dabashi, where he says, 'the greatest shortcoming we have in our country is the absence of a history of people'.[8] This position can be analysed with reference to Walter Benjamin's analysis of the task of historical materialists in contrast with chroniclers and historians of official discourses:

> without exception the cultural treasures [. . . that a historical materialist] surveys have an origin which he cannot contemplate without horror. They owe their existence not only to the efforts of the great minds and talents who have created them, but also to the anonymous toil of their contemporaries. *There is no document of civilization which is not at the same time a document of barbarism.* And just as such a document is not free of barbarism, barbarism taints also the manner in which it was transmitted from one owner to another. *A historical materialist therefore dissociates himself from it as far as possible. He regards it as his task to brush history against the grain.*[9]

This brushing involves using archival, artistic, literary and folk resources to reveal the silenced voices of 'the anonymous' majority who have lost power in the present. It confronts the official discourses that promote the idea of the causal progression of history towards 'the perfect present', or their equally reductive opposites that offer political alternatives without revealing how systematic distortion of history and culture produces dominant discourses.

The idea of constructing cultural histories based on material culture, folklore and sporadic historical evidence about the lives of people has its roots in the gradual deconstruction of sociocultural and political hierarchies towards the end of the eighteenth century in the process that Jacques Rancière calls the rise of 'the aesthetic regime of arts'.[10] The reconciliation of the opposite ends of social hierarchies within the same cultural space was, in fact, a common practice in informal literature before it became frequent in formal literature from the 1780s. However, it was its dominance in formal literature and its glorification in critical writings that lent its power to history and sociology in such approaches as *histoire des mentalités*, *Annales* or cultural anthropology, which found their micro-cultural forms in *Alltagsgeschichte* and other similar approaches to studying human lived experience.[11] Beyzaie's outlooks, therefore, are not unique in the context of the critical approaches of the last seventy years. They are, however, exceptional in their conscious probing and reformulating momentum through which Beyzaie has produced an impressive oeuvre and has set the stage for an artistic tradition which is in touch with the marginalized forms, narratives and people of Iran.

Two years later, in another interview with Iranian National TV, Beyzaie reiterated the same position with more references that suggest his deepening self-identification with a form of being Iranian that endeavours to decolonize the artistic life of the country.

> I search for forms of expression inspired by Iranian civilization: miniatures, myths, *ta'ziyeh* and *tamāshā* (comic forms). I am a carrier of these forms in the era I live in. All my works deal with Iranian history and culture and with what we can do with it at when the influence of western culture and civilization is felt in all areas of our lives.[12]

Beyzaie's anti-colonial tone is probably intensified here due to the revolutionary zeitgeist of the era. His statements, however, are accurate as his scholarly writing and his creative use of Iranian forms before and after this date had major impacts on the reformulation of Iranian art forms from the late 1950s. In fact, an inspection of his articles and books on Iranian, Chinese, Japanese and Indian performance traditions published during the 1960s shows that he was very systematic in his approach to bringing Iranian forms to the centre of modern Iranian theatre and cinema and introducing non-Western dramatic traditions to help transform Iran's artistic life from being obsessed with Western forms to being conversant with Iranian and other non-Western traditions. Thus, one of my major lines of inquiry as I examine Beyzaie's life and works in this book is to analyse the transformation of traditional Iranian form in Beyzaie's works and their functions as products of a creative mind that has been anti-colonial and anti-hegemonic in its vision but works through cross-fertilization and creative borrowing.

As suggested in the last sentence, Beyzaie has never shied away from creative borrowing. However, I argue that, like most creative individuals, he has been influenced only by the cultural practices, narratives and forms which have had the potential to echo the experiences through which he has defined his own identity at personal, cultural and sociopolitical levels. Since these original concerns have been the product of the zeitgeist and the challenges that he encountered in his forming years, I also examine the environments in which Beyzaie grew up and began writing to identify the origins and the descent of his creative impulse.

Theory or no theory

During the late 1980s, the foremost practitioner of cultural studies, Stuart Hall, who was worried about the adoption of cultural studies by US universities in a way that would inundate this meta-discipline with money, theoretical fluency and 'textual ventriloquism', wrote: 'The only theory worth having is that which you have to fight off, not that which you speak with profound fluency.'[13] Hall's concerns about maintaining the political force of cultural studies in the face of what he construed as self-congratulatory 'theoretical excess' indicates the presence of a dangerous space of complacency where excessive theorizing robs humans and their cultural products of any agency in transforming the systems in which they function. Since my primary methods are semiotic explication and cultural analysis, in my chapters I avoid excessive theorizing and reshape the theories I use to make them reflective of my Iranian context. To this end, I use theory not in the sense of 'the will to truth', which is nothing but a figure of speech, or with the intention of etching my work in the 'meta-narrative of achieved knowledges, within the institutions', 'but theory as a set of contested, localized, [Gramscian] conjunctural knowledges, which have to be debated in a dialogical way' and is culturally and politically charged while aware of its perspectival limitations.[14]

Given the qualities of Beyzaie's oeuvre, I use theories that help me inspect the juxtaposition, reconciliation and reformulation of aesthetic and social opposites as carnivalesque, artistic processes and means of challenging the hierarchies that perpetuate oppression and distort people's lives with claims of exclusive access to truth. To this end, I use diachronic and synchronic methods to construct a genealogical approach for analysing Beyzaie's films with due attention to his life, monographs, plays and screenplays. My primary purpose is to analyse their innovative aesthetic structure and their artistic and sociopolitical functions. The process, thus, also includes identifying the multiplicity of locations these works have occupied in the Iranian discourses on art, modernity and emancipation since the late 1950s. Nevertheless, prior to engaging with individual works, I introduce theoretical perspectives that are relevant to the totality of Beyzaie's oeuvre and the type of creativity he displays in them as an artist concerned with the politics of culture and marginalized ideas and people.

With the utopian illusions of communist and Islamist replacement of capitalism failing to fulfil their promises of emancipation due to their obsessions with absolute power and control, the post-political reform movements, which aspire to reform capitalism and other dominant discourses from within by institutionalizing the rights of marginalized groups and promoting egalitarian mentalities among people, have gained momentum. Thus, most emancipatory movements are now concerned with the types of outlooks that Beyzaie has been representing since the 1950s. While identifying some of these mentalities, next I reflect on why and how such forms of creative thinking have emancipatory functions, display how Beyzaie's ideas are similar to the ideas of some of the leading theorists of the contemporary era and introduce my own theory about the type of creativity observed in Beyzaie's oeuvre. Those of my readers who have no interest in cultural theory can directly go to the next section in which I outline my own theory of creativity. Nonetheless, knowing the theories I discuss here and the links that I have identified in them will situate Beyzaie in a global context and enable the reader to realize the positions he has occupied in Iranian cultural production.

Regimes of truth, regimes of art and regimes of belonging

Rancière argues for the existence of a form of political art which is not political in being openly committed to a theory of emancipation but works better precisely because it is more concerned with making visible and voicing things that were not formerly seen in art.

> There is [. . .] an 'aesthetics' at the core of politics that has nothing to do with Benjamin's discussion of the 'aestheticization of politics specific to the age of the masses'. This aesthetics should not be understood as the perverse commandeering of politics by a will to art, by a consideration of the people qua work of art. If the reader is fond of analogy, aesthetics can be understood in a Kantian sense – re-examined perhaps by Foucault – as the system of a priori forms determining what presents itself to sense experience. It is a delimitation of spaces and times, of the visible and the invisible, of speech and noise, that simultaneously determines the place and the stakes of politics as a form of experience. Politics revolves around what is seen and what can be said about it, around who has the ability to see and the talent to speak, around the properties of spaces and the possibilities of time.
>
> It is on the basis of this primary aesthetics that it is possible to raise the question of 'aesthetic practices' as [. . .] forms of visibility that disclose artistic practices, the place they occupy, what they 'do' or 'make' from the standpoint of what is common to the community. Artistic practices are 'ways of doing and making' that intervene in the general distribution of ways of doing and making as well as in the relationships they maintain to modes of being and forms of visibility.[15]

For Rancière, moments of emancipation occur only when individuals temporarily exit their pre defined professional roles or social models and ways of seeing, doing and hearing things to think about the phenomena, processes, social practices or discourses hovering around them not practically as it is relevant to advancement in their professions, but aesthetically as constructs that can be analysed and transformed rather than accepted as given. This argument becomes easier to understand in the context of Pierre Bourdieu's conception of 'habitus':

The habitus is the product of the work of inculcation and appropriation necessary in order for those products of collective history, the objective structures (e.g. of language, economy, etc.) to succeed in reproducing themselves more or less completely, in the form of durable dispositions, in the organisms (which one can, if one wishes, call individuals) lastingly subjected to the same conditionings, and hence placed in the same material conditions of existence.[16]

For Bourdieu, the habitus is 'a system of internalized structures, schemes of perception, conception, and action' comprised of practices, beliefs and mentalities of the original purpose and the historical origins of which have been forgotten. This makes Bourdieu's position like that of Foucault, who also refers to the inevitable formation, development and entrapment of the individual in the network of power relations. Since this system is internalized in a process that triggers a sense of belonging in individuals before they are capable of thinking and is maintained by society through constant manipulations of truth and power relations reinforced by emotional violence, surveillance, ostracizing and physical punishment and incarceration; it seems impossible to transcend it. Thus, one can argue that emancipatory innovation can only occur if the individual is pushed onto 'multiple habitus' or 'on multiple axes of networks of power relations' so that their identities hover between marginal and central identities where they become capable of divergent thinking and also have the confidence to use it.[17] I will build on this point when discussing my theory of emancipatory creativity. However, what is significant here is that for Rancière this space is where the actual politics of art lies as it is the divergent, transgressive aesthetics of modern art that equips it with emancipatory potential.

To further theorize the relationship between art and politics, Rancière replaces the usual periodization of modern European literature – neoclassicism, romanticism, realism, naturalism, modernism, surrealism, expressionism and postmodernism – with his ideas about the presence of coexisting, overarching regimes of arts. Among the three regimes he introduces, 'the aesthetic regime of art', the generator of the modern conception of art and literature, is the most important one because like its origin, Foucault's conception of 'regimes of truth', it highlights the political nature of something that is normally considered to be pre-political or apolitical, such as perceiving beauty or understanding natural phenomena.

'Regimes of truth' is the concept that Foucault introduced to puncture the philosophical myth about the existence of autonomous truth:

[T]ruth isn't outside power, or lacking in power, [. . .] truth isn't the reward of free spirit, the child of protracted solitude, nor the privilege of those who have succeeded in liberating themselves. Truth is a thing of this world: it is produced only by virtue of multiple forms of constraint. And it induces regular effects of power. Each society has its régime of truth, its 'general polities' of truth: that is, the types of discourse which it accepts and makes function as true; the mechanisms and instances which enable one to distinguish true and false statements, the means by which each is sanctioned; the techniques and procedures accorded value in the acquisition of truth; the status of those who are charged with saying what counts as true.

In societies like ours, the 'political economy' of truth is characterised by five important traits. Truth is centred on the form of scientific discourse and the institutions which produce it; it is subject to constant economic and political incitement (the demand for truth, as much for economic production as for political power); it is the object, under diverse forms, of immense diffusion and consumption (circulating through apparatuses of education and information whose extent is relatively broad in the social body, notwithstanding certain strict limitations); it is produced and transmitted under the control, dominant if not exclusive, of a few great political and economic apparatuses (university, army, writing, media); lastly, it is the issue of a whole political debate and social confrontation ('ideological' struggles).[18]

Thus, 'truth', as described by Foucault, is 'a system of ordered procedures for the production, regulation, distribution, circulation and functioning of statements'; a system which is interconnected 'by a circular relation to systems of power which produce it and sustain it, and to effects of power which it induces, and which redirect it'. Consequently, the greatest challenge of the contemporary era 'is not changing people's consciousness . . . but the political, economic, institutional regime of the production of truth'. The issue is 'not a matter of emancipating truth from every system of power (which would be a chimera, for truth is already power) but of detaching the power of truth from the forms of hegemony, social, economic and cultural, within which it operates at the present time'.[19]

Using this Foucauldian analogy, Rancière reveals the political nature of aesthetics by using the idea of 'a regime of art' as 'a mode of articulation between three things: ways of doing and making, their corresponding forms of visibility, and ways of conceptualizing both the former and the latter'.[20] Rancière's regimes of art are 'the ethical', 'the representative' and 'the aesthetic'. The first which is concerned with images rather than art/s requires that images are distributed according to communal ethos and arranges them based on their origin, purpose and function. The ethical regime distinguishes between artistic simulation and true arts (crafts), which are 'imitations modelled on the truth whose final aim is to educate the citizenry in accordance with the distribution of occupations in community'.[21] The second regime, 'the representative' or 'poetic' regime, of art originates in the axioms offered in Aristotle's critique of Plato, which evolved into a full theory of arts during the classical age. This mode of articulation released art from its ethical, religious and social standards and 'separated the fine arts, qua imitation, from other techniques and modes of production'. By 'defining the essence of *poēsis* as the fictional imitation of actions and isolating a specific domain for fiction', it also went beyond producing 'a regime of resemblance':

Rather than representing reality, works [created or read] within the representative regime obey a series of axioms that define the arts' proper form: the hierarchy of genres and subject matter[s], the principle of appropriateness that adapts forms of expression and action to the subjects represented and to the proper genre, the ideal of speech as act that privileges language over the visible imagery that supplements it.[22]

While the ethical regime of art continued along the representative, the dominant regime of art during the neoclassical era in Europe was the representative regime, but the later stages of the Renaissance also observed the rise of 'the aesthetic regime of art'. Although already present in the transgressive masterpieces of all literary traditions including *One Thousand and One Night* or the works of some Renaissance writers, such as Miguel de Cervantes (1547–1616) or Giambattista Vico (1668–1744), the aesthetic regime of art became dominant from the late eighteenth century, and the first attempts to theorize and popularize it occurred in Friedrich Schiller's *On the Aesthetic Education of Man* (1794). In Rancière's terms:

> It is this notion [the aesthetic education of man] that established the idea that domination and servitude are [. . .] part of an ontological distribution (the activity of thought versus the passivity of the sensible matter). It is also this notion that defined a neutral state, a state of dual cancellation, where the activity of thought and sensible reception became a single reality. They constitute a sort of new region of being – the region of free play and appearance – that makes impossible to conceive of the equality whose direct materialization, according to Schiller, was shown to be impossible by the French revolution. It is this specific mode of living of living in the sensible world that must be developed by 'aesthetic education' in order to train men susceptible to live in a free political community. The idea of modernity as a time devoted to the material realization of a humanity still latent in mankind was construed on this foundation. [. . . The] 'aesthetic revolution' [therefore] produced a new idea of political revolution: the material realization of a common humanity still only existing as an idea. This is how Schiller's 'aesthetic state' became the 'aesthetic programme' of German Romanticism, the programme summarized in the rough draft written together by Hegel, Hölderlin, and Schelling: the material realization of unconditional freedom and pure thought in common forms of life and belief. It is this paradigm of aesthetic autonomy that became the new paradigm for revolution, and it subsequently allowed for the brief but decisive encounter between the artisans of the Marxist revolution and the artisans of forms for a new way of life.[23]

The aesthetic regime of art 'abolished the hierarchical distribution of the sensible' ingrained in the representative regime, 'the privilege of speech over visibility' and 'the hierarchy of the arts, their subject matter and their genres'. The consequences of this rise, which came along with the Industrial Revolution, the French anti-monarchical Revolution, the gradual division of human knowledge into disciplines and the radical changes in the hierarchical structure of west European societies, were numerous. As Rockhill states:

> By promoting the equality of represented subjects, the indifference of style with regard to content, and the immanence of meaning in things themselves [rather than just words], the aesthetic regime destroys the system of genres and isolates 'art' in the singular, *which it identifies with the paradoxical unity of opposites: logos and pathos*. However, the singularity of art enters into an interminable contradiction

due to the fact that the [egalitarian impulse in the] aesthetic regime also calls into question the very distinction between art and other activities. Strictly speaking, the egalitarian regime of the sensible can only isolate art's specificity at the expense of losing it.[24]

This paradoxical regime of art/arts blurred the borders of art and life as it gave birth to 'art' in singular as a discipline along other evolving subjects, such as psychology, sociology, philology and so on. This occurs because the aesthetic regime considers everything worthy of being presented as art in the space dedicated to art in the community and creates a momentum for creativity in which the artist endeavours to reflect the chaos of life while inevitably forming it into a meaningful whole. Thus, everything goes so far as it can be pulled together at presentational and communal levels (due to promotion or change of taste, etc.) to be viewed and interpreted as art. Within this scheme, the differences between the typical styles of different periods occur because new discoveries or cultural trends encourage artists, who later influence the public taste, to bring into art what has been neglected – for instance, the working of human mind as in interior monologues in fiction, the geometrical shapes hidden in human face as in cubism, or the new forms that ancient myths may take when reinterpreted to display female agency. The momentum, however, is always the form-conscious, egalitarian urge to manipulate and change established binaries, reconcile the opposites, display the world from different perspectives and provide a space to reflect aesthetically on the experience of life – which can be present even if the artist's views are not egalitarian, as in Gustave Flaubert's case, for instance. This mode reinforces the transgressive nature of art and its momentum for redistributing 'the sensible' – the range of images and sounds that can be seen, heard and construed as image and voice rather than ugly shape and noise in society. Within this regime, overtly political or presumably unpolitical art can both lead to the transformation of the public space and the public and private lives of individuals.

Most of Rancière's books are attempts to show continuities in apparently dissimilar artistic processes or refute declarative pronouncements, such as 'the end of history' or 'the death of tragedy'. He argues against the existence of breaches between, for instance, classical and modernist cinema, or modernist and postmodernist art, by highlighting the differences between the artistic works of the same era and the presence of the same elements in the works of previous practitioners. In *Film Fables*, in a passage which analyses aesthetic features that remind the reader of Beyzaie's films, he demonstrates how directors play with realistic and surrealistic imagery to produce meanings which are independent from the main narrative of their films, and how this autonomous functioning of independent or metonymic image, which is assumed to be unique to cinema, is shared by all products of the aesthetic regime of art. Rancière deconstructs Gilles Deleuze's arguments about the primacy of 'movement-image' (narrative, action based) in classical cinema and 'time-image' (non-narrative, thought-based) in modernist cinema by demonstrating that they display the same types of reconciliation of opposites that one can observe even in the fictional masterpieces of the nineteenth century: *'The camera's fixing on the hand that pours the water and the hand that holds the candle is no more peculiar to cinema than the fixing of Doctor Bovary's gaze on*

Mademoiselle Emma's nails, or of Madame Bovary's gaze on those of the notary's clerk, is peculiar to literature.'[25]

Rancière's analysis is, of course, mostly focused on west European cultures in general and France and Germany in particular. It is, in fact, possible to argue that the history of the emergence of the aesthetic regime of art is to some extent different even in Britain. However, I argue that despite their differences, Beyzaie's oeuvre and those of several other Iranian filmmakers, dramatists, novelists and poets – including among others Sadeq Hedayat, Nima Yushij, Ahmad Shamlou, Forough Farrokhzad, Gholamhosein Sa'edi, Bijhan Mofid, Abbas Kiarostami, Mohsen Makhmalbaf and Rakhshan Banietemd – made major contributions to the rise of the form-conscious kind of creativity essential to the aesthetic revolution in Iran.

Creativity, in general, but particularly in the aesthetic regime of art, involves intercultural and intracultural reformulations of old and new templates, ideas, characters, narratives and lived experience and yoking them together to produce loci of aesthetic contemplation about human life. Beyzaie has excelled in both, and his mastery in reformulating indigenous narratives and forms and yoking them to global ones to create modern templates suggests that he has been instrumental in the rise of the aesthetic revolution and its emancipatory codes in Iran. Having situated Beyzaie's style within the global trends in the transformation of art, I will investigate the qualities and sources of the type of emancipatory creativity observed in his works.

The outline of a theory of creativity: Culture, trauma and narratives of redemption

. . .for behold he comes!
Not like the shepherd with his rural pipe
And cheerful song, but groaning heavily.
Either his wounded foot against some thorn
Hath struck, and pains him sorely, or *perchance*
He hath espied from far some ship attempting
To enter this inhospitable port,
And hence his cries to save it from destruction.[26]

In Sophocles' rereading of the myth of Philoctetes, the lonely hero suffers from an infected wound whose stench has led to his ostracization by Odysseus and his compatriots who have left him to die in the Island of Lemnos and continued their journey to wage their war against Troy. However, when ten years later, an oracle states that the Greeks must have Hercules' bow and Philoctetes' arrows to conquer Troy, Odysseus and Neoptolemus, Achilles' son, go on a quest to obtain the arrows and retrieve the bow which is in Philoctetes' possession. Despite this heroic setting, however, Sophocles' imagery, 'rural pipe', 'cheerful song', 'groaning heavily' and 'the idea of saving others from a similar fate' projects the image of Philoctetes as a tragic artist. The bow and the arrows, therefore, become the ultimate artefacts and Philoctetes the ostracized artisan/archer whose art is desperately needed. Sophocles uses an honourable youth to juxtapose political opportunism, represented in Odysseus, who wants to rob Philoctetes of the bow and the arrows, with the generous inclusiveness of Neoptolemus, who decides to take Philoctetes along and gives him the chance of being healed and reintegrated into Greek society. The myth, therefore, becomes a metaphor for an artist whose sought-for art provides him with the chance to be loved, find a sense of belonging, overcome his hate, the wound that separated him from society and return to his homeland as a hero.

In Adrian Rich's revisionist allusion to the myth, the poetic voice becomes a female Philoctetes, who no longer craves to be integrated in society or make a career from her pain.

> What kind of beast would turn its life into words?
> What atonement is this all about?[27] [. . .]

* * *

> I can see myself years back at Sunion,
> hurting with an infected foot, Philoctetes
> in woman's form, limping the long path,
> [. . .]
> yet all the time nursing, measuring that wound.
> Well, that's finished. The woman who cherished
> her suffering is dead. I am her descendant.
> I love the scar-tissue she handed on to me,
> but I want to go on from here with you
> fighting the temptation to make a career of pain.[28]

Rich sings about leaving a suffocating milieu to attain a form of creativity that sublimates obsession with past suffering and poetic self-pity into emancipatory poetry and love, which, I argue, is at the centre of the form of creativity that characterizes artists of Beyzaie's type.

Celebrations of such forms of creativity are also present in Iranian legends. For instance, in the legend of Zāl and Simurgh, as reported in Ferdowsi's *Shahnameh*, the albino boy, Zāl is left in the wilderness to die, but his adoption by Simurgh, the mythical incarnation of wisdom turns him into the wisest hero and the greatest lover and father of the *Shahnameh*. Despite all dogmatic objections, he falls in love and marries Rudābeh, a descendant of Zahhāk, the monstrous embodiment of monarchic cruelty, and she proves to be the best female lover and mother of the *Shahnameh*. Even though his world is rife with fathers who fail their sons, and his own father, Sām leaves him in wilderness to die, he becomes the ever-supportive father and spiritual guide of Rostam, the greatest hero of the *Shahnameh*. The legend, thus, celebrates difference, reflects an epistemic shift that opens the culture to cross-fertilization, prioritizes love over war and rejects religious and ethnic marginalization. Zāl's ostracization and intercultural or interspecific nurture, thus, places him in a position which I, building on Bourdieu's theory of habitus, argue to be 'on multiple axes of networks of power relations'.[29] He can see failures where others cannot, and he has unprecedented solutions due to his exposure to divergent forms of being. In other words, he has what I call 'epistemic privilege' – access to divergent ways of seeing and doing which can expand the progressive resources of a culture.[30] The outcast albino child of the Iranian legends, therefore, is like an artist whose vision and wisdom become sources of emancipatory blessing.

These two anecdotes are apt metaphors for a condition in which the post-traumatic growth that may follow traumatic marginalization or ostracization leads to a form of creativity that generates individual and national narratives of redemption and emancipation. In both cases, the ostracized comes back as a saviour whose creativity wins him recognition. The legends, thus, imply that those who lose their sense of belonging because of marginalization or sociopolitical and family problems may regain recognition – among the people with whom they have a love-hate relationship – not by bending to the rules or craving for it but by creating ideas, artefacts and narratives that become essential to their culture. The legends, particularly Zāl's, also imply that people who survive life-threatening marginalization will also become more creative, not just because their mental resources are heavily tasked in the process but also because they develop an outsider gaze, which, when discussing arts, means that works produced by such individuals always reflect and critique the failures of their culture, the mentalities and practices that lead to marginalization and loss of human resources in society. I argue that Beyzaie's creativity is characterized by the two qualities I specified for Zāl, epistemic authority and outsider gaze as well as what Edward Said calls 'amateur gaze' with the latter two reinforcing the former.[31] However, before analysing the way these qualities further to see how they lead to creative reconfiguration of culture, below I provide my perspectives about culture in a bid to specify the points that are important for my discussion without claiming to offer a comprehensive definition of this complicated term.

Culture is the ever-evolving sum of the mentalities and practices that determine people's assumptions and behaviours and make the production and consumption of meaning possible. It evolves as historically and geographically determined responses to real needs but expands to institutionalize its own impact by creating and suggesting ways to fulfil imaginary needs.[32] Though it changes by intercultural contact and adaptation for survival, culture is also hereditary and contains outdated elements that people staunchly adhere to because they are either sanctified through religion or justified as part of the public common sense, although the reasons for which they were invented may no longer exist. However, as Williams states, 'A culture, while it is being lived, is always in part unknown, in part unrealised', and the making 'of a community is always an exploration, for consciousness cannot precede creation, and there is no formula for unknown experience'. Thus, 'a living culture' will 'not only make room for but actively encourage all and any who can contribute to the advance in consciousness'. 'Wherever we have started from, we need to listen to others who started from a different position. We need to consider every attachment, every value, with our whole attention; for we do not know the future, we may never be certain of what may enrich it'.[33] William's prescription for guaranteeing the growth of a culture is hard to fulfil as dedicating one's 'whole attention' to assessing one's culture by listening to others requires a zeal for learning and openness which cannot be imposed on people. This is where the necessity of rereading the past and analysing the oeuvre of writers like Beyzaie's reveals its significance.

Since culture also provides the space and the means for producing meaning, and therefore the relations of power, any study or critique of culture must also involve making assumptions and suggestions about how human beings have been producing and consuming meaning through the systems of signs that they have created and how they have used these systems to process and produce relations of power as well as other human beings as cultural products that in turn produce culture. In the sentence above, I defined human beings as cultural products, who are themselves capable of producing culture. Let me now unpack these two concepts.

From an existential outlook, humans are creatures of becoming. They are not born human; they rather have the potential to become human through acquisition and education, which involves imitation, inculcation and reformulation. This process exposes the individual to countless linguistic and non-linguistic codes that have been in making for thousands of years. From birth, therefore, human beings are exposed to so much culture that by the age of 18 they are thousands of years old, and that is what makes them human and how the process continues. Many of these codes enter the mind with assumptions that determine the nature of thought and interpretation even before the individual is capable of thinking. Every human being is, therefore, a cultural product produced by being exposed to the codes and practices that hover around in the intra- and intercultural interactions around them. This product, however, is also capable of reproducing culture by reformulating these codes in accordance with the specific experiences that are themselves determined by individual and collective factors such as heredity, environment, gender, religion, nationality, ethnicity and location. Human beings, thus, produce culture through culture-specific reformulations and syncretic adaptations of indigenous and non-indigenous sources. These constant reformulations are essential for individuals' survival and growth and can be examined both at personal and collective levels. At personal levels, the theory of narrative identity, which was propagated by Erik Erikson and later expanded by Dan McAdams and others summarizes the situation.

According to the theory of narrative identity, everyone has an internalized, semi-imagined, personal history which is continuously reshaped, mostly subconsciously, but sometimes consciously, in response to external stimulants and mental processes, which are, in turn, shaped by the clusters of memories and their associations in the mind. This process creates a narrative which gives a sense of stability to the fluidity of a person's ranges of identities and enables them to have a sense of purpose and make sense of their presence in the world. This story-like medley of reconstructed pasts, perceived presents and imagined futures is at any given moment of a person's life at the verge of beginning again 'in medias res'. It also has reassembled beginnings, middle possibilities surrounding the individual (ongoing responsibilities, endeavours and foreseen and unforeseen consequences), points of suffering due to which imagined or real moments of redemption and transformation occurred, and potential denouements. Characters come and go, scenes and settings change and turning points, motives, recalled or imagined imagery and climaxes occur. Life, however, also has moments of personal or collective crisis and traumatic disasters which force individuals to change their narratives not in the normal, gradual, minimal ways but drastically to enable them to cope with the new givens that have denied the truth value of their former narratives.[34]

This theory is relevant not only for individuals but also for collective groups such as nations because collective identities acquire their elements from collective narratives, which have the same qualities as individual narratives of selfhood. A nation's elites and their rivals create contradictory senses of past, present and future by consolidating the narratives that support their outlooks and marginalizing those that do not. This occurs in a dialectical process that generates a nation's rivalling discourses of togetherness and their numerous subdivisions. Like individuals, nations undergo traumatic experiences that require changing the collective narratives of belonging and togetherness. Thus, the institutions in charge of producing the dominant regimes of truth or those that promote their rivalling discourses change their narratives, replace one another or make sense of the present while redefining a people's past and its potential futures. Like individuals, nations also produce narratives of trauma and redemption in reaction to wars, occupations, revolutions, reform failures or military coups. Thus, rivalling narratives that have more followers due to their power over the institutions that manufacture truth may define the past, present and future of a nation at any given time.

It is at this juncture of rivalling discourses that a major form of creativity originates when an individual experiences traumatic marginalization due to the limitations of both the systems that define the criteria of truth, belonging and integration and those that confront them. Such a position leads to a form of marginalization that among other things produces minority perspective, which, though in many cases, occurs to people from minority backgrounds, it is not limited to them. My clarifying anecdote for minority perspective is the metaphor of the door as a portal of opportunity. As part of our human training, we learn early in life to open doors as a basic rite of passage by turning a handle or a knob and then pushing or pulling. We also learn to be goal oriented and focus on what is behind the door rather than the door itself. Thus, if we turn the handle, and the door opens, we do not think about the handle or the door. However, if we turn the handle, but the door does not open, we start thinking about why the door does not open. In a rapid succession of ideas, we think about the structure and the potential issues with the handle or the lock. If that does not resolve the issues, we focus on the door, then the frame and ultimately even the walls and the building as a crack may have distorted the frame. Our conception of life is also like that. If the doors open, as it does for those who have the privilege of cultural centrality, the individual never thinks about the handle, the door, the frame or the building. However, if the door does not open, as it happens to marginalized people due to the unfairly rationalized hierarchies of race, gender, ethnicity, religion, age, looks or even accent, the individual automatically thinks about what is wrong with him or her or society, and how it can be resolved. This is minority perspective.

The immediate reaction to such situations is that we start to adapt because since childhood we have been taught that life is unfair and if we attempt to change it, we lose our opportunities. As the Persian song, written by Iraj Jantai Ataei and performed by Dairush Eghbali, goes, 'Bend your head as when the doors open, if you say no, you remain behind the Concours.'³⁵ However, one may also engage in violent reactions against such forms of injustice or shelter in a minority cocoon. In some cases, however, traumatic marginalization occurs to those who have qualities that are essential to the culture – intelligence, economic potential, special skills and cultural capital. This creates a desire for regaining a sense of belonging not by bending but by achieving recognition, which, in turn, enhances the individual's special abilities. Thus, to be wanted by the people rejecting them while culturally admonishing them, they push their limits, become more creative and articulate cultural positions that aspire to make their culture more inclusive by extracting and reformulating cultural elements whose authenticity no one can deny. This is a status that I call epistemic authority, the ability to see and understand problems that others do not perceive and to articulate new perspectives that challenge the accepted norms and sociopolitical constructs that cause those problems.

Epistemic authority is rooted in what is called epistemic privilege in philosophy, the idea that certain forms of knowledge are perceived directly by a person or a group of people but not others. Whereas in psychology, this suggests that only an individual has privileged access to his or her thought processes, in social sciences it entails that those marginalized and deprived of their rights by a sociopolitical, religious or cultural system apprehend the problems of the system much more acutely than those ripping the benefits or remaining unharmed by the system. In other words, the only person who can know that there is something wrong with a door is the person for whom the door does not open and perhaps the ones that have set up or maintain the door in that way. As seen in the previous paragraph, however, rather than calling this status epistemic privilege, I call it minority perspective and argue that epistemic privilege occurs only when such individuals transcend the limits of their minority perspective and perceive the problems of those in other marginalized positions and the outlook of those in the centre by understanding the way the system works. Indeed, the mere fact of seeing cannot be a privilege if it pushes such people into the trap of individual or group self-pity and make them unable to see how other groups of people are also systematically suppressed.

However, to achieve epistemic authority, it is also often the case that though identifying with the marginalized and rebelling against marginalization in general, the individual develops unique intellectual or physical qualities (creativity, beauty, power, etc.) that make him or her appealing to the centre. This can occur only to those in whom marginalization does not lead to bending, sheltering in their minority group, or engaging in violent reaction but to a situation in which they transcend the centre-margin or majority-minority binary and articulate inclusive visions of togetherness in ways that influence the centre. To gain the means to do the latter, those who have epistemic privilege typically look at the origins and historical evolution of the present mentalities and practices which marginalize people or those which can be reformulated to produce inclusive mentalities. They also examine other cultures to see how they have failed or attained inclusive togetherness. It is somewhere along this search that the ideal holders of epistemic privilege achieve 'epistemic authority' and establish a type of recognition that convinces people to adopt new ways of seeing, hearing and doing things.³⁶

The ability to see and offer corrective views about the failures of one's culture, either because of having epistemic privilege or the experience of living in other cultures or both, has always been vital for cultural progress. However, since the late eighteenth century, with the rise in the range of global cultural encounters, the collapse of sociopolitical, economic, religious and cultural hierarchies, the branching of fields of knowledge into disciplines and the drastic change in the transgressive function of art which made it a field open to all subjects, such an ability has found a wider space of expression enabling leading thinkers from marginalized backgrounds, including Marx, Freud, Einstein, Arendt, Foucault, Lorde, Butler or Said to adopt and reconfigure the language of the centre to articulate new positions that have transformed dominant discourses on religion, science, social classes, politics, economy, human mind, governance, women, heroism, religious and ethnic minorities.

Disciplines work by gradual revisionism, but those with epistemic privilege are likely to introduce new forms of revisionism that initiate epistemic shifts. Analysing this further, however, suggests that one of the reasons such individuals achieve epistemic authority is that their epistemic privilege prevents them from adhering to a single future-directed narrative of identity for themselves or simple revisionist views about a discipline or culture. This failure is a major source of creativity as it forces them to constantly create alternative narratives about reality. Thus, because their epistemic privilege questions their own narratives of belonging, they constantly engage with the world and create new narratives as scientific or scholarly theories, discoveries and inventions, or stories, poems, plays or films to negotiate new positions which change the rules of the game or evade self-deception about rivalling narratives of identity by mixing them. Thus, it seems that only those who have had traumatic experiences of marginalization and obtained the mental and technical means of sublimating them into artistic, scholarly or scientific reformulations have stories worth telling.

Of course, to transform these into artistic or scholarly creativity, they also need to acquire the skills needed for such purposes. The latter entails absorbing the codes of their cultures and other cultures to which they have access and reformulating them with many non-specific narratives from their memories, daily experiences, dreams and nightmares to create a space of relations and characters that may have the potential to redeem their lost sense of belonging and purpose. While doing so, their divergent approach to thinking also allows them to create intriguing forms that engage their readers or viewers and conveys these experiences to them. Since this form of creativity is rooted in the failure of the individual's narrative of selfhood to reconcile with an unfair world and the people maintaining it, it also always involves creating parallel narratives which may combine contradictory personal and collective narratives hovering around the artist to articulate positions that may help the culture exit a deadlock.[37]

In Beyzaie's case, as reflected in my following chapters, one observes the previously discussed type of creativity which he shares with such generators of new ways of seeing as Shakespeare, Ibsen, Brecht or their Iranian counterparts Hasan Moqaddam, Hedayat, Sa'edi, Mofid, Farrokhzad or Zoya Pirzad. However, Beyzaie's type of creativity also contains what Said calls perceptive amateur gaze. Said's analysis of the concept begins by discussing Russell Jacoby's claim in *The Last Intellectuals* that modern professionals are chiefly 'buttoned-up, impossible to understand classroom technicians, hired by committee, anxious to please various patrons and agencies, bristling with academic credentials and a social authority that does not promote debate but establishes reputations and intimidates nonexperts'.[38] Said contends that this is an overgeneralization, but he modifies it to discuss the pitfalls of specialization and argues for the necessity of engaging with subjects as amateurs. This amateur gaze occurs when a perceptive individual with advanced training in one field engages with another field and deconstructs the presuppositions of the recycled materials of the latter field. Since artists regularly engage in evaluating other fields from aesthetic or cultural angles, such a gaze is like the one Rancière refers to when he specifies the nature of emancipatory gaze and its role in the aesthetic regime of art.[39] However, it also occurs in other fields to produce revisionist readings of the past. In humanities, it often leads to challenging the truth value of assumptions or arguments that dehumanize certain groups of people to justify domination. This is what Foucault, a philosopher, does with history in *The History of Sexuality* (1976) or Said, a literary critic, does with the Western discourses on the Middle East, Asia or Africa in *Orientalism* (1979).

Though different in its manifestations, the mechanism at work in the amateur gaze is like that of the informed outsider gaze. In both, if the individual is well informed about the discipline or born and bred in the culture they examine, the result is epistemic privilege. The individual approaches a subject from a divergent viewpoint that is external to the established mentalities and practices of the discipline or culture. Indeed, both can be said to be reinforcing elements functioning within an overarching epistemic privilege. They allow the individual to spot the failures of the practices that the upholders of dominant discourses propagate, their followers habitually accept and the people who know they are wrong reluctantly accept to avoid losing their opportunities. Foucault and Said's projects were theoretically charged historical studies, in which their defamiliarizing amateur gaze as non-historians and their sublimated minority gaze (epistemic privilege) made them work like artists who constructed forms of looking that identified some of the failures of the recycling processes involved in writing history. Such theoretically and artistically charged reconfigurations are not immune to mistakes in details or evaluating specific situations.[40] However, due to their divergent types of foregrounding, they have the potential to deconstruct established perspectives and introduce new methods and marginalized outlooks that may change any field of study. In his examinations of Iranian ways of doing things, Beyzaie does the same. He combines the roles of a perceptive amateur, an outsider born and bred inside and thus knowledgeable about details, and an artist of the aesthetic regime of art, who displays cultural failures and suggests life-affirming solutions, which even when retrospectively looking naïve in his early works, suggest the precociousness of a young artist who asked essential questions far before anyone thought about them.

Thought does not know borders and intercultural cross-fertilization with a mind to adapt non-native theories to transform pre-existing assumptions within one's culture has always been a major vehicle of progress. The argument remains valid even if one does not believe in progress. The passage of time and new economic and political urgencies necessitate change and attachment to old paradigms produces more suffering than adapting to new ones, especially if one is aware that the new ones do not eradicate misery, may create other problems and may later become as rigid as the ones they replace. Progress may be a myth, but change is not. Furthermore, although the ethical and representative regimes of producing and interpreting art continued in twentieth-century Iran, in numerous propaganda works produced by some of the leftist and some Islamist writers before the revolution, and were given a new momentum with the imposition of the Islamic codes of production after the revolution, most of the intellectual and economic triggers that gave rise to the aesthetic regime of art has been present in Iran since the mid-nineteenth century and modern Iranian art harbours all the markers of what Rancière calls the aesthetic regime of art. In this context, examining Beyzaie's works by adapting contemporary theory to an Iranian context may help highlight some of the neglected aspects of Iran's journey of transition since the 1950s.

Origins and qualities of Beyzaie's creativity in form, narrative and language

Beyzaie's life has been influenced by the opposing conceptions of modernity and nationhood in Iran's political discourses since the 1890s. He passed his childhood during a time when the end of Reza Shah's dictatorial rule (1925–41) and the domination of the Allies over Iran's politics, economy and culture (1941–6) urged some Iranians to create new discourses on modernization in which the nation was to acquire its meaning and forward trajectory not from gathering around a visionary, authoritarian monarch or religious patriarch but from its people and a historically rooted future-directedness (1946–53). His teenage years coincided with an era of political suppression, which began with the 1953 coup and became systematic with the foundation of SAVAK (Iran's intelligence and security organization, 1957–79). This era was doubly difficult for Beyzaie due to the heavy-handed suppression of the Bahais in 1955. Although the Pahlavis followed a nationalist agenda in which religious minorities were to have equal rights, the state allowed Mohammad-Taqi Falsafi (1908–98) to deliver anti-Bahai speeches on national radio in April and May 1955. This led to widespread atrocities committed against the Bahais across the country and the demolition of their religious centres. The Shah's bending to Shi'i extremism was probably due to his fear of communism, but he also felt indebted to the ulama due to their support for the coup and wanted to reconcile with them to avoid the rise of militant groups like *Fedāiyān-e Eslām* (self-sacrificers of Islam).[41]

Though he has regularly worked with the mythology of Iranian and Abrahamic religions as sources of inspiration and his expertise in *ta'ziyeh* has made him a major reformulator of Shi'i mythology, Beyzaie has never practised Bahaism or any other religion.[42] However, his family background meant that since early childhood, particularly between 1955 and 1957, in his late teenage years, when individuals constantly reshape their narratives of selfhood to find their place in society, he not only suffered the impacts of political suppression but was also ostracized for a religion he did not practice and observed the daily sufferings of his parents. These years were then followed by a period of social and economic reform and relative relaxation of censor in the years leading to the White Revolution and its early years (1959–69), when Beyzaie began his creative career. Though the state failed to deliver the democratic promise of the reforms, he and more than forty other playwrights and theatre practitioners produced one of the golden ages of Iranian drama and theatre. This golden period, however, came to a gradual decline as the country moved towards a revolutionary era in which the armed struggles of opposition groups against the state and the state's obsession with rapid Westernization and single-party rule in the 1970s gradually pushed Iran forward through the channels of anti-communist, authoritatian Westernization and brought it inadvertently to the dawn of a revolution which led to the establishment of a fundamentalist Islamic state.

Beyzaie's youth, therefore, was rife with the sounds and images of radical suppression and change, which demonstrated to his young mind 'how global economic and power relations and native, ideologies of salvation and growth transform the face of cities and alienate their populations' and 'how internal failures help foreign powers [. . .] exploit a nation'.[43] He also personally suffered the consequences of the way the proponents of dominant religious and political discourses distort history and life, deprive people of the chance to live normal lives and marginalize alternative narratives of belonging and togetherness. Thus, 'the experience of being placed in the margins of belonging made him aware of how the centre can be blind to the failures of the structures it creates'. However, since he had a high level of cultural capital due to his parents' literary interests and observed the costs of religious and political extremism, his minority vision was sublimated into a secular epistemic privilege equipped with the perceptive gaze of a professional amateur, an informed, internal outsider. He perceived problems that others neglected or justified and endeavoured to reveal how the promoters of dominant discourses suppressed others to reinforce their reductive narratives.[44]

Examining Beyzaie's works from such an angle enables a viewer to identify dense texts that reformulate and reconcile opposite elements – from the inherited hierarchies of carnival, ritual and elite forms, as well as mythical, historical and folk narratives – to expand the horizons of visibility in society while redefining art and pushing new forms into the space dedicated to art in ways that redraw the borders between art and life. In other words, since 1958 Beyzaie's works have functioned as loci of revelation of marginal voices in ways that expand what is visible and audible or conceived permissible in society due to the limits imposed on minds by the dominant regimes of truth. Last year, for instance, he published a filmscript *Mahi*, in which he uses a self-reflexive form, films within the film, to display how the miseries and hopes of a street girl turn her into an unlikely saviour. The script, however, also reveals how the givens of toxic masculinity may rob women of the chance of having normal lives and analyses the *parastu* (swallow) phenomenon, the state's criminalization of attractive women to use them as bait for trapping dissenting intellectuals or artists in Iran.

His works, therefore, often involve displaying the victimization or survival of marginalized characters and rereading historical and mythical accounts to undermine reductive narratives of nationhood, leadership, modernity, modernization, war, heroism, sacrifice, intellectuality, manhood, womanhood, childhood, myth, history and culture. They also refashion traditional Iranian forms and narratives in works that achieve high levels of linguistic and poetic virtuosity while creating alternative narratives on the formation of human identity at personal, existential, psychological, social, religious, political, family and cultural levels. Among these forms of refashioning, the first point to examine is Beyzaie's use of language which has remained unique in Iranian drama and cinema and has not faced much competition in fiction. This is essential as this book, being in English, is doomed to work with translation rather than the original Persian, and thus, remains limited in its analysis of language.

Beyzaie's experimentations with language began with pure Persian in his early recitation plays such as *Ārash* and *Azhdāhāk*. In these works he used a style of expression that he gradually improved for his plays that were set in pre-Islamic Iran, to produce masterpieces such as *Death of Yazdegerd*, *Reciting Siyāvush* or *Ardāvirāf's Report*. As Mehdi Hashemi, who played the miller in the film version of *Death of Yazdegerd*, states, combined with the characters' shifts between the roles, this poetically charged yet intensely dramatic language, in which 'the words seem to fly' with contradictory emotions and create the content out of the form with their conflicting discourses, turns the play into the best play of the Persian language and the film into one of the top five films of Iranian cinema.[45] Beyzaie's sensitivity to language and mastery of dialogue, however, go beyond pure Persian to create masterpieces in which the language is always appropriate for the characters and the historical eras of the settings. This is important as in his works, due to the range of his historical settings and the gender, class, education, ethnic, profession or cult or subcult backgrounds of his characters, one faces a multiplicity of linguistic idiosyncrasies. Moreover, whether topically realistic or heightened and unrealistic, his dialogue remains vivid and multi-layered and often a few brushes of his mastery are enough to make tertiary characters tangible. Due to these qualities, scholars who have engaged with analysing Beyzaie's language or translating his works compare his use of language and approach to dialogue to Shakespeare's.[46] To me this is correct at the level of dialogue but not the language. Beyzaie's use of language is like Shakespeare's in its poetic playfulness, use of irony and sarcasm and inventiveness and the range of characters' speech qualities in terms of class, education, profession and occasional regional idiosyncrasies. Beyzaie's language, however, also has historical and period reverberations and inflections. Shakespeare never tried to create a language that echoes aspects of Middle English as he probably knew that it would sound stilted and incomprehensible on the stage. With Modern English, he only had a maximum of 100 years, and his maximum depth would probably take him to two centuries earlier to Chaucer, Gower and Langland. Beyzaie, however, has had more than twelve centuries of New Persian to work with and knew that, if purged of Arabic and Turkish words, this Persian can be conventionally accepted by readers or viewers to echo the speech of pre-Islamic Iran. Thus, being concerned with creating the best form of language for each character in every play or script, Beyzaie uses the linguistic idiosyncrasies of different eras but makes the language more familiar and performable by inserting modern expressions that do not conflict with the typical speech of those eras.

To give an example, part 1 of *The One Thousand and First Night* uses pure Persian with epic qualities and courtly banter to display Zahhāk's court, part 2 mixes Arabic and Persian with a section in pure Persian for a passion play to focus on the victimization of an intellectual and his wife and sister during the Arabs' rule in Iran and part 3 uses the language of *taqlid* and female performances of the 1900s to reflect on a woman's success to civilize her dogmatic husband during the late Qajar era. Or in *Parchment of Master Sharzin*, he uses the scholarly language of the eleventh century with a poetic power that has remained unrivalled in Persian literature.[47] Thus, besides its literary qualities, Beyzaie's language has a unique range that makes translating his works difficult. This is because it is impossible to approximate this range in English, and even if one does so, it may end up becoming unperformable. In translation studies, when it comes to drama, the balance between faithfulness and naturalness is problematized by performability. For instance, in Shakespeare's case, it is often the case that the poetically excellent translations lose their performability in Persian. Thus, most theatre practitioners insist on having a performable translation. In Beyzaie's case, the best example is to compare Manuchehr Anvar's *Death of Yazdegerd* with Soheil Parsa and Peter Farbridge's translation of the play. The former is powerful and poetic but misses the comedy, the latter is easier to follow and more performable but again misses the comedy of the priest's droning and the girl's and the woman's carnivalization of the performance.[48]

In the first decade of his career, this form- and language-conscious creativity was dedicated to theatre. Beyzaie wrote fifteen and directed four plays and produced four monographs on Iranian (1962–5), Japanese (1964), Chinese (1969) and Indian (1971) performing traditions. Then in 1969, he expanded his vision to cinema and established himself as a leading figure of the New Wave. Since then, he has made thirteen films, directed nine plays and written more than eighty plays and screenplays, which, though remaining unproduced due to lack of funds or censor, have been among the most read in Iran because of their literary merits. As stated earlier, Beyzaie uses forms inspired by popular performing and ritual traditions. One significant case is his use of *ta'ziyeh* passion plays.[49] As the product of the popular reshaping of the principles and techniques of several Iranian art forms, '*ta'ziyeh* represented for Beyzaie the best that he, as a dramatist, could have had, but did not, because [. . .] its secularization had been disrupted due to misguided understandings of modernity'.[50] Thus, to create modern dramatic forms, he used its techniques but subverted its narratives to display the humanity of mythical heroes and confront political and religious suppression by depicting life-affirming individuals or creative intellectuals as sacrificial heroes. After the revolution, when the state began mythicizing its activities by comparing them with the deeds of *Shi'i* saints and depicted dissenting groups and secular intellectuals as stooges of the West or like the killers of Shia saints, Beyzaie enhanced this template in several tragic counter-narratives that depicted secular thinkers and artists as sacrificial heroes, and Shia saints as thinkers in conflict with dogmatic institutions. He also extended this tragic template to history and myth to produce alternative narratives for Iran's cultural identity and glorify real or fictional figures such as Ferdowsi, Sharzin, Siyāvush, Sohrāb and Sennemār as sacrificial heroes.[51]

This tragic paradigm, however, is only one of the templates that Beyzaie has created for the rejuvenation of Iranian dramatic forms. In fact, an examination of his *Theatre in Iran*, the result of his research between 1961 and 1965, suggests that from the early years of his playwriting, he has been adopting the forms that he analysed in the book to recreate them for a modern audience. His systematic approach to refashioning these forms began with *naqqāli* dramatic storytelling, *kheimeh-shab-bāzi* puppet plays and *ruhuzi/taqlid* satiric forms in his early plays and continued with *taʿziyeh*, fertility and healing rituals in his later works where these forms were creatively combined with Asian or Western forms to create the most extensive oeuvre in Iranian theatre and cinema. He, thus, steadily experimented with old and new forms even when he was not allowed to make films or direct plays. After the revolution, several major Iranian playwrights fell silent, and three of them, Saʿedi (1936–85), Bijhan Mofid (1935–84) and Abbas Naʿlbandiyan (1947–89) drugged or drank themselves to death as a result of the stifling circumstances of the 1980s. Beyzaie, however, used writing as a means of survival and created a body of works that transferred his experimentation of the 1960s and 1970s to the post-revolutionary Iran of the 1980s, 1990s, 2000s and 2010s. The use of these forms is also important as the reappearance of mythical or folk figures in new dress signifying new concepts or the use of archetypal narrative structures for modern and social concepts turns such works into loci of negotiation between the past and present.

Raphael Bassan divides Beyzaie's primary concerns into three thematic categories: the stranger in a strange land, unfulfilled love and explorations in individuals' histories and memories or the nation's collective, cultural and mythical histories.[52] Baqer Parham refers to children, women, strangers and historical necessity or fate as Beyzaie's favourite subjects.[53] Hooshang Azadivar argues for the same issues but states that the forming principle for these concerns is a quest for identity,[54] which in Jamshid Arjomand's terms also includes an attempt to create an authentically Iranian epistemology.[55] These critics briefly discuss nearly everything that has been central to Beyzaie's world until 1979, but apart from failing to offer detailed analyses of Beyzaie's works, they also give no adequate overview of the types of works he has produced in various eras and their relationship with each other, the works of other writers and the sociopolitical conflicts and aesthetic debates of the time of annunciation. Therefore, before analysing his films in my chapters, I will here offer an overview of Beyzaie major techniques and subjects and then provide a chart reflecting the impact of different political eras on Beyzaie's major works. This will help the reader to have an overview of Beyzaie's activities before I commence my analysis of his major works.

As all innovative authors, Beyzaie's artistic creativity is designed to fulfil three impulses: (1) personally political and existential self-expression, (2) communication with people about the problems of public and private lives in Iran, (3) responding to a perfectionist impulse for creating the best forms for subjects that have clearly evolved along the forms. These three have in turn given shape to special moods and tendencies in his works which I have specified next in a chart in which I have arranged Beyzaie's major works on the bases of eight historical eras and six expressive moods. Any form of artistic production has its own history. Thus, my intention is not to analyse Beyzaie's productions based on their historical periods, but such an overview reveals the worldliness of his works as responses to the zeitgeist of the years in which they were produced, and when that aspect has become clear, the analysis can move more freely to engage with the other aspects of his artistic vision.

The first era (1958–66) is the era of reform and hope for democratic change during the years leading to and the first years of the White Revolution. The second (1967–76) is the apex of Mohammad Reza Shah's power when SAVAK was in control, and the Shah was 'passing through the gates of the great civilization', neglecting the gulf that his top-down development plans was creating between social classes and the intensification of people's reactions against modernity due to his refusal to engage in political reform. The era is also significant in that several equally exclusionist rivalling discourses of emancipation, with Islamist and Marxist tendencies engaged in militant confrontation with the Pahlavi state. The third period (1976-9) is an era of instability and revolution, when the Shah's terminal illness wore him down, and the chaos of unresolved conflicts resulted in the 1978-9 revolution. Then comes the years of Islamization, state and party terror, suffocating censorship and war (1980-8), which began with the 'Cultural Revolution' - which deprived Beyzaie of his university job - and concluded with Iran's acceptance of Resolution 598 which ended the war. The next was the era of post-war reconstruction (1989-96) which was characterized by corruption and the move towards a form of predatory capitalism, which in the absence of social freedom deepened the social ills that the Islamic Republic claimed to have stopped. The following era (1997-2005) was that of attempts by the enlightened forces within the state to engineer democratic reform and return to the original ideals of the revolution, which had been distorted by a dogmatic obsession with Islamic fundamentalism. Yet, these attempts came to a dead-end due to the restrictions imposed by the powerful non-elected side of the state and the economic and political clout of security and military organizations. The result was an era of populism (2005-13) that used propaganda to get support from lower classes to try to return the country to the oppressive policies of the 1980s under the pretext of security exigencies imposed by international imperialism.[56] During the second phase of this period as the conflicts over the rigged presidential elections of 2009 continued, Beyzaie received an offer to become a guest lecturer at Stanford University, where he has so far published a monograph and a filmscript and staged four of his plays. The final era of my classifications (2010-21), therefore, registers Beyzaie's work in the United States. In 2013, a new political era began with Hasan Rouhani's presidency and his bid for reform and reconciliation, which, due to the influence of the non-elected part of the state and the shenanigans of the Trump administration, failed.

Though not exhaustive in listing Beyzaie's works or the moods they reflect, the chart offers an outline of Beyzaie's major works and the mentalities they display towards the events in these periods. These expressive moods are not absolute and works characterized by certain moods contain elements central to the others. However, the moods specified for each work are dominant and can be used as guidelines to find the metaphoric backgrounds that Beyzaie creates for each work, which, in turn, suggest the mentality with which they were written. In all these cases, Beyzaie's critical gaze is not fixed just against the state but more so against the inherited or hybrid dominant discourses that turn people into opportunistic agents of religious or military tyrants and distort culture by limiting progressive ideas and aggravating retrogressive mentalities and practices. I have used grey shading and underlining to make distinctions that show though women played important roles in his works from the beginning, they became more central from around 1975 as he found that the salvation of a culture is dependent on the emancipation of its women. I have also used bold fonts to mark the works that due to their innovative forms and the range and power of their linguistic registers and

Table 1.1 The Political Eras and Their Reflections in Beyzaie's Major Creative Works Female Protagonist [Underlined], Male and Female Protagonists [Shaded], Male Protagonist [Normal].

Era	Year	Plays (Year of Writing)	Films & Filmscripts (Year of Writing)	Expressive Moods
1. The Era of Social and Economic Reform	1959 1960	1. Ārash the Archer; 2. Azhdāhāk		1 & 2. Deconstruction (of Archaist Royalism) & Myth and Identity
	1961	**3. Account of Bondar, the Premier**		3. Deconstruction, Myth, Identity & Deploring
	1962	**4. The Marionettes; 5. Sunset in a Strange Land**		4.5. Deconstruction (of hero worship)
	1963	**6. Tale of the Hidden Moon;** 7. So Dies Akbar the Hero		6.7. Deconstruction (of hero worship and cultural demonization)
	1964	8. The Eighth Voyage of Sinbad		8. Deconstruction (heroism/history)
	1966	9. Journalistic World of Mr Asrāri; **10. The Snake King**		9. Injustice (victimization of Talent); 10. Myth & Identity, Deconstruction & Resistance
2. The Apex of Mohamad Reza Shah's Absolute Power: Rapid Development	1967	11. The Legacy; 12. The Feast; 13. Four Boxes		11. Deploring; 12. Injustice 13. Injustice (Monarchy) & Resistance
	1968	**14. Court of Bactria**		14. Injustice and Resistance (women)
	1969	15. The Lost		15. Injustice (Social Hierarchies)
	1970	16. Stormy Path of Farmān the Son of Farmān	17. Uncle Moustache; 18. Downpour; <u>19. Lonely Warrior (Ayyār-e Tanhā)</u>	16. Deploring (Colonialism); 17. Injustice Resistance and Transition; 18. Injustice (Victimization); 19. Resistance (women)
	1972		**20. The Journey; 21. Stranger and the Fog**	20. Injustice; 21. Myth & Existential Identity (women and men)
	1975		<u>22. Truths about Leila, the Daughter of Edris; 23. Ballad of Tārā;</u> 24. The View	22. Injustice (Victimization/women); 23. Myth & Identity (historical and existential/women); 24. Injustice (Poverty)
	1976	**25. Āhu, Salandar, Talhak and Others**	<u>26. The Crow</u>	25 & 26 Injustice, Resistance, Myth & Identity (Rereading the past/women)

3. Instability Revolution	1977	**27. Mourning Wail (Nodbeh)**	27. Injustice, Resistance &Transition (women)
	1978	28. Writing on the Wall (Graffiti) (Neveshteh-hā-ye Divāri)	28. Resistance &Transition
	1979	**29. Death of Yazdgerd**	29. Transition & Deconstruction (of Monarchy & Patriarchy); 30. Resistance and Transition;
4. Fundamentalist Islamization, Suffocating Censorship, Terror & War	1980	**30. Tales of Shroud-Wearing Leader (Qesseh-hā-ye Mir-e Kafanpush)**	31. Resistance & Transition
		31. Sable's Night;	
	1981	32. Memoirs of the Actor in a Supporting Role	32.33.34. Deploring, Resistance and Transition; 35. Myth & Identity (historical)
		33. Facing Mirrors; **34. Occupation**;	
		35. The Unbelievable Story	
	1982	**36. Conquest of Kallāt Kallāt Claimed**	36 & 37. Resistance and Transition; 38. Transition & Identity
		37. Day of the Event; 38. The Earth;	
	1984		39. Transition; 40. Resistance and Transformation; 41. Transformation; 42. Myth and Identity (Historical) and Deploring; 43. Myth & Identity (Individual/ National
		39. Pir-Abad's Old Case; 40. Warrior's Account/Ayyār-Nāmeh; 41. Mobārak's Shoes 42. Secret History of the Sultan in Abaskun; 43. Maybe Some Other Time;	
		44. Covered Interiors (Pardeh Khāneh)	44. Resistance (Women); 45. Identity/National
	1985	**45. Bashu the Little Stranger**	46. Deploring; 47. Myth & Identity; 48. Deploring, Myth & Identity
	1986	**46. Parchment of Master Sharzin**; 47. Gilgamesh; **48. The New Preface to the Shahnameh**	
	1988	50. Mr Lear	49. Deconstruction & Resistance; 50. Deploring
	1989	49. Battle of Slaves	51. Deploring, Myth & Identity; 52. Resistance
5. Post-war Reconstruction	1992	51. Travellers; 52. Journey to the Night	53. & 54. Injustice & Resistance (Women)
		53. Reed Panel; **54. Killing Rabid Dogs**	55. Deploring, Myth & Identity
	1993	**55. Reciting Siyāvush (Play)**	
		55. Reciting Siyāvush (Filmscript)	
	1994	56. Book of Merriment (Tarabnāmeh, original 2006) Part 1 and Part 2	56. Injustice, Resistance and Transition
		57. The Songs of Mama Arsu	57. Deploring & Resistance
	1995	58. Hurā in the Mirror	58. Deploring
	1996	59. The Destination; 60. The Protest	59. & 60. Injustice & Resistance

(Continued)

Table 1.1 (Continued)

Era	Year	Plays (Year of Writing)	Films & Filmscripts (Year of Writing)	Expressive Moods
6. Attempting & Failing to Deliver Democratic Reform	1997	61. Congregation for the Removal (Majles-e Basāt Barchidan); **62. Afrā or the Day is Passing**	63. The Last Days of Sadeq Hedayat	61. Resistance and Transition; 62. Deploring; 63. Deploring
	1998	64. The Sacrifice of Sennemār	65. Conversation with the Wind	64. Deploring; 65. Deploring
	1999	66. Congregation for Killing Sohrab 67. Jānā and Balādur (A Shadow Play) 68. Ardāvirāf's Report	69. Conversation with Water; 70. Con. with Soil; 71. Con. with Fire	66. Deploring, Myth & Identity; 67. Transition, Myth and Identity; 68. Myth and Identity, 69., 70 &. 71. Deploring, Myth and Identity
	2000	72. Congregation for Striking Ali	73. Saljuq Station	72 &73. Deconstruction, Myth & Identity
	2003	**74. The One Thousand and First Night**	75. Accident Does Not happen by Itself	74. Resistance, Deploring, Myth & Identity, Transition; 75. Injustice and Deploring
	2005	76. The Sufferings of Professor Navid-e Mākān and Architect Rokhshid-e Farzin	77. Mahi (Heroine's Name: Fish/Moonlike)	76. Deploring; 77. Injustice and Resistance
7.Extremist Populism	2006		78. Edge of Cliff; 79. Speaking Rug	78. Deconstruction; 79. Myth and Identity
	2007		80. When We Are All Sleeping;	80. Deconstruction & Deploring (the loss of cultural values)
	2009	81. The Crossroads		81. Deconstruction & Deploring (lying)
Stanford	2010 2021	Staging 67 (2012), 1 (2013), 68 (2015) 56 (2016), and 81 (2018).	Publishing 77. Mahi (2020)	

visual motifs have become unrivalled masterpieces or changed the course of modern Persian literature, drama and cinema (Figure 1.1).[57]

The following table provides a panorama of the recurrence of expressive moods in various eras.

Table 1.2 The Recurrence of Expressive Moods in Various Eras

No	Expressive Moods	1960–6 6 Years	1967–6 10 Years	1977–9 3 Years	1980–8 9 Years	1989–96 8 Years	1997–2005 8 Years	2006–9 4 Years
1	Deconstruction	9	1	1	1	General	1	4
2	Injustice	1	11	1	3	5	2	General
3	Deploring	1	2	1	7	6	11	3
4	Resistance	1	6	2	10	5	3	0
5	Myth & Identity	4	3	General	6	3	9	1
6	Transition	0	1	4	9	1	3	0

As reflected in Table 1.2, the zeitgeist of each era is mirrored in the recurrence of expressive moods. Yet, short-term conflicts are also reflected in works written immediately after some events. The first mood, deconstruction, which is present in all Beyzaie's works but occurs extensively in his early works, shows his attempts to influence his audience by subverting dominant beliefs about love, women, heroes, sacrifice, religiosity, fate and justice. Though influenced by the aftermath of the 1953 coup in its bid to use simple forms to communicate with the masses, it often goes deeper to examine the obstacles to constructive citizenship and inclusive nationhood. The second reflects the feeling of injustice in a society where values are bent to satisfy the elite, who include not just the members of the state but also the holders of economic and religious power, the landlords, the clergy and their cohorts as the agents of injustice. Central to this is the idea that with the failure of the state to deliver the democratic potential of the White Revolution, the country was going towards a more undemocratic form of governance. It also reflects on how the Shah organized international shows to prove Iran's grandeur as the reincarnation of ancient Iranian empires, although the country's rates of illiteracy and poverty were still high. In other words, at political level, it criticizes a mode of modernization concerned with showing off Iran's grandeur to Western countries instead of real modernization. Later returns of the mood reflect on similar poses during the 1990s, when the state exploited Iranian resources to buy support among global Islamic movements or glorify itself as the leader of Islamic revival. Like myth and identity or deconstruction, injustice is an ever-present mood with various motifs associated with it. I have, therefore, marked these as 'general' even when they are not central to any works. This injustice might lead to individual determination as in *Downpour* (1970) or *The Crow* (1976), collective resistance as in *Court of Bactria* (1968) or giving up as in *The Feast* (1967).

'Deploring' reflects on aggravated forms of injustice, victimization of human beings or loss of moral values, knowledge, love, freedom, national treasures and chance of progress due to regressive mentalities and practices, ignorance, corruption, utopian illusions or petty grudges between people, the traditional holders of power or officials. In the second period, it often critiques the failure to ward off colonialism. For instance, Farmān in *The Stormy Path of Farman the Son of Farmān* (1970), who is preoccupied with turning a village girl into an ancient queen, loses all his resources in his dealings with materialistic dealers and usurers. The highest occurrence of this mood is between 1980 and 2005, particularly during the years of execution, terror and war (1980–8) and then between 1997 and 2005 when the relative relaxation of censor allowed writers to comment on the 'chain murders' of the dissenting intellectuals.[58] The conditions were so severe that in two occasions, from 1988 to 1989 and 1996 to 1997, Beyzaie preferred to live outside the country. As a momentous example, *Travellers* (1989), which was written after the loss of hundreds of thousands of young people in the war or in political executions, works like a *ta'ziyeh* ritual to commemorate this loss while hoping for rebirth. The film's narrative also suggests how, following the revolution, people expected a blissful sacred marriage of heaven and earth but went through ten years of terror, war and loss. Similarly, *Reciting Siyāvush* (1993),[59] *Congregation for the Sacrifice of Sennemār* (1998), *The One Thousand and First Night* (2003) and *Sufferings of Professor Navid-e Mākān and Architect Rokhshid-e Farzin* (2005) reflect on the victimization of creative intellectuals and artists to comment on the chain assassinations of the 1990s. Or *Congregation for Killing Sohrab* (1999) reflects on how political opportunism demolishes Sohrāb, the hero of meritocracy, to comment on the failure of Khatami's political bid for democracy and meritocracy. Thus, Siyāvush represents the youth's desire for honour and tolerant spirituality, Sennemār creativity and progress and Sohrāb justice and meritocracy, and together they represent thousands of educated people who stood for the same values but lost their lives or left the country in fear of persecution or in search of a better life.

The fourth mood, which reached its highest frequency during the revolution, focuses on resisting the machination of political and religious opportunism, hypocrisy, deception and cruelty. For instance, *Four Boxes* (1967), which was written immediately after the Shah's crowning ceremony and a few months after the strikes of Chitsāzi Textile workers, uses a stylized puppet form that reflects on the failure of social classes to curb the power of a scarecrow and displays the victimization of the lower classes in the process.[60] Or *Occupation* (1981) focuses on how a repressive regime is replaced with a more brutal one that crushes any dissenting voice. It uses historical distancing to compare the atrocities of the era of the Allies' occupation of Iran (1941–7) with the post-revolutionary situation and to celebrate the bravery of a woman who embarks on a quest in the Tehran of the 1940s to find her husband who has been kidnapped by the agents of an unknown security organization.[61] Thus, both are concerned with rising against seemingly indomitable enemies.

The fifth responds to Iran's contemporary problems with symbolic studies of people's national and mythological identity. It is also the locus of Beyzaie's discovery of women as vanguards of emancipation, which is essential in his films. Yet, the works reflecting this mood are also philosophical, commenting on man's existential predicaments, historical failures, patriarchy, nationalism, conflict resolution, spirituality, leadership and the psychology of human love. The works reflecting this mood are written during periods of extreme censorship when the only way to convey emancipatory ideas was through symbolism.

The last mood concentrates on periods of transition, signifying how resistance might lead to breaking the vicious circles of injustice, victimization, cruelty, hypocrisy and corruption. For Beyzaie, this successful transition or initiation into a higher state is usually the fruit of an individual determination, as in *Killing Rabid Dogs* or *Sable's Night* rather than a collective movement with utopian illusions. Yet, even this individual determination is always in danger of being aborted, distorted or destroyed.

Epilogue: Closing the chapter and introducing the book

Of the thirty works that I marked as unrivalled masterpieces in Table 1.1, eight are films and twenty-two are plays and scripts that have continued to be read as literary works due to their special qualities. If one compares this range and his scholarly works on Iranian myths with any other writer's playwright's or artist's oeuvre, the unique role Beyzaie has played in expanding the resources of Iranian literary, visual and performing art and mythological studies becomes clear.[62] My two monographs on Beyzaie are intended to reveal some of these unique qualities. I have organized the two books as stand-alone spaces of analysis which go through Beyzaie's creative worlds chronologically to reflect on their dialogue with Iranian culture, society and politics as well as world cinema and drama. The timelines of the two books with one focused on the era between 1959 and 1979 and the other on the years after the 1979 revolution suggests the revolution as a turning point. While I do think that 1979 was a turning point in Iranian cultural production due to the impacts that it had on the aesthetics of everyday life and cultural production in Iran, this division does not deny the continuity of the emancipatory discourses that have shaped the nature of artistic activities in Iran since the early 1900s.

The present book, therefore, is focused entirely on Beyzaie's activities between 1959 and 1979. The first chapter, which you just read, introduces Beyzaie, clarifies why his works are significant and outlines the approaches I will be using to examine his oeuvre, particularly his films. The sections on regimes of truth and art and the types of creativity that originates in trauma theorize how Beyzaie's sublimation of his life experiences has shaped the trajectory of his vision. The overview of Beyzaie's works provides a chronological panorama of his contribution to Iranian cultural production and suggests the worldliness of his creative impulse, which is, nevertheless, not to be interpreted as a map for reading Beyzaie because his works always transcend the conditions of their production and examine their subjects from different angles and through forms that highlight what is universal and to some extent timeless. This is particularly so as many of the expressive moods and themes that I mention are projected through forms that reframe the mythic, mystic and historical narratives taken from the cultural memory of Iranian people. It is thus often rewarding to reread them to see how they reflect on some of the most endemic problems in human societies.

Chapter 2, *The Puppet Trilogy* (1962–3): Deconstruction of the hero/villain binary, analyses Beyzaie's engagement with the dominant discourses of heroism in his early puppet plays in which he modernizes Iranian *kheimeh-shab-bāzi* to create an emancipatory aesthetics about heroes and villains as victims of the machination of marginalization and exclusion. Beyzaie's penchant for self-reflexive theatricality is central to the form as the actors walk and talk like puppets, the hero and the demon refuse to fight, the girl and the black servant begin to act like heroes and the puppeteer embodies the obsession of dominant discourses to control people's lives by surveillance and punish or destroy them if they refuse to bend.

Chapter 3, *Uncle Moustache* (1970): Carnivalesque deconstruction of hegemonic masculinity, focuses on how Beyzaie's first film uses comic, carnival and grotesque elements to trace the journey of a middle-aged man from the seclusion and intellectual poise of hegemonic masculinity and its obsession with controlling other to love, sociability and youthful playfulness in a context in which children act as agents of emancipation.

Chapter 4, *Downpour* (1971–2): The creative intellectual and the meta-cinematic subversion of hegemonic masculinity, argues that by focusing on the quest of a teacher for belonging, recognition and love in a film saturated with images of films, film posters and frames, *Downpour* engages in a self-reflexive dialogue with Iranian culture and cinema about the absence of women, intellectual and child protagonists in mainstream films and replaces the tough guy of Iranian cinema with characters with heroic potential from these three categories.

Chapter 5, *The Journey* (1972): A Sisyphean quest for belonging in a world of toxic masculinity, violence and blind obedience, analyses Beyzaie's first ritualistically charged film in which he uses the perspectives of two marginalized orphan boys whose quest for a lost identity and a sense of belonging takes them through the streets of a violent megacity from the lower depths to the high-rise buildings that promise protection. Their quest of initiation, however, takes them through twelve labours in a world of blind obedience, superstition, violence and consumerism only to prove that the city's superficial façade of modernity is fake and its high-rise buildings mask its alienating lack of support for the marginalized.

Chapter 6, *Stranger and the Fog* (1974), rituals of existence: Homecoming, becoming and departing, analyses Beyzaie's first film in his village trilogy. It demonstrates how Beyzaie's film functions like a feast of reformulated agricultural rituals which confront the sanctification of patriarchal values and the obsession with afterlife in religion by finding the roots of modern egalitarian perspectives in pre-religion natural agricultural rituals. The arrival of an individual from the unknown, his quest for belonging, love and recognition and his depiction as a sacrificial hero of fertility and prosperity subvert the ideals of tough guy masculinity and depict him as an agricultural dying and resurrecting god, in par with Tammuz or Siyāvush. His departure in search of the meaning of the unknown, however, suggests how the energy that must be spent for happiness and prosperity is lost to an obsession with the unknown and the inherited conflicts that continue to distort human life.

The final chapter, Chapter 7, *The Crow* (1977): City, home and the pitfalls of Iranian modernity, offers a close reading of the first film in which Beyzaie's epistemic privilege displays itself in a female intellectual protagonist, whose centrality suggests Beyzaie constant aspiration to redefine the roles of women in society. The chapter argues that the film is the first of four films which use mystery/thriller elements and surrealistic journeys in time or to different parts of a violent city to contemplate the rise and the pitfalls of Iranian modernity. It also reveals that the film subverts the tradition-modernity binary that neglects the aspects of Iranian tradition whose reformulation for the present is essential for homegrown modernity and suggests that a constructive approach to modernity requires a thorough rereading of the past and transcending the obsession with copying Western modernity.

Follwing my chapter on *The Crow*, I will close the book with a conclusion in which I sum up the main points of the book and suggest how the revolution marked the end of an era which led to major changes in Iranian cultural production and Beyzaie's works.

As observed in the above outline, my second chapter focuses on Beyzaie's plays of the early 1960s to analyse the evolution of his deconstructive emancipatory aesthetics before he began making films. But the following chapters go on to provide scene-by-scene analyses of the semiotic structures of Beyzaie's films and identify their multiple levels of realistic, surrealistic, metaphorical, psychological and mythological suggestiveness and the intricate restructurings of cultural codes which enable Beyzaie to establish a dialogue with the past and present and reformulate the meaning of being Iranian in a modern world. Depending on the form and the main experiences mirrored in each film, I also use a series of theoretical perspectives to highlight the unique qualities of the film's expressive grammar and reveal the significance of the cultural beliefs and codes that are de- and re-mythologized in the films. Whenever the forms and the subjects of the films require tracing their evolutions in his plays, the chapters also provide brief analyses of Beyzaie's earlier or later plays. The purpose in each case is to extract the aesthetic and cultural dialogue that the film and its associated plays establish with Iranian cinema, theatre, literature, culture and politics in their situations of annunciation. The unifying themes of the two volumes include (1) trauma, marginalization and creativity, (2) outsider gaze, epistemic privilege and epistemic authority, (3) transgressive and emancipatory framing and reframing, (4) redistributing the sensible by introducing new ways of seeing, hearing and doing things, (5) the modalities and transformations of human identity at personal and collectives levels, (6) desire for belonging and recognition (7) modernity, modernization and democracy, (8) citizenship and leadership, (9) gender relations, (10) hegemonic masculinity and femineity, (11) patriarchy and power, (12) social and political surveillance and control, (13) the impact of indigenous artistic forms on the poetics and politics of Beyzaie's drama and cinema and (14) his reshaping of these forms to create emancipatory forms and outlooks that subvert the dominant exclusionist and suppressive discourses on life, art, human identity, belonging, power, heroism, masculinity, intellectuals, women and children. As specified earlier, my approach is characterized by textual analysis and thick interdisciplinary investigative description informed by aesthetic, political and cultural histories of Iranian cinema and theatre, as well as theories of performance, reception, psychoanalysis, gender relations, translation, post-colonialism and cultural semiotics. However, I also avoid overtheorizing as such an approach masks the true nature of Beyzaie's oeuvre and decreases my readers' enjoyment of my writing on Beyzaie.

2

The Puppet Trilogy (1962–3)

Deconstruction of the hero/villain binary

A young artist in search of authenticity: Human puppets and the birth of a new form

In an interview with Mohammad Abdi about his teenage encounters with cinema and theatre, Beyzaie states that he failed to pass his exams in years seven and eight of his school years, which coincided with the chaotic years between 1951 and 1955. However, what Beyzaie recalls beyond these conflicts marks the achievements of some of his classmates despite the poverty and disciplinary violence endemic everywhere. It was also during the same years that Beyzaie discovered his passion for cinema and later theatre. In 1958, he told his father who was worried about his future that he intended to study theatre, and, to convince him, took him to see a few plays and films that he thought were relevant to his plans. Some of these experiences proved disastrous because although he had introduced Mostafa Oskouei and Houshang Kavousi as people educated in the field to high levels, Kavousi's film, *Hefdah Ruz be E'dām* (Seventeen Days to Execution, 1956–7) and Oskouei's staging of Shakespeare's *Othello* (March 1959) fell below his expectations.[1] Beyzaie stopped urging his father to join him in his trips to Tehran's cinemas and theatres, but he soon saw Abbas Javanmard and Ahmad Bratlou's staging of Ali Nasirian's *Bolbol-e Sargashteh* (*The Wandering Nightingale*, first act performed 1956, full performance March 1959) whose magical world remained essential in determining his vision of theatre. Conjuring the magic of folktales with poetic words, incantations, songs and traditional performing techniques, the play dramatized a folktale about a boy murdered by his foster mother and metamorphosized into a nightingale.[2]

Determined to study Iranian performing traditions but finding no relevant degrees, he began studying Persian literature at Tehran University, with the hope of writing a dissertation on the subject. However, once he realized that his professors do not support his vision, he dropped out to conduct his research by himself. Thus, from 1961, with Ghaffary's referral,[3] he began publishing his articles on Iranian and Asian performing traditions in *Music Journal*. Then, having realized that his creative experiments with *naqqāli* and mythic narratives could not be performed with a proper level of expertise, he began frequenting the performances of *Goruh-e Honar-hā-ye Melli* (National Arts

Group, 1956–78). The result of this experience and his research was a series of plays that reformulated the tales, cliché characters and stylistic features of Iranian puppet plays, *kheimeh-shab-bāzi*. These included a one-act play entitled *Matarsak-hā dar Shab* (Scarecrows at Night, 1961), which Javanmard (1929–2020), a founding member, of *National Arts Group* performed and then recorded for television. Beyzaie, however, later excluded this play from his published works as he thought it 'did not reflect his dramatic vision'. The case of *Arusakhā* (The Marionettes), *Ghorub dar Diyāri Gharib* (Sunset in a Strange Land) and *Qesseh-ye Māh-e Penhān* (The Tale of the Hidden Moon), however, was different. 'Intended for live actors or puppets',[4] they went beyond Nasiriān's works to introduce a new form drama in which Beyzaie's deconstructive reframing introduces three metatheatrical situations to subvert the inherited ideology of Iranian culture and his linguistic versatility sublimates the folk poetry of the form to create a poetically magical world which many scholars count as the most poetic plays of Persian literature.[5]

Knowing about the emancipatory significance of what happens in the trilogy due to having actors instead of puppets, in one of my interviews with Beyzaie, I asked him abouthow he came up with the idea of using actors instead of puppets. He confirmed that his original purpose was to revive a dying form by writing a modern piece with the technical and character resources of *kheimeh-shab-bāzi*. However, as he was writing the play, he realized that it can be performed by actors. Thus, after finding that traditional puppeteers, being used to improvisation, were not open to memorizing and performing, he decided to find a way to have it performed by actors.[6] The idea of using actors who acted like puppets, therefore, was one that gradually dawned on Beyzaie before submitting the text to Javanmard.

Beyzaie specifies that his fascination with the form may have originated in 'seeing in 1950 or 1951 a local performer in regional clothing with a portable box on top of which two colourful puppets, a man and a woman, on horseback were placed'.[7] As to the sources of inspiration for using actors instead of puppets, although similar techniques have been used in theatre and cinema, Beyzaie's reframing creates an entirely new momentum which makes it hard to find a particular source. Though Beyzaie began his research on Japanese theatre two years later, one such example can be found in Kabuki. During the seventeenth century, Japanese puppeteers, *kugutsu mawashi* began to use larger puppets to create *bunraku* or *ningyo joruri*, which mixed puppet theatre with dramatic recounting of popular legends and *shamisen* music. This new form became so popular that during the eighteenth century *kabuki* performers adopted its narratives and techniques in *kabuki* plays in which live actors acted like puppets.[8] Another likely source is *The March of the Wooden Soldiers* (aka *Laurel and Hardy: Babes in Toyland*, 1934), in which actors act as puppet soldiers fighting against the bogymen invading the Toyland.[9] Beyzaie combined this human-as-puppet method with the already intriguing metatheatrical techniques of *kheimeh-shab-bāzi* and made them serve his own deconstructive gaze. The process produced a situation in which humans acting as puppets achieve a level of agency and face a puppeteer-narrator, who embodies the way dominant discourses perpetuate the marginalizing narratives that deprive people who are different of the chance to have normal lives and society of the chance to benefit from the divergent views of these people.

At the time, Jalal-e Al-e Ahmad criticized Beyzaie's choice of 'Japanese-style titles'. Echoing what Dariush Ashoori (1938–) had referred to as a possibility in his friendly discussion with Beyzaie, he also reduced Beyzaie's emancipatory gaze to its raw origin and criticized what he called Beyzaie's defence of a minority. He also assumed that Beyzaie was blaming God for problems that he himself blamed on the state and concluded that the plays contributed to 'the state-run [propaganda at] Sanglaj theatre'.[10] The first issue with his critique was that, like many others, he thought that where even men's rights are violated, one must not focus on women, children or minority's rights. This was one of the failures of many people associated with Iranian opposition, but it was particularly problematic in Al-e Ahmad's case as the state itself had nationalistic tendencies which made it more advanced regarding women and minorities than the Islamic fundamentalists whom Al-e Ahmad had begun to support. A more important issue, however, was that either purposefully or due to his zeal for rabblerousing, he ignored that Beyzaie's emancipatory gaze was directed at the whole idea of minoritization and marginalization and the way dominant discourses, and not God, use exclusionist narratives to crush anyone who thinks differently regardless of their origins.[11] This accusatory approach to criticism was Al-e Ahmad's trademark, but it was later adopted by other intellectuals, who, like Al-e Ahmad, aspired to become the sole authority of taste and culture. Though seemingly secular, they never seemed to have transcended the minority/majority binary or see that those who originate in a so-called minority but have transcended the minority-majority binary may see the failures of their culture more efficiently.[12] As Beyzaie himself states,

> Does the opposite of his words mean that everyone else was representing the majority instead of, as we all wished, expanding our cultural resources and ideas to recognise our self-constructed dead-ends? Yet even if his readings were correct, why should I not have the right to defend minorities and how does defending minorities mean helping state-run theatre. Indeed, the state itself was itself a part of a larger governing system which had Al-e Ahmad as its intellectual and later its unofficial representative. *The conflict over power did not really hide the essential, tyrannical unity of the two sides.* [. . .] Al-e Ahmad failed to remember that more than two centuries before I was born, the black men of *kheimeh-shab-bāzi* and *takht-e huzi* have been the minority on the stage, have turned their lives into a source of entertainment for the elites: kings, premiers, commanders, heroes, merchants, and clerics and have ridiculed the whole system in the process. That is the same Black, who, at the end of *Sunset in a Strange Land* and *Four Boxes* rebels. Nevertheless, what Al-e Ahmad did with his pen was to leave a bad example that led to the renewal of the accusatory approach of dogmatics towards arts. *I do not even want to count how many intellectual trials I have gone through with the leadership of renowned writers who imitated Al-e Ahmad with the hope of becoming the Master of Jurisprudence for intellectuality and literature and give decrees on limits and customs of being a writer of literature.*[13]

My italics in the quotation highlight how Beyzaie explicitly states the similarity of the activities of some intellectuals and those of Shi'i clerics in establishing their own cults and followers. In Beyzaie's trilogy, the use of actors as puppets and the hero and the demon's decision to die rather than kill each other created a new discourse in which what was being criticized was not just the state but the discourses that perpetuated the exclusionist and dictatorial obsessions of people, the opposition and the state towards their 'others'. Indeed, even in their political suggestiveness, the plays went far beyond Al-e Ahmad's views. As Beyzaie recalls, a well-educated man, named Masoudi, whom Beyzaie knew from Ghaffary's Cine Club (1949–51 and 1959–79) told him that for him the character Demon was a leftist activist, and Hero an honest officer who realizes the leftist man is not evil, refuses to kill him and is thus destroyed by the state.[14]

In any case, Javanmard directed *Sunset in a Strange Land* in 1964 in Tehran and several other cities and received support from the Ministry of Culture and Art to rehearse *The Tale of the Hidden Moon* and take both to *The Theatre of Nations' Festival* in Paris in 1965. Through building the décor and training the actors to act as puppets with masks and elastic bands attached to them was beyond the habitual capacity of Iranian theatre, the performance was a success in its impact on raising the standards of staging in Iran and its momentum for the rise of indigenous-style modern plays. As Javanmard specifies in his account of staging the plays in Iran and France, it was also praised by Le Figaro's theatre critic Jean Jacques Gautier:

> In the heat of the intense music, as the play moves towards tragedy, this mythic morality play begins to blossom with the captivating aroma of a distant land with a simple yet beautiful and charming poetry that reminds us of Iranian miniatures. [...] How amazing these puppet-like actors who are hanging from ropes with their painted eyes, crimson cheeks and mechanical moves are! [...] The puppeteer [...] depicts the eternal battle between the angelic and demonic forces which occupy the conflicting sides of human soul, but suddenly, the puppets who are tired of these unending conflicts [...] realize that the demons have been created and placed in their minds by this very adroit narrator. In a rebellion that ends with their lives, they rebel and shout this truth in the ears of the person who has created their fate.[15]

Gautier's reductive reading of Asian theatre as medieval European plays reduces the play into a morality play, but his closing words imply that despite Javanmard's approach for promoting his own political idea of the play, Beyzaie's vision had been conveyed.

After this experience in which he acted as a stage manager, Beyzaie continued reframing the form in plays that handled topical subjects, including a significant scene of a puppeteer enacting the essential conflicts of the constitutional revolution in *Mourning Wail* (1977) and a full-length puppet play *Congregation for the Removal* (1997).[16] Echoes of puppet forms can also be seen in his *taqlid* plays such as *Four Boxes* (1967) or *Battle of Slaves* (1988). These latter plays are different from his trilogy in that while carrying the same deconstructive vision, they introduce new characters. Together with the first three, they also sublimate comic folk forms to release their potential for tragic aesthetic contemplation while preserving their power to communicate with ordinary people. As in Ahmad Shamlou's folk poems, *Pariā* (The Fairies, 1953), *Shabāneh: Yeh Shab-e Mahtāb* (Nightly: One Moonlit Night, 1954), or

Qesse-ye Dokhtarā-ye Naneh Daryā (The Daughters of Nanny Sea, 1959) and Forough Farrokhzad's *Ali Kochulu* (Little Ali, 1963) or Bijhan Mofid's play *Shahr-e Qesseh* (Tale City, 1966), Beyzaie's first puppet plays were among masterpieces that originated as attempts by dramatists, painters, novelists and poets to rework folk songs, tales and paintings to transcend the fixation on Western forms and modernize Iranian artistic forms. The approach was not unprecedented as echoes of such a vision can be found in Mirza Aqa Tabrizi's (1870s) and Hasan Moqaddam's plays, M. A. Jamalzadeh and Hedayat's stories and Nima Yushij's poetry. Now, however, the adoption of this approach had found political urgency. The 1953 coup had shown them the cost of their inability to communicate with people, and such an approach functioned as a creative bid to do so for emancipatory purposes. The process, however, evolved into a return-to-the-roots discourse and a corresponding eastward gaze, which ranged from reactionary nativism to emancipatory cosmopolitanism. Beyzaie's fascination with these forms, however, was not just because of the rise of this originally marginal discourse in the 1950s as due to his background in a family of poets and his older cousin's research on Iranian chivalric tradition, he had already developed a taste for the *Shahnameh* and a modern gaze with a high degree of curiosity about indigenous forms and ideals of heroism.[17] Thus, rather than shaping the people of Nasiriān or Beyzaie's type, this new discourse was partly shaped by them, and in time, Beyzaie's research on Iranian and Asian forms and his creative works for reformulating indigenous forms made him a leading figure in the progressive side of this movement which aspired to create dramatic and cinematic masterpieces which were rooted in Iranian indigenous performing traditions.

The origins and forms of Iranian comic and puppet traditions

In the case of his puppet-style plays, the forms that Beyzaie used share their origins and rise with those of Iran's comic forms, which began to be called *taqlid* from the 1840s. The first references to these forms identify them as *maskhareh-bāzi* (Farce Plays) and suggest that they became more popular during the Mongol era when the Mongols' execution of the last Abbasid caliph in 1258 ended the religious influence of the Arab Caliphs on Iranian Muslims and paved the way for a total disengagement under the Safavids (1501–1726). According to Beyzaie, though such shows have ancient origins, under the Mongols pressure on itinerant musicians, puppeteers, jugglers and dancers decreased, so they settled in cities where people could hire them for house celebrations.[18] Their shows were usually of three major types:

1. *Motrebi* (musical entertaining) referred to dance and song routines accompanied with music and comic acts which mimicked regional dialects, gestures of local dignitaries or traits of people of different professions. In the second half of the seventeenth century, due to the state support, such forms of entertainment developed dramatic aspects. Though mostly performing for rich families, the players also preserved the right to perform for common people. This change of venue and audience gave variety to their work because to draw laughter, they had to improvise and change

the dialogue of their scenarios or the subjects of their satire in accordance with the occasion and the taste and social class of the audience.

Taqlid evolved from these forms in the next two centuries, particularly by music entertainers and *dalqak(s)* (jesters) who had since ancient times entertained courtiers or common people with jokes or music and dance plays. As in *Commedia dell' Arte*, these performers improvised based on satirical folktales and topical scenarios.[19] During the last Safavids and the Zands (1750–96), these players were joined by itinerant entertainers to create comic interludes, which in the Qajar era (1796–1925) dramatized full-length scenarios, called *taqlid*. The actors normally performed on boards covering small pools in the middle of yards of houses and inns, and thus their plays were called *ru-hozi* (on the pool) or *takhteh-hozi* (on the pool board). *Taqlid* was innovative: the scenery was minimal and the conventions symbolic, but the costume and make-up were crucial. The scenarios were enhanced by witty improvisations and dance moves, exaggerating the physical, psychological and linguistic features of people in various professions, age groups or regions. The most popular form of *taqlid* was *siāh-bāzi* (black-face play), which dramatized the relationship between a witty servant and his stupid master. In the houses of officials, players toned down their crude jokes and anti-elite satires, but in normal parties or coffeehouses, everything depended on the taste of the viewers. In the twentieth century, *taqlid* players established *Bongāh Shādmāni* (Happiness Agencies), where people booked them for shows, and from the 1920s, they also performed in small theatres.[20] Women had their own *taqlid* troupes who performed dance and song plays and sometimes lewd interludes of anti-patriarchal satire in female-only house parties.[21] With the alterations in Iranian public space from the 1900s, women began to perform in *taqlid* troupes in house parties and from the late 1920s on public stages. Due to its popularity, *taqlid* had the potential to generate modern forms, but the Pahlavis' push for Westernization and the intelligentsia's preference for Western-style theatre distorted the course of its growth, and the new regulations requiring texts for *taqlid* plays blunted its topical satire. Thus, *taqlid* degenerated into a basic comedy of manners, yoking insipid moral teaching with repartee and local intrigue. Despite this degeneration, however, the form experienced artistic revival from the 1960s.[22]

2. *Ma'rekeh Giri* (Performing Feats) included activities such as juggling, telling tall tales, riddles and jokes, making animals dance to music, exhibiting physical strength and skills such as breaking chains, walking on ropes or somersaulting.[23] Having described these feats, Sir John Chardin, who visited Iran between 1673 and 1677, states:

> Besides these Exercises [...] *Persians* [...] also have of those who Dance upon the Ropes, *Poppet-Shows*, and doing Feats of Activity as adroit and nimble as in any Country whatever.[24] [...] The puppet-shows and Juglers ask no Money at the Door as they do in our Country, for they play openly in the publick places, and those give 'em that will. They intermingle Farce and Juggling with a thousand Stories and Buffooneries, which they do sometimes Mask'd and sometimes Un-mask'd, and this lasts two to three hours: and when they have done, they go round to the

Spectators and ask something. [...] For two crowns the Juglers will come to their House. They call these sorts of Diversions *Mascare*, that is to say *Play, Pleasantry, Raillerie, Representation*; from whence comes our Word *Masqurade*.[25]

Despite the dubious etymology he offers for 'masquerade', Chardin provides the reader with an overview of the forms of entertainment one could observe in seventeenth-century Iran. It also highlights that at the time puppet shows were an integral part of these activities.

3. Thus, the third type was the puppet tradition whose various forms were in dialogue with the above. Beyzaie classifies these puppet shows into three types: *sāyeh-bāzi* (shadow play), *kheymeh-shab-bāzi* (puppet show) and *pardeh-bāzi* (puppet shadow play), which, respectively, used hand shadows, puppets and puppet shadows to show the movements of characters. Puppets were moved with nearly invisible threads with the puppeteer hiding in a cloth-covered frame above them and distorting his voice with a whistle-like device to suit the size of the puppets and a narrator interacting with both the audience and the puppets. Measuring between 20 and 50 centimetres, puppets were made of wood and cloth. The plays dramatized folktales which in some cases included fifty-three characters,[26] suggesting how puppet shows were the fertile grounds for transcending the Islamic restrictions against impersonation and acting. The regular main characters included *Pahlevān* (the kind young hero), *Pahlevān Kachal* (the bald and wily but generous champion), *Negār* (the beautiful girl), *Diev* (the demon), *Mollā-ye Riācār* (the hypocritical clergyman), the sage. Though honourable, *Pahlevān Kachal*, who is also the ancestor of the fifteenth-century Turkish puppet Kargoz, has a typically Iranian sense of humour, reminiscent of Ayyārs' disguising tricks and subversive charm.[27] In his *Theatre Persan*, Alexander Chodźko, a Polish officer in the Russian service, who was in Iran between 1830 and 1844, offers an account that reflects this carnival quality:

> There is a favourite piece in which *Pahlavan Kachal* betakes himself under the guise of a most pious Muslim to the house of a certain *Akhwund*, or rector of a parish. He sighs, weeps, groans, prays, recites verses, from the Koran or elsewhere, and quotes scraps of morality after the most approved fashion. The *Akhwund*, delighted with his visitor and edified by his religious zeal, begins to imitate and to emulate him. *Pahlavan Kachal* displays his theological knowledge, his acquaintance with the traditions and the patristics of Islam and recites legends in favour of the virtue of giving alms. Voluntary charity meets his highest panegyric. He quotes many lines of the mystic poetry so dear to the Persian heart, the poetry which under the profane semblance of love and wine, celebrates the activity and wisdom of Allah the all-merciful. Then *Pahlavan* begins to describe the delights reserved for the charitable in paradise. [...] [He] speaks as an eyewitness. He sings of heaven and its *houries* [heavenly nymphs] with the graces of antelopes, of its splendid banquets and its sparkling wine. The *Akhwund* is in ecstasies. He tastes already those rivers of milk which never grow sour, and those seas of clarified honey which never become dry.

He reposes already under the perpetual shade, or couches whose linings are of thick silk interwoven with gold. [. . .] He sees damsels advancing to meet him, with complexions like rubies and pearls, beauteous damsels with eloquent deep black eyes. He dances with delight. [. . .] [Finally,] he gives *Pahlavan* [. . .] his purse, bids him buy a banquet, and produces *Khullari*, the most excellent wine of Shiraz, which by some strange chance is found in a corner of his room, hidden away with a guitar. The two drink and play, until at last the pious *Akhwund* becomes drunk, and drops his Kuran and his rosary. The piece of course may be extended at pleasure. It is a vivid and never ill-timed representation of the *Tartuffe* of the religion of Islam.[28]

Chodźko's summary in Mew's translation suggests that these plays carried in them the seeds of carnivalesque resistance against cultural hierarchies. This was probably because their performers were marginalized people who suffered the opportunistic morality and double standards that characterize the figures of power and their cohort. Thus, when they performed for the royalty or the rich, they drew laughter from the audience by changing their dialogue and scenarios to mock the clergy, the rivals of their audience or the common people of different professions or ethnicities, but when they performed for commoners, they would add comic scenes about the police or the rich. Nevertheless, they also had sentimental plays with moral messages that they performed when their profession was in danger of being demonized by the clergy. In any case, they still preserved the givens of the dominant discourses by operating within a sentimental form of morality in which there was the possibility of having an ideal clergy or an ideal king.[29] Thus, these performances often used, what J. C. Scott calls, the gaps of pretended benevolence in the official discourse, to satirically protest injustice and claim rights for people 'in the prevailing ideology without appearing in the least seditious'.[30]

Framing and reframing in Beyzaie's reformulations

Beyzaie used similar characters but deconstructed the themes and suggested either using live actors or life-size puppets with the puppeteers in black working on the stage or with ropes from above. However, what distinguishes these plays besides the emancipatory aesthetics of live actors as puppets and their rebellion against the puppeteer/narrator who insists on preserving his exclusionist narratives at any price is the deconstructive gaze at cultural memory and rituals which is partly created by this form. In the trilogy, demons are victims of cultural stereotyping and economic deprivation which has also distorted the lives of heroes with unwanted battles with these demonized figures. Here, the hero wants to reconcile with and help the demons, but the narrator, though conscious of the injustice, is too conservative to approve of this aberration. More significantly, then, the qualms of the hero and the violent conservatism of the narrator, however, is that during the play, the black servant and the girl begin to gain agency, love each other and try to change the story. The play, thus, reformulates the metatheatrical technique of puppets talking to the narrator to redefine fate, heroism, demons and the position of underdogs.

Essential for analysing Beyzaie's reformulations is to master the concepts of 'framing', 'keying' and 'key change' in social sciences. As specified by Erving Goffman, a frame is a paradigm of interpretation, an assortment of acquired narratives, statements and stereotypes that human beings rely on to recognize and react to situations and events. Any act may have a variety of meanings depending on its intrinsic form (its shape, artistry and arrangement of parts) and external 'framing', which signifies the set of relationships and symbols through which individuals and institutions perceive, establish and communicate 'reality' in different interpretive communities. In the mundane life, for instance, a pair of shoes has generic and specific meanings and practical and aesthetic functions, but once it is placed on a platform in a museum, it becomes an object of aesthetic contemplation with potential to produce historical, philosophical and sociopolitical meanings. It may also find functions that have nothing in common with the original intentions it was made for. Placed among other objects, it may also generate a few statements in a narrative about the past, present, future or an aesthetic tradition. This framing is done through a process of 'keying in' as the object is promoted to become capable of being received by people to produce new meanings.

Framing has always been the main factor in generating meaning in social life and giving transcendental meanings to rituals. Yet, with the rise of the aesthetic regime of art to dominance,[31] new forms of framing emerged to subvert social and cultural hierarchies through a reconciliation of opposites from the conflicting ends of these hierarchies. These have often involved 'key change', a process of altering, rearranging or even revoking a frame, through which 'a given activity, one already meaningful in terms of some primary framework, is transformed into something patterned on this activity but seen by the participants to be something quite else'.[32] To give an example, a puppet play produced in early modern Iran had entertaining, cultural and sociopolitical functions, but despite the technical abilities and the framed inventiveness of its practitioners, it was not art as we understand it today. It was also limited in what it could do with the tradition in which it worked because it operated within a frame that made communication possible through special channels. Beyzaie's encounter with Nasiriān's *The Wandering Nightingale* triggered in him the idea of creating a new frame, which would subvert the dominant discourse to reflect his marginalized perspective.[33] Nasiriān remained faithful to the limited carnival force and the habitual framework of the traditional practitioners of the craft, but being familiar with Western-style drama, he increased the plausibility of the plot while preserving the uncanny elements of the folktale.[34] He, thus, adapted the folktale for a new stage without subverting the ideology of the tale. The creative change, therefore, was not in the vision, but in recrafting the old for a new stage in which the audience could not participate beyond a certain level. They could not, for instance, address the director to stop the father's new wife from killing his son or question the ending. Unlike the traditional audience of folk plays or puppet shows, the modern audience were not there just for entertainment or emotional catharsis achieved through a moderate dose of sociopolitical satire or sentimental morality. They were rather in a modern public space to explore the vicissitudes of human experience through aesthetic contemplation. Thus, though crucial in heightening the passion for indigenous forms, Nasiriān's adaptations lost the power of participation without offering the heteroglossia required for releasing the emancipatory power of drama.[35]

In Beyzaie, however, the change was historic. Between 1846, when Ākhundzādeh began writing plays, and 1959, when Beyzaie wrote his recitations, Iranian drama had produced several major plays. Yet, apart from some exceptions, like Ahmad Mahmudi's *Ostād Nowruz-e Pineh-Duz* (Master Nowruz, the Cobbler, 1919), what was deemed proper theatre remained aloof from indigenous forms.[36] The plays were significant as they addressed Iranian problems through Western-style theatre either by performing translated plays or by adapting Iranian topics for Western-style theatre. With Beyzaie's experiments with Iranian and Far Eastern forms, however, the sapling of Iran's indigenous-style modern drama began to grow in plays in which his epistemic authority enabled him to question the hierarchies of belonging.[37]

The puppet trilogy[38]

Beyzaie uses some of the stock characters of puppet shows: a narrator/puppeteer conversing with the puppets and the audience, a hero, a girl who is to be protected and loved, a demon whom the hero is to slay to gain recognition, a witty sidekick (the black of *taqlid*), a mystic traveller and the representatives of the town that requires saving: a merchant, a clergy and a poet. Yet, instead of creating a metatheatrical satire that ultimately reproduces sociopolitical, artistic and moral norms, Beyzaie mixes the puppeteer and narrator's roles and uses the conflict between this puppeteer-narrator and a few dynamic puppets to subvert the ideology that pushes unique people into the binary roles of heroes and outcasts. In Parvin Loloi and Glyn Pursglove's terms, Beyzaie creates 'a striking and multivalent image, interpretable in' terms of various 'types of power relationships – between a writer and his characters, between a political leader and his people, between God and man'.[39] More notably, however, he depicts how dominant discourses produce the people who become the products, victims, consumers and reproducers of inherited exclusionist relations in all aspects of the culture.

The Marionettes: The dawn of a tragic awareness in the heart of a comic tradition

The Marionettes begins with the narrating puppeteer, Morshed (the spiritual guide), addressing the audience in a conventional form of keying. He explains that the puppets only do what he wants them to do which is to entertain the audience, that the hero has a Black friend whose funny words will make people faint with laughter, and that the hero is to fight the bad guys 'who are always bad'. Then, he engages in a poetically charged discussion with Hero, who, disillusioned with his acts, breaks the illusion of reality by commenting on the stage and complaining about the act remaining unchanged for over a thousand years with him slaying whomever he has been told to be bad. Hero's account of his loneliness echoes Rostam's in the Shahnameh: 'When have I ever had rest?/ The earth has been my mat, and the sky my quilt'.[40] Though the narrator tries to twist his arguments to urge him to play, his existential questions about his role in life suggest that he has started questioning his own assumptions about others and his obsession with glory which has trapped him in endless wars. Though seemingly personal, this dilemma also has a social side:

> **Hero:** But what am I saying? For whom?
> **Narrator:** For me; for us.
> **Hero:** For those who watch but do not see!
> **Narrator:** This reminds me of the pain that is my life. In the famine year I heard an old woman say: 'A big wound crushes a man, but what kills him are the small ones!'
> **Hero:** Well said!
> **Narrator:** Thanks. So, from now you –
> **Hero:** I am nearly done for.
> **Narrator:** That is too bad.
> **Hero:** Why? Because I can't entertain people?
> **Narrator:** The people who only watch;
> **Hero:** the death of heroes!
> **Narrator:** Those who only count, after the battle –
> **Hero:** the corpse of the dead![41]

Narrator changes the discussion into love to suggest that Hero suffers from unrecruited love. The stratagem, which reflects the suppressive idea of reducing all problems to the personal, works well because Hero's dilemma is that he feels he has ruined his life for uncaring people without receiving any sense of belonging. Thus, having a beloved, which is suggested to be the cure as 'life is what it is and people cannot be changed', is, indeed, a treatment intended to make him leave social hierarchies and failures alone. Meanwhile, Black, whom Hero calls 'my only friend' arrives to display his typically poetic jests and deriding attitudes to power. Before being censured by Narrator for being too noisy, however, Beyzaie's black displays, in an aside, a level of poetic insight that associates him with spring and fertility, while implying his potential for being a saviour and the depth of his character when he is alone and not playing the clown. Making him the only character with a name, Yāqut, which means Rubi, Beyzaie associates Black, who was traditionally merry and dressed in red, with the common people's potential for growth, the blackness of fertile earth and the heat of the sun:

> **Black:** I heard someone calling me a hundred times. /I heard the tree, the mirror,/ the wind,/ the deer of the meadows,/ the flowing water calling me.
> **Narrator:** Don't try to be too cute, Yāqut (Rubi). Where are your manners?
> **Black:** As I was escaping, I left them in the lurch.
> **Narrator:** What about greeting?

> **Black:** (singing) Master dearie, hello, hello, hi, hi! Master dearie bring headie high. Master dearie, you see me sha-ki-n! Of your moustachie, I am fea-ri-n! (84)

Humour in *taqlid* extends from subtle sarcasm to bawdy jokes. Apart from making sarcastic remarks or interrupting the master by speaking, crying or laughing, professional *taqlid* actors who play the servant or the black often improvise and employ the following methods to incite laughter. In *pakari* (pensive deflation), 'the blackface hero engages his victims in serious discussions' only to mock their reactions in the end. He may engage the targets of his joke in a conversation about unemployment and ardently suggest that they must apply for a new job located in Ferdowsi Square, and then puncture their enthusiasm by explaining that the job is to act as a substitute for the statue of Ferdowsi whenever it feels like taking a break. *Navā dar āvardan* (copying the voice) is to imitate a person's speech qualities (accent, tone, word choices) to exhibit their inanity. *Hamdardi* (sympathy) is to ironically express compassion for a person or join them to do something stupid only to prove them stupid. In *tahammoq* (fooling) 'the protagonist pretends to be stupid' so that he can say whatever he likes about rich or powerful people. In *taqlib* (twisting), he ridicules his boss by malapropism, repeating the name of an object or food they loathe to disarm them, approvingly comparing them to beasts, flattering them for qualities they lack, turning their exclamations of 'pain or anger into funny songs', or interrupting their 'serious speech by crying or laughing noisily'.[42]

As seen in the excerpt, while maintaining the intellectual thrust of his play, Beyzaie uses these techniques well, but twists them to emphasize Black's superiority to Narrator in intelligence, linguistic skills and poetic creativity. His rapid switching between the poetic and the bawdy and his ability to insert folk songs and rhythmic, narrative clichés into every conversation also reflects Beyzaie's skills in using and enhancing the carnivalesque functions of his role. In any case, Black is there to tell them a *diev* (demon/ogre) has attacked the town:

> **Black:** A desert giant with bells on his feet; an incubus like a strap-legged demon! A spotty, skirt-wearing monster, who caught the cattle; changed the water's path; looted caravans! The pot-on-head, head-on-belly giant; the I-shape-eyed demon! Our girls saw and laughed at him, so he changed into seven shapes and blocked the seven gates. What a disaster! Everyone is about and around looking for Hero; yelling for help. (85)

The etymology of the term *div* suggests that in the original cosmology of Indo-Europeans it referred to a group of divinities who were later demonized in Iranian religions.[43] The writing and architectural skills attributed to some *div*(s) in the *Shahnameh* and *Garshāspnāmeh* also suggest that, regardless of being more civilized than their conquerors or less, the term was also used to refer to the original peoples of the regions Iranians conquered.[44] Black's report, however, also suggests how folktales may depict *div*(s) in line with the dragons of drought and famine in Indo-European agrarian myths, as like them, the *div* disrupts the flow of water, kills men and steals women and cows as emblems of fertility.[45] Beyzaie, however, disrupts this narrative by showing that Demon is a man whose appearance has led to his ostracization.

With Hero's assertion that he is done fighting for a people who just watch; three characters – Clergy, Merchant and Poet – arrive and, using their own priorities and speech styles, try to convince Hero to fight 'just one last time' as this 'Demon is the last of his kind'. Aware of their games, however, Hero ignores them and leaves. Here, as Black is mocking the three, a covered person, presumably a woman, enters to look for Hero and is beaten up by Black until she starts claiming that she is the prettiest woman in her clan. However, when Black removes the cover, the audience faces Demon, who begins bragging as everyone is escaping.

Demon is depicted as an individual who is aware of being Hero's double, without whom Hero would be nothing. Beyzaie shows that he hates people and grabs everything because he has been deprived and pushed out of the borders of belonging by those in power. In the middle of the chaos, with Merchant, Clergy and Poet worrying about their specific assets, there appears a girl to whom the three respectively offer coins, prayers and poetic praises to urge her to make Hero fight the demon. Though their attitudes differ, they all want to use her in ways that depict them as agents of patriarchy. For Merchant she is like a merchandise; for Clergy, a means of procreation and private joy that must be covered from everyone except him; and for Poet, an idol on the pedestals of praise which limit her agency and diversity. Girl, however, has a fluid character with elements ranging from the stereotypes of the gypsy fortune-teller to the comely beloved and the intellectual sage. She engages Hero in a conversation about his future, which leads to his discovery that she cannot read his future because she may well be his future. Hero talks of the conflict between honour and love and of how he buried his love to fight for people. He, then, explains how he has realized the futility of his triumphs: 'I began to pity my enemies as they are also the toys of this ever-watching people.' Beyzaie uses poetic suggestiveness to push this Pirandello-like, Brechtian, or indeed Beyzaiean, metatheatrical moment to its full potential: 'My home is a box of loneliness, and my battlefield is a tiny leather spread. Every day an enemy appears with a new face, and uproars arises from the viewers. Alas that a curtain stands between me and them, which they do not want removed. A hand pushes me forward, another in me searches inside' (98). The play keeps the ambiguity of the encounter to preserve its existential, social and aesthetic implications. Yet, having found to her wonder that 'the dice, the cards and the book all say the same thing', Girl pleads with Hero not to fight as 'this battle would lead to his death'. After a thousand years of absurd fighting, however, death is what Hero craves: 'This heart is still hot [. . .] with a burning desire for my blood, which I have craved to spill for a thousand years' (99). Having said these words, Hero exits leaving others to discuss their worries about Hero's ability to preserve the means and the market spaces that guarantee their status: Merchant (exchange corners), Clergy (preachers' and funeral food corners) and Poet (bookbinders and paper sellers' corners). Black directs his carnival laughter against their obsessions. To Clergy, he suggests going to 'paramours' corner', and to Poet, who sentimentally wishes to be like Hero and 'chase demons in mountains and forests like lightening, winds and clouds', he suggests killing the demon inside him to save time.

Hero and Demon now engage in a battle displayed on the stage or through their shadows on a back curtain. Heavy drumming and the characters' frightened arrivals and departures intensifies the idea of a war. With Demon presumably killed, Hero, who is injured, perhaps by a self-inflicted strike, declares his joy about seeing his own blood. He, then, deplores, 'while we are standing here, other heroes and demons are in making', and having advised Poet not to ever wish to be like him, he drops his sword as if ready to die and leaves the stage to Black, who has now realized the absurdity of the role he has been playing for a millennium. Worried about the continuity of his narratives, Narrator now asks for volunteers to take the sword to replace Hero. Each makes his own excuses, and Poet, having failed to move the sword, cannot imagine carrying its burden in the loneliness of restless, loveless journeys and endless battles. Beyzaie, thus, turns the sword into a metaphor for the burden of heroism in a culture in which the ideals of citizenship are still to be achieved and thus people watch rather than do things. In this context, Narrator's attempt to continue the narrative as if love or a personal obsession has led to Hero's death reflects his role as the guardian of the inherited culture and its hierarchies; Black's refusal to continue his jolly function suggests the rise of his agency which also urges him to guard the sword as a token of his desire for a still undefined type of heroism; and Poet's aspiration and failure to achieve the commitment required to act selflessly for others reveals the futility of using empty rhetoric for subverting dominant discourses. His fascination with playing Hero's role, however, echoes the existence of the same issue in the culture where poets, writers and filmmakers continue to celebrate the demon/hero binary like children who cannot put their dream toys away. Unlike Hero and Black, who have, for thousands of years, suffered the consequences of the narratives promoting such binaries, he is still engrossed by them and helps perpetuate them.

Narrator, then, closes the play in an epilogue that apologizes for this metatheatrical resistance against predefined roles: 'They failed to forget themselves; and I am not sure why no one can forget himself' (101). Beyzaie, thus, concludes that the hegemony of dominant discourses may silence people but cannot guarantee that they forget. The idea of remembering is then used more openly in the next play to subvert the ideological hierarchies of folktales by depicting Hero as a victim in a society characterized by the apathy of people, opportunism of the elites (Merchant and Clergy) and the inanity of those who have a voice in society (Poet).

Sunset in a Strange Land: The banality of evil and the crushing of the demonized

Sunset in a Strange Land begins with a prologue in which Narrator highlights the position of humans as puppets controlled by invisible threads of sociocultural relations and necessities: 'Every spectator [. . .] is himself an actor wishing to go on a path, while the threads are taking him to another path. Every spectator is also a player who remains confused; among so many threads and paths – visible paths and invisible threads.'[46]

Though a hasty reading may suggest that these statements are just youthful comments on life and fate, the play that follows introduces to the Iranian stage a perspective on social life which is like what Bourdieu later presented in his idea of 'habitus'. However, rather than just describing it as a social state, Beyzaie endeavours to transform the 'doxa' which, according to Bourdieu, maintain the invisible, taken-for-granted threads of inherited class-based assumptions and acquired educational views and relations that shape an individual's habitus. He, thus, turns his play into an intersection of several opposing 'habitus' to offer a locus of divergence and intellectual resistance that promotes agency among those banished from the hierarchies of belonging. Since aesthetic is at the basis of politics at its larger cultural level, this is also true of what he does for Iranian theatre. In his *Distinction: A Social Critique of the Judgement of Taste*, Bourdieu argues that 'taste' is an integral part of cultural hegemony, and that social hierarchies operate through social institutions to provide certain groups of people with the tools to access cultural codes which enable them to comprehend and appreciate 'elite' types of art. Moreover, since these codes are inculcated in the minds of individuals at a young age, they are internalized as 'taste', a kind of social conditioning that makes class an integral part of a person's identity. Thus, the way individuals present their social identity reflects their aesthetic dispositions which is determined by their status and causes a form of distancing or even disgust towards lower groups and their aesthetic tastes and behaviours.

> Whereas the ideology of charisma regards taste in legitimate culture as a gift of nature, scientific observation shows that cultural needs are the product of upbringing and education: surveys establish that all cultural practices (museum visits, concert-going, reading etc.), and preferences in literature, painting or music, are closely linked to educational level (measured by qualifications or length of schooling) and secondarily to social origin. The relative weight of home background and of formal education (the effectiveness and duration of which are closely dependent on social origin) varies according to the extent to which the different cultural practices are recognized and taught by the educational system, and the influence of social origin is strongest – other things being equal – in 'extra-curricular' and avant-garde culture. *To the socially recognized hierarchy of the arts, and within each of them, of genres, schools or periods, corresponds a social hierarchy of the consumers.* This predisposes tastes to function as markers of 'class'. The manner culture has been acquired lives on in the manner of using it: the importance attached to manners can be understood once it is seen that it is these imponderables of practice which distinguish the different – and ranked – modes of culture acquisition, early or late, domestic or scholastic, and the classes of individuals which they characterize (such as 'pedants' and *mondains*). Culture also has its titles of nobility – awarded by the educational system – and its pedigrees, measured by seniority in admission to the nobility. The definition of cultural nobility is the stake in a struggle which has gone on unceasingly, from the seventeenth century to the present day, between groups differing in their ideas of culture and of the legitimate relation to culture and to works of art, and therefore differing in the conditions of acquisition of which these dispositions are the product.[47]

Bourdieu's evaluation is focused on what is understood as the upper-middle class idea of taste and social conduct. In its actual manifestations, however, taste can be defined as having sets of rivalling regimes that impose their importance on individuals, interpretive communities, artists and artistic groups. Taste in 1950s and 1960s Iran was a rapidly changing phenomenon as the newly acquired taste for European- and American-style music, theatre, cinema and visual arts was conflicting with the evolving mostly leftist intellectual expectations that required works of art to criticize the state symbolically or realistically. The religious idea of high taste was also a force to reckon with, as although occasionally approving the intellectual anti-state idea of taste after Al-e Ahmad's success to yoke leftist and Islamist ideas together, in general it remained aloof to most artistic activities except those which served religious purposes such as *ta'ziyeh*, *noheh-khāni* (elegy recitation) or *manāqeb-khāni* (religious storytelling).[48] All these categories of taste, however, denigrated Iranian forms as either backwards and uncivilized or cheaply entertaining and lewd (*motrebi*). The idea of working with Iranian forms, therefore, could also be easily denigrated as decadent, form-obsessed or rooted in nostalgic obsessions with the past.

Indeed, Beyzaie's summary of how policing and censor work in Iran in his speech during Goethe Institute talks in 1977 or the following excerpts reflect these contradictory ideas of taste:

> [When arguing with the managers of the office of theatre about directing Zeami Motokiyo's *Atsomury* (1190s) in 1964], I said, 'it is our duty to experiment and help people understand alternative forms, and it is not too early as the text was written six hundred years ago'. They said, 'It is new as it is unusual. It is an attractive experiment, but it is too early for common people'. I think it was one of those cases in which both left and right agreed against.[49]

> During the production [of *Death of Yazdgerd*], every few days or so we received a threatening letter from an unknown political group that considered our existence against some values and told us to stop. It is good that in this country all rivalling political groups at least agree on stopping cultural activities.[50]

> From left-looking right and right-looking left or even the left of the right and the right of the left to the rightmost side of the right and the leftmost side of the left; they are not different from one another [in suppressing cultural activities].[51]

Despite these pressures which were doubled for Beyzaie due to his family background, his still-evolving epistemic authority allowed him to appropriate the scarcely tested resources of popular forms for the cultural space of elite art. His early experiments, however, were only staged because the leftist practitioners involved in National Arts Group read his emancipatory discourse in terms of their own political agendas.[52] Thus, the dominance of these regimes of taste meant that the staging of divergent plays faced major challenges and became possible only if they could be read in the light of one of these regimes, and the fact that Javanmard performed the latter two plays of the trilogy but not *The Marionettes* suggests this issue.

Using popular forms to create new trends in elite art is not a new practice, as the aristocracy, the church and then the bourgeoisie have since ancient times expropriated and transformed folk forms to their advantage while denigrating the original ones under the name of religious or elite art. The process has often involved distorting their subversive discourse, while giving them glamour, poise and a lofty language, which is possible only when the class involved in the reception and, to some extent, production of the form has been through the type of education that Bourdieu refers to as a surplus of disposable capital, and has the leisure time which it can then dedicate to what it calls elite culture. In the process, of course, it often romanticizes their motifs and characters or transforms them to reflect social, religious and aesthetic hierarchies. As the spectre of Antonio Gramsci puts it in Dario Fo's *The Worker Know 300 Words, the Boss Knows 1,000 – That's Why He's the Boss* (1975):

> We must stop thinking of the working class as marionettes, who don't know, who can't know, because they don't have culture. The working class knows because they are at the vanguard of the people, because the people have a great culture. Bourgeois power, aristocratic power, and the Church have in great part destroyed it, buried it. But it is our duty to help them retrieve it.[53]

In 1950s Iran, which had gone through several decades of West-inspired modernization and six years of occupation by the Allies (1941–7), this onslaught on popular culture had also been intensified by the forces that later came to their full potency in the capitalist globalization of the 1980s which in Iran joined religious philistinism to uproot many aspects of popular culture. Fo's solution to this suppression or 'stealing and falsifying' is to encourage all intellectuals to 'reconstruct the folk culture', 'in order to give it back to the people and make it the highest and most progressive instrument of the revolution' as he does himself.[54] Popular culture, of course, has its own ways of restructuring and recuperating to confront the pressures of official culture, but there is always the possibility that these restructurings, even the ones like Fo's are cornered within the official culture as 'safety faucets'. In time, however, when the number of 'safety faucets' increases the current becomes impossible to control and an era of cultural renewal may force the official culture to transform its methods of domination. This is exactly what happened in 1960s Iran as the tolerant side of the state realized the implications of the return-to-the-roots movements in arts and began to accommodate it through the cultural organizations run by the king's wife, Farah Diba (1938–), who had herself studied fine arts in France. The result was an era of cultural rejuvenation which despite its paradoxes produced one of the greatest eras of modern Iranian drama, cinema, literature and visual arts.

Though harbouring no romantic illusions about working-class heroes and leftist revolutions, Beyzaie's restructuring were like Fo's in their emancipatory gaze. Since his family were from a demonized religious group, he knew from experience how the dominant discourses spread distorted images of the beliefs and rituals of unwanted groups to make them look demonic.[55] Thus, his reformulations were geared towards challenging the cultural aesthetics for which he prepared his piece. This was achieved by radicalizing and tragicizing rather than neutralizing or romanticizing the counterhegemonic force of these forms. Beyzaie's Black was no longer the clever, subversive observer who saw the underbelly of the hypocritical holders of power while being ultimately submissive; he was also not like Fo's ideal working-class hero. Functioning in the space of elite art, he was now a witty downtrodden character capable of heroic feats and mistakes, a man who could enlighten and be enlightened by Girl and work with her to change or fail to change his milieu. Beyzaie had serious problems with the shenanigans of Iranian left and right and their derivative cultures which distorted artistic activities by referring to their unreal idea of people's taste or to 'capitalist' or 'anti-capitalist' propaganda. His own vision, however, was more in line with adopting and elevating the culture of the lower classes who had produced Iranian performing traditions. It, therefore, had the high emancipatory potential of the ideal left without the superficial obsessions of the real left with toppling states and establishing communist utopias.[56] It also challenged the dominant discourses that turned left-wing or right-wing ideas into excuses for tyranny and exploitation.

Set in a green land, *Sunset* begins with Girl and Narrator offering a romantic description of a Herculean hero whom the audience will soon see. This conventional 'keying in' creates an idyllic pastoral ambiance where the love between Hero and Girl unfolds with a combination of poetically reformulated and sublimated popular expressions which suggest Beyzaie's mastery of the language even at this very young age.

> **Hero:** In this meadow, I see a morning glory rising to the shining circle of sun.
> The sun has casted its light on the flower,
> And the flower has granted her fragrance to the light.
> My love is the sun,
> And the morning glory is your body.
> **Girl:** This flower is picked for you.
> **Hero:** And these hands have come for holding it.

To this idyllic world, Narrator introduces the possibility of disaster, which, as in puppet plays, the two lovers hear as a thunder.

> **Narrator:** But is there any mirror which will not break one day? And is there any pond whose water is never muddied?
> **Girl:** What was this sound?
> **Hero:** Maybe, thunder.
> **Girl:** No, it's not thunder; the sky is clear.
> **Hero:** The wind shook the flowers. But why are you shaking, my flower?
> **Girl:** We shall not build our hut near the green pond.
> **Hero:** Why? Is the green pond not beautiful?
> **Girl:** It is beautiful, but –
> **Hero:** Is the bank of the green pond not the paradise itself?
> **Girl:** Yes, yes –
> **Narrator:** But people say just on the other side of this pond a demon lurks, sleeping.

> **Hero:** A demon?
> **Girl:** The demon that everybody is afraid of, but on one has seen.
> **Hero:** People are always afraid of things that cannot be seen, but tell me of one thing that is invisible and yet believable?
> **Girl:** The demon!
> **Hero:** Forget about it!
> **Girl:** The demon is believable, and what is believable is unforgettable. (113–15)

The legend states that beyond the pond is an orchard with golden apples, which no one dares to approach as a demon lives on the path leading to it. But Hero reveals that his father and his grandfather, both great heroes, visited the other side of the pond and did not find anything although they searched for both the demon and the orchard. Though Hero explains there are no demons, Narrator insists that they are everywhere, and Girl, who believes him, insists that they can only build their hut on the bank of the pond if Hero slays the demon. Thus, Beyzaie depicts how cultural inculcation (Narrator) and desire for happiness (Girl) push individuals to play predefined roles and perpetuate the process of 'othering' and demonization.

> **Narrator:** This is love itself! It is a rose blooming on the bank of a green pond; you can approach it, but next to it, a black demon is lurking!
> [Black enters.]
> **Black:** the dialogue was about blackness so Black showed up; I'm sure if the dialogue was about something else, 'something else' would appear. (119)

Thus, though Hero has realistic views, he is framed by the inherited culture to embark on what he is required to do to prove himself. Narrator also maintains the status quo by suggesting that the conflict is existential and eternal rather than cultural and sociopolitical. Black's entrance, however, adds a different level to the plot. He engages in a repartee with Girl in which he clarifies how he is expected to play a social role which has enabled others to become heroes: 'Whatever Hero has learned he has learned from me. You disagree? Let's count; from my fear, bravery; from my rashness, poise and reflection; from my greed, contentment; from my restlessness, patience; from my bragging, modesty; from my talkativeness, reticence!' (121). His dialogue also reveals a mystically practical sense of humanity that does not see ideas as more important than humans or life: 'I have no idea whether this orchard exists or not; but I won't swap the red apple on my side with all the apples of that orchard! They talk of a golden orchard; I of the thirty birds (*si morgh*) looking for the Thirtybird (Simorgh)!' Beyzaie's allusions are not hard to follow. The first alludes to Omar Khayyam's poem which prefers the earthly joys of life to the promise of paradise,[57] and the second to the mystical journey of the birds for finding their divine prototype in Attar's *Manteq-ot-Tair* (*The Conference of the Birds*, c. 1177) which implies that our idea of the divine may just be the totality of our ideas of goodness and wisdom in time. Once more, these may seem simple figures of speech but placed on the lips of Black who may embody folk culture; they propose him as the producer of the two types of heroism, spiritual and physical, which have been consistently celebrated in Iranian culture. Simultaneously, however, Black also becomes the child of a homegrown, down-to-earth form of enlightened modernism which rejects all forms of religious or non-religious superstition through Khayyam's poetry. The repartee between Black and Girl also reveals how much they have in common both in speech and the way they feel they are controlled by fear.

Beyzaie, thus, transforms Black into a new type of character, the talkative, down-to-earth, popular picaresque trickster who may finally win the heroine with his honest, generous love.

> **Black:** If the sky had a tiny bit of your heart, I wouldn't be black.
> **Girl:** Do you have pain in your heart?
> **Black:** Pain has me in its heart! But there is no way out; I have to bear it.
> **Girl:** We have to bear it.
> **Girl:** There is no colour beyond blackness; except for blackness itself.
> **Girl:** I wish I could do something for you.
> **Black:** Be happy, this is enough for me. (124)

Thus, Black whose selfless love suggests he doubts he can make Girl happy changes the subject to inform her about trouble in the city.

> **Girl:** What was going on?
> **Black:** Like it was before, like it will be afterwards: coming, going, fearing, shaking, catching, shackling, running, seeing, and saying nothing. (125)

Then, he says that people visited the oldest man in the city and discussed signs in the sky, the lost orchard, the necessity of killing the demon. The use of 'some said' and 'others said' suggests the discords between the sociopolitical groups of the time. But the fact that 'all said they want to see the other side of the green pond' highlights a general obsession with utopia, which takes the existence and the necessity of destroying demons to fulfil the contradictory dreams of utopia for granted. The paradise imagery also refers to the rise of religious utopianism in 1960s Iran. Beyzaie wrote the plays at a major turning point in Iranian history when with the clash of the political side of religious establishment with the state, which was in making since Ayatollah Boroujerdi's death in March 1961 and reached its zenith over the White Revolution in 1962 and 1963, from within the return-to-the-roots ideas of the 1940s and 1950s, a new form of nativism which upheld Islam as the way to uproot imperialism was born. Thus, while maintaining a dark comic aspect, Beyzaie moves between confronting the ideology of cultural marginalization and a political culture of social surveillance and violence, which has failed to transcend the vicious circle of oppression and violent outbursts.

To understand Beyzaie's take on the politics of post-coup era, a reference to the political situation is necessary. Following the coup, the premier Mohammad Mosaddeq (1882–1967) was put under house arrest until his death and his minister of foreign affairs, Hossein Fatemi (1917–54), was sentenced to death. Many National Front and *Tudeh* (Iran's pro-Soviet leftist party) leaders were also imprisoned and many army officers with *Tudeh* or pro-Mosaddeq links were executed. As Derek Jones reports, in 'the witch hunt' that followed

Up to 5000 supporters of Mussadiq were rounded up, tortured, imprisoned, or killed at the behest of the 'Committee for State Security'. The list is outstanding and typically Iranian in the number of poets who suffered: Morteza Kayan was killed; Nima Yushij, Mehdi Akhevan, Ahmad Shamlou, and Houshang Ebtehaj ... were tortured or imprisoned. Many newspaper and individual journalists were banned: the 600 publications which had existed under Mussadiq were reduced to around 100.[58]

A period of suppression followed, and power concentrated in the hands of Mohammad Reza Shah who, in fear of the USSR and internal conflicts, increasingly edged towards the United States. Martial law continued until 1957 when SAVAK (Iran's security organization) and other forms of modern policing were established with US assistance. In 1962, the Shah, who had good ideas for modernizing the country but was too concerned about losing power, was finally urged by John F. Kennedy to initiate large-scale modernization reforms.

In January 1963 over six million voted in a referendum, approving by about 12 to 1, six reform measures sponsored by the ruler. These were, the land reform bill, the sale of state-owned factories to finance land reform, sharing of workers in up to 20 percent of industrial profits, nationalization of forests, amendment of election law to include female suffrage, and establishment of a Literacy Corps. These measures were followed in subsequent years by a Health Corp, Reconstruction and Development Corps, Houses of Justice, nationalization of water resources, and the decentralization of administration. In its entirety these actions were described by the regime as the Shah's White Revolution, or Shah-People Revolution.[59]

The reforms were hailed by many people, but the opposition felt betrayed because power had remained undivided. The Islamic groups, however, were the only ones that openly opposed the reforms. Some, led by Ruhollah Khomeini (1902–89), opposed the referendum itself as they believed that it was their own rather than the people's right to determine the legitimacy of the reforms. They also criticized the handling of the land reforms and opposed female suffrage, granting equal rights to women and the possibility of having non-Muslims and women elected to Local Houses of Justice positions.[60] However, after the state's suppression of the clerical students' protests against the reforms in Qom in spring 1963, which led to the deaths of several protesters and Khomeini's first arrest, his approach changed so that in his speech of October 1964, he focused on the US influence in Iran, putting Iranian generals at the behest of American corporals, paying astronomical salaries to foreign experts and belittling Iranian ones, advocating Israeli occupation of Palestine and granting immunity from prosecution to the US citizens in Iran, which he called a renewal of the law of capitulation.[61] Known as 'the law of capitulation' the state's agreement to relinquish jurisdiction over American citizens working within Iran's borders was one of the most controversial issues of the time.[62] In 1928, Reza Shah, who had been secularizing and modernizing the Iranian legal system for the purpose, abolished this law which had been somehow observed since the 1820s. However, with the reduction in death penalties in major Western countries from the late 1950s and the Iranian states' dependency on US support from the 1940s, the US government which had many advisory and military personnel in Iran pressed the Iranian state to extend the Vienna Convention of 18 April 1961 on the immunity of diplomats in their host countries to these military and development advisors. With Khomeini's confrontational character already earning him support in seminaries and the bazaar due to the conflicts of 1963, this speech, which was delivered a few days after the endorsement of the agreement by the Iranian parliament, functioned as a turning point in the history of the Islamist movement in Iran. The agreement had little to do with the 'anti-Islamic' reforms of the White Revolution, but it was the Achilles heel that the political side of religious establishment had discovered against the state.

In any case, following this speech, Khomeini was arrested and exiled, but in the next fifteen years, living in Turkey, Iraq and France, he continued his campaign against the Shah, which, in the light of the 1979 revolution, has been construed as heading a campaign for the institution of an Islamic state.[63] Meanwhile, in the absence of alternatives, some political and cultural activists, including Al-e Ahmad, who had leftist nationalist tendencies prior to 1962 and was already set against the Pahlavi approaches to modernization, began to promote Islam as an anti-imperialist ideology and contributed to the rise of a form of nativism in which Islam was the path to Iran's salvation.[64] For Beyzaie, however, the tactical or honest utopianization of Islamic beliefs and the Islamic state was as calamitous as the Pahlavi's royalist nationalism and its idealization of the political structure of ancient Iranian empires and the leftist obsession with fashioning a communist utopia.[65] It ignored the nature of religion as a body of amassed dogmas, fallacies, superstitions and contradictions that, though psychologically fulfilling for some, could be exploited to justify violence against those who think differently. Thus, in his reformulation of popular traditions, among other things, his Khayyam-like protagonists celebrate earthly life and 'scoff at the reification of the ineffable' in organized religions,[66] which fuel the salvationist zealotry and the supremacist myth of those claiming to have exclusive access to truth.

In the scene that follows, Beyzaie's Black, the protagonist of this subversive gaze, explains that he has been told if Hero embarks on a battle with Demon he will die. Thus, Girl and Black rush out to save Hero as he is the only one who understands them. Placing Hero, Girl and Black in one camp is one of the key elements suggesting how they are similar in that they have been deprived of normal opportunities because of the roles imposed on them. The scene, then, changes to a hill and a cave where Hero who has been walking the whole day is sleeping. Demon, a dishevelled black man, wakes him up, gives him his sword, assures him he is one of the worst demons ever and encourages him to do the job faster.

> **Hero:** So, I am supposed to –.
> **Demon:** And I'm waiting! Come on, grab this, and kill me.
> **Hero:** Why this hurry?
> **Demon:** So, you can return faster.
> **Hero:** And when I return?
> **Demon:** You will throw this black head before the walls of your city and shout: 'one of its seventy-seven heads! I am the cleanser of your paradise!'

Hero: I assumed you would be a different sort of thing.
Demon: Not your fault.
  [Hero lifts his sword.]
Hero: And no one told me that a demon may be so fair!
Demon: To bring his neck down and to say 'strike'!
Hero: 'Kill'!
Demon: And let me rest in peace.
Hero: What did you say?
Demon: We were talking about letting me rest in peace; something I've never had.
Hero: We are so similar. (130–31) (See Figure 2.1.)

Worried about what comes next, Narrator expresses his surprise at the unforeseen turn of events. This metatheatrical moment is reinforced when Demon explains that people are afraid of him 'because they must have something to be afraid of' and that they think he is a bloodsucker because fiction influences perception. Once more, Narrator tries to twist the events to his advantage by stating 'this is a tale that no one has ever heard in the city' as 'criers only repeat timeworn tales and boring, sleep-inducing narratives'. His position, thus, is that of a clever manager who manipulates unexpected events as if they are just to intrigue the audience, a strategy that echoes the ways flexible cultural and political institutions maintain their hegemonic hold on society. Thus, the characters may be permitted to do whatever they like so long as it may be shown to reflect the values of the system.

Demon contradicts the official claim that 'demons cannot cry' by stating 'the green pond' from which so many flowers and trees have been created 'is the product of my

Figure 2.1 Hero decides not to kill Demon. From Hamid Amjad's collection.

father's tears'. Beyzaie, thus, explicitly asserts that the marginalized have the potential to become the greatest artists and sources of blessing if they can transform their anger into creative care.[67] He, then, constructs the story of demon's ostracization with reference to a traditional method of shaming used by Iranians to degrade enemies or unwanted social types.[68]

> **Demon:** Our great grandfather became ugly in the dungeon! With long hair and dirt on his face. They attached a tail on him and put horns on his head! Making him naked with marks of burns and brands all over his body, they made him wear a skirt!
> **Hero:** Come on! Do you think I'm a fool!
> **Demon:** *My father used to say: humans created demons to save themselves. They exaggerate the demon's ugliness to make light of their own ugliness.*
> **Hero:** Your father's words made me drop my sword.
> **Demon:** My father and his father used to say that the most tyrannical ruler of the town kicked them out of the town. Our ancestor was ugly; the ruler tyrannical; the town small and the world large!
> **Hero:** Why did he kick out your ancestor?
> **Demon:** A gatekeeper had told them it was because our ancestor had not stopped playing his pipe when he had seen the ruler passing with all his glory and entourage.
> **Hero:** That ruler died, but his tyranny is alive. (133)

With a body deformed by brands and tattooed with the verdict, the demonized man, then, resided in a cave and played his pipe to sublimate and communicate his pain. Thus, as his tears were making the pond, state propaganda linked his pipe-playing to magic and famine, and those who killed their friends or massacred others for power and money claimed that the demons did it. Then, as Demon is explaining that he left his cave looking for a hero to kill him, Narrator addresses the audience to claim that Demon is malingering. Hero, however, foils his attempts to turn this situation into a subplot and twist everything back to normal.

> **Demon:** And now we are confronting each other.
> **Hero:** *As narrators want it; confronting rather than standing beside each other.*
> (136)

The story of the pipe and the downtrodden being pushed outside the hierarchies of belonging echoes Beyzaie's depiction of Azhdāhāk in his second recitation play, but it is, here, adapted for a folk play rather than an epic monologue. This folk aspect, however, is sublimated by Demon's philosophical gaze as an outcast observer of human treachery, a man whose father ate 'the golden apples' of patient wisdom in loneliness as no human beings dared to share it with him. Demon restates his desire to be killed by Hero as he prefers to die rather than do the same and die in loneliness like his father. He does not want to kill himself either, for this is what the ruler wants. Hero is, thus, his best chance. He has met Girl and Black and knows that Hero has promised her to kill Demon. He is also unable to accept Hero's offer to return to the town to be honoured, as he knows that people have not changed. He is, thus, like a Philoctetes, who is completely disillusioned with all humanity and has transcended his desire for return. So, he attempts to arouse Hero's jealousy by saying that he has also been in love with Girl. Narrator is overjoyed with this, but Hero being capable of generous love is determined to return to the town not with the claims of false honour, but with a narrative of truth, love and brotherhood that annuls the stale tales of the past. The dispute that follows reflects on how real heroes are born not to fulfil a utopia, but to help others:

> **Narrator:** Then, why do you think I made Demon?
> **Hero:** Let me ask you! Why?
> **Narrator:** So that you fight him! This people like watching you two fight!
> **Hero:** I have nothing in common with this people, but a lot with a demon who faced me like a mirror.
> **Narrator:** Mirror of what?
> **Hero:** The cruelty with which you had dealt with him.
> **Narrator:** Are you talking about justice?
> **Hero:** I am talking about cruelty and oppression; and if you had made my sword longer and sharper, I would cut your hand with it. (141-2)

Narrator, then, threatens that he would throw Hero into the puppet box rather than allowing him to go back to the town. Their arguments about the existential duty of Hero escalates and in a moment of anger Narrator grabs and tears Hero into pieces.

Rancière argues that moments of emancipation occur when individuals see their status not through the lens of their customary needs and functions but through a detached, aesthetic lens which enables them to see their lives from outside their inherited norms.[69] These moments occur when one is temporarily placed on multiple axes of Foucault's networks of power relations and becomes aware of the possibility of participation in multiple 'habitus'. These liminal positions enable one to identify the failures of the system and venture to change the sociocultural templates that delimit one's cultural, existential and sociopolitical habitus,[70] by creating new templates which those benefiting from the hierarchies of power relations may try to accommodate or resist to continue their hegemony. Hero's decision occurs in such a moment. His father and his grandfather had seen Demon's father and grandfather, but being gripped by the truth of cultural inculcations, they assumed real demons existed and had brushed away the possibility that these people could be the so-called demons. Hero, however, being already full of questions about the role imposed on him by an apathetic society, sees the truth of Demon's account, perceives the treachery of received narratives and is ceased by a desire for defining new roles for himself and Demon. He now sees demon as he sees Black and himself, victims of an absurd system of exclusion and glorification which robs people of the chance of having normal lives. In this context, Narrator's violence which may be interpreted existentially, artistically or sociopolitically reflects what Zizek identifies as 'systematic violence', 'the often catastrophic consequences of the smooth functioning of our economic and political systems'.[71] For Zizek, systematic violence works through physical and economic victimization and exploitation of those at the margins of the system, but in Beyzaie's play, soldiers (heroes), who suffer the consequences of wars justified in terms of national or international 'common sense', are also victims. Yet, as expected, the moment of realization for Hero leads to his death.

With Narrator tearing Hero into pieces, Hero achieves a level of heroism like other individuals of unique qualities victimized by an unsympathetic system in Beyzaie's works. Yet, as in his other works, this sacrificial act may or may not have revolutionary outcomes.[72] When Girl and Black arrive, Black realizes what has happened; Narrator kills Demon, who calls him a brutal animal; Girl dies of desperate sorrow as she is calling Narrator 'the real demon', and Black who identifies himself with Demon reinforces Girl's final words with the folk song of demons, 'Break, break, it's breaking time!' (145–6) in a variation that signifies the absurdity of living under such conditions. Having broken the stage into pieces, the exhausted Narrator, then, expresses, in an epilogue, his sorrow over losing everything and his surprise that he himself may have been the real demon all along. Having praised the power of the play's poetic idiom and its philosophically tragic gaze at the inevitability of human fate, Ehsan Yarshater uses this closing to argue that 'Beyzaie denies us an absolute villain' as Narrator, 'having destroyed the tools of his trade and instruments of his power, remains a defeated and broken demon'.[73] While this is correct as the trilogy does transcend the conventional hero-villain dichotomy, I argue that the ending of *Sunset* signifies that an inherited culture that fails to modernize and expand its borders of belonging to generate more inclusive artistic, cultural and sociopolitical narratives will collapse. The trilogy, however, goes on to complete a circle of three unsuspected types of villains who are more dangerous than the easily perceived conventional types as they think their cause is fair, sacred or rational: the banal meticulously-doing-my-job kind (Narrator), the obsessed saviour type (Traveller) and the watching nothing-to-do-with-me type (the audience). This becomes clear when Narrator returns with another stratagem, Traveller becomes the ultimate generator of the vicious circles of power and the people are reported to still watch. Thus, though Narrator is not a villain in the conventional sense of the term, he is a villain in Hannah Arendt's sense of the term, which is worse, as he justifies himself by thinking he is just fulfilling a duty to avoid trouble and earn a living, even if it means destroying others.[74]

The Tale of the Hidden Moon: Failures of knowledge and rise of two new protagonists

The Tale of the Hidden Moon, the last play of the trilogy, begins with Narrator's prologue about a community that has forgotten all its tales except that of Hero and Demon. Then, the curtain moves aside to show a dark stage, from which a shout has just been heard. Immobile but awake, Girl and Black are talking about how the god of whites overcame the god of blacks as he had more might and about Hero, still fighting Demon while others are asleep. Beyzaie's description of eyes gazing through the back curtain suggests the existence of a surveillance society in which the puppets watch each other as a means of control and the movements of Black (the lower or working class) and

Girl (women in a patriarchal society), are monitored. Girl urges Black to help wake up the puppets. Beyzaie, thus, uses the metaphor of light and dark, asleep or awake and moving or motionless to suggest the condition of a culture which needs awakening. The song of naming, as they noisily try to awaken the dilapidated puppets, has multiple functions. Referring to the characters of Iranian puppet tradition in a blithe spirit, it signifies the unique character range of a vanishing dramatic tradition. Yet, it also reminds the audience of the hypocritical holders of economic, political and religious power and their cohorts before moving to typical loudmouth characters in society and disreputable entertainers within the public space: the King and King's Soldier, Guard, Horseman, Artilleryman and Army Clergy; Hypocritical Clergy, Jarring Koran Reciter, tricky Prayer Caller, Talkative Witch, Ugly Demon, Desert Giant, Sweeper, Porter, Juggler, Lantern Lady, Promiscuous Lady Dancer, Big-bellied Long-nosed Mulla, Taymour the Horse groom, Indian Yogi, Womanizing Bald Hero and next to him Lady Falaknāz, Lady Taiyāreh (Flying) News Manager, Mobārak of Zanzibar, Sleepy Sholi (slack), Champion of Zurkhāneh, Donkey-riding Lady, Wicked Merchant, Foxy Nanny, Philosopher Nonsensical (Hakim Zerzeriāns), Cotton Champion, Blackman Beshārat and finally Traveller. The box, therefore, is a microcosm, and their discussion over Blackman Beshārat (glad tiding) and his pointing finger, the list of tales that are no longer told, the static state of the puppets, and Girl's endless waiting for Hero's return evolve into a comically philosophical debate over the meaning time and waiting for the apocalyptical coming of the saviour.[75] The swing between the comic and the philosophical is also seen in the dark comedy of Black's desire for becoming a hero and the worries of living in a society in which the fear mongering of those in power and their rivals and the uncertainty about the future prevent people from having intellectual maturity or a minimum of happiness.

Their discussion, then, turns to the new puppet, Traveller who wakes up with a thunder to explain that outside this city spring is in bloom, a sentence that Narrator tries to exploit to make the play more intriguing. Traveller, however, continues with his poetic story:

Narrator: Here we can touch darkness.
Traveller: And a dead person in the grave dreams of life.
Black: How funny! Ouch my tommy!
Traveller: Today I came out of a distant crypt and began my search for a lost object. Walking uphill near a trench at a crossroad I asked myself, 'which way?' And dark clouds covered the roads. I came towards your town, and now I am asking myself: 'where in this town can one find a lost person?'
Black: Pay a visit to the graveyard; you may find your lost person there.
Traveller: But that thing is in the heart of a living man. That man is alive! That man is me, myself!
Girl: Who?
Traveller: Myself!
Black: So, make sure to visit to the graveyard. It is full of people who were once looking for themselves. People who one day stopped at a crossroad and shouted, 'which way?' But there was only one way!

Girl: It is not funny at all!
Black: I know. I haven't forgotten that I have forgotten laughter.
Traveller: In this darkness one cannot take a black man's jokes seriously. I will go back to sleep. (158-9)

With Hero absent, the stage direction and the dialogue are teeming with images of darkness, doubt, death and bad omen. The imagery is reinforced with references to sleeping to conjure the idea of apathy and ignorance, not in their usual political sense but at an epistemological level that signifies the inability to perceive due to inculcated assumptions and preoccupations. The presence of the mystic Traveller, a new puppet, however, also suggests that Narrator may have initiated a new stratagem to restore his hegemony. Worried about the ongoing battle between Hero and Demon, Black pretends jumping on a horse and after suggestively joking with Girl about riding along, sets off for the battlefield. With Black gone and other puppets sleeping, Narrator explains why the two are fighting. Echoing the Zoroastrian myth of Ahura Mazda and Ahriman's battle and the other myths of fraternal rivalry,[76] he states the two were born as antagonistic doppelgängers who were to rule the world in alternate years. Hero kept his oath and relinquished power when his year ended, but Demon extended his reign of tyranny. Hero asked for help from 'merchants', 'muftis' (high clerics), 'hajis', 'stoics', 'bosses' and 'head of treasury', who did not help, and from 'the oppressed' and 'lovers' who had little power to offer. Thus, he gained might from faith and faced Demon and his entourage. While amplifying these mythic motifs with the song-like expression of folk plays, Narrator uses poetic adoration which places Hero on a pedestal that precludes the prospects of questioning the role. Girl's outlook also displays how a seemingly innocent and marginal gaze is engineered by the machination of cultural inculcation to turn even love and desire into means for guaranteeing the unthinking reproduction and the generational persistence of the vicious stereotypes and hierarchies of power and belonging. Thus, with Hero and Demon cast unfairly in roles whose origins are beyond their understanding, their battle continues.

The discussion is disrupted by a cry which wakes some puppets up. While Narrator delivers a moral cliché about hearts closed to the cries of others, Beyzaie propels the dialogue towards echoing two of Nima Yushij's poems 'Mitarāvad Mahtāb' (The Moonlight Beams 1948) and Dārvak (Hylidae, 1952), which use metaphors of sleeping and draught to reflect the challenge of initiating growth in unproductive and stagnant societies burdened by apathy, tyranny and ignorance.[77] These allusions, however, are given in an understated style as if Narrator and Traveller are only reporting. This approach echoes the characteristic puncturing style of folk forms, but Traveller's comments, which maintain the philosophical level, also signify that both Traveller and Narrator are unable to care at human levels for what is happening.

Traveller: I read in a philosophy book that the length of a war diminishes the importance of its cause. But what cause is more essential than the fact that we are human beings, subject to the ebullition of our elements, subdued to the rebellion of our nature!

Narrator: In every human being there is a hero fighting with a demon, and the demon and the hero are always fighting! Always, ever since they have been, ever since we have been. *For years; ever since they have gone, ever since we have gone.*
[Black enters.]
Black: With that loud cry, the last demon and the last hero slayed one another. A grave opened its mouth and a wall collapsed from middle. The moon went under a cloud and the night became darker. (165)

The dialogue between the two highlights the philosophical, intellectual and folk continuity of the idea of what Henry Corbin calls 'the imaginal', the unseen, yet real land of secular and religious heroes awaiting to be conjured in cultural products.[78] The term 'gone' suggests that they are all dead, but their reverberations are present in our lives. One opens a book or turns on a TV set, and the eternal battles of heroes and demons rush to reinforce the patterns that structure our minds since birth. The human cost of this continuity, however, seems irrelevant to Narrator and Traveller as they consider it an eternal given that is impossible to change. Thus, as the two are philosophizing and mystifying the events in a discourse void of any humane aspect, Black intrudes to speak about his own sorrow, his origins, his bond of a thousand years with Hero, and the people's joyous belief that they can now build their houses with confidence. Significantly, the third play occurs with Hero absent and then reported dead which means that the sunset that occurred in the previous play may or may not promise the rising of a new moon, but whether this moon will be found or not depends entirely on Girl and Black as the new protagonists. Black's reference to a thousand year is, thus, twisted to refer to the millennial battles of good and evil in Zoroastrianism and the metatheatrical status of puppets in a dark box in which time and action are circular. A myth of creation, then, traces the origins of Black and Traveller in a hazy past, with the former ending up in an uncaring town where he became a jester and the latter in a cave learning philosophy and magic. It also specifies that with the black people's god dead, they had to be either demons or clowns. Thus, though Girl has always liked Black, she never took his love seriously. The accounts of the two and Narrator's interjections are orchestrated as parallel monologues rather than a dialogue. While Narrator reiterates his assumptions about what people want for entertainment, Traveller shows signs of having the potential to be a sympathetic intellectual or artist by speaking about his sense of alienation and his desire to use his magic to serve people and be understood by them. Having expanded Khayyam's metaphor of humans as puppets into a myth of creation,[79] Black refers to Hero as the only one who could understand his situation and expresses a desire to revive him as 'Hero is needed more than Black' (169). Here Black and Traveller's parallel monologues reach a shared point to turn into a dialogue.

Traveller: I can revive Hero!
Black: What?
Traveller: With my knowledge and incantations Hero can be brought back to life.
Black: Really?
Traveller: I can begin as soon as someone wishes for him to come back to life.

Black: I do!
Traveller: But beware that if Hero comes back to life, Demon will also be revived.
Black: No?
Traveller: Yes!
Black: And again fighting!
Traveller: The only way – are you ready?
Black: I only want Hero alive.
Traveller: Science of miracles and miracles of science; alas, they have their limits.
Black: Only Hero!
Traveller: It is impossible without Demon.
Black: Remember that a girl has been waiting for him her whole life.
Traveller: Maybe there is someone who has been waiting for Demon.
Black: No – that's impossible!
Traveller: I have read in the philosophy books that one half of the self in each of us is demonic; and we love that demonic half. So you see it is not impossible. (169–70)

The dilemma pushes Black to a higher level of self-awareness. Hero and Demon, being tired of their absurd war, wished to die, and with the end of the war, people now have the stability they lacked for a thousand years. Thus, Black refrains from wishing their revival. Narrator's insinuation, however, leads to Traveller's accusations that the motivation for Black's choice is his love for Girl. Narrator, therefore, uses Black's love for Girl and Traveller's obsessions with showing his knowledge and skills to muddy the situation. Black would lose Girl to whoever wins the war, but their death also does not help him as with Hero gone Girl may not even want to stay with him. Then, as Narrator speaks poetically about death, darkness, light, happiness and the puppet box, Girl shows up. Once more, the Shiite idea of waiting for the saviour as a belief providing an illusory meaning for life is raised and questioned in her speech. Now conscious of the absurdity of her life and waiting, she is void of any hope. This despair promises the rise of her agency, but the moment of realization is ruined when she is presented with the same choice for reviving Hero. Her decision is sacrificial. Like Admetus' wife, Alcestis in the Greek legend involving Heracles' wrestling with death, or Domrol's wife in the Azeri legend, Girl volunteers to die instead of her beloved, yet when she realizes what the hero's revival entails, she hesitates. Now, both Black and Girl, Iranian subjects at the verge of becoming citizens, declare their willingness to die instead of Hero but refuse to do so if it means restarting the absurd battle that Hero and Demon detested. Traveller, then, goads her on by saying that Black let them remain dead because he loved her. This infuriates the girl. She had waited for Black's expression of love and could have loved Black, but his decision means he has been unfaithful to the memory of his friend. Beyzaie belabours the moment of decision by highlighting the qualms that make her unable to decide: 'they will cry: "what was this life that you gave back to us? And why were you shedding tears? What requires tears is not our death but our life!"' Traveller, however, continues with arguments about the value of life and finally convinces her by agreeing to put them back to death if they did not want the revival. Thus, Girl makes the wish, and Traveller embarks on the act of reviving, which becomes a frightening ritual of necromancy, at the end of which he states: 'I learned about everything and came to know everyone from books; but I really don't know what I did tonight – was to test the souls of others or my own knowledge?' (176–7).

Metaphorically, the process implies the human obsession with demonization and idealization represented in bardic epic and folk narratives and their echoes in cultural products, which offer role models for every generation. It also shows how some intellectuals are so obsessed with displaying their knowledge of the inherited culture that they revive the old templates of heroism which need demons and the inevitable demonization of those who have no voice in society. Beyzaie's play, thus, reformulates the form in a way that asks the working class, women and men of knowledge about the sense in reviving processes that lead to demonization. In the three cases specifying Black's, Girl's and Traveller's motives for their choices, Traveller is not sure whether the choice was made due to a sacrificial, social impulse or a selfish one triggered by opportunism, jealousy or illusions about ideals, love and knowledge. Thus, Beyzaie reflects the contradictory nature of our motives to ask the audience the same questions, highlight the difficulty of judging our choices and show how even not choosing is a choice. Yet, he also shows how the dominant discourse undermines human thought with the structural impulses it has already planted in the mind.

With the moment of euphoria passed due to the revival of violence, Black shows up and unaware of the revival of the two kills Traveller with Hero's sword to stop the history from repeating itself. However, as Traveller lies dying, he offers another perspective:

Traveller: [to Narrator] Say something!
Narrator: I didn't know.
Traveller: You are the one responsible for the final drumming and drawing the curtain!
Narrator: Yes, I am! But I am not responsible for what goes on in the world!
Traveller: Did you see everything and remain silent?
Narrator: What's the use of asking questions or responding to them? I'm only a spectator; the spectator of an unaccountable principle or passage!
Traveller: You see and ignore; you shun responsibility! In the book of philosophy, I have read that there are no spectators!
   [Traveller collapses; Black is still yelling.]
Black: [Singing] The sky is decorated; death is arisen! I'm hitting the drum of suffering; I'll go to God! You, our guide to the chosen one; what happened to your promises? Your promise of the good days; your enemy killing verses!
   [A thunder claps. Girl enters in a hurry, shouting.]
Girl: Kill them! [To Black] They don't want to live. [To Traveller] Kill them!
   [Since Traveller does not respond, she goes forward and shakes him, shouting] They don't want to live! [Suddenly she steps back, looks with terror at Traveller's corpse and the sword in Black's hand, and realizes what has happened. Shocked--] Death found its quarry; and the tale of this war till the end of the world . . . [To black with sarcasm and pity, sobbing] My lover, look at my hands: they are red with blood! [Black turns his head away] My helpless

lover, look at me: this man was the only one who could give death back to them.

[The sword falls from Black's hand. He remains dazzled and mute staring at the Girl.]

Girl: [Yelling] Now they are cursing us; shouting what kind of life was this that you returned to us? What kind of life?

[The Curtain falls.] (178–80)

Significantly, the curtain closes with a sword falling from Black's hand and Girl acting as the speaker against distorted heroic narratives. Narrator, then, closes the play with a prologue in which he talks about the continuity of war and suffering, now with a Black who has become a hero and a hero who has turned his sword towards himself. Thus, Beyzaie suggests that although Narrator has got what he wanted and has closed the curtain once more, in the puppet play, Black and Girl have become fallible heroes who may or may not find a way forward.

In her analysis of the trilogy, Gisele Kapuscinski focuses on Beyzaie's stylized approach to characterization and poetic dialogue. However, coming from within the same literary tradition that Beyzaie subverts, she fails to perceive the plays' emancipatory meliorism. She, thus, echoes Narrator's words by specifying that embittered at having wasted his life, Hero feels lonely and has lost his zeal for life and recognition. She, then goes on to identify embittered loneliness, desire for love or personal happiness and war as the respective subjects of the plays and 'the human condition and the individual's inability to influence his or her destiny' as their 'central theme'. While avoiding Al-e Ahmad's disparaging tone, she, thus, makes a similar conclusion by linking the plays to the reductive orientalist idea of 'Iranian traditional fatalism' and by asserting that Beyzaie's tragic vision is pessimist: 'destiny is absurd, and the only respite from suffering is death'.[80] Though fatalism has always been one of many discourses in Iran, as in every other country, one may ask how can a fatalist nation engage in two major revolutions and several major reform movements between 1906 and 1988, when she wrote the article, and how is it possible for a pessimist to write more than fifty plays and playscripts and make nine films between 1959 and 1988. Having a tragic vision is not pessimism, it is meliorism at its best, particularly in Beyzaie's case.

Conclusion and reception

Having given three alternative accounts of the encounter between the puppets and the forces that have defined their past, Beyzaie leaves the audience with a choice to continue or stop the distorted expectations about the binary-confirming tales of heroes and demons. This self-reflexive dialogue with the audience which continued in Beyzaie's later works suggests his ongoing dispute with those who, like Narrator, perpetuate inherited fallacies by insisting that a work of art must entertain the audience by bending to their taste. For Beyzaie, people's taste is determined by the distribution of the sensible and the audience's inherited cultural capital and class origins, and thus, must be transformed rather than reinforced by exciting repetitions of past formulas. The trilogy, therefore, offers a modernist critique of and a series of alternatives to the discourses that reduce human conflicts, contradictions, needs, hopes, fears and issues to a battle of good and evil. Instead, it suggests, among other things, that the real evil is misrepresenting the needs of marginalized people in narratives that demonize those whose needs contradict 'the smooth functioning of our economic and political systems' (Figure 2.2).[81]

Since its first performance, the trilogy, which can be performed individually or together, has been occasionally performed in Iran and abroad both as stage plays and as puppet plays, including one directed by Jody-Anne George in the Joot Theatre in Dundee in 2004.[82] In 1986, Kapuscinski published an abridged translation of the trilogy. Later, two other English versions of 'The Marionette' were published.[83] Writing in March 1963, Akbar Radi was astounded by the dramatic force of having a Hero of the past appear on a stage of the present to question his own role and realistically gaze at his unrealistic role and his indifferent audience to reveal 'the injured nature of reality through the coloured prism' of a puppet show.[84] Beyzaie's research, the trilogy and his *Four Boxes* had tremendous influence on the artistic revival of the form, the attention given to puppet shows in the Shiraz Arts Festivals, and the activities of such practitioners as Parviz Kardan, Marziyeh Brumand, Goli Taraqi, Medhi Faqih, Sadeq Ashurpur, Behruz Gharbipur and many others still active in the field.[85]

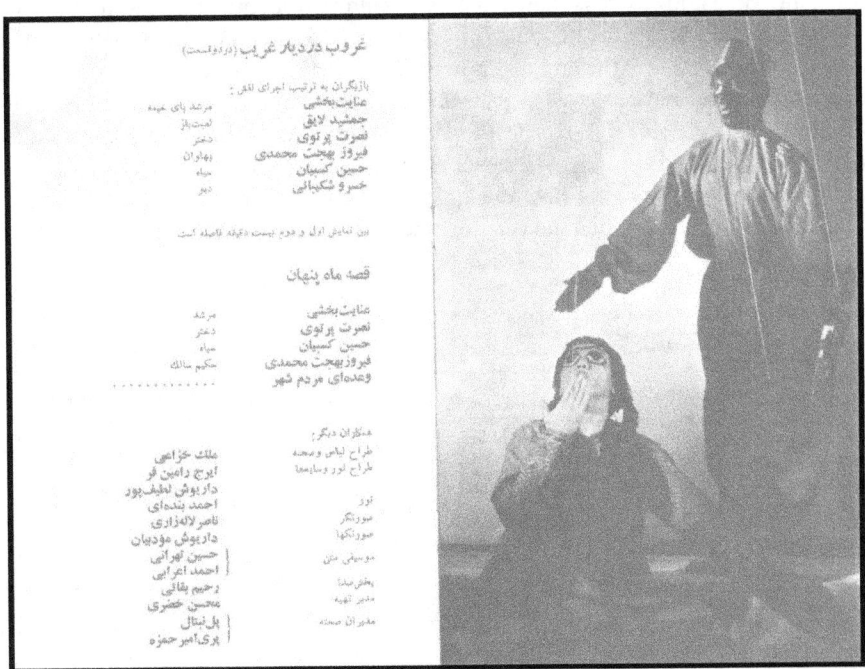

Figure 2.2 Brochure of Abbas Javanmard's staging of *Sunset* and *Tale*. From Amjad's collection.

Though Beyzaie considered Javanmard's staging of the plays an opportunity and a successful example of relatively good interpretation, he was not entirely happy with the result.

> In Javanmard's staging what is good and bad is the nervous force, the stresses, which enable Javanmard to make the main motifs of the play serve his ideas. He subdues and supresses the normal thinking of the audience. Under this nervous domination, which is created by the overwhelming presence of the actors, the stage loses its openness to multiple meanings, fluency and flexibility in a process that replaces the latter with intensity and constant hammering. Nevertheless, he has personal ideas which makes him much better than thoughtless and self-alienated directors.[86]

According to Beyzaie, this was particularly the case with *The Tale of the Hidden Moon*, in which the intensity of the staging with its emphasis on heroic walking and speaking and the overwhelming use of sound and light techniques had buried the ideas and the poetry of the play.[87] The play examined the meaning of heroism in the soul-wrenching doubts of Hero and his determination to change everything prior to his murder by Narrator in *Sunset in a Strange Land*. The same is true of the complicated relationship between Girl, Black and Traveller in *The Tale of the Hidden Moon*, in which the ineffable intricacy of human intentions is highlighted, and the obsession with accumulating and using inherited knowledge is shown to derail a culture from moving forward. In 1967, Beyzaie himself went on to direct and record *Arusakhā* for Iranian national television in a production that due to the limitations imposed on it due to shortage of time, facilities and proper performance space fell below Beyzaie's standards. However, even now after fifty-five years, it holds a mirror to the idea of heroes as victims of a society which fails to stand up to the standards it sets for others,[88] a theme that Beyzaie continued to explore in *So Dies Akbar the Hero* to high acclaim and went on to examine in several later works in which he often indicates that heroes are made rather than born.

3

Uncle Moustache (1970)

Carnivalesque deconstruction of hegemonic masculinity

Introduction: From theatre to cinema

As reflected in the previous chapters, in 1970, when Beyzaie commenced his film career, he had already established himself as a major playwright and since January 1970 had started teaching at the Department of Dramatic Arts at Tehran University. The dramatic and literary success of *So Dies Akbar the Hero* continued to attract the attention of writers and students of Persian literature, drama and cinema to the extent that Houshang Golshiri (1938–2000), who was very form-conscious and interested in various registers of Persian, was curious about Beyzaie's sources for the language of the play, his father's poetry society and the books he had in his library.[1] However, the rivalries between practitioners, the tedious bureaucracy of chaining creative work to office work, the politically charged milieu of theatrical activities, the pressures enforced by the state and the increasingly violent Marxist and Islamist revolutionaries negatively impacted the lives of theatre practitioners.[2] As evident in the debate that occurred between Beyzaie and the Marxist poet and theatre practitioner, Saeed Soltanpur (1940–81), during the post-performance review of Beyzaie's staging of *Mirās* (The Heritage) and *Ziyāfat* (The Feast) in autumn 1967, such critiques could have had positive outcomes for Iranian cultural production if they had remained in the realm of practical performance and social theory.[3] However, in the decade leading to the 1978–9 revolution, such critical animosities went so far as they added a radical leftist form of policing and censorship to the official and Islamic forms of censor already in place, and in several occasions, leftist groups organized by Soltanpur disrupted cultural activities.[4] They were particularly antagonistic towards the activities of those involved with *Kārgāh-e Namāyesh* (Workshop Theatre,1967–79), whose works they considered decadent, formalist state-run shows. Yet, other practitioners were also not safe. In one occasion, for instance, in autumn 1969, during Beyzaie's staging of *The Snake King* in Mashhad, radical leftists, who had been organized by Soltanpur, tried to disrupt the performance. They chanted slogans, accusing Beyzaie, who had long been involved in the campaign for freedom of speech and was one of the founding members of the *Kānun-e Nevisandegān* (Writers' Association, 1968–), of selling himself to the state and threatened to kill him.⁵ Such debilitating attitudes suggest why in his speech on censorship during the famous gatherings in the Goethe Institute in 1977, Beyzaie criticized non-governmental forms of censorship as much as the governmental ones.⁶

The volatile status of theatre and his passion for cinema urged Beyzaie to accept the offer of the Centre for the Intellectual Development of Children and Young Adults (Kānun) to make his first film, *Amu Sibilu*, which also enabled him to gradually distance himself from the toxic milieu of the Iranian theatre of the late 1960 and early 1970s. Cinema was Beyzaie's first passion. He developed an intense love for cinema, the foremost vehicle of intercultural cross-fertilization in 1950s Iran, during his high school years (1951–7) to the extent that two of the spaces in which he sheltered from the marginalizing and often violent attitudes of ignorant people, including some of his classmates and teachers, was cinema and drowning himself in film journals.⁷ In 1959, he joined Ghaffary's *Kānun-e Film* (Cine Club/ Film Centre), the foremost promoter of international art films in Tehran, and without any formal education won the first prize of their film facts competition. Here Beyzaie got engaged in critical discussions run by Ghaffary, Hagir Daryoush, Houshang Kavoussi and several others on films and on how words and images of static and moving objects and people can produce meaning when placed in loci of aesthetic attention and how these meanings proliferate once projected in the minds of spectator. Despite a short closure, Cine Club continued working under different names until 1979, enabling the young Beyzaie and many others to watch films by leading directors such as Ingmar Bergman and Orson Wells, and film adaptations of plays by leading dramatists such as Shakespeare and Ibsen between 1959 and 1969. Beyzaie, however, did not limit his viewing to these art films and continued visiting public cinemas and their mixed screenings of mainstream or artistically interesting films.⁸

This early familiarity with Shakespeare and other Western dramatists and directors involved him in reading, seeing and writing about Iranian and non-Iranian plays and films. Another aspect of this interest was the magic allure of cinema as the foremost vehicle of intercultural artistic interaction in the country. If until the early 1940s theatre was the major carrier of the new forms of producing art and the new models of heroism and behaviour, now it was cinema that negotiated such forms and images in the minds of people. In these early years, however, Beyzaie was unable to obtain a camera or find any other path to the world of cinema. Initially he was too young, but the main reason was that the world of Iranian cinema was too commercially driven to be open to a playwright whose ideas were deemed to be too intricate for viewers.⁹ Thus, after he was exempted from military service in the formal recruiting lottery, he launched his playwriting career and his lifelong research on Iranian performing traditions and mythology. Nevertheless, as reflected in previous chapters, he first experimented with forms that bore similarities to the magic box of cinema, with *pardeh-dāri* and *naqqāli* (dramatic storytelling with paintings) and puppet forms being the first. It was also his determination to understand Kurosawa's *Seven Samurai* that urged him to embark on studying and teaching Japanese and then Chinese, Indian and Indonesian theatre traditions.

> *Seven Samurai* marked a turning point in my mind not due to its form, but due to the spectators. In Cinema Park everyone was laughing at it. Being addicted to western manners [in films], they ridiculed the manners, actions, and shouting of the Japanese. I don't know. Perhaps because they rejected it, I identified with it. I saw it four times and tried to understand its world. After a few days of hesitation, I approached a famous actor [. . .] to ask about Japanese theatre, but he said the east does not have a theatre [. . .] From that moment, I began to look for articles on Asian theatre forms.[10]

His first articles on cinema appeared in *Elm va Zendegi* (Science and Life) journal in 1959, and he continued writing about cinema even when he was a full-time playwright. He also intensified his studies on Iran's pre- and post-Islamic culture, literature, myths, miniature and folk narratives on *ayyārs* and *javānmard* to identify the potential ways the codes of the culture could be reformulated for a modern stage or screen.[11] The result was several plays, which, as reflected earlier, deconstructed the illusory ideals of tough guy heroism and without negating the possibility of human heroism depicted heroes as victims of a society in which people have not yet become citizens and thus wait for others to save them. These experiments were important because at the time Iranian cinema had entered an era of obsession with tough guys as heroes saving damsels in distress in the context of street and cabaret fights, and irrelevant dancing and singing. This film type, which began to evolve in 1958, reached its zenith in the mid-1960s and created alternative realistic types in the late 1960s. The modern tough guys of Iranian cinema were primarily of three types: (1) the strong silent type who echoed the qualities of legendary *pahlevāns* (heroes of Iranian epics),[12] (2) the fast talking, streetwise and often happy-go-lucky lower-class hero who echoed the qualities of the *ayyārs* (Robinhood-like heroes of folktales)[13] and (3) the angry rebels who combined the qualities of the first two, revenged the loss of honour, family or land and lost their lives in the process.[14]

Deconstruction of hegemonic masculinity: An ongoing project

Beyzaie's first concern in cinema, therefore, was to deconstruct this obsession with violent masculinity, which was being reinforced even in alternative films with New Wave elements such as Masoud Kimiaei's *Qeysar* (1969) or Ali Hatami's *Toqi* (Woodpigeon, 1970). However, penetrating the world of cinemagoers whose idea of cinema had been distorted by mainstream Hollywood films, and their Iranian, Indian, Egyptian and Turkish offshoots was different from engaging theatre enthusiasts. He had to develop new tactics to create or attract new types of spectators while making new types of films that could carry the deconstructive vision of his epistemic stance. In his first two films, therefore, Beyzaie refrained from mythical and folk subjects, simplified his plots, chose comedy as a means of attraction and focused on city life. His deconstructive gift to Iranian cinema in these two films and in *The Journey*, which replaced comedy with archetypal quest, was subverting the ideals of masculinity in mainstream cinema.

These three films were also characterized by self-reflexive theatricality to contemplate marginalization and the margins of human observation.

To reveal how Beyzaie's subverting of the retrogressive ideals of masculinity evolved, in the next three chapters I examine *Amu Sibilu* (Uncle Moustache, 1970), *Ragbār* (Downpour, 1971) and *Safar* (The Journey, 1972) as films in which he reflects on the crisis of masculinity in Iranian society and cinema through narrative techniques and meta-cinematic scenes in which he explicitly engages with cinema and reflects on its obsessions with such forms of hegemonic masculinity. I argue that prior to focusing on the roles of women in society at realistic, mythic and metaphoric levels, Beyzaie embarked on redefining the ideals of masculinity in films in which the rights of non-hegemonic men, children and women were central, and the ideal man was a compassionate and persistent provider whose masculinity was displayed not in his ability to inflict pain on or kill enemies but in constructive productivity and making the people around him happy. I also argue that *Downpour* is significant in that while engaging with Iranian cinema at meta-cinematic levels, it also reintroduced the figure of reformist intellectual who had disappeared from Iranian cinema.

As observed in the dates given in the first part of this chapter, the years between 1969 and 1973 were the heyday of the streamline tough guy films and the alternative films with rebellious tough guys. This is when Beyzaie made *Ragbār*, in which the protagonist is a teacher with a staunch desire to win recognition, love and a sense of belonging among the people that he loves. He is, thus, inspired by his hardworking beloved Ātefeh and the hard lives of two of his own students to engage in systematic hard work to encourage children to enjoy cultural activities rather than fight in the streets, spy on others or cause problems.

The interest in examining the ideals of masculinity reflects Beyzaie's own journey of self-discovery as a marginalized young man. As reflected in Chapter 2, Beyzaie's early plays were among the first Iranian cultural products which critiqued the polarization of tortured souls into the conflicting roles of hero and villain and asked existential and cultural questions about why a society needs heroes. Thus, in the puppet trilogy, the demon is given a voice and is found to be a potential hero victimized because of his appearance or tribal background, the black and the girl's heroism is revealed when the puppeteer destroys the hero for refusing to kill the innocent demon, and the narrator, who maintains the hierarchies of power through narratives and embodies the ethos of surveillance, marginalization and victimization, proves to be the villain as he cannot tolerate the emancipation of his puppets. Or in *So Dies Akbar the Hero*, instead of glorifying the heroic deeds of the *luti* cliché, Beyzaie creates a multisided character by depicting the genealogy, the values, the failures and the psychological needs of a lonely man in a culture in which if an individual of special qualities does not play along the official or religious lines of power or their violent alternatives, he will be portrayed as a villain and is marginalized and destroyed. Thus, instead of depicting Akbar as a champion of survival, he creates a Kafkaesque plot in which the machination of existential, social and political givens makes a man of unique qualities unable to fulfil his potential.

Similar reversals of roles occur in other plays and screenplays by Beyzaie, particularly those in which he reflects on the history of Turkic and Mongolian invasions, including *Court of Bactria* (1968), *Lonely Warrior* (1970), *Tales of the Shroud-Wearing Commander/Leader* (1979) and *Warrior's Account* (1984). Though using *javānmardi/ayyāri* narratives to achieve a dialogue with the ideas in circulation about resistance against tyranny between 1967 and 1988, these works were all set in the past, commented on the present through historical distancing and never depicted the modern lumpen *luti* type as an embodiment of historical *ayyār/javānmard*. Indeed, in Beyzaie's contemporary city films or plays such as *The Journey* or *Afrā Or the Day Is Passing*, the *luti* type is usually a negative figure,[15] except for Rahim in *Downpour* and Mirkhān in *The One Thousand and First Night* (2003), where they redeem themselves,[16] and Einollāh's son in *Occupation* (1981), where the young man displays good qualities from the beginning and is open to progressive ideas reflected in his resistance against occupation and tyranny and his support for men of knowledge, women and children.[17]

One of the key appearances of this figure in Beyzaie's oeuvre is in *Downpour*, where Rahim is neither the honourable *luti* of the popular cinema in any of the forms observed earlier nor his vulgar antagonist *lout*. He is rather a normal tough guy who carries the signs of both. More important, however, was that the same reversal of clichés happens in the case of a unique figure, the intellectual reformist, who had remained absent in Iranian cinema since the early 1950s. Moreover, these reversals create a clash between the two figures which suggests that Beyzaie's first concern in his early films was to redefine the ideals of masculinity. Prior to this time, Beyzaie's creative intellectual and his encounters with the hierarchies of power and belonging were only present in such characters as Bondār in *The Account of Bondar the Premier* (1961/1997) and Mahmud Shirzād in *Journalistic World of Mr Asrāri* (1966). In *Downpour*, however, the encounter was so aesthetically well pronounced that one is urged to read his first film *Uncle Moustache* in a similar light. The rest of this chapter, therefore, will analyse Beyzaie's deconstruction of hegemonic masculinity in *Uncle Moustache*, arguing that Beyzaie's epistemic authority displayed its first cinematic vision in a symbolic orchestration of events in a plot that focused on the emancipatory and reconciliatory power of sports and youthful energy and their potential to modernize a culture obsessed with the past.

Uncle Moustache: Subverting the main manifestations of hegemonic masculinity

Uncle Moustache, which was commissioned by the Centre for the Intellectual Development of Children and Young Adults (Kānun), began with a one-page synopsis that Beyzaie turned into a 29-minute comic masterpiece. A retired man, who has moved to the outskirts of Tehran to avoid the clamour of the city, faces a group of noisy boys who use the field opposite his house for football games. He uses intimidation techniques and guards the field from his roof to scare them away but encounters their light-hearted, yet persistent, resistance. They call him 'Uncle Moustache' when seeing his fuming face gazing at them through his window, make posters to protest and run away when he comes down to catch them. Then, they work quietly for a few days to clear the field of rocks and prepare it for their noisy competition. Soon, the man, whose routine includes gazing at old photos, playing solo card games, reading books, talking on the phone and napping, finds their noise too disturbing. He confiscates their balls several times, but they keep returning with new balls. Finally, during an important match, their ball breaks one of his windows. He comes out with a knife, stabs the ball and chases the boys. One of the boys falls from a wall and is badly injured. The boys vanish. The man assumes he can finally be in peace but soon he realizes that he is missing them. He also feels guilty for hurting the boy. During a shopping trip, he sees four of the boys and wants to talk to them, but they run away. He follows them to the clinic where their friend is hospitalized. He takes a bunch of flowers from a trash can and enters the room. They hide behind the curtain and the bed, but the man tricks them by opening and closing the door. When they come out, they see a smiling man who has bought them a ball. The boys return to the field. The final scene shows the man returning home from shopping. The boys sing a song, asking him to shoot their ball which is in his way: 'Uncle Moustache, kick it to us!' The man brings down his shopping bags which he has been using to hide his face. He reveals a face with no moustache and a smile. The film ends as the ball that he has kicked breaks his own window.[18]

The first binary that *Uncle Moustache* deconstructs is that of the old, wise spiritual guide and the inexperienced youth who is to be initiated into the culture as a disciple. Ghazaleh Alizadeh states that this is one of the first filmic expressions of Beyzaie's lonely and secluded characters encountering a community of equally wretched and thus revengeful people.[19] To me, however, Alizadeh's emphasis on the characters' misery reduces Beyzaie's sublimating gaze to one focused on people as victims rather than one interested in showing the failures of society while suggesting how people may survive and evolve. In *Uncle Moustache*, the man has gone through the journey of life and, disillusioned, has chosen the mask of independent, secluded masculinity, and the boys are still busy making trouble to revenge the oppression they suffer in a patriarchal society. The conventional obsession with spiritual guides, which has its origins in ancient cultic practices and is echoed as an archetypal motif in Iranian epics and folk stories, was sanctified in the medieval era through mystic and religious rituals and has found its reconfigurations in modern cultural products and contemporary secular, spiritual and religious cultural practices in which individuals may still act as disciples of leading figures in their field or aspire to have disciples.[20] It is, thus, one of the major manifestations of hegemonic masculinity, whose examples range from the Shi'i Master of Jurisprudence as a source of emulation for the faithful to the master-disciple attitudes that writers such as Āl-e Ahmad or musicians such as Mohamad Reza Lotfi displayed in their cultural activities. The film's life-affirming, comic narrative, however, creates a situation in which instead of the old man saving and guiding the youth, the boys emancipate the old man from obsession with his top-down gaze, and being drowned in seclusion, silence and the past. At this level, the film uses differences in the height of the building and the field to reflect the old man's original top-down gaze and displays his ultimate descension not as a defeat but as a rebirth.

At one level, therefore, the film is about the old man's rebirth, which can also signify the rebirth of an old culture. Through an energetic comedy which also subverted the obsession with seriousness which marked *Kānun's* products for children, Beyzaie scrutinizes human behaviour to reflect on how healthy relationships can evolve when personal fixations and outdated mentalities and practices that fail the reality of life are discarded. Along with Beyzaie's *The Journey* (1972) and Abbas Kiarostami's *The Bread and Alley* (1970) and *Break Time* (1972), the film created a template, which, due to the rise of new forms of censorship after the revolution, became the foremost path for questioning the inherited power relations and beliefs that impeded emancipation. The template functioned like Mark Twain's *Huckleberry Fin* (1884) or Lewis Carroll's *Alice in Wonderland* (1865) in displaying the absurdity of outdated conventions by testing them against children's vision. However, the dynamic character from whose perspectives the camera records the events is a secluded old man with a dormant *ayyār* trickster vivacity buried under layers of convention and desire for authority, poise and respect. This suppressed vivacity which leads to the old man's ultimate rejuvenation embodies the life-affirming qualities that Beyzaie celebrates when examining Iranian culture. This signifies that besides offering a critique of distorted indigenous or imported practices and mentalities, Beyzaie suggests a path for rebirth, a quality missing in the films produced with similar forms of critique such as Golestan's *Khesht o Ayeneh* (Brick and Mirror, 1965) or Sa'edi and Mehrjui's *Gāv* (*The Cow*, 1969).

The absence of women in the film suggests the man's intense loneliness. This is signified at the beginning of the film. Speaking on the phone, the man declares his joy at having escaped the uproar of the city in a shot that displays two photos in the background. One is the photo of his wedding, and the other a group photo of a graduation ceremony. This suggests that though boasting about enjoying his seclusion, the man suffers from nostalgia and loneliness. This is also reinforced by his longing gaze at his wife's photo.[21] Thus, his final decision to befriend the children suggests that despite the illusion of resourceful masculinity being the saviour of women and children, here children act as the saviours of an old man who, as discussed later in this chapter, displays the motifs of both the tough guy and the spiritual wiseman.

The man's life is static: photos, books, newspapers, radio programmes, with little human interaction. His encounter with the boys, therefore, also displays how human interaction, mutual respect and dialogue can open new horizons. His transformation, however, occurs in a metaphorically suggestive, yet comically realistic and non-romantic process. The minimal dialogue and fast-paced narration pay homage to silent comedies. The initial exposition, with the man speaking on the phone about his new life in a quiet district, rapidly establishes the setting while drawing laughter by dramatic irony as the audience has already seen what is happening outside. The plot, then, evolves swiftly in the rising action by jump cuts that signify repeated encounters, as in the shots that show him putting several confiscated balls in his cupboard one after another, or children shouting, 'Look at that moustache! You scare me!' or making fun of, reacting to or booing him for his actions or retaliations. These scenes also echo those of alternate hitting in slapstick comedies or Tom and Jerry cartoons.

The film's deconstructive comedy is also reinforced by the soundtrack which includes two types of music as well as the noisy energy of the boys' voices, horns and drums when they play football or conduct their carnival procession, and their booing and chanting against and finally singing in praise of the man which remind the viewer of street demonstrations. The first type of music is comic and energetic with elements associated with spring rituals due to its melody and use of *dohol* and *sorna*. This music is diegetic at first when heard from the radio but becomes non-diegetic for scenes of action and fun. The other is elegiac with motifs borrowed from *ta'ziyeh* mourning rituals. Occurring in the scenes in which violence thwarts the relationships between the man and the boys, this music is also intertextual as it echoes the score of Kimiaei's *Qeysar*, which was also composed by Esfandiyar Monfaredzadeh (1941–). In *Qeysar*, the eponymic *luti* vigilante embarks on a quest of revenge against three brothers who have killed his brother after one of them has raped his sister. This music comically corresponds with the scenes in which the window breaks enticing the man to use violence and the one in which the man sits down in despair after stabbing the ball, chasing the children with a knife and causing one of them to fall from the wall. Like a *luti* tough guy, who has completed his gory task, the old man wipes his forehead and allows the knife to fall from his hand in a gesture suggesting exhaustion and regret. The elegiac music also reflects the mood when the injured boy is carried by his friends like a martyr in the war against tyranny.[22]

Thus, the comedy is realistic, but the orchestration of events, mise en scene, costume and music suggest cultural, political and cinematic symbolism. At cultural level, the film is primarily about hegemonic masculinity. The man appears in two types of costumes reflecting the three major types of hegemonic masculinity: the modern official, the religious patriarch and the violent tough guy. The first is the costume of the official intelligentsia of the Pahlavi era, representing the authoritative patriarchy of the modern man wearing a suit, vest and tie. In this role, the man is modern: he brushes his teeth, listens to radio, talks on the phone, reads newspapers and plays cards.[23] He, thus, embodies modern-looking masculine types such as headteachers, state officials, SAVAK agents or even the second Pahlavi king himself. His methods of creating docile bodies with no voices/noises are also modern: light punishment (bucket of water which suggests the use of water cannons to scatter protesters), confiscation of 'unwanted' material (the balls) and surveillance (guarding on the roof).[24] This is, of course, useless, because the children refuse to take him seriously. They set up their own surveillance group for confronting his threat, use a ladder to gaze at him through his window and make faces, keep buying new balls, and in response to his guarding the field from his roof, make a poster with a big moustache and a pair of glasses representing surveillance and chant slogans to ridicule him.[25] Beyzaie uses the poster as an effigy, which in conjunction with the scene that follows, creates a carnivalesque space with motifs associated with some of the spring rituals that he analyses in his book on Iranian dramatic forms.

The Bakhtinian grotesque and the Iranian carnivals of dethroning and ostracization

The earliest mention of the qualities of such festivals in Iran occurs in *Histories*, when Herodotus discusses the revolt of Darius and his confederates against Gaumāta, the Median magus who had usurped the Persian crown by impersonating Cyrus's son, Bardiyā.

The other Persians, once they had learnt of the exploits of the seven confederates and understood the hoax which the two brothers had practiced on them [...] drew their daggers and killed every Magus they could find [...]. The anniversary of this day has become a red-letter day in the Persian calendar, marked by an important festival known as the Magophonia, or Killing of the Magi, during which no magus is allowed to show himself – every member of the tribe stays indoors till the day is over.[26]

Based on Plutarch's account of how the Parthians celebrated their victory after crushing Crassus, one may assume that people made processions in which a person, dressed up as Gaumāta, was ridiculed by singing and dancing people. Plutarch's passage deserves proper attention as Beyzaie uses the elements of such a procession in the following scene when the children make a carnivalesque procession for their actual football match.[27]

XXXII. Surena now took the head and hand of Crassus and sent them to [the Parthian King] Hyrodes in Armenia, but he himself sent words [...] to Seleucia that he was bringing Crassus there alive and prepared a laughable sort of procession which he insultingly called a triumph. That one of his captives who bore the greatest likeness to Crassus, Caius Paccianus, put on a woman's royal robe, and under instructions to answer to the name of Crassus and the title of Imperator when so addressed, was conducted along on horseback. Before him rode trumpeters and a few lictors borne on camels; from the fasces of the lictors purses were suspended, and to their axes were fastened Roman heads newly cut off; behind these followed courtezans of Seleucia, musicians, who sang many scurrilous and ridiculous songs about the effeminacy and cowardice of Crassus; and these things were for all to see.[28]

J. G. Frazer argues for a link between such festivals, especially Megaphonia, and the Jewish Purim in which the effigy of Haman was burnt.[29] The myth recounts how Ahasuerus (Xerxes) (R.486–465BC) designated the Jewish Esther as his queen and her uncle or brother Mordecai, rather than Haman, the enemy of the Jews, his premier. This is probably a mythicized account of the Persians preferring the Jews over the Babylonians and giving them special privileges in the empire. Ahasuerus, like Cyrus, became a hero of the Torah, Esther and Mordecai were sanctified as saviours and a ritual like Megaphonia developed among the Jews.

Using Gaon's account of the festival as performed in Babylonia and Elam in the tenth century, Israel Abrahams writes that boys make effigies 'resembling Haman' and 'suspend them on their roofs', a few days before Purim. 'On Purim day they erect a bonfire, and cast the effigy into its midst, while the boys stand round about it, jesting and singing. And they have a ring suspended [on] the fire, which they hold and wave from one side of the fire to the other.' Abraham then goes on to suggest the ring represented the sun, and Frazer builds on this to link the ritual to ancient spring rituals and argue that 'the kindling of the Purim fires was originally a ceremony of imitative magic to ensure a supply of solar light and heat'.[30]

Based on (Abu Reihān) Mohammad Biruni's report about Purim, *Haman Suz* (Burning of Haman) or *Haman Sur* (Feast of Haman) – which Frazer mistakenly translates as the Burning of Haman – and the associated burning of the effigy took place all over Iran and central Asia.[31] It is also clear that the use of comic impersonators or effigies was an interchangeable practice with the former probably occurring before the latter, but existing simultaneously as well. This can also be argued if one examines the other Iranian carnival processions which involve dethroning and ostracizing a force of sterility or destruction, including such rejuvenation, purgation or spring rituals as *Dey-be-Mehr* (January to September) performed with clay or dough effigies on the day of Dey-beh-Mehr, fifth day of January (15th Dey), *Kuseh bar Neshin* (Ascendance of the Beardless One) or *Omar Koshān* (Killing Omar), performed with effigies. As Beyzaie himself and others have reported, such festivals seem to have been frequent in Iran both before and after Islam.[32] The comic narrative behind these rituals highlights the rise to the power of a usurper and his final downfall. They, thus, suggest the temporary nature of power, display the power of the carnivalesque to resist tyranny and celebrate the fall of the usurper.

In the film, children's activities are intensified after the poster scene to suggest a traditional carnival, the critical space in which hierarchies of power are challenged. Realistically, this is completely plausible as their actual competitions with other teams have just started. They use noisy drums, horns and pipes, wear masks representing animals, political figures or Iranian *Mir-e Noruzi* characters – *Ghul Biābāni* (Desert Giant) and *Ātash Afruz* (Fire Juggler) – as well as non-Iranian figures – such as the raven mask and the mask of dancing death. To intensify these grotesque elements, which are essential to the carnivalization of the scene, Beyzaie even includes a scene of bodily fluids when a boy takes a pee on the wall of the old man's house.[33] In all of these, however, as in the motif of setting up the goal or collecting the rocks, the hard work required for constructing a soccer field is celebrated, which reflects on how the children's energy is used for a constructive activity, which gives shapes and life to a featureless and dry landscape. Like all energetic activities, this is noisy, but it has no destructive element, and the seeming anarchy is at the service of creating joy in life.

As Mikhail Bakhtin puts it when discussing Wolfgang Kayser's 'The Grotesque in Painting and Poetry', 'the grotesque liberates man from all the forms of inhuman necessity that direct the prevailing concept of the world'. Thus, in the carnivalesque, imposed regulations are 'uncrowned by the grotesque and reduced to the relative and the limited'.

> Necessity, in every concept which prevails at any time, is always one-piece, serious, unconditional, and indisputable. But historically the idea of necessity is relative and variable. The principle of laughter and the carnival spirit on which grotesque is based destroys this limited seriousness and all pretense of an extratemporal meaning and unconditional value of necessity. It frees consciousness, thought, and imagination for new potentialities. For this reason, great changes, even in the field of science, are always preceded by a certain carnival consciousness that prepares the way.
> In the grotesque world the *id* is [. . .] transformed into a 'funny monster.' When entering this new dimension [. . .], we always experience a peculiar gay freedom of thought and imagination.[34]

In other words, the shattering of artificial limits and fake needs, which have made the old man aloof and incapable of rejuvenation, requires the awakening call of carnival noise. Thus, to rejuvenate an old culture, the nation should be capable of breaking the shackles of the past and should use the energy and the voice of the youth even if they look chaotic at first.

Shedding the mask of modern authority in reaction to carnival resistance

Beyzaie reframes the motifs that he borrows from these carnival rituals to turn the fall of the effigy and the old man's suicide-like stabbing of the poster with his walking stick into a comic locus for marking the failure of the old man's mask of modern hegemonic masculinity. Thus, his show of modern civility, which is a borrowed identity, collapses to reveal his underlying mask of old-fashioned violent authority. Beyzaie comically politicizes this old form of hegemonic masculinity while maintaining the references to social surveillance and control-obsessed masculinity with the old man embodying an authoritarian regime aspiring to silence its subject to maintain the established power relations and social hierarchies.

In this context, the comic radio scene finds a new sense. The radio is transmitting a male singer's voice delivering a long *tahrir*, a free-rhythm melismatic type of singing. The man who is furious with the children's noise slaps the radio, but, to his surprise, this leads to an automatic change of channel to one on which a woman is screaming at the top of her voice as in a crime drama radio play.[35] This comments on the state and anti-state religious or Marxist forms of censor in 1960s–1970s Iran and the idea that if the voice of the artist or the people is supressed, it may turn into a frightening noise. The radio scene functions like a reinforcing motif to remind the spectator of the centrality of the interplay of noise, voice and dialogue in the film. Let me develop this point further. When an individual is sitting in a room focusing on a subject of interest, any sound coming from outside may function as a disturbance, a noise. However, if the same individual exits his or her comfort zone, approaches the source of the sound and understands the reason and the function of the sound, the same sound may reflect a point that the individual identifies with. Thus, removing the physical or metaphorical distance between an individual and the source of a sound and engaging with the origin of the sound may transform it into voice, which, in turn, may make sympathetic dialogue possible. Alternatively, if the needs of a group of people is neglected, and their voice, their freedom of expression is marginalized or silenced, the voice may become shrieking, the noise of angry chants and breaking objects. The idea of noise sublimating into voice and then speech and dialogue is significant in any emancipatory discourse and one of the best spaces for reflecting the desire for such transformations is in artistic products which have the potential to be transgressive with the hope of shifting the borders of suppressive norms.

As discussed in Chapter 1, an emancipatory product of the aesthetic regime of art expands what Rancière calls 'The distribution of the sensible', the range of voices and images – ideas, mentalities, practices, images and so on – which are aesthetically, politically, religiously and socially allowed to be heard and seen in society and understood as acceptable. They can also simultaneously train the ears, eyes and minds to hear, see and understand them. Thus, art has the democratic potential to introduce a marginalized or neglected perspective through its form even when they do not seem to be reflected in the dialogue or images[36] (Figure 3.1).

Figure 3.1 Screenshots from *Uncle Moustache*. Minutes 2′–14′.30″

Time-image-sound: The emergence of the religious judge and his executioner

In the film, the interplay of noise and voice promotes an emancipatory, democratic discourse reflected in the transformation of the main character. Prior to this transformation, however, the situation is aggravated by a regressive change in the old man. Thus, the scene of stabbing the poster functions like a turning point following which the old man embarks on enforcing medieval forms of control. This corresponds to a change of costume. Now, the man wears an *araqchin* (a religious skullcap) and an *abā* (a traditional cloak). He also sinks into the role of serious masculine loner and engages in a different set of activities. He gazes at old photos of 'the good old days' and reads a book which looks like the *Quran* or the *Shahnameh*.³⁷ This change of attire may seem implausible, but it is realistic as it was common for men even until the 1980s to wear a suit to work and an old-style cloak when at home or going to the mosque.

In response to Zaven Qukasiyan's question about the reason he made the film after his complex experimentation in theatre, Beyzaie states, 'I owed something to the child [himself] who never had the chance to live like a child, owed him a film like *Uncle Moustache*, a film that he needed then but could not see.'³⁸ He then switches to the question of the emancipatory power of laughter: 'It does not make sense if we laugh in our everyday life but frown when creating an artistic work. This fake frowning, which is there to deceive ourselves and others, is [. . .] the consequence of a culture in which laughter is said to be the product of foolishness; [. . .] these are wrong conventions.'³⁹ In the context of the late 1960s when the film was made, the experience was unique. It transcended the vicious circle of the trivial mainstream cinema and the bitterly serious literature produced by some leftist writers for children in Kānun with the intention of creating politically responsible, committed adults. Thus, the idea of laughter, gaming and children acting as agents of emancipation is centralized to empower and inform children and act as a wake-up call to transform the intellectual zeitgeist of the time. However, as specified earlier, before this emancipation happens, the film displays the machination of regression. The old man, who, in his first role, displayed some trickster qualities and was capable of laughter cannot even laugh now. Beyzaie who owed himself a film about laughter and fun displays some of the embodiments of unhealthy and tyrannical seriousness. The first form of regression in the old man makes him a crossbreed between a medieval jurist judge and a cruel executioner. This regression is also suggested by a technique that highlights the flexibility of time in the mind. Beyzaie's unrealistic extending of time in the scene in which the children's ball breaks the man's window recalls Deleuze's idea of the time-image. The 20-second sequence is shaped by the medium shots of the ball in the air juxtaposed with the close-ups of the children's anxious eyes and heads tracing the ball's path to the window to mark a Bakhtinian 'chronotope' in which 'time [. . .] thickens, takes on flesh, becomes artistically visible' and 'space becomes charged and responsive to the movements of time, plot and history'.⁴⁰ The ball holds in itself the memories of the past trauma, the conflicts that the children have had with the old man and predicts a now inevitable, more frightening future. Beyzaie himself explains this in terms that recall the distinctions made between psychological and chronological time in narratology:

> If you remember the ball is in the air on its way to hit the glass. Everyone is looking, and they all know that no one can prevent the event. For a second, the scene becomes like a nightmare; it is simultaneously real and unreal, and it is also an allegory for the collapse of any hope of reconciliation. Well, this is the cinema that I like. Its various dimensions are at the service of the subject; and the maker is not restricted by visual verisimilitude. It shows both the factual event and what is behind it.⁴¹

Thus, here, though in a less stylized or surrealistic form than Beyzaie's later films, the reflection of emotions, feelings and non-linear psychological time stretches the space-time continuum of an action and transforms the mis en scene. In the scene the man stabs the ball, Beyzaie even manipulates the soundtrack to imply and then subvert an intriguing personification of the ball. As the knife is impaling the ball, the soundtrack delivers the sharp shriek of a crying baby that a moment later is revealed to have been that of a baby whose mother has been watching the soccer game. The impacts of such moments, however, transcend the emotional status of the characters because it also leaves an impact on the spectators by making them share the ordeal. If one compares a filmic scene to a statement, such scenes are like 'performative' linguistic statements, the types that perform an action on the addressee or a third party rather than just state something – such as a priest stating, 'I pronounce you husband and wife' or a judge stating, 'I condemned you to 10 years of imprisonment'. Such scenes intensify the experience of the moment for the spectator. More notably, this manipulation of time and space marks the man's regression. The strict judge is already in him as in anyone with internalized religious or non-religious dogmas. Thus, prior to the incident he is shown sitting in a cloak and a skullcap, reading an old book. The ball that breaks his window, however, becomes the ultimate violation of his masculinity, pushing him to the past to conjure the violent jurist executioner in him.

The scarecrow of hegemonic masculinity asserting his power by violence

Thus, the filmic elements – the man's costume, mis en scene, cinematography and music – are orchestrated to introduce the two other forms of hegemonic masculinity: the clergy-jurist, who believes he has a divinely ordained right to decide what is forbidden or allowed, and the tough guy, who conducts the acts of violence, either due to personal vendetta or to fulfil the decrees of a clergy or a master. Besides his costume, the religious aspect is also highlighted by the man's reading of a book which resembles the *Quran* when his window is broken and then by his ceremonial stabbing of the ball on a hand barrow set up like an altar, which suggests an execution. The scene is also comically festivalized by echoing the *shemr-khān* character (Imam Hossein's murderer) of *ta'ziyeh* plays in the judge-executioner. Sadeq Bahrami's embellished *ta'ziyeh*-like acting when he brandishes his knife and walking stick in pursuit of the children and his violent encounters with two of them reinforce this referencing. This echoing reverses the roles that judges and their executioners define for themselves because it suggests that, rather than upholding justice, they are obsessed with maintaining the status quo by force and believe in power as worthy in itself, which means they are just villains, at least when they act as tools of tyranny. The old man's big moustache and knife, therefore, also present him in his third role, the most physically violent form of hegemonic masculinity, the knife-brandishing tough guy. The scene that follows confirms this. While chasing the children with his knife in one hand and his walking stick in the other, the man extends his hands open to frighten the children. A series of close-up, medium shots and long shots then establish his image as that of a scarecrow to reflect the role of violent masculinity in society.[42] Finally, as specified before, the sequence ends with a burlesque reference to Kimiaei's *Qeysar* through music and the way the old man eventually throws away the knife.[43] Here, Beyzaie's mis en scene joins the musical motifs to create a parody of *Qeysar* and suggest the end of a vendetta with disastrous results (Figure 3.2).

Figure 3.2 Screenshots from *Uncle Moustache*. Minutes 14′.30″–19′.30″

The birth of the new ideal of masculinity: Fun, provision and support

The sequence is the film's climax and second turning point as the man must now face the consequences of his vendetta. The boys leave the field, never to return, which reflects how authoritarian regimes and dogmas lead to brain drain. Beyzaie, however, does not end the film on this negative note. The man embarks on a journey of reconciliation. This journey has its obstacles, but he becomes increasingly modern and compassionate to create an image of ideal masculinity. Trying to return to his normal preoccupations, he realizes the emptiness of his life without the lively children. He returns to his modern costume but must now call the 'speaking time' to have a semblance of human interaction. He gazes at the deserted site of the dusty football pitch being in danger of obliteration by construction material, guards an empty field from his roof and walks in the empty field to the crowing of crows[44] (Figure 3.2).

The scene of the encounter in the city has been designed to imply the significance of distance and the resilience of the youth. Though they have abandoned the field due to the old man's behaviour, and they escape from him in the town, the children, like the Iranian students who lived abroad during the late 1960s and 1970s, use any opportunity to remind the patriarch of the absurdity of his behaviour. Thus, once they maintain a distance, they resume their 'Look at that Moustache, Oho!' The idea of setting a safe distance between oneself and the source of tyranny suggests both physical distancing and artistic distancing, because their resistance takes the shape of a song. Nevertheless, the man has now realized the necessity of change, and the fun-loving trickster has been revived in him. He traps them in the hospital room and intrigues them and the spectators with a combination of calmness and unpredictability to establish his power and resourcefulness, but instead of punishment, he proceeds to offer gifts.

Beyzaie uses a Hitchcockian approach to create tension and suspense, which again stretches the time-space continuum through a nightmarish situation of fear and helplessness. The juxtaposition of the close-ups of the bandaged face of the injured boy, who is like Jeff in *Rear Window* (1954) in not being able to do anything against a dangerous intruder,[45] with close-ups of the old man's naughty smile and intense gaze and the medium shots of his approaching steps, the handle of the door and the boy's desperate covering of his head with the sheet builds up tension only to subvert it with irony, the interplay of what is expected and what happens. This time the situation is resolved not by violence but by gifts of compassion: flowers, instead of a knife and a ball to roll life back to a desirable situation. The old man's trickster side also functions to endear him. He tricks them by opening and closing the door, but once they are out of their hiding place, he surprises them with a smile, a hat greeting and a deep bow as a juggler who has just completed a wonderful act of conjuring a ball and a bunch of flowers. His trickster trait, thus, now entertains rather than rob or punish people. Thus, Beyzaie highlights the versatility and resourcefulness of Iran's inherited culture and its institutions but suggests that the only path to salvation for everyone involved is to employ these resources to support the younger people's freedom of movement and expression rather than limit it so that both the older and the younger people can learn from one another.

The final scene even goes one step further, as his unexpected appearance, with the moustache gone, reveals a kind-hearted smile and eyes instead of the evil-looking laughter and inscrutable gaze that the moustache gave him. He remains playful but has now been reborn with a new form of masculinity that has transcended his obsession with being intimidating. His hands are also full of grocery, which along with the ball that he already gave to the children suggests the ultimate image of a providing agent and patron of happiness (Figure 3.3).

Figure 3.3 Screenshots from *Uncle Moustache*. Minutes 19′.30″–29′

Reception and conclusion: *Uncle Moustache* as a New Wave prototype

In two brief reviews published in the journal *Zamān* and the *Etelāʿāt* newspaper about the film when it was first released during the Fifth International Festival of Children's Cinema in Tehran, two anonymous critics – or perhaps one, as they were probably written by the same person – specified that the film should have ended with the old man remaining alone in the middle of the field, and that since everything from that point onwards was predictable, the film fails to achieve the potential greatness that the first part had built.[46] Parviz Davaei praised the film's power to capture the reality of a situation but considered the ending artificial and the satiric gaze inconsistent.[47] Sirus Tahbaz also praised Beyzaie's ability to make 'the festival's most loveable film' but criticized the old man's exaggerated acting, which made him like a '*taʾziyeh* antagonist', (Shemr-khān) and 'the hasty shots in the city and the hospital'.[48] To my understanding, however, though Tahbaz's critique may be said to have a grain of truth about the scene in which the man chases the children in the city, the man and the children's ritualistically exaggerated acting and the episodes following the injury of the boy are integral to the film's coherence. Indeed, without the reconciliation and the transformation of the two sides of the conflict, Beyzaie's film would not have been a children's film but a mediocre film for the adults with a serious problem with coherence as the ending would have violated the energetic and comic tone that characterizes the film. It is also exactly because of this comic tone and the man and the children's ritualistically exaggerated acting that Beyzaie manages to work with and subvert the three stereotypes of hegemonic masculinity.

With these ritual elements, Beyzaie creates a carnival world to suggest that the so-called masculine qualities of taciturnity, aloofness, controlling others and ability to engage in violence are not the accurate markers of masculinity but destructive elements that must be transformed so that the real qualities of a man can surface and make him a supportive, flexible provider who serves the continuity of life by serving women and children. In its sociopolitical suggestiveness, the film also light-heartedly engages with people's resistance against a tyrant, who is intelligent enough to adapt himself to the new age rather than end up lonely in a death-in-life of silence and obsession with the past at religious or political levels. The idea of rejuvenation, of course, is essential here and has been treated realistically. The man's shrewd theatricality, when he tricks the children to pour a bucket of water on them, when he pretends interest in the ball to get it from one of them, or when he fakes a heart attack to capture one of the boys suggests his young spirit and his potential for change.

Like the earliest prototypes of the Iranian New Wave, Ghaffary's *Night of the Hunchback* and Golestan's *Brick and Mirror*, one of the subjects that Beyzaie examines in *Uncle Moustache* is fear. This fear which is also reflected in his earliest plays, such as *Ārash* or *So Dies Akbar the Hero*, can be existential, religious, psychological and sociopolitical. *Uncle Moustache* focuses on existential fear in the old man, and sociopolitical fear in the children. As reflected in my analysis, it also critiques the institutionalization of fear and violence in religion and politics as means of external and internal control. In the case of the old man, however, it is implied rather than depicted. As Beyzaie himself puts it, 'he feels he needs tranquillity and solitude, but he is also afraid of it'.[49] Thus, the dominant discourses of masculinity have created in him a desire for independence, self-sufficient resourcefulness and not being afraid of loneliness or other people, which together generate a strong fear of losing reputation. In other words, the old man's fear is rooted in his constructed need for strength, tranquillity and aloofness which maintain his aura of dominant masculinity. In Freudian terms, his socioculturally constructed superego has a hold on him, but when his id, the child in him, is reactivated and he realizes the vacuity of this fabricated needs and the violence they exert on him and others, his ego finds a middle path enabling him to exit this death-in-life status. His final fear, therefore, which makes him reconcile with the children, is the real fear of death-in-life, of rejecting the present acts of kindness, companionship and fun for an obsession with the unreal past of photos and books and a constructed image of masculinity symbolized in his alternative costumes, moustache and knife. Thus, his real needs, the lived experience of the present and the games he is willing to play reignite his passion for life and lead to the emancipation of his soul from the requirements of fabricated masculinity in a process in which children become the agents of emancipation.

Another motif which became frequent in Beyzaie's later films is the presence of a disabled boy in the visual landscape of the film. In *Uncle Moustache*, the motif reinforces the neo-realist and the carnivalesque elements of the visual world of the film. However, the energy displayed by the disabled boy who is carrying noisy tin cans to celebrate the game is also a call for attention to an often-neglected type that if treated appropriately have high potential for society. This unique inclusive vision in which the neglected are always given visibility is unique to Beyzaie and a review of his earlier and later works signifies how children with disability continued to become more significant in the films that he made in the 1970s.

Beyzaie's film was generally received well and continued to be a favourite film with children, particularly because it was energetic and funny and thus different from the sombre books and films produced by Kānun. Being the only film in Beyzaie oeuvre which he wrote based on a story by another person, the film was never duly analysed even by those who loved Beyzaie's work, but to me *Uncle Moustache* is as much the product of Beyzaie's divergent gaze as any of his other films, and even in the case of the story, Beyzaie wrote the script on the basis of a one-page story, which he changed a lot. When it was first released, Nader Ebrahimi celebrated its unique power to communicate with children and insisted that Beyzaie, being highly talented from the beginning in matters related to cinema should have been given the chance of making films far earlier. Ebrahimi also recounted how 'the spectator's chants of Beyzaie, Beyzaie . . .' after seeing the film in the cinema theatre was long due as it was directed towards a lover of cinema who 'was duly tasting the fresh water of acceptance and praise for his first film'.[50] Recounting the time when at the age of 18, Beyzaie used a 4-minute-long film and a rented 8-mm camera to create a wonder with recording the unnoticed moments of life in the city, Ebrahimi was one of the few people who had, by then, seen what Beyzaie's divergent gaze could do to a field of vision. Beyzaie, however, did not become complacent with this success and never repeated this template. Instead, he went on to make this gaze more striking in *Downpour* which, while addressing some of the themes he had worked with in *Uncle Moustache*, expands the field by introducing several new characters into Iranian cinema and using a unique range of ritual and reflexive techniques to produce his first filmic masterpiece.

4

Downpour (1971–2)

The reformist intellectual and the meta-cinematic subversion of hegemonic masculinity

Introduction: Position of *Downpour* in Iranian culture and cultural production

As argued in the previous chapters, in his first two films, Beyzaie's deconstruction of inherited dogmas and the systemic violence through which they function focused on hegemonic masculinity, a subject that he also handled in his early plays where he depicted the pitfalls of hero worship and portrayed heroes as victim. Beyzaie, thus, demonstrates that hegemonic masculinity distorts the lives of all men, even when they seem to be winners, as much as it victimizes marginalized men, women and children. This preoccupation reflects his own desire as a young man to find a place in society. It also suggests how he sublimated his own experience as a marginalized individual to identify the processes that urge people to maintain dogmatic and marginalizing attitudes towards others. In *Uncle Moustache*, his outsider gaze enabled him to defamiliarize the motifs associated with three types of hegemonic masculinity and subvert the Iranian master-disciple obsession by showing how an old man is emancipated from his aloof obsession with the past by the energy of the youth.

Beyzaie's main method for presenting this outsider gaze is to construct a plot in which the arrival of a stranger disturbs the normative ways of seeing and doing in a community. He also contrasts the public and private spaces in which individuals' roles reflect how their dreams and desires evolve in a symbiotic relationship between their public and private lives. In *Uncle Moustache*, the border between the stranger and the one who belongs is vague. The stranger can be the old man who has recently moved to the neighbourhood or the children whose noise in the public space penetrates the old man's private space. However, although in the end both sides change, the direction of emancipation suggests that it is the children's outsider gaze and noise that intrudes the old man's private space and changes him for better. In *Downpour*, however, the stranger is marked as a teacher who comes to transcend his own intellectual and middle-class limits to personify Beyzaie's ideal form of manliness in contrast with figures embodying different forms of hegemonic masculinity in a microcosm of 1970s Iran. The film's motifs, however, are orchestrated to suggest that the hardworking emancipator in him evolves only due to his encounter with the emancipatory gaze of a hardworking woman and his realization of the hardship of the lives and the high potential of his pupils.

Emanating from the inherited resources of patriarchy which evolve along the dominant sociopolitical, cultural, religious and economic discourses, hegemonic masculinity defines the most esteemed modes of being a man. As its tenets originate in conflicting sources, it often produces rivalling manifestations or ideals, which are, nevertheless, similar in that they are embodied in men whose power makes them role models for other men. The system created thereby is a crossroad for gender, religious and cultural values, and a locus of reformulation for producing men. It forces all men to adopt, adapt or oppose the models it offers for the individual and collective roles that men play in their lives. Its ideals are normally conveyed through a top-down hierarchy so that the men in the lower levels of society are to be modelled after those who are physically and militarily equipped to embody or support the patriarch or the ideals of manhood that he represents. In pre-revolutionary Iran, this patriarch was represented by the king, who aspired to be the wielder of absolute power, and the ideals of official manhood were reflected in officials as conveyors of top-down power, and men of action in the army or the police who maintained the order. However, there also existed religious, politically dissenting or street-level types who, while being in dialogue with cosmopolitan and indigenous forms of being Iranian, evolved alongside or in contrast to those reflecting the dominant political discourses. Thus, for instance, the clergy had their own claims to being the sources of wisdom and role models of emulation. Or the semi-literate streetwise youths, who grew up with the inherited codes of street masculinity and had tough guy aspirations, considered themselves the heirs of Iran's ideals of heroic manliness.

As evident in the rise of tough guy protagonists to centrality in Iranian cinema, a major locus for reflecting and renegotiating these and other contradictory vestiges of modernity during the twentieth century was cinema. Iranian cinema had inherited physical and trickster heroism from epics, romances and folktales. This, however, was not unique to Iran as most of the imported films that young Iranians were exposed to also had tough guys as protagonists, and the forms of masculinity in sword-and-sandal, gangster, Western or alternative Western films between the 1940s and 1960s were not different from the ones observed in tales recounted in coffeehouses, the *zurkhāneh* spaces or their hangouts. The adoption of Western-style drama and fiction in the late nineteenth century played a central role in introducing new characters and changing the old ones. Their popularization, however, was due to the power of moving pictures. Filtered through the intellectual and emotional agency of the viewers, foreign films gave a new momentum to the reformulation of cultural mentalities and practices, which, in turn, reinforced the cultural impacts of the sociopolitical and economic changes that had begun in the 1810s and had become overwhelmingly fast due to the Pahlavis' authoritarian approach to modernization. These films established an ongoing dialogue with the country's evolving systems of value, which due to the popularity of tough guy cinema across the globe focused on negotiating new forms of tough guy masculinity. Cinema, however, was also a site for promoting or resisting the hybrid identities and power relations produced due to the rise of modernity. This latter role was mainly performed by indigenous films in which non-Iranian types and social relations were adopted and mingled with their indigenous or already hybrid counterparts to produce new role models for the cinemagoers who then distributed these hybrid mentalities, relations and character types in the population.[1]

The purpose of this chapter is to demonstrate how *Downpour* opens a meta-filmic dialogue with Iranian cinema about masculinity. I argue that he subverts 'toxic' masculinity – greed for domination, possessive and protectionist attitudes towards women, misogyny and marginalization of nonconforming forms of masculinity – and reformulates the positive aspects of the ideals of manhood, such as 'pride in [one's] ability to win at sports, to maintain solidarity with a friend, to succeed at work, or to provide for [one's] family',[2] to construct his own ideal masculinity. This ideal, however, is not just a revisionist form of masculinity that guarantees the evolution of patriarchy and postpones the possibility of gender equality,[3] as the film also portrays the lives of seven women and shows the emancipatory synergy that arises from new forms of bonding among hegemonic and non-hegemonic men, women and children. In compression to his later films, the film's celebration of women's agency is less conspicuous, urging some scholars to assume that the film is limited in its vision about gender equality.[4] Nevertheless, it offers a realistic panorama of women's lives in 1970s Iran and even identifies the issue of 'toxic femininity', the type that uses conventional forms of charming or undermining to control or exploit both men and other women.[5]

Thus, if examined with attention to the reproductive cycle of patriarchy which I have provided in Figure 4.1, Beyzaie's first two films are like interventions that subvert

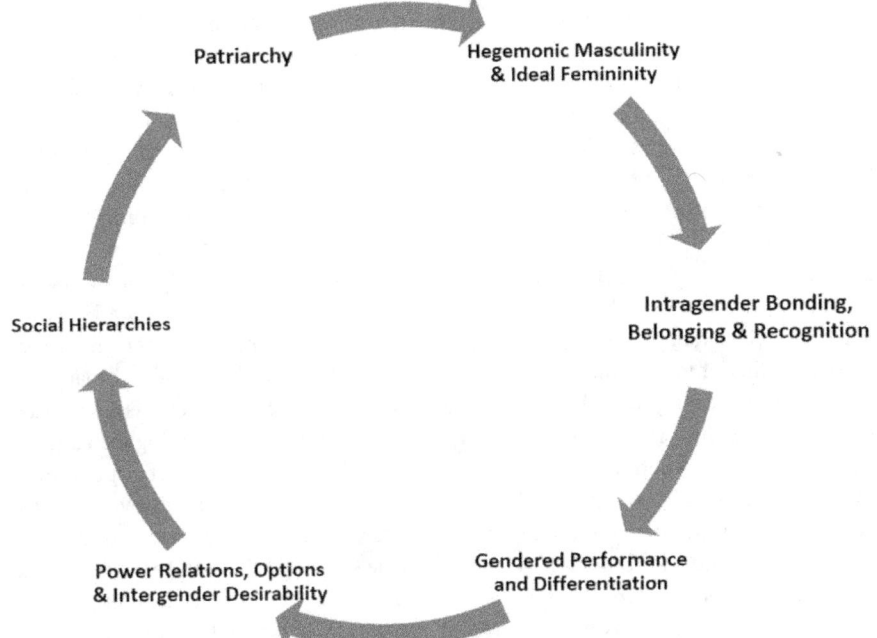

Figure 4.1 The cycle reflecting how patriarchy reproduces itself

gender relations in the space between 'Intragender Bonding, Belonging & Recognition' and 'Social Hierarchies' to produce new forms of masculinity and femininity that may confront gender inequality. In *Downpour*, this intervention is meta-filmic as the film uses several self-reflexive techniques that make cinema one of its subjects. Thus, Beyzaie establishes a dialogue with the filmmakers and spectators of Iranian cinema to transform their obsession with hegemonic masculinity, which, among other things, guarantees the continuity of culturally, politically or religiously justified violence against marginalized groups, women and children.

Downpour is also significant in reintroducing the character of reformist intellectual, who had been relegated to invisible corners in Iranian cinema. The reasons for this invisibility are multisided and beyond the focus of this book. However, an overview of the evolution of the contradictory depictions of modernized men – as intellectuals or spruced-up womanizing *fokolis* (dandies) – and the tough guy – as the honourable *luti* or the crooked *lout* – suggest that depicting the reformist intellectual as an agent of emancipation was probably risky between 1953 and 1979.[6] This was primarily because during this period the state promoted itself as the source of reform, modernization and emancipation with the king embodying both the intellectual reformer and the military defender of the nation. Thus, the suggestion of any alternative with the same qualities was likely to create reactions, which producers were not ready to risk. Moreover, such a protagonist ran the risk of being unpopular with common cinemagoers for three main reasons: (1) the image did not correspond to the self-image of the main Iranian cinemagoers, the streetwise youth who had tough guy aspirations; (2) due to censor, such figures, even when present in films, had to become neutral or like state officials, which meant that those who resented the state or the status quo did not identify with them; and (3) due to these issues such figures were never properly reformulated to enable them to compete with the tough guy types that had captured the screens in their various forms.

Educated people continued to appear in minor and, occasionally, major roles as nurses, teachers, doctors, judges, officers, but they never acted as agents of emancipation. They were around to do a job or, if central, acted as saviours for honourable, romantic or official reasons. A good example is Kimiaei's *Bigāneh Biā* (Come Stranger, 1968), whose protagonist, Ahmad is an aloof educated man. When Ahmad's brother, Mahmud impregnates Farangis, a girl that their parents raised, and then callously goes abroad to continue his education, Ahmad saves Farangis from suicide and marries her. However, when a lonely and depressed Mahmud returns years later and realizes that he has a son, a brief conflict of love ensues. Feeling that Farangis still loves Mahmud, Ahmad ends the dispute by killing himself and leaving a note stating he sacrificed his life to save three lives. The film introduced a new type of hero worthy of psychological analysis. Behrouz Vosoughi's acting was, as usual, special, and his stepping out of popular films to be the lead in an 'alternative' film was a positive change. The plot, however, uses the cliché of a seduced girl caught between her duties as a mother, her relationship with a corrupt dandy and her obligation to an honourable supporter. It, thus, resembles Majid Mohseni's *Lāt-e Javānmard* (Chivalrous Lout, 1958), but the setting is in an upper-class milieu in which the *luti* is an educated man, and the dandy is his brother. Kimiaei alludes to Golestan's *Brick and Mirror* in the scene Ahmad talks about the child as an abandoned responsibility.[7] The depiction of love and lust also echoes and aspires to surpass Golestan's film. Whereas Mahmud is initially like Hāshem in Golestan's film and believes that he is a passer who should just enjoy life, for Ahmad the desire for sex is linked to love and duty. This also enables Kimiaei to include voyeuristic scenes of lovemaking to contrast the two brothers and attract viewers in the absence of cabaret scenes.

However, as Parviz Davāei specified in 1968, the plot is too trivial to carry the burden of the philosophical ideas projected onto the dialogue, and each time the director attempts to unpack the underlying causes, the sentimentality of the events undermines his work.[8] The film music is irrelevant, the voice-over with Farangis's voice is sentimental, the dialogue is uneven with lofty ideas inserted between trivial incidents, Ahmad's mentalities and values remain unclear and his suicide is implausible. Rather than being an intellectual, he happens to be educated. In action, he is a self-effacing noble man obsessed with doves and capturing and releasing birds which symbolize his relationship with Farangis, a man who has lost hope in society but has remained honourable. The core of the film, therefore, resembles Kimiaei's later films as it glorifies an honourable man in a world which has no place for larger-than-life, heroic people. The difference is that whereas in his later films the protagonist is a tough guy like the eponymous heroes of *Qeysar* (1969) and *Dāsh Ākol* (1971) or an intellectual who loses everything and becomes a tough guy as Nuri in *Sorb* (The Lead, 1988), here he is an educated aristocrat. As Kimiaei himself puts it, Ahmad is 'the embodiment of a type of heroism, which can no longer exist, and is, therefore, annihilated. As stated in the film "the world is too overcrowded, too busy; no emotional situation can lead to the rise of a hero anymore"'.[9]

Kimiaei's film, therefore, introduces a type of masculinity that transcends the violence of the tough guy, the master-disciple cults of religious, mystic or official traditions and the triviality of Westernized dandy. However, it promotes a morbid form of masculine honour and fails the test of time in reflecting the roles of educated men in society. It also carries no emancipatory force in its form and has no clear critique of the world in which the events occur. Moreover, if examined with attention to the depiction of gender relations in 'alternative' cinema, it falls behind earlier films. Whereas in Golestan's *Brick and Mirror* the moral ground is given to a modern-looking compassionate and responsible woman, in *Come Stranger* as in other films by Kimiaei, the moral ground is given to a man whose sense of honour transcends the triviality of modern men and women, and women are often blamed for their wrong choices.

Thus, the reformist intellectual remained absent from Iranian cinema despite the scattered appearance of pseudo-intellectuals in films. With *Downpour*, however, the borders began to shift as the film reinforced the emancipatory discourse of *Uncle Moustache* by introducing realistically depicted female characters and an intellectual whose qualities surpassed those of the intellectual reformist that Mortezāqoli Fekri depicted in his plays between 1911 and 1916.

Like Beyzaie's other films, *Downpour* contains aesthetic stylization which according to some critics makes some of his scenes 'unnecessary' or 'forced'.[10] However, if such viewers discard their assumptions about the dependency of cinematic reality on verisimilitude and accept that cinema, like literature, can adopt various forms of expression, they find that his films present more reality than most realistic films. Beyzaie's insistence on turning proverbs or mental images into scenes, on slowing or hasting the action to reflect the mood and on making his dialogue multi-layered and his action and background dense and evocative turn his films into poems, which communicate at various levels with different types of people. The density of motifs at realistic and surrealistic levels may seem to undermine the unity of his films with ideas that propose subplots, but they gradually create a master plot that addresses the totality of the experience rather than reducing it to its realistic essence. His films are, thus, like musical compositions with point-counterpoint structures that introduce images and later develop them into contexts that help the viewers reinterpret the events from new perspectives.

However, though rare at the time, such forms of stylizations, which were already present in Ghaffary's *Night of the Hunchback* and Golestan's *Brick and Mirror*, became central to Iranian New Wave. Hamid Naficy argues that 'the marriage of gritty realism and uncanny surrealism (such as a man becoming a cow) became a hallmark of some of the best new-wave products'. This is correct as such a 'marriage' was crucial to 'Golestan's *The Secrets of the Treasure of the Jenni Valley* (*Asrar-e Ganj-e Darreh-ye Jenni*, 1972), Parviz Kimiavi's *The Mongols* (*Mogholha*, 1973), Baizai's *Stranger and the Fog* (*Gharibeh va Meh*,[11] 1974) and *Ballad of Tara* and many other New Wave films. However, self-reflexive stylization without disrupting narrative continuity, which is crucial to Beyzaie's work as a major plot element or minor motifs, has also been central to Iranian New Wave, and its evolution in Kiarostami's *Close-Up* (1990), Jafar Panahi's *Āyeneh* (Mirror, 1997) or Asghar Farhadi's *The Salesman* (2016) are rooted in Beyzaie's experiments with such forms in his plays and in *Downpour*, *The Crow* (1977), *Death of Yazdgerd* (1981) and *Maybe Some Other Time* (1986). In the films that Naficy mentions, surrealistic elements 'interjected fantasy into the realistic plots and narratives, but unlike in commercial movies, it was driven by the psychology and internal urges of diegetic characters, not by the extradiegetic directors' desires, market forces, or genre conventions, or by chaotic and improvised narratives'.[12] In Beyzaie's film and those I mentioned before, another layer is added to this psychological turn by self-reflexive and intertextual motifs which expand the films' thematic and formal structures while commenting on the meaning and function of art, the impacts of recorded sound and image on the meaning of existence and the constructed nature of history, memory and narrative identity.

The meta-filmic aspect is essential in *Downpour* as instead of a chivalrous tough guy as its hero and a nightclub dancer or a rich or poor damsel in distress as its heroine, it depicts the love story of a teacher and a dressmaker. This choice is significant as the film depicts the rise of a constructive intellectual as he finds his place among people in a process of mutual emancipation. Hekmati, an educated man from a middle-class background, falls in love with Ātefeh, a lower-class intelligent woman, in a narrative context in which the gradual rise in Hekmati's awareness about his students' life pulls him down from the ivory tower of higher education and middle-class mentalities and makes him a hardworking man with a constructive mission. His desire for love and belonging activates his constructive aspiration for recognition and displaying his worth by refurbishing the school hall where the children can have non-violent entertainment, play music and perform plays. Thus, love, responsibility and hard work transform a bookish man into a reformist hero. Nevertheless, he is separated from them by forces beyond his control. At this level, Hekmati's victimization by Rahim, though suggestive of the structure of hegemonic masculinity, is only a hurdle which leads to the children's identification with him, as they already know his worth. However, his victimization by the principal who represents the abuse of power and his sense of mission and innocence make him a sacrificial figure. This is metatheatrical in that, like his *Puppet Trilogy* and *So Dies Akbar the Hero*, it reformulates the archetypes of sacrificial heroism and the motifs of spring rituals and *ta'ziyeh* for existential, cultural and sociopolitical purposes.

At meta-cinematic level, Rahim reminds the spectator of the protagonist of Ismail Kushan's *Kolāh Makhmali* (1962). He even wears striped suits that visually echo the latter. Like other specimens of the type, he is generous and has ethical prestige, physical strength and obedient disciples. Beyzaie, however, demythologizes the character by contrasting his strength and honour with his obsession with violence, his maltreatment of his disciples and his hypocrisy. He also uses parody to suggest he is trapped in a cliché that has distorted the other aspects of his humanity. The school principal is also like the politically correct officials of mainstream cinema. He is well dressed, articulate and modern-looking, but Beyzaie's metonymic framing catches him with his finger in his nose and displays his nosiness, pretentiousness, opportunism, hypocrisy, obsession with control and malice towards true talent.

Downpour: Meta-filmic framing and the rise of new characters in a feast of light

The opening credits of *Downpour* appear with the sound of downpour. Then follows a sequence that begins with a metonymic close-up of the wheels of a cart surrounded by children running around and annoying or helping the cartman in uphill places. The fast-paced, energetic music accompanying the images of the wheels, the cart, the children and the old man suggest normal movement in life and establish an intertextual dialogue with *Uncle Moustache*. This is also confirmed later as the primary change in the film is Hekmati's self-identification with the children and his resolve to improve their lives. The film proceeds to show the cart has been carrying the personal stuff of Mr Hekmati, a teacher, who has just arrived at a poor district in early 1960s' Tehran. The children offer to help and are rejected, which leads to their making fun of and annoying the newcomer with their catapults and Bic Pen Blowguns, fooling around with the cart and finally finding a way to help. The cartman nags about the fare, a woman shows up to reprimand the cartman for splashing her and the cartman giggles and escapes into Hekmati's room. The framing of the household objects then confounds this multi-layered, down-to-earth realism with ritualistic symbolism. Carried in a line as a procession with sombre music, the objects signify Hekmati's inherited identity. Old photos of women in modern clothing with no or little hijab and men in suit with ties or bowties suggest Hekmati's modernity as a gift of generations; old books, antique lamps and a huge mirror suggest his intellectual identity as a product of love and the identity-building legacy of enlightenment, and the empty frame signifies Hekmati's still-evolving identity.

Beyzaie's meta-filmic playfulness starts with shots that, like the still images at the beginning of *Uncle Moustache*, suggest them as the continuation of the credits. In the first, Hekmati meets Ātefeh's employee, the dressmaker, who criticizes the cartman, links his rudeness to the demise of chivalrous manliness and specifies that she is from the upper parts of the city before testing Hekmati's class background. Hekmati tries to calm her, and the shot-reverse-shot that follows through the picture frame he has been carrying frames the woman and the intellectual as central characters. Another self-reflective framing follows, with Rahim, the district's wealthy butcher, reflected in the large mirror in Hekmati's hands. Beyzaie's mise en scene places Rahim, the tough guy, on an upper step to accentuate his stature.[13] Thus, standing tall in a pose exuding confidence with his full reflection in the mirror, Rahim talks like an indisputable hero, the cock in the roost, to Hekmati whose pose implies subordination. The emphasis on his good qualities suggests Beyzaie's usual avoidance of black-and-white characters and his reluctance to demolish a social type that still had positive impacts on some people. The breaking of the mirror, however, reflects the complications to come. The scene suggests that although set up by educated individuals, the mirror of cinema has become obsessed with chivalrous tough guys and hegemonic masculinity. Rahim's saving of the mirror the first time it falls confirms this reading. Yet, the scene also indicates Hekmati's fascination with the power, charisma and status embedded in hegemonic masculinity, and the breaking of the mirror prefigures the possibility of change in him and his society (Figure 4.2).

Thus, the first paragraph of this filmic novel implies that both men and their cinematic image must change and declares that its goal is to display the prospects of this change. The sequence also depicts the tough guy aspirations and speech habits of the children to propose that with the current educational system, street culture will continue to determine their lives and push them into the hierarchy of master tough guy and obedient disciples. However, it also proposes the possibility of change by displaying their positive qualities. Towards the end of this sequence as Hekmati is lifting the frame of the broken mirror, he appears in a medium shot in the middle of the frame. This occurs as a boy who is trying to annoy him reflects the sunlight into his eyes by a broken piece of mirror. Though realistic, the combination functions like a cinematic spotlight which highlights the children's role in engineering Hekmati's centrality.

The children's fooling around with the cart leads to its rolling down the sloping alley with the beautiful lamp that Hekmati has inherited from his mother at the top like a ritually charged artistic object, a legacy that must be saved. The scene has been extended to highlight the lamp as a motif of love and enlightenment. The lamp and its bulb survive, but the bulb falls from Hekmati's hands when he sees Ātefeh, and he shatters the lamp itself while shouting angrily at the children. The poetic motifs, thus, signify how Hekmati's past ties and illusions of enlightenment will be replaced with a new form of love and social responsibility.

Beyzaie's penchant for poetic reality rather than realism and using background to enrich his semiotic references turn the first sequence into the opening of a poem and foreshadows love, rivalry, a chaotic mixture of old and new, the accidental nature of our encounters with life-changing experiences and the psychological tendencies that determine our reactions to outside stimulants. As in Beyzaie's other works, emotions and moods are suggested by objects, music and events. Thus, like the cart that is set free by the children and roles down the alley totally out of control, Hekmati is emancipated and becomes an emancipator by the energetic children and the dazzling Ātefeh. The cart stops where Hekmati sees Ātefeh, and the lamp, the memory of the past, does not break until Ātefeh's gaze, embodying Beyzaie's fascination with the positive aspects of his culture takes Hekmati's breath away (Figure 4.2).

Figure 4.2 Screenshots from *Downpour*. Minutes 3'–9'

Distribution, discipline and the official hierarchy of power

The next sequence focuses on the principal, who embodies official, authoritarian masculinity. While normal office types are presented in the constantly bowing teacher or the woman who laughs at everything, the principal appears as a figure of authority as he distributes cigarettes among the teachers. Thus, having control over and distributing what others need is implied to be the source of his power, and the cigarette motif highlights this position and the subservient attitudes of the others towards him. The scene displaying his power over Hekmati, however, is the one in which they enter the classroom. The juxtaposition of pupil's noise and their sudden silence, his poised entrance in a medium shot ahead of Hekmati and his patronizing patting of Hekmati's shoulder while introducing him to the pupils indicate that he wants everyone to know that he is the one making it possible for Hekmati to be visible. He then delivers what is to Hekmati, the children and the camera an endless speech about Hekmati and the

Figure 4.3 Screenshots from *Downpour*. Minutes 10′–15′

duties of pupils and teachers. While Hekmati suffers under the burden of his official clichés and the mocking gaze and whispers of the pupils, the music and the camera highlight Hekmati's position as a stranger to such affected presentations. With the principal gone, the mocking questions of the pupils and their noisy games continue to challenge Hekmati until he invades them with the method they are used to. Using his penknife, symbolizing his small leverage, as a pointer, he smiles and randomly throws one of the naughty pupils out. These events happen in a room decorated with ruined-mirror and coloured-glass decoration and delicate stucco, suggesting the richness of a cultural tradition that remains neglected even in an educational institution. The same emphasis on art and culture continues in the foreground and background, even in the decorations of Rahim's butcher's shop (Figure 4.3).

The bookish man and the strong woman: Fate, love and comic surveillance

Then comes the first conversation between Hekmati and Navvāb, the teacher representing the collapse of idealism under the pressure of life. Together, the two continue to construct the film's existential discourse about life, love, intellectuality and responsibility. These discussions suggest human identity as partly pre-determined due to what Martin Heidegger defines as human *Geworfenheit* (thrownness), the birth and upbringing conditions beyond human control, and partly determined by a type of free choice that is bound by human *Befindlichkeit* (disposition or attunement) – temperaments, desires, goals, skills and specific ways of perceiving the world which originate in thrownness.[14]

> **Navvāb:** How did you come to this school?
> **Hekmati:** It was not my choice.
> **Navvāb:** Yes, everybody is like that.[15]

For his first teaching position, Hekmati had requested to be sent to a school near his home, but because he was single and the school was a girls' school, he was sent to this school. Thus, personal history, social circumstances and incidents push the individual towards directions or choices whose consequences cannot be chosen. This shows that, at one level, the film reflects on how human beings are thrown into their worlds and use their resources to either exploit or gain recognition by serving or trying to change their communities. As the shot of his books implies, Hekmati is characterized by a desire for knowledge and change, and knowledge is the resource he has for serving others. As the camera moves over his books, his interest in literature and history is emphasized. His conversation with Navvāb also reveals two other aspects of being a man in Iran: the likely death of intellectuality due to family responsibilities and smoking as a masculine obsession. While dropping the ashes of his cigarette in an ashtray held by Hekmati, Navvāb refers to his interest in books as a past habit and justifies his apathy by stating that he is married, and his knowledge is enough for the school.

Beyzaie uses smoking to mark the absurd habits that people, especially men, adopt to display their adulthood, independence or power. The physical education teacher, for instance, smokes and reads newspapers in the yard as counting or whistling to pace the pupils' exercise. Such ritual forms are also linked with metonymic motifs of masculinity, femineity, work, culture, art and agency signified in close-ups of hands. In the scene before Hekmati's meeting with Ātefeh, these include the tattoo of a female face on the school servant's hand, Hekmati's hand covered in chalk or moving with a pen as he is marking coursework, the hand of a girl holding a pen or needle in the painting on the office wall, or Ātefeh's hands injured due to sewing. This art-life link is reinforced when a parallel is created between Ātefeh and the girl in the painting. Echoing a later scene in which Ātefeh brings her hands near Hekmati's face to show him her injured fingers, the camera captures Hekmati thinking in front of the painting in a shot that suggests he is kissing the girl's hand as she is writing on his lips or, as in the Persian saying, she is punishing his rude words by putting needle on his lips.

Ātefeh's active entrance into the film is as tumultuous as that of her employer, the dressmaker. Like her, she thinks that her rights have been violated and enters the school office like a heroine to punish the new teacher by delivering a speech that reveals a multi-layered character. Thus, in two short scenes, Beyzaie introduces two working women who are positively assertive outside home, ask for their rights, support themselves and their families and without being adventurous openly censure men. Like the dressmaker, but at a more intellectual level, Ātefeh dazzles Hekmati, this time, not by releasing a rapid succession of ideas and dreams, but by displaying a deep awareness of social inequality and the emancipatory power of education, and by her assertive showing of her hands as a sign of hard work which magnifies her already established appeal as a well-spoken young woman. The dramatic irony created by Ātefeh not knowing Hekmati is 'the new teacher' enhances the comedy of a practical woman beating an awareness of the world into a bookish man. Her scattering of Hekmati's papers is, therefore, not just a plot device to make her pause and enable Hekmati to tell her who he is, but also a motif suggesting that she is an agent of emancipation forcing him to exit the world of papers.

Hekmati: [Looking at the papers and her] It doesn't matter. [He sits to collect the papers in a pose that resembles kneeling and then looking at Ātefeh in admiration.]

Ātefeh: [Sitting to help him.] I am sorry this happened.

Hekmati: I'm not the principal.

Ātefeh: You're not?

Hekmati: No, you made a mistake. [Smiling] I'm the new teacher.

Ātefeh: Look at me, talking to someone like you. How can you get what I'm saying? (18′.30″–19′.20″)

Turning to leave, Ātefeh finds that her chador is stuck under Hekmati's foot. While paying homage to the comically intriguing bathrobe scene between the lovers, George and Mary in Frank Capra's *It's a Wonderful Life*, Beyzaie slows down the action to emphasize the budding of love between his equally magnificent protagonists.[16] She pulls it a few times as the clock chimes, marking the moment's emotional intensity, but Hekmati is too dazzled by her and her critique of his understanding. When he finally lifts his foot, and she leaves, Beyzaie hits the nail on the head by a meta-filmic shot showing that, like the man on the veranda in Capra's film, four pupils have been watching them through a window the whole time.

With the tug of war between Hekmati and his pupils, this moment leads to complications. A boy that Hekmati kicks out of the class exonerates himself from

Figure 4.4 Screenshots from *Downpour*. Minutes 15′.30″–24′.30″

the accusation of daydreaming by stating that Hekmati himself is constantly daydreaming as he is in love. The rumour of Hekmati's love then reaches the teachers through an eager principal. In the same sequence, the sycophantic attitudes of the PE teacher when delivering the boy to the principal reinforces the motifs that highlight the distorted hierarchy of hegemonic masculinity, a motif whose tough guy manifestation appears in the scene in Rahim's shop. The gossip complicates Hekmati's life with his pupils' romantic paintings on the board and his colleagues' and pupil's knowing glances, smiles and whispers. Though suggested earlier with the boy on the lamp-post reflecting light on and watching Hekmati, the cartman and his friends, these scenes suggest how the gaze of others and surveillance may lead to self-discipline (Figure 4.4).

Ubiquitous in Beyzaie's films, this motif predicts Foucault' use of Jeremy Bentham's idea of 'panopticon' to clarify how modern societies use surveillance to produce compliant people. In Beyzaie, surveillance occurs in both modern and old settings. It may be a neutral yet regulatory form of communal observation which may sometimes even lead to empathy and support, or a means of religious, sociopolitical, and cultural suppression, punishment and marginalization. When dealing with modern life, however, Beyzaie's use of light, mirrors, glasses and top-down gaze give a Foucauldian sense to surveillance, and his protagonists' anxiety for being under threatening or judging gazes creates Kafkaesque ambiances.

Ostracization, desire for control and upward gaze

The film, then, changes perspective to focus on Ātefeh's brother, Mossaiyeb, who becomes the second victim of this system of surveillance and ostracization. Beyzaie highlights the impact of such experiences on the child by depicting him going down a downhill alley with tens of steps before sitting on a step to play with two cockroaches that he controls with black threads. The boy smiles, pushes and pulls the cockroaches and then casts a sad gaze at the sky. The game is realistic, and the gaze means he notices it is getting dark, and he must go home. The scene, however, suggests the erratic nature of events that determine human life and Mossaiyeb's desire for having control over something. The threads on the cockroaches also intertextually refer to the puppet trilogy to signify the invisible hands of an exclusionist ideology that functions like fate at sociopolitical, cultural and existential levels (Figure 4.5).

Figure 4.5 Screenshots from *Downpour*. Minutes 25′–26′.10″

Mithraic ritual of light, tough guy hierarchies and cultural ambiguity

Mossaiyeb's upward gaze is then juxtaposed, in a ritualistically stylized scene, with close-ups of five men looking up not at the sky but at what the camera reveals to be Rahim and the lamp that he turns on. Rahim's light is, thus, what they are looking up to. With the decorative tiles of *Shahnameh* figures, musicians and Qajar kings on the walls of Rahim's shop, the camera traces Rahim's hand as he extends his cleaver and turns on the light, which illuminates a mural of Fereydun, the dragon-killing hero-king, and his army of men with Persian headgears fighting Zahhāk and his army of men with Arab headgears. The mural depicts Zahhāk from behind, and the lamp has covered Fereydun's face which, while making him appear like a haloed Shi'i saint, marks the difficulty of deciding whether the people of Rahim's type are like Fereydun or Zahhāk. The ritual of 'light time' is then finalized with a *salavāt* – a brief Muslim prayer for the prophet and his family performed to thank God for a blessing (light) or ask for protection. The ritual also signifies the continuity of pre-Islamic celebration of light in Islamic rituals. With Rahim's apprentice included, seven people, aged between 14 and 60, partake in the ritual, which marks the seven ranks of Mithraic mysteries.[17] The framing of the mural and the men suggests the origin of Iran's tough guy culture in Mithraism but questions its current form by juxtaposing the *salavāt*, an Arabic salute, with the headgears of the two sides of the battle.

Figure 4.6 Screenshots from *Downpour*. Minutes 26'.10"–26'.40"

With Rahim's communal and cinematic centrality established, the camera follows Mossaiyeb to Ātefeh's workplace. The spectator now finds that Rahim has been financially supporting her family with the hope of marrying her, but she is reluctant to do so. Ātefeh's reaction to Mossaiyeb's news about Hekmati having fallen in love suggests she likes Hekmati. Beyzaie, thus, completes the focal love triangle of Rahim-Ātefeh-Hekmati. However, he gradually also expands the field to the lives of Navvāb, Ātefeh, Ātefeh's mother, the dressmaker, Hekmati's landlady, a few of Hekmati's pupils, the principal, his wife and his daughter to offer insights about several aspects of life previously neglected in Iranian cinema (Figure 4.6).

Meta-filmic sequences of solidarity, love, misogyny and toxic masculinity

Shots of Ātefeh and Hekmati's matching gestures in their daily activities are then accompanied with a calm sad flute melody, which suggests the hardship of their lives, their suitability for one another and the sad ending. The plot then moves forward with Hekmati's refusal to accept Navvāb's innuendos about his love for Ātefeh, Navvāb's celebration of love and equation of having eight children with being dead, Hekmati's accosting of Ātefeh to explain why he does not greet her in public, Ātefeh's glance of desire at Hekmati, Hekmati's confession to Navvāb about rumours making him think about her, Ātefeh's nervous denial of having any interest in Hekmati and her accidental wounding of her finger as she is embroidering a wedding dress.

> **Ātefeh:** People just gossip. They never leave anyone alone.
> **Dressmaker:** Don't be upset about it.
> **Ātefeh:** It is upsetting. They just babble and babble. I don't know in how many ways I must pay for trying to earn my living. [Ātefeh injures her finger with a needle.]
> **Dressmaker:** [Looking at Ātefeh's finger with her glasses and commenting like a specialist] If you like him, go away with him. I have to stay here, but what about you? Think more about yourself. Don't spoil your life. (30'.50"–31'.30")

Beyzaie uses Navvāb and the dressmaker as confidantes to reveal the budding of love between the two and imply that while they are still in denial, the dice are already cast. The two are also similar in that though highly skilled and still in their early forties, they think that they are done for: one because she is probably alone and has failed to achieve class mobility, and the other because he married too young and has eight children. Ātefeh's words about the reason people gossip about her also highlight gossip as one of the methods for controlling the women who work outside. Building on the experience of his characters, Beyzaie also turns the desire for leaving into a statement about leaving a particular way of life.

This is reinforced in Ātefeh's house where the mother's constant weaving is symptomatic of a society in which women's labour remains underpaid. On the two sides of the window, two small statues suggest the inherited vision of male and female collaboration: with a toiling man and a water-carrying woman. The toil implies breadwinning, and the vessel on the woman shoulder the womb and the acts of nourishing and caring for children. The mother, however, has had to carry the burden of life by herself by a lowly job or by works usually done by women, such as clothes and carpet weaving. The mother, now, weaves jumpers that Ātefeh sells in her workplace. Thus, one of the neglected insights that Beyzaie introduces is that by providing work, the dressmaker has been helping Ātefeh much more than Rahim. She even comes out as more chivalrous than Rahim as her help is not linked to demands. The mother's fate, however, also contains another social implication. Towards the end of the film even when she is apparently dead, with her lips sealed as always, her hands continue weaving to testify to the hard work of women and their silenced past. The spectator does not know why Ātefeh's father is absent, or her mother is so prematurely old although her son is only about 10. However, the film clearly suggests that if Ātefeh does not marry Hekmati, her fate will be either like her mother, the one who married, or the dressmaker, the one who did not.

A meta-cinematic scene then furthers the motifs about the tough guy culture of desire, possessive protectionism and misogyny towards women. The scene opens with schoolboys using a hired airgun to shoot at a seductive picture of the typecast actress of femme fatale roles in European films, Marisa Mell (1939–92). With the gun and the darts as metaphors for power and phallus, the boys' intense pleasure at hitting the picture depicts how due to the separation of the world of boys and girls and the use of women as sex idols in cinema, the typical obsessions of hegemonic masculinity are reproduced to make the object of desire the target of overpowering. Desire, thus, turns into violence and misogyny if the target of desire is unattainable. Beyzaie's use of Mell's picture also proposes that femme fatales, the ultimate products of toxic femininity, are the reactionary results of the same system.

A scene of fight between children, then, illustrates the impacts of violent masculinity. While building a playhouse and talking about action films, a boy tells Mossaiyeb that Hekmati gives him high marks because he 'wants' his sister. The fight that ensues destroys their playhouse, signifying the way macho bragging and rivalry distort productive friendship. Frustrated with such allegations, Mossaiyeb tries to fulfil 'social expectations' by playing the action hero. He picks up a rock and goes to 'kill' Hekmati, but while waiting for Hekmati, he cools down, and his crying and their friendly talk suggest his love for Hekmati and young boys' potential to communicate their concerns without violence when not goaded by peer pressure.[18]

Further allegations of nepotism make Hekmati so furious that, to everyone's amusement, he asks Mossaiyeb to arrange a meeting with Ātefeh to prove that there is nothing between them. This leads to one of the most memorable sequences in Iranian cinema, which begins with Ātefeh waiting in a park and Hekmati reciting a declaration of no interest with his landlady listening from another room and Hekmati's medium shot corresponding with images of Ferdowsi and a cat with a ball of yarn in the background. Thus, Beyzaie alludes to Hekmati's comic intellectuality, the centrality of unexpected love in several *Shahnameh* legends and his similarity to a cat with a yarn as his next move further entangles him in love. Despite this rehearsal, when trying to deliver his declaration to an impatient Ātefeh, with her first glance, his nerves fail, and his frown of detachment is replaced with a smile of endearment.

Hekmati: [With confidence.] Dear Lady –
Ātefeh: [Turning her head towards him.] Ha?
Hekmati: [Hesitating to continue. He bends forwards to rub his knees, pulls himself together and raises his hand to make his declaration] Dear Lady –
[Ātefeh's glance disarms him.]
Hekmati: [Smiling, he brings his hand down to his hair] Nice weather, isn't it? It's really good that we are alone here together away from those intrusive eyes.
[The camera zooms out to show Hekmati's pupils watching them from behind.]
Hekmati: Dear lady! [Pause.] I love you.
[Ātefeh looks concerned. She raises and runs away with the wind in her chador creating the image of a bird flying. Hekmati follows her, but then stops to look at his pupils who have been chasing them and are now hoarding behind him.] (38′–41′)

This meta-cinematic scene comments on surveillance and the accidental nature of human love and identity formation and uses cinema-loving boys as voyeuristic viewers of a comic love scene between an intellectual and an intelligent, hardworking woman, an odd mixture they have never seen in cinema. It also subverts the teacher-student binary by placing the pupils in the position of invigilators and the teacher in the position of an examinee in the trial of love.

The next sequence, then, parodies the reaction of the chivalrous tough guy in folktales and popular films. Like Western films, Rahim juggles his weapons, two knives, which also evoke Zahhāk's two snakes in the mural. Like medieval knights, he is dressed by his apprentice. Like thugs, he spits into his palms to straighten his hair. As in folktales, he pulls out a brick out of a wall, and as in popular films, he pushes the handles of a strength machine so hard that its hand turns twice around the face. The parodic incongruity, however, is strong, as despite his silly reactions and naivety, Hekmati's caring and calmly determined disposition has already established him as an invincible hero who cannot be defeated by being beaten.

Having no clues about Rahim's intents, Hekmati is then beaten by this incarnation of violent masculinity with his pupils acting like film spectators. Rahim rudely removes and puts Hekmati's glasses, the markers of his intellectuality, in Hekmati's pocket before beating him. This shows his coolness when using violence, but it also implies he cannot beat Hekmati as an intellectual. This is confirmed when, after the fight, a bruised and bleeding Hekmati picks up the untouched glasses from the ground and goes to classroom to create one of Beyzaie's stylized scenes of redemptive anagnorisis. Hekmati enters the class and slowly limps towards the blackboard with six columns of concerned pupils appearing column by column in the camera frame watching him like a tragic hero. On the board, fading words suggest his interior monologue: *khoshbakhti* (happiness), *divār/divāneh* (wall/mad), *pāydāri* (steadfastness), *moqāvemat* (resistance), *khol* (crazy) and *hesāb* (account). As he is sitting on his chair with the mirror ornament and stucco in the background and solemn looks on pupil's face, a sharp spin top on his chair makes him jump with a shriek. This final comic relief marks how he has been treated by his pupils until now, but it also suggests a new beginning (Figure 4.7).

Figure 4.7 Screenshots from *Downpour*. Minutes 33′.30″–43′.40″

Master-slave binary and the quest for ascendancy: From bookishness to violent masculinity

Now that Hekmati, the hero of the romantic plot that the pupils have created, has been beaten as they are beaten every day, they begin to identify with him. The transformation, however, is mutual. As reflected in the mirror scene, Hekmati begins to discover a new redemptive self. The trauma of being watched by his pupils when beaten has enabled him to watch himself from outside, discover some of his own absurdities and define a point of resolution for himself. In the mirror scene, Hekmati, who is in desperate need of talking to someone as a process of self-rediscovery, asks Navvāb to stay with him. Navvāb, however, has a family.

> **Hekmati:** Just a few more minutes. I really want to talk.
> **Navvāb:** Okay. Talk.

Hekmati: You know that there was nothing at first.
Navvāb: Yea, yea. I know.
Hekmati: When I told her I loved her, I was just curious to see her reaction.
Navvāb: Did it hurt a lot?
Hekmati: [Grumbling in pain as putting his head on the back.] *Hurt? Did you say hurt? I don't know, but yes. Let me confess to something strange.* [Navvāb sets a chair before him] *On the contrary, I somewhat enjoyed it because then and there, I began to discover a feeling in myself.* [Navvāb sets a mirror on the chair and leaves.] [...] *You know what I mean. I began to feel that I cannot live without her. Where are you?* [Hekmati looks at himself in the mirror.] *It's good that you're here.* (46'–47'.25")

In realistic terms, the presence of a violent adversary who crushes Hekmati's reputation forces him to exit his ivory tower to compete for Ātefeh, who has now become more desirable as she is also wanted by the neighbourhood's alpha male. From a psychological perspective, being beaten like a child due to his love for a woman has placed him in an Oedipal situation, with Ātefeh as the mother and Rahim as the father. Examined through the Lacanian idea of the 'symbolic order', this means that Ātefeh is now his *objet petit a*, the desired phantasy and a replacement for his mother.[19] One must, however, remember that the *objet petit a* is not the ultimate object of desire. It is rather 'the little other', 'the cause of the desire', 'the object of anxiety', which translates desire into action because it is also 'the final irreducible reserve of libido'. Hekmati's actual object of desire, therefore, is gaining ascendancy and asserting his masculinity by competing for the girl that he loves, but more important, is also loved by Rahim. In this context, the mirror scene also echoes Lacan's idea of 'the mirror stage', which begins as 'a stage in the development of the child' but becomes 'a permanent feature of the structure of subjectivity' or 'imaginary order' which works with 'the real' and 'the symbolic' orders to form a coherent self.[20] Therefore, the mirror scene, with its ultimate declaration, 'It's good that you're here', announces the recognition of the old self in the structure of a new self, which, unbeknownst to everyone else, results from the alignment of his desire for Ātefeh with a desire for recognition that has, at this stage, been translated into a desire for assertive masculinity and ascendancy. Hekmati is, thus, set to assert a new form of masculinity which can overpower Rahim and become worthy of being desired by Ātefeh.

This can also be analysed in terms of the master-slave cults that the film subverts. In his analysis of 'aggressivity' in the context of desire for recognition, Lacan uses Alexandre Kojève's reading of Hegel, which specifies that 'the DIALECTIC of the master and the slave is the inevitable result of the fact that human DESIRE is the desire for recognition', which requires the subject to impose 'his idea of himself' on another. Such a desire, however, results in conflict as 'this other also desires recognition', and the willingness to risk one's life in the 'fight for recognition' or 'pure prestige' is the marker of being human. However, since 'recognition can only be granted by a living being', and the drive for preserving one's life is equally strong, the conflict usually ends before one of the rivals dies. Thus, the defeated person 'gives up his desire for recognition', 'recognises the victor as his "master" and becomes his "slave"'. Both Kojève and Lacan discuss the dialectical variability of this relationship and identify the sources of fulfilment open to the slave but not to the master, but they assert that the process is inevitable as it is impossible to have a community of masters.[21]

The film displays two master positions: the official one embodied by the principal and his circle of sycophantic teachers, and the tough guy one embodied in Rahim and his disciples. The scene after the mirror monologue exemplifies the way the film displays this master-slave hierarchy. Rahim's young apprentice comes out of Ātefeh's workplace and gives a package (the meat portion that Rahim provides for Ātefeh) to a man of about 30. The man takes it to Rahim, who is lighting a cigarette, and states that she has left. Rahim slaps him, holds him by the collar and shakes him as he has failed in his duty. Then, noticing that the dressmaker is closing her workshop, he passes his cigarette to the man, combs his hair and goes to talk to the dressmaker. The man takes a deep pull of the cigarette and joins him as a silent confirmer as Rahim ironically reminds a defiant dressmaker of Ātefeh's desperate conditions. Then, in another scene, the head of the wandering musicians distributes the money they have collected during the day. The regular appearance of these musicians in several scenes from this point onwards suggests Beyzaie's meta-filmic playing with diegetic and non-diegetic music while reinforcing the motifs that highlight the role of art and music in all aspects of life and the desperate conditions of Iran's artistic heritage and folk artists. Here, however, he also uses them to suggest that leadership does not necessitate a master-slave hierarchy.

Rahim's crass references to Ātefeh's 'dumb mother' and 'ill-disciplined brother' and the dressmaker's emphasis on Ātefeh's desire to see a film that make her laugh signify Hekmati and Rahim's difference. Both need her to assert their masculinity, but whereas Rahim does not like her family, loves her tears, wants her to need him, and treats his disciples in ways that suggest he will be a violent husband, Hekmati, as the film gradually demonstrates, loves her laughter and wants her free and flying. Ātefeh's restlessness in the next scene reflects her awareness of this difference and suggests the conflict between her desire for growth and freedom and the reality of her situation. When Mosaiyeb expresses his worry about Ātefeh's marriage, Beyzaie's camera uses Mosaiyeb's upward gaze to frame Ātefeh with the picture of their father signifying that Ātefeh has been occupying the position of the absent father and has thus gained insights that transcend the limits of her community's gender roles.

In its meta-cinematic aspect, the mirror scene echoes two scenes in Mohseni's *Chivalrous Lout* which ushered in the initially splendid template of *luti* as a new hero. In both films, the mirror scenes reflect the solitude of men who exemplify a caring and egalitarian masculinity. In Mohseni's film, every Friday, Dāsh Hasan's entertainment evening, after he gets drunk in a cabaret, his friends who cannot comprehend his cultural chat about etiquette and honour, leave him to talk to himself in the mirror: 'Cheers! Thanks! These are fair-weather friends. I honour you as whenever we're together, you won't leave me until you take me home. Cheers! [he clinks his glass against mirror and drinks.]'[22] Beyzaie, thus, sets up a dialogue with the neglected, egalitarian intellectuality of Mohseni's hero to suggest Hekmati as a new hero whose dynamic, constructive intellectuality may transform Iranian cinema. At this stage, however, the pressures are so that even Hekmati himself neglects his intellectuality.

The first viewing of the dilapidated school hall which determines Hekmati's future occurs here. Hekmati's theatre-loving female colleague talks about what they need to stage a play in the hall and delivers a turgid monologue about 'the awakening of one's conscience'. The monologue which comments on infatuation makes others smile in derision or surprise, but it makes Hekmati nervous, and since he has been restructuring his identity to become more masculine, he borrows a cigarette from Navvāb. The principal, however, asserts his position by putting it out as if Hekmati needs permission to smoke before him. Hekmati leaves the hall in anger stating that he has no interest in the hall or the performance. He then goes to the school yard to start working out along the pupils with the hope of defeating Rahim.

A sequence, then, focuses on Hekmati and his pupils. Three of them emerge from a cinema screening Amin Amini's romantic comedy *Four Dervishes* (1968) and Ignacio Iquino's cheap Western *Five Dollar for Ringo* (1966). Excited by seeing the Western, they break Rahim's window with stones. As in *Uncle Moustache*, Beyzaie includes a limping boy in the attack. Hekmati's angry throwing of his bookcase is then contrasted with a boy's tearing of a huge poster of Jalal Moqaddam's comedy *Seh Divāneh* (Crazies 3, 1968).[23] Reinforcing the motifs of laughter, the sequence shows Beyzaie's preference for comedies rather than tough guy dramas as entertainment. Like Iran's mainstream cinema, Hekmati and his pupils are now done with comedies and books and are obsessed with violence as a solution. The pupils support him, and Hekmati now works out hard and punches his punching bag with the images of *Zurkhāneh* wrestlers and *Shahnameh* war scenes on his walls. However, as observed in the exam scene in which Hekmati is distracted by seeing Ātefeh and Rahim together from a window, the relationship between Hekmati and his pupils is not yet constructive. The pupils still cheat, and Hekmati continues to punish them.

Ātefeh and Rahim's conversation slightly shifts the film's emotional centre. He promises to support Ātefeh's family if she marries him. Ātefeh remains reluctant. She feels indebted to him but does not see him as a man with whom she can live her whole life. At realistic level, the dialogue depicts her as a woman with creative potential, who knows that time has changed, and she must have a choice. At another level, however, she embodies a people, a nation, at a turning point, where they must choose between the status quo, Rahim, and the promise of change due to the rise of education and the possibilities of modern life, Hekmati. The background displays the vacuity of the constructs Rahim represents by a ladder on a high wall of empty fruit crates which resemble unstable houses and a huge, dilapidated building, ironically called 'Robat Karim's Joint-Stock Company of Reconstruction, Renovation and Light: Power Plant 1953'. The year 1953 marks a turning point in the Iranian journey to modernity in which the Shah united with the clergy, Tehran's tough guy groups and the army to topple the constitutionalists headed by Mosaddeq, one of the few groups that could help him sustainably modernize the country. It was also the beginning of the era in which the tough guy culture found centrality in cultural products, with such novels as Hosein Madani's *Esmāl in New York* (1953–5). This centrality was because the state felt indebted to and wanted to modernize and use the formidable street force tough guys held. Thus, it urged cultural products with such potential. The process, however, led to the marginalization of the intelligentsia in mainstream cultural products. Thus, although Rahim, Ātefeh and the district may be said to represent Iran's local culture, and Hekmati the modern intellectual in the process of gaining an in-depth knowledge of this culture, it is equally valid to state that Hekmati and Rahim represent the two sides of Iran's grassroot modernity, with Rahim signifying the gradual modernization of the tough guy culture, and Hekmati that of Iran's intellectual tradition. In this latter context, rather than being exclusionist towards the tough guy culture, Beyzaie proposes that constructive intellectuals must be given more centrality.

Hekmati's punishment of his pupils for cheating leads to a debate between Hekmati and Navvāb, in which Navvāb reminds him that they have no entertainment and that Hekmati has never tried to recognize their needs. Navvāb's passive idealism, thus, functions like an intermediary between Hekmati, the intellectual, and his pupils, the people and joins Ātefeh's no-nonsense, hardworking attitude to stir Hekmati's potential as a constructive intellectual. This discussion is linked to a poetic sequence in which a line that the pupils have drawn on the walls of their alleys with the words

Figure 4.8 Screenshots from *Downpour*. Minutes 54'.40"–65'.30"

'follow this line' and 'come' function like the arrows of cupid to bring Hekmati and Ātefeh together in a narrow alley. Ātefeh's concern about another fight, however, urges Hekmati, who has been exercising, to go to 'settle his accounts with Rahim'. As expected, the fight leads to another defeat with an unconscious Hekmati carried to the hospital with his token of intellectuality, his glasses, on his chest in the same cart that brought his stuff to the neighbourhood. If one interprets the first defeat as the death of his soft self and his rebirth as a man aspiring to man up by exercising, the second defeat signifies the death of his illusion with violence as a solution and the birth of the man who aspires to gain recognition and prove his worth by constructive work (Figure 4.8).

Quest for belonging: From violent masculinity to sympathetic intellectuality

With the motif of rebirth emphasized in the barber's shop, Hekmati is reborn as a sympathetic intellectual, a man with epistemic authority, capable of noticing his pupils' hard life. In the shop, when he sees his pupil is sweeping the floor, he kneels before him in a ritual of compassion and humiliation signifying the character-building importance of work. He now realizes that their cruelties towards each other and other people are symptomatic of a society which has no planning for children's free time, where their energy is wasted for creating intrigues to entertain themselves. This illumination enables him to see the difference between doing a job and working for a purpose, leading to his decision to refurbish the hall as a space of constructive entertainment for the pupils and communal meetings for people. The principal emphasizes that they have no budget for the hall, but Hekmati does all the job himself.

The full circle of Hekmati's identity from bookish man to tough guy and then sympathetic intellectual is in dialogue with Elliott Nugent and James Thurber's *The Male Animal* (1948), in which the evolution of Professor Tommy Turner's character originally makes him try to be a 'tiger' to win his wife back, but then makes him realize that his fight for the freedom of speech in academia is more 'manly' than punching his rival. Beyzaie, however, reframes Hekmati's journey of self-discovery in an archetypal frame with biographical references. The hall, thus, signifies Beyzaie's own mission to reconstruct Iranian theatre by reformulating its indigenous forms. The significance of work is also stressed in shots reflecting the change of season along those of Hekmati's labour which leads to his happiness despite his isolation. Hekmati is shown building a stage with old desks and then washing and painting in shots that signify a spring cleansing ritual, with the agent of purgation, Hekmati acting like a sacrificial carrier of the dirt of decades on a cultural space. This sacrificial trope is stressed by shots marking the comments of Hekmati's colleagues, who, instead of praising his work, display their misguided understandings of the cause which from their view is limited to his grief over losing Ātefeh. While displaying the way people brush away such achievements or excuse themselves from working, the film, thus, also reflects the ignorance of those critics whose analysis of an artistic work is limited to its cause or message rather than its emancipatory aesthetics. The words of the pretentious, female colleague, 'from psychological perspective', 'from sociological perspective' (69′–69′.20″) is particularly relevant in this regard (Figure 4.8).

The principal's house: Superficial religiosity and borrowed modernity

Hekmati's dedication convinces the principal that Hekmati can be a good son-in-law. He, thus, invites him over, leading to a sequence in which he and his wife treat Hekmati as a suitor for their daughter Pari (Fairy), whose name implies her unreal world and her distractive function. As expected from the epitome of Iran's 1970s' official masculinity, the principal's life is filled with the clashing vestiges of cultural imitation, borrowed modernity and West-obsessed consumerism in a house decorated with a blend of religious and Western motifs. Their television is, thus, contrasted with its cover depicting the folktale of Imam Reza saving a deer, and the made-up appearance of his wife with her outdated beliefs about marrying her daughter young. The machine gun scene of a war film on their television, then, reflects Hekmati's feeling of being blasted by her verbose hospitality. Pari's method of attracting Hekmati by wearing high-heel shoes indoor and a doll as necklace, making spoiled gestures, displaying her albums of butterflies and actors' photos, or her puerile show of her English by 'This is my hand' joins with the principal's pretentious display of interest in Strauss's *Blue Danube* on his gramophone, his bragging about shaking hand with a higher official and his wife's attitudes to highlight superficiality, imitation and pretention as the main failures of borrowed modernity and its point of similarity with imitative religiosity and traditionalism.

When Pari's mother forces Hekmati and Pari to sit together alone, Beyzaie ritualizes the way Pari turns on the television by making her go forward on her knees as if she is approaching a shrine. Beyzaie, thus, shows that the family has just replaced one form of superficiality with another: obsession with religious tales and imitating a Shi'i Master of Jurisprudence signified in the cover with a fixation with fashions and ideas set by TV series. While Pari is babbling about a soap opera, Hekmati takes his raincoat and leaves in silence. Her garrulity in front of the TV screen and her empty gaze have been arranged to imply she is intellectually blind and unable to see or utter anything beyond the vestiges of consumerism. Juxtaposed with the noise on the TV screen and its audio, this suggests that such forms of modernity are just visual and auditory noise. Her mother's garrulity and controlling attitudes also indicate her toxic femininity and the opportunistic nature of those who adopt borrowed modernity. The two women's garrulity is also contrasted with the silence of Ātefeh's mother, the dressmaker's romantic yet outspoken use of language and Ātefeh's non-erudite, yet calm and precise use of language, which suggest authentic generational progression in women's voices (Figure 4.9).

Walking in the rain: Epistemic privilege, poverty, surveillance, work and love

Hekmati, thus, steps out of the house into the downpour which gives its name to the film. In the title, the term most likely suggests the brief yet fertilizing impact of Ātefeh on Hekmati and Hekmati's new self on the district. Yet, the downpour sequence also signifies the downpour of contradictory events, relations, ideas and practices that Hekmati's new epistemic privilege has enabled him to see and be positively changed by. While standing under two pillars, he sees a boy under the rain without a raincoat pleading with a passer-by to buy some of his lottery tickets in a shot with empty barrels of crude oil in the background. The background, thus, once more, expands the field of motifs, with the pillars representing the failure of state and religion, the pillars of power, to address people's suffering in an oil-rich country. Since the principal is now determined to punish Hekmati, the film also provides the first glimpse of the Bespectacled Man, a Kafkaesque figure who, like his counterpart in *So Dies Akbar the Hero*, may represent psychological, existential or social fate, the looming presence of death, oppressive surveillance or abuse of power.[24] As if in a reverie of self-criticism, Hekmati stops him by accident to ask if he saw the boy's suffering, but the man states 'the rain is too heavy', suggesting he has other concerns. At its sociopolitical level, this means he is not concerned with the boy because the mission of such people is not to report people's misery or solve problems but suppress those who raise a concern about them. At its cultural level, however, it displays the issues of a cultural discourse that rationalizes human suffering as fate which leads to people's apathy towards it.

Hekmati's new vision is then used to highlight how hard Ātefeh works. Under the rain, he visits Ātefeh's workplace and, like a butterfly riveted by a source of light, watches her through the window working late due to their dress orders for New Year's Eve (21 March). She has now replaced the lamp, the light of love, that fell from Hekmati's hand in the first sequence. Thus, using the principal's daughter as a foil, Beyzaie depicts Ātefeh as the epitome of the ideal form of authenticity that is now Hekmati's ultimate desire. While remaining significant as a realistic figure, she now also represents the potential of a nation if it becomes capable of productive work. In his analysis of Golestan's *Moj, Marjān, Khārā* (Wave, Coral and Rock, 1962), after calling the film an epic of 'machinery' and 'work', Beyzaie states, 'if this film is Iranian, which is, one must regretfully state that the troubadour has not made the machine'. He, then, explains that the film has been made by resources that belong to Iranians but celebrates work that is controlled by foreigners: 'In the future, the existence of this enduring and expensive film will suggest a nation that did not work, but spend 300,000 dollars to make an epic about work.'[25] Beyzaie's critique, here, does not mean that Iranians do not work because they do. It rather refers to the emancipatory power of work when it does not originate in doing a minimum to obtain a salary but in an aesthetic vision that uses one's limited life span and resources to change life for better, one that expands cultural, social and economic resources rather than just use them. Work is art when it does what Rancière calls a 'redistribution of the sensible', by opening the path for new ways of seeing and doing things and displaying the invisible.

Beyzaie stylizes the scene Hekmati takes Ātefeh home by contrasting the gracefulness of the dressmaker's matchmaking style with the principal's wife. Although her dreams of success and perhaps marriage have been shattered and she is outspoken when wronged, because she has worked in a productive field all her life, she is a gentle romantic who wants happiness for others. Thus, noticing the twinkle of love and honour in Hekmati's eyes, she urges Hekmati to escort Ātefeh to her home. Beyzaie depicts the joy embedded in love and contrasts Rahim's insistence on offering patriarchal support to gain Ātefeh's approval to Hekmati's desire to make Ātefeh happy and full of laughter. Beyzaie states that the music of the sequence is to imply 'happiness in a memorable dance of two, which also echoes the dressmaker's dreams'. The use of Ātefeh's umbrella to protect both of them from rain in several shots, as Beyzaie himself states, 'suggests that Hekmati's only moments of happiness occur when he and Ātefeh are under a single emotional umbrella'.[26] However, aligned with her refusal to accept Hekmati's raincoat, her umbrella also suggests her independence, subverts the cliché of the chivalrous hero protecting his beloved from the elements, and registers their relationship as one of equals in which her emotional care, reflected in her name, can protect and sublimate Hekmati's intellectuality, also suggested in his name. The scene, therefore, suggests that Hekmati's vision of love is egalitarian and wants Ātefeh to be a hardworking, productive and happy woman who can dance to the music of life, but Rahim's vision wants her to be dependent on him and housebound. One offers meat, shelter and patriarchal love, the other a life of productive work, collaboration, hope, freedom and mutual love. Hekmati's reference to 'the boy with no raincoat' during his dialogue with Ātefeh once more reminds the viewer of his newly gained epistemic privilege and his vision of joining social responsibility and love. Hekmati wants to be worthy of both Ātefeh's love and his pupil's support. Thus, whereas Rahim's idea of leadership requires him to be the master of obedient followers, Hekmati's vision of leadership wants no mastery as he equates himself with his pupils and takes off his raincoat to share their pain. Ātefeh's potential for sublimation is also reflected in the statues of the angels and birds in their path. Thus, the stylized way Hekmati states 'Come with me' or 'Live with me Ātefeh' offers a vision of equality and building together, which, nevertheless, does not mean leaving.

> **Ātefeh:** I wish I were a typist. I wish I had nobody. Then, I was free to get away from here. What about you? I am sure you also wish you were free to get away from here.
> **Hekmati:** Get away from here? Why? I have just begun to know this place.
> **Ātefeh:** Do you like it here!?
> **Hekmati:** I don't know; here I can do things that would not make a difference anywhere else. I have realized that I can make the children happier. I'm not a poet or an actor, but I can do other things for them. We're refurbishing the school hall. Repairing the hall is not important if it is elsewhere, but here it is. Isn't it enough that I am being useful?

Ātefeh: *You're lucky, then. You miss nothing in your life.*
Hekmati: I miss you in my life, Ātefeh. Live with me. Would you live with me, Ātefeh?
Ātefeh: I am indebted to him.
Hekmati: To that bully.
Ātefeh: Yes, I'm indebted to that bully. God, how can I make him change his mind?

Ātefeh's desire to leave and her love for Hekmati signifies she longs to transcend the burdens of the past and its patriarchal relations and use her resources in a modern relationship in which social mobility and progress are conceivable. This love scene is punctuated by shots of Ātefeh's mother struggling to stand up and turn off the light to avoid Ātefeh's wrath about the light of their other room being pointlessly on. This builds on earlier signs marking Ātefeh as a provider, which later became central to Beyzaie's focus on the rise of women's agency in the absence of men. Thus, Ātefeh's mother's critical gaze, when meeting Hekmati, implies her fear of losing her provider. Hekmati's meta-filmic words, however, highlight a type of happiness which has been inaccessible for the old woman. Emphasizing his awareness that cliché acts of heroism involve exerting violence on others, Hekmati specifies that though he is 'not a hero' and has 'not even killed an ant', he truly loves Ātefeh. Violent masculinity is, thus, weighted against loving manliness. Ātefeh's words, here, show her own happiness with the concept and her mother's distance from the idea of love by asking him to speak louder. Hekmati also rejects Ātefeh's feeling of indebtedness to Rahim by 'You think you'll be making up for his generosity, but you're ruining your life'. This is a new vision of love that offers caring mutual love rather than violent, patriarchal protection. Later Ātefeh also tells his mother why she loves Hekmati: 'He is different, educated, energetic. He has no hero stuff in him but can save me from this district.' She says saving but in a way that signifies he can provide the means with which she can save herself. She adds, 'he has funny qualities that I like – But I shouldn't leave you, I know'. Then, she laughs and echoes what Hekmati says in a parallel shot: 'he said, "When I think of you, I feel I am invincible"' (80'–85').

The use of a policeman as Hekmati's accidental interlocutor when declaring his invincibility in his ecstasy of love completes the 'homage' of the sequence to Stanley Donen and 'Gene Kelly's *Singin' in the Rain*' (1952),[27] whose protagonist, Don, sings and dances in the rain after seeing Kathy home, and stops only when he faces the authoritative gaze of a policeman who is amazed by his actions.[28] The fact that the latter film is a meta-filmic musical satirizing earlier musicals shows Beyzaie's interest in self-reflexive films and echoes what he himself does in *Downpour*. His neo-realist vision minimizes the use of music, but his use of itinerant musicians as the only observers of the couple's brief happiness musicalizes the film. Yet, he uses their silence and their implied blindness to foreshadow how tragedy emerges from the heart of this romantic comedy due to the limitations imposed on their lives. He also includes a dialogue in the policeman scene which makes the policeman a foil for the Bespectacled Man. Thus, from this point onwards, the two appear several times to display the two roles associated with policing: the protector of people and the tool of tyranny. Yet, with the policeman looking modern and gentle and the Bespectacled Man looking like a medieval executioner or the blindfolded mule of the mill of death – mask-like goggles, handlebar moustaches like Zahhāk's snakes and a black medieval shirt like those worn in religious mourning rituals – the film transcends the political allegory that some critics argued for by reducing the Bespectacled Man to a SAVAK agent.[29] If anything, the Bespectacled Man is an agent of drought and destruction, the assassin of religious, social and political exclusionism.

Though the irony of Hekmati's invincibility is revealed by his later sneezing, his words also function as an archetypal metaphor. Geared towards productive work and innovative thought rather than just books, his intellectuality now promises a failproof future for himself and others, but like all invincible heroes, his fate has already been put in motion with his honesty being his Achilles' heel in a crooked world of opportunism (Figure 4.9).

Figure 4.9 Screenshots from *Downpour*. Minutes 69′.20″–85′.30″

School hall: The crowning and de-crowning of a carnival temporary king

With the downpour sequence marking the emotional climax, the school performance becomes the climax of the action where Hekmati rises to his highest position in a 'carnival of temporary king', in which his walk of fame is visually designed to suggest he is walking on clouds. Beyzaie celebrates the hall as a public space for aesthetic contemplation about art, discussion about children's future and democratic competition for recognition. The sequence displays the people preparing for the event, and Ātefeh's happiness suggests the progressive potential that a free public space can provide for a nation. The film also momentarily displays the dressmaker's workshop as her upper-class customer finally visits her. Thus, here and later when Ātefeh's mother suffers a stroke, Beyzaie suggests that, like many Iranians, despite her positive qualities, the dressmaker's obsession with class hierarchies and waiting for saviours deprives her of being a modern citizen by displaying her agency in public activities.

With the circles of sycophants around Rahim and the principal trying to assert the centrality of their masters, the hall becomes the scene of rivalry between Rahim, the principal and Hekmati for occupying the central position among people. Already applauded by the gas station attendant for having bought the next-door shop, Rahim shows off his generosity to Ātefeh by giving a large sum to the school. The principal has also set the stage for taking credit for refurbishing the hall. They also display mutual support: the principal acknowledges Rahim's contribution and declares he must be a role model for the community, and Rahim applauds him louder than anyone else. While everyone, even the compassionate policeman, is captivated by the magic of the stage, the principal, his wife and Rahim are desperate to attract people's attention to themselves. Realizing that they are stealing the fruit of his labour, Hekmati rises to leave, but in one of his typical bullying feats, Rahim stops him and loudly proclaims that Hekmati must appreciate other people's glory rather than be jealous. Beyzaie, then, further displays how officials or rich people claim the fruit of other people's labour and creativity. With Rahim already applauded, the principal's sycophants begin to hail him as the engineer and sponsor of the refurbishment. Beyzaie lengthens the scene by the speech of the pretentious literature teacher who is to invite the principal to distribute the pupil's prizes. He also shows that only Navvāb, the passive idealist, is upset about this situation.

The film then enters a carnival zone when the limping boy bravely declares Hekmati as their benefactor and other pupils in their military, sport and civilian stage costumes shout his name as in a rally. Even Navvāb briefly exits his stupor of passive idealism to applaud Hekmati and shout 'go up'. His clapping becomes contagious, and the stage and auditorium unite in a carnival spirit to subvert the hierarchies of being and belonging. While shouting Hekmati's name with noise and laughter, the pupils also lift the limping boy to their shoulders to celebrate his bravery. Walking on the handles of the chairs he was painting a few days earlier, Hekmati goes forward and climbs the stage. Reluctant to applaud Rahim's generosity, Ātefeh applauds Hekmati with joy and laughter. Even the gas station attendant celebrates the success of this gentle soul. Thus, the outcome of the competition for recognition in the hall, which echoes the rivalries of pre-revolutionary Iran, is a triumph for Hekmati whose compassion and perseverance are rewarded by his pupil's love. Ironically, however, this success is also the cause of his future downfall foreshadowed by the principal's assurance to his wife: 'he will be transferred soon'. The light in Hekmati's eyes is, then, shadowed as the camera zooms in from his perspective to display the Bespectacled Man, who, amid the people's excited clapping, ominously stares at Hekmati with his hands on his chest.

In his analysis of European fiction as a genre, Bakhtin predicts Rancière's notions of 'the aesthetic regime of art' and 'redistribution of the sensible' by finding a carnival core in the 'heteroglossia' and internal diversity of styles in novels from different literary movements. To grasp this sense of carnival, he argues, one must 'dispense with that narrow theatrical-pageantry concept of carnival' and see it in its ritual sense with 'the world as one great communal performance' and carnival as where a 'new mode of man's relation to man is elaborated' to disrupt social hierarchies by an aesthetics that ignores boundaries.[30] It is in this context and the time of the pupil's performance in spring that the carnival acts of 'de-crowning' the two 'masters' and 'crowning' Hekmati as 'the carnival king' become visible. By carnivalizing the film's climax, Beyzaie transforms the aesthetic sense of his parodic and spring cleansing motifs and turns the film itself into a *Mir-e Noruzi* carnival.

Mir-e Noruzi was an Iranian New Year carnival performed between 20 March and 2 April probably until the early 1950s in different parts of Iran. Mohammad Qazvini's research on the topic provided by a physician about the festival as it was held in Bojnurd in Spring 1923:

> On March 30, I saw a large procession of people on foot and horseback. One who was clad in an expensive costume had an umbrella over his head and rode on a splendid horse. People walked in front or behind him [. . .] as if they were his entourage. Some had long sticks in hand with shapes of animals' heads on them [. . .] as if the king was returning from a conquest [. . .]. Other people also followed them making a lot of clamour. . . People said 'during the *Noruz* festival, one becomes the ruler of the town and is obeyed until deposed on April 2.' Apparently, the job was kept in the family.[31]

This account describes the carnival as performed by professional actors and people for entertainment. The details, however, suggest that though it was a spring ritual whose origins and outcomes differed from the more violent feasts of *Mogh-Koshi* (Magophonia), *Kuseh bar Neshin* (The Ride of the Beardless One), *Hāmān Suz* (Burning Haman) or *Dasteh-ye Surenā* (Surena's Procession), which, as discussed in Chapter 3, celebrated the fall of a pretender or seasonal demon, it was like them in mixing stationary and ambulatory forms and displaying the nature of power. However, its carnival elements were more pronounced because during the ritual (1) people identified with a temporary ruler and (2) disrupted social hierarchies to signify the impermanence of worldly power in the grand scheme of life and death.

Beyzaie reinforces these two functions to turn the former into a locus for the revelation of marginalized voices and inserts the latter's rebellious laughter into the centre of a tragedy of sacrificial heroism which begins to unravel from this point onwards.[32] Thus, spectators, like his pupils, laugh at Hekmati, but this is an ambivalent, carnival laughter that along with his victimization endears him so that by this point, his pupils, and perhaps the spectators, achieve the status of ideal citizens and realize that Hekmati, the only man with a white raincoat, can actually be their ideal leader rather than a funny temporary king. The cleansing and sacrificial elements also gradually heighten to suggest him as a Christ figure, a saviour king of hearts, like Iraj or Siyāvush, whose future suffering is presaged by the ominous presence of the Bespectacled Man at the peak of his crowning and his pupils' rebellious laughter.

Beyzaie's juxtaposition of a constructive intellectual with the two incarnations of hegemonic masculinity makes *Downpour* a site of negotiation about modernity and leadership, but these two figures and others also function as foils to display the formation of an ideal intellectual. Thus, Navvāb's attachment to outdated modes of life, which has distorted his life with eight children, is in contrast with Hekmati's childlike energy and desire for 'becoming' the useful product of his own imagination in response to the challenges of his milieu. This energy may be wayward as it originally makes him exercise to fight the district's tough guy, but it also enables him to serve people by refurbishing the hall. The principal's blend of superficial modernity and authority-obsessed conventionalism is also in contrast with Hekmati's genuine modernity which reformulates and refurbishes the cultural resources of his people for a new age. Rahim's boorish bravery as well as hypocritical generosity, though real and at times useful, is also contrasted with Hekmati's courage in opposing him, his honest confession that he is not a hero and his determination to help people in new ways that Rahim could not even think of. Nevertheless, Beyzaie also highlights that it is Ātefeh and the pupils' work ethics and cultural energy that transform Hekmati from a bookish man into this ideal intellectual.

The sequence of collecting goods for earthquake victims is another public space for showing the communal centrality that Hekmati has achieved through hard work. Echoing the accounts of Takhti organizing a procession for collecting goods and money in Tehran's Bazaar after the 1962 Buin Zahra Earthquake, the scene displays Rahim in the front row of the procession acting as a role model. Unlike the other teachers, Hekmati joins the procession, with a black blouse of mourning under his white raincoat. Ātefeh watches both in admiration. The kind policeman is also present. Carrying a bag like Takhti's to collect money, Rahim puts in all his earnings of the week to display a positive aspect of Iranian *javānmardi* tradition. Thus, whereas in *So Dies Akbar the Hero*, Beyzaie depicted a *pahlevān* with intellectual leanings and a sublime commitment to human values, a man who resembled and perhaps predicted or inspired Takhti's suspicious death, in *Downpour*, he divides Akbar into a tough guy and an intellectual to suggest that both must be reformulated for centrality in culture[33] (Figure 4.10).

Figure 4.10 Screenshots from *Downpour*. Minutes 89'.20"–102'.30"

The sublime poetry of ascendance, light and love: Ātefeh in Hekmati's room

With Rahim and Hekmati waiting for Ātefeh's reply, the film displays one of its unique portrayals of women when Ātefeh goes to deliver the dress of Hekmati's landlady. The landlady has, so far, been a prop, who listens to Hekmati's conversations or makes comments that suggest she is kind and curious, but now she talks about her dreams and her son who has left her. She inspires Ātefeh to visit Hekmati's room by saying she also once secretly visited the room of the man who later became her husband. Here, Beyzaie's focus on a woman's experience of love is in dialogue with a similar scene in Max Ophüls's *Letter from an Unknown Woman* (1948) in which Lisa's visit to Brand's flat displays the nature of a young woman's love for an intriguing stranger who proves to be a scoundrel.[34] Beyzaie, however, empowers women by focusing on a hardworking, wise woman whose love for a worthy man transcends Lisa's naivety. Rather than a victim, she is a survivor with a choice that she makes with awareness and responsibility. This reframing also uses steps, sounds of birdcalls, rays of light and shadows to evoke on the screen the sense of ascendance in love which is central to Persian poetry. Beyzaie slows down the action and focuses the camera on Ātefeh's upward gaze, followed by close-ups of her shoes and chador touching the steps as she slowly climbs up the steps as if engaged in an act of sublime transgression. In the room, the play of light from the window on her face and torso becomes like a spotlight and works with the shadows of her movements to give a sacred aura to her presence and the sublime form of desire she represents.[35] With the surrealistic soundtrack echoing the sound of flying and birdcalls to suggest her desire for freedom, she looks at the poster of the birds flying over the sea. She examines the photos featuring the wedding of Hekmati's parents and his mother at an old age. The scene displays Ātefeh's desire to open the path of mutual belonging and signifies how photos record the passing of time and echo the similarities of human emotions. In a unique scene of desire for intimacy reinforced by a magical melody of clarinet and flute, she, then, sits on Hekmati's bed and touches his pillow. The chaste shot makes her desire visible while inspiring admiration for Ātefeh's calm beauty in a way that subverts cinematic voyeurism.

Hekmati's landlady appears, and Ātefeh shares her fears with her: the burdens of her life may ruin Hekmati's potential for growth and the possibility of their happiness. The landlady, however, is preoccupied with her own loss as a letter she has just received confirms that her son, who signifies another form of alienation, is ashamed of her life and will never return. Thus, Beyzaie asserts Hekmati's authenticity by contrasting his longing to stay with the shame of his landlady's son. This also proves that Ātefeh's fears are pointless as Hekmati has already realized that his real growth can only happen here and with her (Figure 4.11).

Figure 4.11 Screenshots from *Downpour*. Minutes 103'.30"–106'.30"

Meta-filmic and theatrical rivalry between the intellectual and the tough guy

Having delivered the goods they collected for earthquake victims, Hekmati and Rahim end up drinking together in a pub which, except for its alcoholic drinks, shares nothing with the pubs of Iranian mainstream films. In a meta-filmic scene, Rahim bullies everyone out to talk with Hekmati, who seems to have risen in stature and strength beyond Rahim's reach.

> **Rahim:** Only you and I understand each other. Don't you agree? Cheers! These people don't get it. A person who has nothing burning in the heart is nothing but brick and mud. Do you like her?
> **Hekmati:** I love her.
> **Rahim:** [Laughing] This is why I like you. You understand me. You know my pain [...] Cheers to you!
> **Hekmati:** Cheers to her!
> **Rahim:** [Surprised by his dedication to Ātefeh.] Yea, yea. (107′–108′)

The film suggests the fluidity of human identity by a scene in which Rahim wears Hekmati's glasses as if wishing to see life from an intellectual's view. Hekmati's holding of Rahim's coat implies the mutuality of this exchange. Manuchehr Farid's ability to display a blend of intellectual curiosity and tough guy speech and assertiveness and Parviz Fanizadeh's display of Hekmati's gradual move from fear to calm confidence adds to the weight of the scene. Like Hekmati, Rahim is not sure why he has been mesmerized by Ātefeh but counts her eyes, anger, crying and beauty as the qualities he loves. Hekmati confirms the eyes, but he loves her laughter and many other things that are impossible to describe. The meta-filmic aspect is emphasized by what Rahim says later as he is vomiting: 'Before you came here, there was only me, but now she no longer accepts the meat that I send her.' Judged in the master-slave dialectics, Rahim has now accepted defeat but tries to gain Hekmati's sympathy by stating that whereas Hekmati has other options and can return to the upper parts of the city, he is miserable and will die without Ātefeh. But Hekmati, who wants to stay in the district, states, 'all of us are miserable', and 'I will also die without her'. He also expresses his awareness of the games of masculinity by 'one of us must step aside, must break', which initiates a parodic drunken combat of recognition with Rahim threatening Hekmati with ever bigger knives, and Hekmati laughing and defending himself with rocks and a long stick. Though Rahim keeps saying, 'I will kill you', he mainly tries to frighten Hekmati, and Hekmati simply defends himself by avoiding or disarming him. This illustrates how creative intellectuals can disarm violent masculinity and win the combat of recognition and love by doing things to raise the awareness of their people. Even Rahim himself seems to have improved. The self-reflexive parody is also enhanced by two bystanders watching their fight and clapping as if watching a film, by Hekmati putting Rahim's jacket on a stick signifying that his type of masculinity turns men into scarecrows, and by Rahim attacking Hekmati's white overcoat by his cleaver. Juxtaposed with Ātefeh's composure in the previous scene, their childish behaviour suggests that masculinity is just a performance which breaks once prohibitions are set aside. The fight ends when the exhausted rivals can no longer chase each other, Hekmati throws Rahim's overcoat over his head and Rahim's fixed gaze on a light that turns off in the house in front of him suggests that he has lost all his hopes for having Ātefeh.

The sequence also parodies the final scene of Kimiaei's *Dāsh Ākol* (1971), a film adaptation of Hedayat's depiction of the downfall of a tough guy because of love. Naficy uses such scenes in *Downpour* to argue that Rahim and Hekmati's rivalry 'replays the archetypal rivalry between a *luti* (Mr. Hekmati) and a lout (Aqa Rahim Qassab)' and in line with the reductive interpretations of the film analyses it as a political allegory with the Bespectacled Man being a SAVAK agent.[36] Although such readings reflect the interpretive tendencies of the 1970s and 1980s, they reduce the intricate motifs that the film sets in motion to a simple replaying of clichés and a reductive understanding of intention. The film replaces the *luti* (hero) of mainstream films with Hekmati, but it is not a replaying of the rivalry between the *lout* and the *luti*. Hekmati never bends to *luti* codes. He is rather the young, intelligent and romantic *javānpush* (young lover) of Iranian *taqlid* comedies, reformulated with attention to but transcending the West-obsessed limitations of Fekri's reformist intellectuals of the 1910s. Rahim also is not a crooked lout but a comically realistic echo of normal tough guys who often mix the qualities of the honourable *luti* and the unscrupulous *lout* to different degrees.

As Rahim and Hekmati display the childish core of masculinity as a rivalry over recognition and being wanted by their 'objet petit a', a series of parallel shots highlight that the actual choice lies with Ātefeh and depict the decline of Ātefeh's mother's health. In the first shot, a worried Mossaiyeb asks a friend to help him find Ātefeh as their mother is dying. He cannot as he must take his blind musician father to perform in a wedding. Then, the dressmaker's illusions are replayed as her upper-class customer appears, again, when no one is around. The dressmaker is good and productive, but old illusions disturb her happiness. The obsession with waiting to be wanted or saved by those from the higher echelons of religion or society is thus marked as one of the debilitating outcomes of inherited religious, cultural and social beliefs (whose hierarchies of god→ prophet→ saints→ clergy/mystic→ men→ women→ children, or king→ prince→ nobles→ the rich → military→ tough guys→ men→ women→ children) must be reconfigured before normal men, women and children can grow to become citizens. Beyzaie's ideal intellectual, who does not claim to be an intellectual, is to replace the 'clergy/mystic' and the 'tough guy' to break the chain of power and initiate the journey towards a more egalitarian society. The final scene of this parallel sequence juxtaposes the physician's matter-of-fact language with his self-medication and odd monologue about the condition of Ātefeh's mother: 'All her organs have failed, but her hands are still moving, as she may still be worried about' her children. Thus, the post-stroke twitching of hands comes to surrealistically reflect how the mother's worry makes her continue weaving after her death. Davāei finds both scenes suggestive of Beyzaie's hasty desire to say a lot in a short space.[37] That may be true to some extent, but both scenes also display Beyzaie's satirical gaze at the typical illusions and prescriptive monologues delivered by educated and uneducated people. In other words, Beyzaie

Figure 4.12 Screenshots from *Downpour*. Minutes 106'.40"–115'.30"

is laughing at rather than using the physician as his spokesperson, and if there is any failure, it is in that the context does not make this more explicit.

The fight scene also suggests the rivalry between the two paths that modern masculinity can take. While giving priority to Hekmati's vision, the film proposes that each side can learn from the other, which subverts the binaries of intellectual/commoner, tough guy/dandy, and *luti*/lout. He also subverts the cliché of the aloof intellectual by a carnival plot that uses the emancipatory force of hard work, common people, laughter, love, women and children to release a bookish man from his ivory tower and create a pragmatic intellectual (Figure 4.12).

Banality of exclusionism and the rise of a sacrificial hero

After the principal gives Hekmati his 'urgent transfer letter' in one of his smug acts of top-down distribution, in response to Navvāb's inquiry about when he will tell Ātefeh, Hekmati philosophizes about the necessity of self-control in love and states that it is Ātefeh's turn to step forward. This is a normal outcome of Hekmati's 'Befindlichkeit' (disposition), which becomes the cause of his undoing as Ātefeh's family responsibilities prevent her from taking such a step without further assurance, particularly because the precarious conditions of their society have already proved that Hekmati's future is not entirely in his own hands. The scene, thus, creates suspense about whether Ātefeh will join Hekmati or stay put. Hekmati's arrival has already changed Ātefeh, the pupils, Rahim and Hekmati himself, and the neighbourhood has observed new ways of doing and seeing things. This may be seen at a social level because the encounter of Hekmati's outsider gaze with his new milieu initiate change in him and others, or at an existential level because his life journey as an individual introduces new ways of seeing and doing to a people in exchange for gaining recognition and a sense of belonging.

The film, however, warns that such changes may be reversed due to the reactionary power of old hierarchies or dominant discourses. Thus, in response to Navvāb's comforting words 'It is good that at least you left something behind, something that will remain', Hekmati picks up the mask of evil death from the pupils' play and says, 'This hall? How long do you think this hall will last? No, it is hopeless.' They then exit the hall and walk in the deserted yard, and Hekmati sounds the school bell to confirm the end of the school year before a whirlwind of dust signifies the end of his hopes for the school and the precarious impossibility of reform in societies in which independent reformists are easy targets for opportunistic leaders or their rivals, who, rather than support the constructive initiatives of such people, either try to use them to their advantage or see them as rivals. Thus, the principal, the embodiment of official hegemonic masculinity, is more concerned with personal vendetta (revenging Hekmati's rejection of his daughter) and his own reputation than with the well-being of the school and the people. He hides behind an official transfer letter that he himself has demanded.

The motifs marking Hekmati as a sacrificial hero become striking if one contrasts the sombre ending of the circular plot with its energetic opening. The pupils watch the Bespectacled Man pack Hekmati's stuff with no music, Hekmati's landlady whose attitudes imply she accepted him as a surrogate for her son sadly states, 'I wished to have a wedding and hear children play in my house'. Hekmati, with a drop of blood on his chest, surrealistically signifying his broken heart, or a Kafkaesque wound inflicted by the Bespectacled Man, sighs in response. He then goes outside and displays his egalitarian spirit by respectfully shaking hands with his pupils. Everyone shakes his hand, except for Ātefeh's brother whose darting off to inform Ātefeh is animated with music. Beyzaie, then, ritualizes Hekmati's exit as a funeral. Rahim's question 'Do you have to leave?' is replied by Hekmati turning his head to his cartman, the Bespectacled Man. Ātefeh and Hekmati's wistful exchange of loving gazes, then, adds to the tension, which is increased when, in reaction to the dressmaker's suggestion, Ātefeh puts on her chador to leave with Hekmati. Mossaiyeb's gaze, however, makes her hesitate. Thus, Hekmati walks uphill, like Jesus on Golgotha, with his burden of past belongings, new experiences and lost love as his cross. The end of the uphill alley becomes like the border of life and death. Everyone stops. When Hekmati stops to look back, the final hope is reflected in the green saplings on the right side of the frame. Ātefeh, however, does not move. Now even the ever-laughing PE teacher is weeping. Hekmati makes a final stop, wipes his glasses, looks back to see if Ātefeh is coming and then moves on to a fading transition in a frame that contains a lamp-post and a sapling on the left, which may or may not promise a rebirth or a continuation of his light and legacy. The last words uttered in the film before the close-ups of the barber, Rahim and Ātefeh's faces, is a neighbour's 'Goodbye, Mr Hekmati!'

This ritualization makes the spectator rethink many of the clues that Beyzaie has left in the film, including his dedication to the refurbishing of the hall, his unconditional love of the pupils when he learns about their hard lives, his sense of mission and his honesty and compassion. Indeed, even the fact that the pupils and people do not begin to love him until he is beaten by Rahim also reveals what Majid Tehranian calls the 'Iranian martyrdom complex'.[38] Yet, as usual, Beyzaie humanizes his heroes. Hekmati gets drunk and fights, fails to tell Ātefeh he will help her care for her family, or is influenced by stupid newspaper articles about love, but unlike the two figures of hegemonic masculinity, once he grows, he is truly egalitarian, modern and honest. His failure, therefore, is not because he fails to display his qualities to his people, but because like most sacrificial heroes, he avoids confrontation with the sources of evil in fear of causing pain in others. If one compares the film with Naʻlbandiyan's *Nāgahān . . .* (Suddenly . . ., 1971), which was written in the same year and works with a similar discourse on the intellectual as a victim or hero, the result suggests that in Naʻlbandiyan's play, the poor, being greedy and ignorant, function as agents of evil and complete the work of opportunistic officials. Beyzaie, however, suggests that whereas people's ignorance is manageable, cultural, religious and political sources of tyranny are not. It is, thus, the Bespectacled Man, the embodiment of fate, death or abuse of power, who functions as the tool of tyranny, and the people are guilty only to the extent of their ignorance and apathy. *Downpour*, therefore, suggests that grassroot reform may be possible if people become aware of the machination of the political, religious and cultural discourses that drain their energy. The master-slave relations depicted in the film suggest how people are trapped in and contribute to the continuity of these discourses in hope of rising in the pyramid of power relations established by them. His emancipatory aesthetics, however, shows how the status quo may be made more egalitarian if new non-violent ways of seeing, doing and constructing things are used to raise awareness among people (Figure 4.13).

Figure 4.13 Screenshots from *Downpour*. Minutes 116′.40″–124′.14″

Reception and conclusion: The rise of marginalized characters

Missing the process in which Hekmati learns from others and acquires his good qualities due to his love for the hardworking and intelligent Ātefeh, rivalry with Rahim's heroic and tough guy gestures, and noticing the hard life of his pupils, Eldad Pardo argues that 'Hekmati represents the conscience of secularly-educated, middle-class Iranians and Atefeh the soul of the traditional masses'. He reproduces one of the reductionist 'messages' attributed to the film: 'Beiza'i [...] views the masses as not ready to allow the middle class to lead them towards a new society, as some intellectuals hoped. Atefeh is too weak and too attached to her mother and the past.'[39] However, as reflected in this book, Beyzaie never bends to the binary cliché of tradition/modernity as any tradition has conflicting layers of conventions which can be reformulated to create a culturally embedded form of modernity. Indeed, Ātefeh is anything but 'weak'. Like Hekmati, she grows due to her contact with Hekmati and can now envision a better life, but her choice demonstrates her mature sense of responsibility towards her family and even Hekmati. Even if examined figuratively, it is the yea-saying West-obsessed sycophancy of the 'middle-class' intelligentsia (Hekmati's colleagues), and the machination of opportunism, exclusionism and corruption, represented in the 'middle-class' headmaster and his wife, which stops Hekmati and Ātefeh from building a better Iran.

This reflects a unique reformist perspective that was at odds with the revolutionary Marxist, Islamist and nativist discourses that aspired to violently replace the absolute power of the Pahlavi with their own utopian illusions of power in 1960s and 1970s Iran. Unlike Al-e Ahmad's 'westoxicated intellectuals', Beyzaie's hero adjusts himself to people's needs, learns from them and achieves emotional and intellectual maturity while trying to improve their conditions, but though always learning from others, he does not embody the Marxist, West-obsessed or Islamist obsessions with obtaining power to fulfil utopian illusions. Thus, the final Hekmati, at one level, represents the Iranian humanist intellectual tradition which has always had high potential for modernity. Indeed, if one examines the poles of power in 1800s Iran, one can see that if it were not for the machination of religious fundamentalism, Qajar tribalism and Western colonialism, the people representing this humanist tradition could have gradually modernized Iran at administrative, educational, economic, military and political levels without bending to the mimicry of the West. The suppression of this tradition, as seen in the assassinations of Qaem Maqam Farahani (1779–1835) and Amir Kabir (1807–52),[40] however, turned Iran into a battlefield between the forces of tribalism, left-wing and right-wing mimicry of the West and religious fundamentalism in a war that still goes on. Hekmati is ultimately banished, which is like being dead to the community that he could have helped and the love that bloomed between him and Ātefeh, but the film signifies that though it may seem hopeless to commit oneself to improving people's status where people only watch and the hierarchies of power do not support change, the very act of sacrificial altruism gives meaning to one's life and may awaken society out of its oblivious mundanity.

Beyzaie, thus, deconstructs the hegemonic masculinity celebrated in Iranian cultural products and presents a dynamic intellectual type. He also demythologizes the tough guy to show a lonely man who gains satisfaction by bullying others and gaining recognition by a carefully engineered cliché persona built on a mixture of genuine or hypocritical codes and deeds. The official saviour, the principal, is also dethroned from his moral high grounds to be revealed as a nosy, opportunistic hypocrite. Yet, these realistically treated presences become more significant if one also notes an important absence. In Beyzaie's film, there are no clergy. This absence is particularly significant in the procession for gathering aid for the earthquake victims. Traditionally, the clergy joined the respected shopkeepers and district champions in such processions. With Rahim representing both the champion and the shopkeeper, the absence of the clergy suggests that Beyzaie replaces them with Hekmati. This may be because the depiction of the clergy in Iranian cinema has always been difficult due to the problems that they themselves cause or because of the anti- or pro-clergy censor before or after the revolution. Nonetheless, it places Beyzaie's intellectual in the position of the moral role model for people. In this context, the emphasis on his human failings increases the significance of his honesty, his devotion to love, his work ethics and his constructive actions and turns him into a reachable ideal which suggests that being heroic is not beyond reach.

As seen in my analysis, apart from subverting hegemonic masculinity and reintroducing the intellectual reformist, *Downpour* is about numerous little beliefs, forces realities and relations that make the lives of human beings difficult while allowing their dreams to thrive. It is about poverty and hunger (the boy selling lottery tickets in heavy rain or Ātefeh's mother weaving even when nearly dead), gossip, ignorance, bullying, marginalization and hypocrisy (the colleagues or Rahim's treatment of Hekmati), the illusions that give meaning to or make life tolerable (the teacher with theatrical pretensions or the dressmaker's pride in having upper-class customers), the possibility of communal responsibility and having a constructive mission in life (Hekmati's discovery of his role and his desire to contribute to the well-being of the community), psychology of love (Hekmati's love, which develops with internal and external influences and accidental encounters, from a simple interest into a tremendous force that reshapes his identity). Beyond anything, however, it records the carnival tragicomedy of life and its associated moments, moods, spaces and relations in a rapidly changing Iranian world in which even in 1971 to create the neighbourhood, Beyzaie had to shoot the film in nine different locations each of which had preserved one aspect of the organic world of the old districts, which, while timeless in what it signifies, no longer exist.[41]

Downpour has continued to be praised as one of the best films made before the revolution. Though with time, it began to attract more positive attention, its difference with other films meant that its original reception in cinemas was lukewarm, and the critics' reviews were also mixed. Whereas Jamshid Akarmi and several others identified the film's uniqueness even then, Parisa Parsi and Mahnaz Khavari, who were probably upset about the film's critique of the people of their type in the pretentious female teachers and the principal's daughter called the film bad influence, sentimental and useless. Houshang Taheri and Mohamad Ali Hashemi praised the film's expressive power and ability to introduce new ideas and protagonists but criticized its unnecessary scenes and dialogues. Davaei did the same but went on to offer a detailed list of technical failures and scenes that were not necessary or functioned like purple patches. Though Davaei's evaluations have occasional valid points, Davaei seems to miss the point-counterpoint structure that Beyzaie achieves in his film by combining tragedy and comedy. Bijhan Mohajer, on the other hand, praised the film's ability to create a realistic ambiance and make a thorough study of the problems of our society but stated that its satiric gaze borders on farce and decided that the scenes of the principal's house and Rahim's arrival in the school hall were unnecessary.[42] Nonetheless, most of these critiques seem to have missed the carnival spirit that contradicts their vision of organic unity but allows Beyzaie to undermine sociopolitical hierarchies of the time and make the film so delightful to watch.

Beyzaie's film won the Judges' Special Award in *Tehran's International Film Festival* in spring 1972 and the Best Film Prize in Sepās Film Festival of 1973. Even as early as 1972, several Iranian and non-Iranian critics identified the film's successful dialogue with Iranian forms and Italian neorealism, but the negatives of the film disappeared and only a damaged positive and a bad quality video copy survived. In 2011, however, after four decades of influencing Iranian cinema, the film was selected for restoration by Martin Scorsese's World Cinema Project and was released and received some international acclaim. In his note on the film, he called the film 'wise and beautiful' and added: 'the tone puts me in mind of what I love best in the Italian neorealist pictures' and 'the story has the beauty of an ancient fable – you can feel Beyzaie's background in Persian literature, theater and poetry'. The renovated copy which was prepared from a positive enabled many people to see the film again and see the details that they missed when seeing the old video copy, but the errors in the subtitles still deprive the non-Iranian spectators of the subtleties of the dialogue.[43]

5

The Journey (1972)

A Sisyphean quest for belonging in a world of toxic masculinity, violence and blind obedience

Introduction: From *Downpour* to *The Journey*

As reflected in my analysis of Beyzaie's first two films, his carnival world for subverting the violent world of hegemonic masculinity began with conflict and comedy in *Uncle Moustache* and became a tragedy of temporary success and victimization in *Downpour*. Carnivalization, however, as Bakhtin states, 'is not an external and immobile schema which is imposed upon ready-made content; it is, rather, an extraordinarily flexible form of artistic visualization, a peculiar sort of heuristic principle making possible the discovery of new and as yet unseen things'.[1] It is, thus, dominant in Beyzaie's world not because of a choice but because it is the essence of his defamiliarizing vision, which is rooted in his outsider gaze and epistemic privilege. He depicts the absurdity of the world around him because his vision is the result of a sublimated gaze that has transcended the centre, its alternatives and its margins. However, what is interesting is that just as in Dostoyevsky's works after his early stories, from this point onwards, laughter lost its centrality in Beyzaie's oeuvre. Now, carnivalized dialogue, background, mise en scene, gestures and actions were 'pushed to' their 'boundaries' to allow everything to 'pass over into its opposite' and create grotesque and nightmarish fears, relations and allusions with dry satire occurring only to enhance these elements.[2]

These dark motifs, which, according to Beyzaie, originate in his own nightmares, are central to *The Journey*. In *Downpour*, as Beyzaie states, 'the teacher's anxiety begins with his fear of not being accepted which later evolves into the fear of being forced to leave. He has fallen in love, and as his desire to stay increases because he thinks he can be useful, the fear that he may have to go overwhelm him.'[3] In *The Journey*, a strong fear of rejection is aggravated by a relentless fear of violence and hunger in a world where billboards suggest affluence and modernity but economic relations allow hungry children to be beaten in streets for a loaf of bread, where film posters reflect an obsession with tough guys saving semi-naked women and poor children but, in reality, they chase children to rape them. While more terrifying, this world is like *Downpour*'s in that its journey does not imply the archetypal scheme of misery, provocation, quest, awareness, redemption and bliss but calicular Sisyphean quests of labour and failure. Like *Downpour*, it also deflates mainstream cinema and shows how its obsession with sex and focus on violence as the marker of superiority reinforce toxic masculinity. In such films, the hero, police or officials defend weaker people against the 'unjustified' violence exerted on them by stronger people, but the hierarchy of violence remains untouched as they can only do so because they belong to a higher level of the pyramid of power. Rather than focusing on a hero who exerts 'justified' violence, Beyzaie focuses on the ceaseless quests of two underdogs for a better life and on how violence reproduces itself in the hierarchy of power relations as it is sadistically exercised by upper layers of society on those in the lower layers. Thus, he subverts the idea of 'justified' violence by showing how it is erected to ignore the way it reinforces the hierarchy of violence by enhancing people's desire to exert violence on others and the master-slave rivalry that I analysed in Chapter 4.

By excluding characters that may be construed as emblems of official power, *The Journey* also confronts the readings that reduced *Downpour*'s multi-layered, poetic suggestiveness to a political allegory. Such interpretations were also damaging because they reduced Beyzaie's chances of filmmaking before and after the revolution. As he puts it, 'the surveillance I suffered then, in the end did not stop the film from being released, but such readings prevent it from being released now [1988] and that for intentions that I did not have, but now stop me from making films'.[4] This phenomenon can be analysed from the angle of what Bourdieu calls symbolic violence. *Downpour* was to reveal how physical and symbolic violence, the toxic cores of hegemonic masculinity, distort life. The revolutionary discourses of the time, however, reduced this revelation to apply only to the state although most of them, especially the radical Islamist and Marxist ones, believed in and exerted violence whenever the occasion allowed it. This was somehow inevitable because as Bourdieu states, 'the state is an X [. . .] which successfully claims the monopoly of the legitimate use of physical and symbolic violence over a definite territory and over the totality of the corresponding population'.[5] This monopoly, however, even when justified for maintaining order, is always open to abuse and transgression of its own standards in ways that are hard to control. Thus, if the legitimacy of a state is under question for any reason, the violence exerted by its agents will be judged as the main source of evil. In the case of *Downpour*, the relative unaccountability of SAVAK as the main source of state violence in justified or unjustified situations distracted interpreters' attention from the medieval, existential and nightmare motifs embedded in the Bespectacled Man, which signified the prevalence of exclusionist violence in Iran.

In his analysis of the conditions of intellectuals in Iran, Javad Mojabi states that, in Iran, due to the absence of free political parties, the roles of theoretical philosophers, creative artists and political thinkers are merged to the extent that the former two are trapped in politics and fail to achieve the philosophical or aesthetic depth their works require.[6] Mojabi's point is correct as the overpoliticization of artistic works distorts the process of their production and consumption and reduces a work of art to its direct political statements. However, what Mojabi does not analyse in this equation is the role of interpretive communities in generating meanings that drastically diverge from the artist's intentions. This inevitable diversion which may expand or limit the meanings associated with the cultural codes embedded in a work had, in the case of *Downpour*, limited its emancipatory aesthetic discourse which questioned the underlying ideology of several rivalling discourses. In other words, people who saw the state as the cause of all their woes prioritized direct political interpretations and ignored the film's critique of culture and its aesthetic dialogue with cinema and Iranian indigenous artistic forms. As Beyzaie specifies in his discussion of why he did not write *Death of Yazdgerd* in 1968, such interpretations may also discourage an artist from certain projects.

> At the time, it was impossible to analyze the givens of a form of power that is rooted in weakness. It would immediately suggest the ruling power. I started it, but before finding a proper form, the subject was associated with something else. So, I stopped. [. . .] Those days we also had another problem. If you were arrested for what you wrote, you were a good writer, and if you weren't, you were bad. The tacit question of some people was 'if you're a good writer, why aren't you arrested?' In fact, we had two forms of surveillance: the absurd official surveillance and the absurd surveillance of the intellectual ambiance, and a writer was trapped between the two.[7]

Apart from the metatheatrical edifice that he sets up to highlight the fluidity of human identity at personal and collective levels by showing relations that had never been depicted in Iranian drama, *Death of Yazdgerd* depicts the unreliability of history and how unbridled power leads to alienation from people, but such a project was likely to be read reductively as an allegory of the Pahlavi state rather than the whole structure of power relations. In *The Journey*, however, Beyzaie decreased the prospects of such readings by excluding anything suggestive of the state and increasing the motifs highlighting a critique of the culture.

Dreary existence and dreams of protection, belonging and flying

The film's title and credits appear along a Turcoman narrative music on a still of two boys holding each other. It then opens with a boy, Tāle (fortune, luck, providence) running as the soundtrack links the wailing of the Turcoman song to the crying of a toddler girl standing next to a lamp-post. As Tāle passes this point, spectators also hear a woman asking the girl if she wants her mother. Tāle runs down some steps in the opposite direction of seven other boys, up other steps in the opposite direction of five fully covered women and then through a ruined building with archways reminiscent of facing mirrors. Having completed his path through the archways, he then faces the poster of a smiling woman on a 7-UP advertisement and then reaches his destination, a shoemaking shop where his friend, Razi (content), works.

The term *safar* in the title evokes connotations that link its denotation – departing, passing and arriving – to the idea of mythic and mystic quests. The viewer, therefore, expects a journey, which, with the still of the two boys and the music that is in the Turcoman melodic mode of *Garyān* (Wailing), evokes the idea of companionship in a painful quest. In this context, the ruined archways may imply the decline of Iranian indigenous architecture in the context of 1970s rapid modernization plans,[8] but together with the crying of the toddler, the archways also foreshadow the unending repetition of quests for finding a mother, and Tāle's running in directions opposite to others suggests his desire for what they may already have. This constant running which is central to the film is also reminiscent of mankind's Sisyphean quest for happiness and achieving recognition and a sense of belonging to a desired other. At its surreal level, the circular running of the two is also like the ceaseless movement of Kafka's K in *The Castle*. The sequence also marks the idea of being chased by their 'thrownness' and 'disposition' as in one scene it is as if Tāle is chased by a wheel.[9]

Tāle's running brings him to a point near a ladder where the camera reflects his gaze in a synecdochic frame of the hands and the sunglasses of Razi's master buying cigarettes and then a long shot of Razi polishing a shoe behind his master's torso. Razi's master is, thus, suggested to control access to Razi and his obsession with 'cool' and violent masculinity is reflected in his sunglasses, cigarettes, cobbling knives and newspaper cuttings of semi-naked actresses on the wall. The dialogue, then, depicts the nature of communication when fear and surveillance distort life and shows Tāle as the dreamy initiator and Razi as the hardworking, streetwise boy who has reluctantly bent to the master-slave binary to survive. Razi's master is, thus, like the Bespectacled Man in *Downpour*, an agent of blind violence and castigation. Tāle's efforts to convince Razi to accompany him highlight their relationship. He has some money and a new address that is 'real, this time'. He promises his parents will help Razi find a better job and insists that he will get lost without Razi. Razi's reluctance indicates that this is a recurrent situation, but when he feels the threat of his 'master's violence', he changes his mind. Here the camera uses the type of synecdochic shots that are usually used in horror films to suggest a looming monster. Ominous movements in the torso and the hands of Razi's master who has been sharpening his cobbling knife suggest danger. The hand picks up a belt to punish Razi for speaking and not working. Razi, therefore, takes off his apron and escapes not because he wants to but because the risk of punishment is imminent. The violence is also displayed by his 'master' throwing a bowl at him and shouting, as his puny bespectacled face is revealed for the first time: 'You have to return anyway, and I will skin you alive.'

Beyzaie uses neo-realist elements to display how the lives of marginalized children may be like our nightmares and how children's exposure to violence reproduces toxic masculinity. At this level, Tāle's words about cinema, 'We can also look at cinema pictures', highlights how in a nightmarish world of poverty cinema functions as a space of escapist dreams. At another level, however, surreal intrusions break the verisimilitude of the action and dialogue to make the film like a *ta'ziyeh* in its incessant shifts between the real and the surreal. Thus, as in Beyzaie's other films, dark glasses and goggles reflect obsession with violence and mundane life, and the camera's framing of its subjects through large glasses conjures the feeling of being under top-down surveillance or a field of vision (cinema) that registers despairs but is unable to help. The two boys also come to embody the aspiration for aesthetic emancipation, the desire to look at one's life as a work of art and redraw its plot not by adhering to norms but by breaking away from them. In Alizadeh's words, the boys 'break away from the frames of mundane subsistence, and thus suffer hunger and poverty'[10] because such transgressions involve thinking outside the box, doing things in ways that others find shocking, disturbing the balance of one's life and exposing oneself to the unknown. Thus, they also poetically represent the two major forms of dealing with life: Razi, the streetwise practical guy, aspires to change his life by working within the given power relations, and Tāle, the visionary one, wishes to find parents/saviours who may help them grow like others. This poetic level can also be read as a people's dream of progress as it becomes a nightmare due to the absence of leadership or an obsession with the idea that a good leader/saviour can resolve all issues.

Beyzaie's use of regional folk music which began in *The Journey* continued in his village trilogy – *Stranger and the Fog*, *Ballad of Tara* and *Bashu, the Little Stranger* – to set a new model for film music in line with his reformulation of Iranian performing traditions. As Kimiaei's *Qeysar* or Beyzaie's *Uncle Moustache* or even *Downpour* show, this choice came after about half a decade of interest in using original and often dominant compositions for film music. Beyzaie's new approach, however, occurred because he concluded that using modern pieces with Western harmony to reshape Iranian music motifs would undermine the archetypal relations and emotions he wanted to reflect in some of his films while folk music contained a natural, raw quality that reinforced such elements.[11] His actual choices in the mentioned films, however, also reflect his inclusive approach to the idea of Iran as he used music from marginalized Turcoman and Arab pieces to reinforce the films' archetypal journeys and rituals of cleansing, fertility, healing, love, marriage, death, rebirth, quest and epic encounter. In *The Journey*, he mostly uses the heightened sounds of the settings of his scenes as music, but in two linked shots *ta'ziyeh* cymbals reinforce the mood and in four occasions two folk pieces suggest continuous action. The main is a Turcoman piece accompanying the credits, the 2-minute eagle-eye shots of the boys running across Tehran's scrapyards and finally the 30-second shot of a disappointed Tāle walking towards Razi after his dreams of belonging have been shattered. The extended wailing and guttural ornaments of this music suggest entrapment in a never-ending cycle of suffering. The other piece, which accompanies the meta-filmic sequence of the encounter with the paedophilic thug and continues with their frantic running across a burning wasteland with the hope of reaching 'the tall trees' and 'the tall buildings', is the music of a *zār* healing ritual and reflects the two boys' attempt to exorcise the vicious relics of a failed history imbued with vestiges of violence and abuse.

The escape scene following this first sequence repeats the incongruity of the smiling woman in the 7-UP poster with the dilapidated milieu. As running away from his master, Razi knocks the umbrella of a man sitting next to oil barrels out of his hand. Razi's question about where Tāle finds these addresses is then responded by Tāle's assurance that this time he has had a dream and that his strong and wealthy father will punish Razi's master and find Razi a good job. The vigour of hope now animates Razi. As they set off, Tāle jumps high over some steps as if flying, and Razi grabs the umbrella of the sedentary man and throws it away. The barrels, the umbrella and the flying subtly refer to imperialism and suggest that oil as Iran's source of wish fulfilment sustains others but not its children. The shot also pays homage to Robert Stevenson's *Mary Poppins* (1964) to highlight how the dreams of escaping a dreary existence sustain people and suggest that Tāle is Razi's Mary Poppins (Figure 5.1).[12]

The Journey, then, begins proper with the boys walking in the streets of poor neighbourhoods in Tehran, craving some fruits and finally buying some bread that they eat while walking. From this point, they go through twelve trials in which they act as anxious observers, active agents, or surviving victims while allowing Beyzaie to turn Tehran into a subject of study by encountering its extreme combination of modern and medieval practices and mentalities.

Figure 5.1 Screenshots from *The Journey*. Minutes 0'.30"–4'.30"

Distraction, loss and ethics: Killing the white demon of temptation

1. The peep box. The boys are attracted to a peep show whose owner is describing a picture of 'Sohrāb', the powerful hero, sightseeing on horseback. Tāle throws a coin flip to decide whether to watch the show or not, but a teenage boy grabs his coin and vanishes in the crowd. After a useless chase, they stop and then laugh at their own stupidity. The peep box sequence suggests that while such entertainments are vital for the mental well-being of underprivileged children and relieve the impacts of their desperate conditions, they are like distractions that decrease their chances in the practical side of life. The reference to Sohrāb, however, echoes the idea of a quest for finding an absent father and the victimization of the youth due to their naivety and the machination of warmongering leaders of hegemonic masculinity. Sohrāb's recreational ride is, then, echoed in their leapfrog game which leads to their encounter with the wiseman. The background of the sequence highlights child labour, and uses mattresses, beds and wheels to associate child labour with homelessness and suggest the way children must carry their wheels of fortune rather than roll along on them to make better futures.

2. The wiseman, the rich boy and skygazing. All quests feature a wiseman guiding the hero. In the *Shahnameh*, this can be an advisor or a father figure as Zāl for

Rostam. If this guide is absent or the hero disobeys him, his failure is inevitable. Thus, Zhendehrazm's death and Rostam's negligence result in Sohrāb's death, Rostam and Pirān's absence results in Siyāvush's death or Esfandiyār's disregard for Pashutan's advice triggers disaster. Such a guide is also vital for mystic quests. As Hafez puts it, 'Without a path guide never quest into the land of love/ I made a hundred efforts by myself to no effect.'[13] The wiseman who may be a retired employee sitting in a corner is dressed in a modern attire, but his face and gestures are reminiscent of clerics, priests and rabbis.

> **The Man:** You are set for a very long journey. Do you have money?
> **Razi:** We'll go on foot.
> **The Man:** On foot is impossible. It is too long.
> **Tāle:** We've made longer journeys.
> **The Man:** Your choice. If I were you, I wouldn't go like that.
> [He looks up, pats his chest and sneezes.][14]

While reflecting the Iranian habit of patting the chest and looking at light to trigger sneezing for health benefits, the gesture of touching the chest echoes performing a crucifix and the sneezing implies the superstitious idea that one must refrain from starting a new activity right after someone sneezes. The man, thus, embodies religion, lore and practical experience which may or may not be valid here because when the conditions of life change, what used to be wise may no longer be so. This encounter set a precedence for similar sequences in post-revolutionary cinema in which the transformative gaze, dedication and energy of the youth are preferred to the useless, dogmatic or inherently unethical visions of sedentary old men.[15]

With the man's warning, Razi becomes more anxious about money. Thus, having noticed a well-dressed boy receiving money from his father, he devises a plot to rob him. While chasing the boy, they pass two *naqqāli* paintings. In the first, a crowd of warriors is staring upwards with their back to the second painting in which Rostam is killing the White Demon. A high-angle shot with no sound then captures Razi and Tāle getting ahead of the boy and pointing at the sky as if noticing something. Soon a crowd gathers gazing at the sky. Then, the eye-level shot of Tāle who has been assigned to pick the boy's pocket is replaced with synecdochic shots of his hand approaching the boy's pocket. The scene's use of silence and manipulation of action-time coordinates reinforce the enormity of the moment. However, just like the painting in which Rostam is killing the White Demon while others are distracted, Tāle kills the white demon of unethical action and greed by refusing to steal the boy's money. The sequence also highlights human impressionability with a high-angle shot of more than forty people gazing at the sky as Tāle and Razi leave the scene surprised by the results of what they have started. The whole market has fallen into silence gazing at the sky. The emphasis on skygazing also suggests how people's dependency on other people's perceptions and their fixation on the supernatural may be used to exploit them, with a classic real example occurring five years later when people saw Khomeini's face on the moon (Figure 5.2).

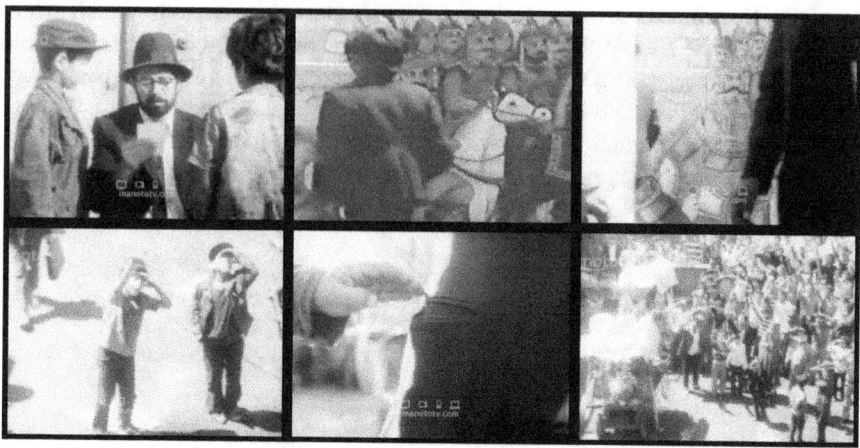

Figure 5.2 Screenshots from *The Journey*. Minutes 6′.30″–8′.30″

Ethical means and ends in the wasteland of hollow men, misery and consumerism

3. The hand barrow. As the eye-level shot of the boys depicts the hardship of finding their way through the skygazing crowd, the soundtrack resumes to capture the market sounds followed by Razi censuring Tāle for failing to rob the boy and asserting that now they 'have to walk the whole way'. This statement is, then, juxtaposed with the shots of a disabled man carried on a hand barrow along with his belongings – a wardrobe, a bed, his beddings and a chair. The same procession appears after the junkyard sequence when they dump the man at the end of the junkyards near railroads. While at realistic level, the scene marks the cruelty of a society with no support for the old or the disabled, Beyzaie ritualizes the scene to generate suggestions about human actions and their outcomes. The sound of cymbal in the soundtrack which echoes *Ashura* mourning processions suggests a tragic end or a funeral, and the words 'spun silk' and the arrow indicating the direction of their movement on the wall alludes to Rumi's poem: If you're injured by a thorn, it is what you planted** If you're in spun or unspun silk, it is what you yourself have spun.[16] Beyzaie's juxtaposition of Razi's concern about going on foot with the ironic portrayal of a man being carried as if on a throne to a terrible destiny and a tacit allusion to Rumi's poem is not concerned with moralizing and afterlife, but with how human agency and choices can change one's fate and how in Tāle's mind worthy ends remain worthy only if the means for reaching them do not hurt others.

4. The automatons. The boys' running around to ask people for direction is then followed by a humming sound in the soundtrack corresponding to the march of more than fifty workers whose identical helmets, large goggle/sunglasses, chalk-covered faces, and shovels joins their apathy towards the boys' questions to imply an expressionistic depiction of bee-like faceless automatons. The scene depicts the absurdity of their appearance and attitudes in the boys' minds, but juxtaposed with the skygazing scene, the scene conjures the image of soldiers or blindly obedient agents of demolition and development, which suggests obsessive obedience for practical purposes to be as dehumanizing as compulsive impressionability and imitation.

5. **The junkyard.** The 2-minute sequence of the vast junkyard uses Turcoman wailing music to stitch together silent eye-level shots of the boys, asking workers for directions and long high-angle shots of the boys running up and down on piles of construction rubble, fruit crates, scrapped cars and broken horse carriages with detached wheels. Here as the music stops, the camera registers the boys' encounter with a coughing man crushed by disease, dust and smoke among broken carriages. Tāle is stunned. The man, who looks like a cartman, is about 40 but seems to be dying. Gasping for air, he grabs Tāle's collar in despair, but Razi helps Tāle escape. This is, then, followed by the horn of a train, the low-angle shot of a train passing as the boys are looking and the sound of cymbals marking the arrival of the seven men who are to dump the disabled man and his belongings near the railroad.

The fear of unknown futures fills the boys' eyes as they begin running again as if avoiding such a fate. The train of a capitalist society aiming for a utopia of machines and high-rise buildings does not stop for anyone. Thus, the fates of the cartman and the old disabled man, as people who are no longer wanted or are masters of outmoded professions, echo that of the carriages, rubbles and cars that fail or fall behind in the relentless path to progress. They are dumped in the ever-expanding wasteland of the modern world which Beyzaie's music and heightened realistic shots poetically evoke in the sequence. Thus, the six first sequences poetically evoke a culture of modern automatons assertively marching and humming and others sleeping, sitting, walking or dying in a process that produces the idea of the wasteland to display the unseen side of consumerism in the margins of urban centres (Figure 5.3).

Figure 5.3 Screenshots from *The Journey*. Minutes 8′.55″–13′.55″

6. **The unknown path to salvation: The mad and the indifferent ones.** The boys, then, enter an open ladder shop. Sitting on a horizontal ladder on top of a scaffolding of ladders and moving his feet like children, a madman in modern clothing merrily states that they 'have come the wrong way and made their trip longer'. But when they ask for direction, he repeats, 'you must ask and search'. This brings them to a shop of salvaged doors where the camera's zooming in and out in lobby-like spaces implies the idea of doors leading to walls or to other doors as silent shots display how the customers and the owner fail to help them.

The Journey contains an abundance of ladders and wheels as motifs implying the desire of the marginalized, here poor orphans, to overcome the discrimination and have social mobility. This sequence, however, in addition to having an abundance of ladders rising to nowhere uses doors that remain closed or lead to walls and hand pointers giving contradictory directions. Having reached the mid-point of their quest, the boys now encounter a childish man who functions like a parallel for the wiseman of the earlier scene. However, whereas the first one was useless due to being too cautious and sedentary, this one is characterized by useless movement, a frivolous ecstasy in other people's suffering and highlighting mistakes without helping to correct them. Thus, along the surrealistic motifs of marginalization and doors as metaphors for a desire for open doors and passing from one state to another, the madman's attitude suggests the apathy of those on the top of the ladder of wealth and power and their frivolous brushing away of other people's problems. While showing their despair due to people's apathy, the door shop episode also functions as a turning point because from this point onwards, the boys' issues escalate from people's apathy or street rivalry to starvation and predatory and sexual violence (Figure 5.4).

7. **The poster, the bread and the violent ritual of public shaming.** As Tāle tries to urge a starving Razi to continue their journey on the wide steps of an unfinished park with empty barrels on site, the camera reflects their gaze by synecdochic stills of rice, coke, kebab, chips and a well-fed child having a piece of bread on a billboard. The boys step back to see the whole picture but are unable to see anything but the food. Then

Figure 5.4 Screenshots from *The Journey*. Minutes 14′.15″–15′.35″

comes the scene in which Razi tries to steal bread. The moment he takes the bread, he is grabbed by a huge man and his two apprentices, whose leather aprons make them like medieval executioners. The limping baker seems to protest but to no effect. Thus, as Tāle, the baker and an old man who has bread in his hand watch in dismay, the camera records the violation of Razi's body while the soundtrack mixes Razi's desperate cries with the sadistic laughter of the execution team and cheery onlookers. The man drags Razi on the ground and then lifts him to the top of his head like a sacrificial lamb. Razi, then, suffers a ritual of shaming in which the executioners hold him while another man cuts the front part of his hair with a blunt hair clipper. Tāle attacks the huge man and is brutally thrown away. Having suffered this violent ritual of shaming, Razi is put back on the ground while the onlookers, including a boy of his age, laugh at his new looks. Here an abrupt silence reinforces the expression on Razi's face. Hardened by his suffering and looking like a Samurai or Post-Mongol Iranian wrestler, he gazes at them and then joins Tāle. The old man offers them bread, but they escape as if facing a trap. After some frantic running, Razi then sits under a huge gear which reflects his crushing under the gigantic machine of toxic masculinity. Tāle gives him his hat to cover his head. He holds the hat on his head and gives out a loud shriek, which echoes Edvard Munch's *The Scream* due to the position of his hands and the intensity of the pain it registers. The shot clearly suggests that he has just suffered what is equivalent to raping his body and brain. The idea of helping a person recovering from violation is also suggested in that Tāle also gives his jacket to Razi.

The episode uses a grotesque carnival in reverse to produce a cinematic portrayal of the sadistic relations of hegemonic masculinity, highlight the helplessness of sympathetic people in such situations, and censure the joy many people get from watching such scenes due to their obsession with physical punishment. If one defines a carnival as a space in which people challenge worldly hierarchies by making visible what is normally not visible in society and ridiculing the holders of power, a grotesque carnival in reverse is one in which a procession of laughing people celebrate worldly hierarchies by victimizing a person at the bottom of the hierarchy of power. Registering how some people, who may even normally complain about the violence of authorities, cooperate with the same authorities to punish a person of their own type, or hurt or ridicule a stranger, a mentally ill person or a person who is just different, the template is one that Beyzaie uses in several plays to reflect the failures of leadership and citizenship. In *Talhak* or *Parchment of Master Sharzin*, the downtrodden victim is a man of visionary intellect who holds a mirror to society, but *The Journey* depicts the victimization of hungry children. He, thus, holds a mirror to Iranian society to show how it fails its own ideals of hospitality, generosity and protecting the weak. However, since the huge man embodies toxic masculinity, he may also signify the attitudes of tough guys or even the state which may punish transgressions without checking the causes. Thus, the sequence asserts that rather than protecting the weak, tough guys and their cohorts exert violence against the weak and that the justice system produced by patriarchy is obsessed with punishing rather than healing.

As the climax of the film's critique of toxic masculinity, the scene uses codes that imply a new layer of interpretation in which the boys represent the main forces contributing to the survival of Iranian culture: Tāle, the intellectual side providing vision, conceptual continuity, moral integrity, hope and ambition, and Razi, the action-focused side providing ritual continuity, societal know-how, craftsmanship, *javānmardi* guilds and warriorship.

In this context, the search for lost parents suggests that Iranian culture has been marked by an original absence or loss of sympathetic leadership and subsequent intervals of victimization that have distorted the culture's potential for progress and led to repeated quests for proper leadership and a coherent cultural identity. An illustrative example is that Razi's appearance after the shaming becomes like his tormentor's, which suggests how the breaking of the military side of Iran's *javānmardi* cults during the Turkic invasions led to a change in the visual motifs of master-slave codes in toxic masculinity. Thus, some who wanted to look like their military masters or mixed with them adopted such Turkic practices as shaving the front of their hair, which continued in some *Zurkhāneh* cults until the twentieth century.[17] In this context, Tāle's act of throwing mud at the food poster and his insistence that if 'we ignore our hunger, it will relieve itself' echo the adages of stoics about ignoring desires and fasting to save the soul.[18] Razi is too worldly to be fooled by such adages, but Tāle's promises and Razi's own hopes that one of Tāle's addresses will finally be real makes him continue. This level, however, remains hidden under the neo-realistic and expressionistic levels concerned with the status of the marginalized in the hierarchies of being and belonging (Figure 5.5).

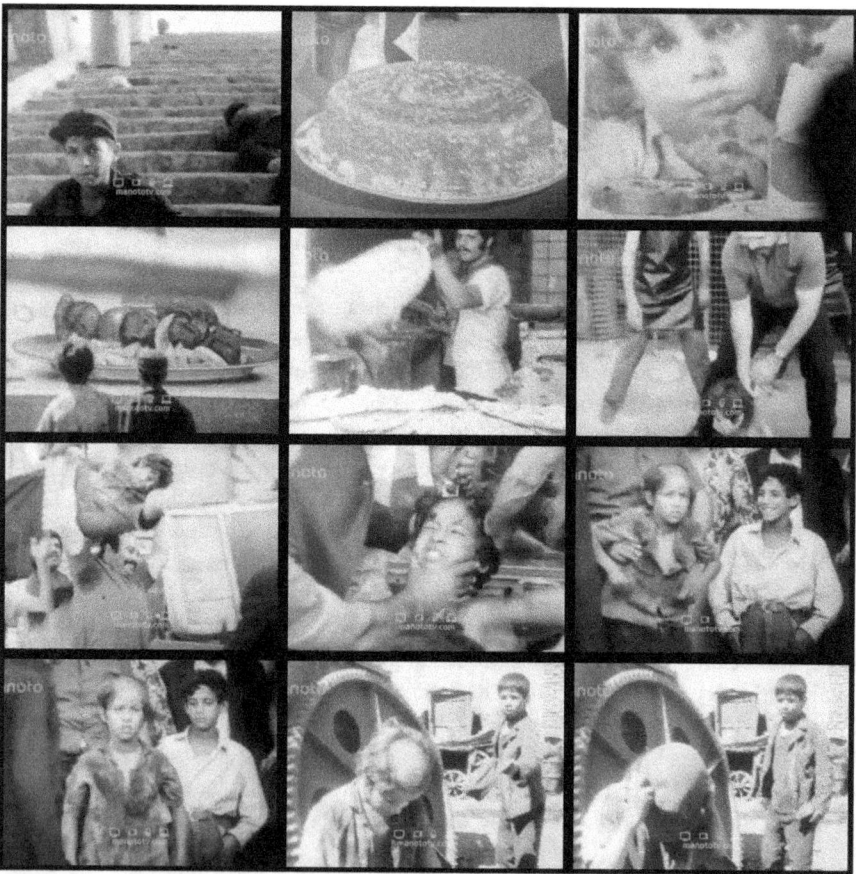

Figure 5.5 Screenshots from *The Journey*. Minutes 15′.40″–19′.10″

8. The bewitched town: Negligence of the future. Unable to calm his hunger, Razi proposes that they take a nap, but Tāle states that if they sleep, they will never reach their destination. As they argue about the plausibility of Tāle's quest for finding his parents, a woman shouts from a window 'Shut up. Don't you see everyone is asleep!' Here Beyzaie stylizes the emphasis on sleep by slowing down the action which turns the scene into a poetic note on negligence and the inertia of traditional craftsmen and labourers in comparison with the bee-like automatons of modernization in the earlier episode.[19] This also echoes the point above as Razi, the craftsman is kept awake and focused on their aim by Tāle, the visionary.

With silence, the wailing of the wind, the howling of a puppy and the final ceaseless crying of a lonely toddler girl walking on rubbles conjuring the eerie ambiance of a bewitched town, for 82 seconds the camera registers people lying everywhere on dusty grounds or rubbles as if dead. The crying toddler parallels the toddler in the film's opening to suggest the absence of a caring parent. Thus, together the two boys and the girl imply the neglected future, but when her echoing shriek is first heard, it breaks the torpor of the horror scene like an extra-diegetic wail that mourns the death-in-life status of the sleeping people.[20] The surrealistic nightmarish shots of the sleeping people also evoke the poetic association of being asleep with being unaware of the movement of history in the Iranian discourse on modernity[21] (Figure 5.6).

9. Burning of the wasteland, and the illusions of light, superficial progress and religion. The boys' escape from this nightmare leads to another junkyard where the sounds and images of a huge fire and smoke punctuate the shots of Tāle and Razi's running and a blind man approaching the camera to sell lottery tickets. With trees and the sky almost entirely absent in the film, as Behnam Nateqi states, 'the momentary glimpse of sky' here suggests 'desolation and darkness'.[22] The episode, thus, stresses the idea of a wasteland fated to burn, and the lottery tickets suggest the blindness of those who assume that such a misery can be fixed by the pipe dreams of grand futures when the chances of such a future is as slim as winning in a lottery. The

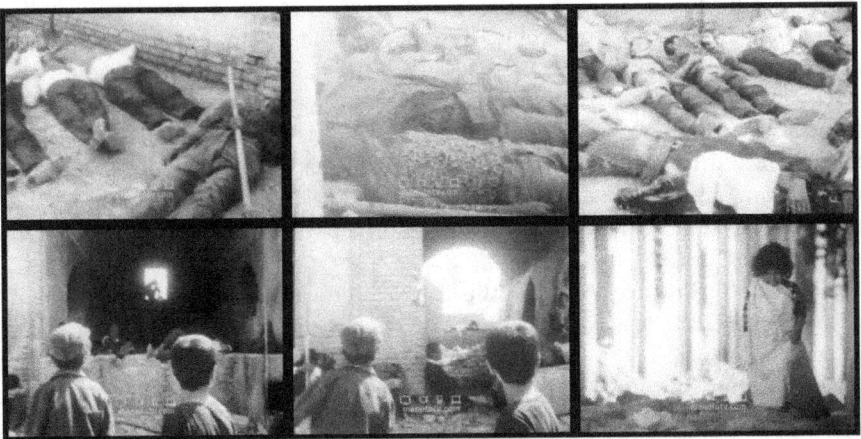

Figure 5.6 Screenshots from *The Journey*. Minutes 20′.05″–21′.25″

noisy fire and the silent blind man, then, provide a transition to a close-up of burning candles in a quiet *saqqākhāneh* (water-dispensing shrine). The camera pauses on a painting in the shrine featuring Abbas, Imam Hussein's brother and water carrier on horseback, Imam Hasan's teenage son Qāsem, the tale of a lion guarding Imam Hussein's body, and a woman, probably Zainab, sitting near a sacred site on top of whose dome is the severed head of a Karbala villain and a scorpion.[23] Tāle grabs the candle of a supplicant and asks God to fulfil his rather than her prayer. The woman puts out all the candles.

Running and long-distance walking later became a dominant motif in Iranian New Wave films about children including among others Amir Naderi's *Davandeh* (The Runner, 1984), Majid Majidi's *Bachehā-ye Āsemān* (Children of Heaven, 1997) or Panahi's *Āyeneh* (The Mirror, 1997). As in *The Journey*, such running bouts mark the resolution of intelligent children to prove their independence and worth or diminish the pressures of a claustrophobic life of poverty and violence by fulfilling a quest or winning a competition. Beyzaie juxtaposes this desire for happiness with a satiric depiction of lighting candles in water-dispensing shrines for divine intervention. The camera pauses on the hybrid motifs of such shrines which provided free water for passersby and worked like sacred spaces for people, particularly women, to pray for prosperity, marital bliss or fertility. The space contains ancient and modern motifs and suggests how the iconographies and functions of Mithra (herald of light and god of oath, heroic pledge and quest) and Ānāhitā (goddess of water, protection, fertility and family) have been transferred to Shi'i figures. The Mithraic candles, thus, combine with the Judeo-Islamic *panjeh* (hand/hamsa) to suggest divine light and intervention which in their Shi'i sense are also linked to the haloed faces of Shi'i saints and Abbas's severed hand.[24] Due to the hybrid iconography of folk paintings, the teenage Qāsem has been depicted as an ideal of beauty, like an uncovered woman, sitting on a modern chair with a shield and a sword in his hands. Thus, he mixes the features of the young heroic Mithra and the beautiful-bodied Ānāhitā. His modern chair, a marker of position, also suggests the use of contemporary motifs in folk paintings which functioned like blueprints for the rise of several modern, nativist styles of painting, including the *saqqākhāneh* style of the 1960s.[25] The shot combines with the earlier shot of the blind man and his lottery tickets to compare the religious pipe dreams of divine intervention with those of borrowed modernity leading to grand futures. The scene also highlights how people sympathize with the victims of violence inflicted fourteen centuries ago but do not do anything when such a violence is regularly inflicted on marginalized people of Tāle and Razi type. The woman's attitude towards Tāle suggests this lack of sympathy in a person who is praying for God's sympathy (Figure 5.7).

10. The kite, the tough guy and the exorcism of Iranian cinema. Tāle's grabbing of the woman's candle and then a boy's kite which leads to the boy's intense crying suggest the inevitable reproduction of toxic masculinity which, in Tāle's case, does not victimize others beyond playing a prank. The kite, however, provides a transition for depicting the bizarre pinwheels and toy-selling tough guy, a paedophile, exemplifying the distortion of Iranian *javānmardi* tradition in meta-cinematic shots that reflect

Figure 5.7 Screenshots from *The Journey*. Minutes 21'.30"–22'.35"

the irony of such a type functioning as the hero of Iranian cinema. Beyzaie reinforces this link by music as the moment Tāle returns the kite to the boy, the soundtrack foreshadows a ritual of exorcism with the drumming of a *zār* ritual marking their steps into a sequence displaying a prime example of toxic masculinity. The man who is wearing the characteristic dark suit and fedora hat of the *dāsh* type begins chasing Tāle and Razi as likely preys. Such people usually chose jobs or had their hangouts near places that boys between 10 and 14 visited, including pet bird markets, parks, cinemas and swimming pools. Unlike most other filmmakers, Beyzaie does not shy away from breaking the illusions of cinemagoers and reminding them of the real habits of such people. He follows Tāle and Razi into a bird market and an area where film posters are displayed and sold. The meta-cinematic shots here highlight the negative impacts of being exposed to sexually provoking pictures in the public space with no proper sex education and juxtapose the tough guy with the heroes featured in these posters.

The posters feature Arhām Sadr (1923–2008), Bahman Mofid (1942–2020) and Morteza Aghili (1944–), three of the most talented Iranian actors playing tough guys with fedora hats. The man keeps staring at and whistling for Tāle and Razi as they walk around fascinated by the pictures of semi-naked women in Iranian and foreign films. The camera, then, shows the tough guy from the view of Razi, the streetwise protector, who has already noticed him. His menacing presence is stressed by the medium shot of his torso approaching which makes him even more monstrous than Razi's master. Razi grabs Tāle's hand and runs with the first frame displaying their running under the gaze of a tough guy, played by Bahman Mofid, in a poster. Beyzaie's satiric gaze, here, makes the tough guy dive onto the picture of a naked woman in a poster of Parviz Nouri's *Hakimbāshi* (The Apothecary, 1972) marking how such figures have catapulted from their world of pederasty and paedophilia into the centre of films where they are depicted as heroes of chivalry and heterosexual attraction.[26] The poster has the apothecary (Nosrat Karimi [1924–2019]), using his cupping therapy trick to seduce Aniseh (Iren [1927–2012]). It, thus, joins the *zār* music to state that Iranian cinema needs exorcizing and that the prescriptions made for it by tough guy films are as deceptive as those of the apothecary.

Beyzaie, then, completes his work by one of his signature eerie presences with a woman in Arabic hijab saying prayer next to this grotesque space of sex and toxic masculinity. The shot corresponds to the Arabic *zār* music, but it also implies how Iranian culture has swung from one extreme in public portrayal of women to another. This is then followed by another shot of the tough guy first in a poster-like mirror shot and then in person watching the boys. Thus, although the boys escape in this case, due to their incessant running, the threat remains ever-present. Modernity, thus, is suggested to have been distorted in such practices as they prohibit any real development in gender relations or the conditions of the marginalized (Figure 5.8).

11. The dream of tall trees and buildings: Running away from a history of abuse to the pipedreams of superficial modernity. The intense running that continues here fortifies the idea of running away from a distorted past with the hope of a better future. Joined with the *zār* music, it also implies that this may function

Figure 5.8 Screenshots from *The Journey*. Minutes 23′.20″–25′.20″

like a ritual of exorcism to rid Iranians of the vicious medieval and modern practices and mentalities that distort their lives. Thus, Tāle and Razi are shown in eye-level long shots running next to high walls, on paved streets or down or up step, and in eagle-eye shots running on paved arenas, dusty roads and parched desert lands. This running is also punctuated by directions given by old traders. One says, 'It is not far. You must reach the tall trees.' Another adds, 'You must reach the tall buildings.' The third one asserts, 'You must reach. You must reach.' And the fourth insists with a peculiar smile, 'You must reach. You must reach. You must reach.' Then just when they reach the steel frame of a tall building, Razi complains of exhaustion, pain in his legs, being afraid of everyone, futility of their quest and the impossibility of returning to his job. Tāle's cure is typical of his role as the visionary intellectual, 'let's imagine'. Nonetheless, they fight, for Razi insults Tāle's unseen parents and insists that if they do not help them, he will curse them and break their door. As they roll on rubble and exchange punches, the dialogue becomes surrealistic. They whine about their old wounds and warn each other about hitting yesterday's wounds. Yet, after becoming like black-face actors due to throwing mud at each other, they suddenly see the 'tall' modern buildings they have been looking for. With their quest complete, the boys reconcile and though they have no money, they ask a photographer to take their photo. They pose, each putting his hand around the other's shoulder as a sign of intimacy, but when the photo is ready, they run away leaving the photographer in dismay.

The motifs of the sequence make these final bouts of running a reflection of the desire for modernity in a world characterized by exploitation. At this level, it is implied that Iranians have been made to run with the hope of recovering their lost identity, fulfilling the promise of their origins, building a better world and gaining recognition. Thus, the insistence on 'you must reach' reinforces the idea that the challenges that the boys have undergone are labours in a quest for happiness, but the process suggests the dog-eat-dog quality of international competition over resources. They are made to run, but their hunger, the fact that they were robbed and unduly punished, the enormous distance that they had to cover with little hope and the confusion over the direction of running and its ultimate purpose have drained their vigour. The last fields that the boys pass through once more mark the enormity of the task, but as the film demonstrates, the modern buildings, with their façade of modern life and technology, do not seem to be the inviting utopian shelter that they have been expecting.

The photo scene is one of Beyzaie's typical meta-filmic jokes about cinema. The man registers their moments of happiness and friendship and develops the film but is left without a reward as his subjects have no money and do not even thank him. With eleven of their labours completed, Razi now displays his honour by saying goodbye as he does not want to burden his friend, but Tāle promises to find and help him in a couple of days (Figure 5.9).

12. Loneliness and Rejection. The twelfth labour of the two is a nightmare of separation in which the practical Razi faces hopeless loneliness and the visionary Tāle undergoes an ordeal of rejection. The scene prior to Tāle's meeting with the

Figure 5.9 Screenshots from *The Journey*. Minutes 25′.30″–28′.35″

couple whom he assumes may be his parents is rich in metaphoric and metonymic orchestration of motifs that deserve analysis.

Defining verisimilitude as a 'function of the metonymic character of the film medium', and our experience of 'time and space' as 'a succession of contiguities', David Lodge states:

> The basic units of the film, the shot and the scene, are composed along the same line of contiguity and combination, and the devices by which the [. . . sequence] of experience is rendered more dramatic and meaningful are characteristically *metonymic devices that operate along the same axis: the synecdochic close-up that represents the whole by the part, the slow-motion sequence that retards without rupturing the natural tempo of successiveness, the high or low angle shot that 'defamiliarizes', without departing from the action it is focused on.* Consciousness is not, of course, bound to the line of spatio-temporal contiguity, in the way that sensory experience is, but then film does not deal very much or very effectively

with consciousness except insofar as it is manifested in behaviour and speech, or can be reflected in landscape through the pathetic fallacy, or suggested by music on the soundtrack.[27]

Thus, Lodge suggests that literature is more tuned to reflecting consciousness. What happens in Beyzaie's case, however, is that he combines a literary genius which tends towards the metaphoric pole with a visual perceptiveness which is metonymic. The result generates dramatic and cinematic situations and shots in which the poles of metonymy and metaphor work together to extract the ongoings of the human consciousness from visual representations.

Thus, the defamiliarizing metonymy of the high-angle shot of a lonely Tāle in an egg-shaped arena with a pipework patch passing through it provides a metaphor for the spectator about the potential for rebirth that this moment holds for Tāle, and Tāle's upward gaze implies the ongoings of his consciousness and his hope for this rebirth. His long shadow, however, foreshadows how this rebirth will be overshadowed by the law of the father. Razi's noble sense of support and disappointment is also reflected in his pointlessly kicking around an empty tin and then wistfully gazing into distance as if listening to Tāle ringing the bell. He knows that their journey may end up being as pointless as his kicking of the empty tin. Thus, he waits for Tāle, and his wistful gaze reflects the desire for belonging which is likely to be crushed as the empty tin. The film also creates an expressionistic moment of waiting by slowing down the action and a synecdochic shot of Tāle's hand pressing the bell in an extended ringing. Razi's distant gaze is, then, framed in a close-up with the earlier bee-like, bespectacled construction workers marching towards the camera to mark the obsession with destroying the old and constructing modern façades without producing modern mentalities.

Tāle's meeting with the couple marks the exchange of accepting glances between Tāle and the woman and the man's execution of the law of the father, the superego that prohibits and postpones. He does not look unkind, but his handlebar moustache signifies an inherited culture of control, and he acts in a matter-of-fact style as if fulfilling a legal obligation:

[Tāle's wishful eyes meet the man's gaze. The woman is behind the man looking at Tāle with sympathy.]
The Man: How old are you?
Tāle: I'm twelve.
    [The man turns and looks at his wife. She looks at him and then Tāle in silence.]
The Man: Our child would be ten if he were around.
Tāle: Isn't twelve possible?
    [The man remains silent, but serious suggesting a negative answer. Tāle looks at the woman in dismay as going down the steps. She looks at Tāle in silent sympathy.]
Tāle: I can sleep in the kitchen or cellar. **The Man:** [Looking through the staircase railing as if he is the guard of a prison.] No.

> **Tāle:** [goes down the steps.] I know how to work, how to sweep the floor.
> **The Man:** [Looking through the staircase railing as above.] No.
> [Tāle and the woman exchange a long sympathetic gaze. Tāle leaves.]²⁸

The woman's sympathetic gaze suggests a kind of modernity which accepts the marginalized and recognizes the joys and skills that an unspoiled, hardworking child of Tāle's type can offer to a family and a nation. With the support of the family, Tāle's qualities may be enhanced through education, familial support and psychological assurance, and both sides may thrive. The law of the father, however, is obsessed with the self and the other and makes such unions impossible. Beyzaie's desire to mark the man as a source of estrangement, a shadowy border separating the emotional contact between the two is reflected in his interview:

> My only regret is the light. I wanted the man's face to be set in darkness, but the cinematographer, being more rational than I was, thought it would be seen as his mistake and although I accepted its responsibility, he did not accept the risk. Maybe in that case the man would look more non-reconciling, cold, inflexible, and strict.²⁹

Using light, shadows and darkness as signifiers for love, hope, rebirth, doubt and despair was a technique that Beyzaie had already used in *Downpour* for poetic purposes as in the scene of Ātefeh in Hekmati's room. Realistically, the scene shows a simple rejection in which the potential mother, the object of Tāle's chaste desire for belonging, is fanatically shielded by her aloof husband. However, having already observed the twelve labours that the boys have suffered for reaching this point, the spectator knows that she is, at one level, an accepting goddess, or an ideal form of nationhood, silenced by the exclusionist laws of patriarchy which have made her male priest or guardian the one passing decrees on her behalf.

The family scene, the final labour which leads to failure, is one of Beyzaie's best depictions of the dismay of the marginalized in an exclusionist culture. The door as a metaphor of acceptance and belonging opens, but this is a temporary opening, which leads to rejection. When the man's response closes the case, Tāle's despair is reflected in his two levels of bending: (1) readiness to sleep in the kitchen or the cellar and (2) working for them. Yet, each level of bending is rejected by a single 'no'. The Turcoman wailing music, then, marks the despair on the woman's face and accompanies Tāle's dejected steps up to the point he sits next to Razi, who has been waiting for him. The film, then, closes with an emotional dialogue:

> **Razi:** You know you don't have anyone. Why do you come after me every day?
> **Tāle:** I'll find another address for tomorrow.

The dialogue implies the Sisyphean nature of their quests and their youthful resilience. Beyzaie, thus, ends the film not with a note of rejection or victimization but with one voicing their survival and eagerness to try again. They have tried many addresses to recover a lost sense of who they are, but they are not willing to stop due to recurrent failures (Figure 5.10).

Figure 5.10 Screenshots from *The Journey*. Minutes 30′.15″–32′.40″

Reception and concluding remarks about the lost boys of Iranian New Wave

Though it was mostly like a wake-up call for adults and teenagers than a children's film, *The Journey* won the first prize of the Seventh International Film Festival for Children and Young Adults (1972) for 'its focus on human values, its courage in depicting life in an unsupportive ambiance, its innovative take on real life and the extraordinary acting of its child actors'.[30] Despite its critical acclaim and influence on later New Wave films, the reception of the film has remained mixed because of Beyzaie's use of the same poetic mix of realism, surrealism and archetypal suggestiveness he found in Persian poetry, *ta'ziyeh* and other forms of literary and folk expression in Iran. These qualities made the film too dense for those who expected a simple children's film, a leftist political allegory, a film in a classical Hollywood style or a European arthouse film. Thus, some critics complained that the film's symbolism and multi-layered dialogue ruined its realistic force and its function as a children's film. Nevertheless, the film's visual power meant that it went on to win the second prize for a foreign film in the Eighth Moscow International Film Festival (1973) and the Silver Hugo Award of Chicago Festival, which suggested that the realistic aspect worked well. It also won the admiration of several critics including Davāei and Nateqi, who commented on how Beyzaie orchestrated his visual motifs and camera frames to produce a powerful comment on violence, poverty and social problems.[31] The film also continued to be considered one of Kānun's principal productions due to its influence on later filmmakers.

6

Stranger and the Fog (1974)

Rituals of existence: Homecoming, becoming and departing

Introduction: From *The Journey* to an archetypal village trilogy

Following *The Journey*, Beyzaie initiated a new template which focused on archetypal forms and functions without diminishing his analysis of contemporary culture. The first product of this template was a mythically charged poetic film about human life and the possibility of using one's potential for innovation, productivity and hard work to serve personal and communal prosperity. This resulted in *Stranger and the Fog*, which examines the existential limits that as Mojabi states, 'breed an anxiety of being',[1] and make individuals bend to mores that distort their lives. Together with *Ballad of Tara* and *Bashu, the Little Stranger*, the film initiates a trilogy whose motifs condense globally suggestive customs and beliefs from different parts of Iran to create a microcosm where myth, history, folklore, rituals and indigenous artistic forms and cinema work together to make surrealistically evocative statements about existential, social and cultural meanings of being human.

Apart from their emancipatory aesthetics which I will analyse in their respective chapters, the timeless microcosms of these films portray the vicissitudes of human relationship with home, love, nature, belonging, marriage, birth, parenthood, productivity, heroism, loss, war and death in contexts that challenge people's attachments to exclusionist norms and highlight the conflicts of divergent individuals with the collective identities imposed on them. *Stranger* focuses on the journey of life and how being human is reduced to anxiety or joy-breeding functions imposed by the real exigencies of survival and the unreal requirements generated by society, theorized by culture and sanctified by religion. *Tārā* analyses mankind's historical identity and shows how obsession with power distorted the past and how fixation on heroes and the past may ruin the present's potential for growth and happiness. Finally, *Bashu* examines national identity and as implied in its climatic *zār* ritual, aspires to exorcise the xenophobic and exclusionist demons of human national identity. Thus, these three films confront the processes through which human existential, historical and national identities are limited by inherited or constructed mores. However, they also gradually enhance their focus on female protagonists in a process in which women achieve a higher level of independent agency and move from failing to control their destiny to being in control.[2]

As Naficy states, in *Stranger*, Beyzaie 'deftly' combines 'the representational realism of the invisible style with the presentational performativity of *taziyeh* passion plays'.[3] This is, indeed, applicable to the trilogy as in these three films Beyzaie reinforces his mythically and ritually charged microcosms with epic, ritual and *ta'ziyeh* techniques and concepts. In *Bashu*, these have more to do with rituals of fertility and rebirth, the circularity of time and nature, an ethical avoidance of compromise with tyranny and protecting the weak in the battle against injustice. In *Stranger* and *Tara*, however, apart from the above, they also include sacrificial, questing or exploring heroism and presentational performance for displaying moments of emotional intensity in the existential cycle of coming from and going to the unknown. Thus, at one level, these films are *ta'ziyeh* performances that instead of commemorating religious figures focus on the marginalization of strangers, women and children and subvert religious, historical and national fixations at philosophical, sociological and psychological levels.

In her brief discussion of *Stranger*, Sheibani rightly argues that 'the film initiated a different kind of cinema that disturbs gender conventions to historicize the portrayal of women, who have generally been depicted in Iranian cinema through a culturally normative lens'. She also makes a few astute points about Ra'nā's evolving character and states that 'Ra'na and Ayat are both strangers to their surroundings'.[4] Dabashi also rightly comments on Ra'nā's courage to face the burden of patriarchal beliefs.[5] Yet, when it comes to the rituals observed in the film, most scholars seem to echo Behzad Eshqi and Naficy's words about Beyzaie's engagement with Japanese rituals although the film's rituals are all Iranian, and Beyzaie's homage to *Seven Samurai* occurs only in the action of the final invasion sequence.[6]

In his analysis of *Stranger*, Naficy states that Beyzaie 'transforms the rather simple Crystalline invaders of *The Cow* into a complex palimpsest, the interpretation of which challenges its spectators, rendering the film an open, if somewhat opaque, text'.[7] Though valid in calling *Stranger* open-ended, this comment is reductive towards both films as it reduces the *bluris* (Crystal-like people) of *The Cow* to their political interpretations and reduces the intrusive invaders of *Stranger* to an 'opaque' imitation of the former. The name of the *bluris* in *The Cow* echoes the term used in colloquial Persian for a person with a white body/complexion.[8] While used as a term of endearment for white Iranians, particularly women, in Sa'edi's story and the film it may suggest Euro-Americans, whose threatening power, like the *bluris*, has been a constant source of anxiety for Iranians since the early 1800s. However, being focused on psychological metamorphosis under pressure, *The Cow* is more concerned with showing how the villagers' ignorance and hypocrisy, and their exposure to the disturbing gaze of the *bluris* transform them, particularly the three pillars of their community, into alienated torturers. It also explicitly displays this alteration in the final scene when Islam's lashing of Mash Hasan causes him to fall from the mountain side, and the final frames from Mash Hasan's position captures three armed *bluris* and the three villagers at the top of two hills to suggest their similarities.[9] Thus, even if one downplays the psychological aspects about metamorphosis and alienation and reduces the film to its sociopolitical ideas, in addition to colonialism, poverty, state brutality and obsession with oil (the cow) as the country's source of income, the film is concerned with how cultural, social and economic failures aggravate the pressure of being under the gaze of outsiders and dehumanize Iranians or make them treat those who are different among them with brutal violence. Thus, the two films' similarities are not at the level suggested by Naficy but at a more complicated level which originates in Beyzaie and Sa'edi's concerns about the position of the marginalized in society and the distortion of Iranian collective identity under the gaze of powerful outsiders.

Though insightful about Beyzaie's focus on women, which had become more important when Naficy wrote his review in 1985, his analysis of *Stranger*, particularly in his later writings, is also marred by his misreading of symbols, characters and relations. He assumes Jeirān is Ra'nā's mother and takes Zakaria for Āshub. He also makes reductive suggestions, such as 'Does Ayat represent Bahaullah, the Baha'i prophet? is Zakaria a symbol of the Mahdi, the Shiite messiah?',[10] which question Beyzaie's agnostically secular vision without any analysis and repeats the dogmatic fixation of post-revolutionary Iranian officials with Beyzaie's family background, which led to his dismissal from his academic position in 1981. He even reads Beyzaie's critique of unbridled Westernization, lack of attention to environmental and cultural preservation and discarding of potentially progressive elements of culture as antimodern ideas: 'Do the violent strangers represent modernity's disruptive forces?',[11] 'Does Beyzai advocate abandoning modernization and industrialization in favor of a return to traditional living?'[12] Eshqi's analysis is also astute in recognizing that 'the film can be interpreted at political, supernatural and psychological levels' and 'works with poetic illuminations rather than a thesis'. However, he fails to chase the motifs properly. He looks for certainty about the unknown although the film argues for the futility of the obsession with the unknown. He also considers some 'beautiful' shots as 'non-referential' just because he fails to link them to the plot and concludes that 'the film leads to dead ends at all its levels.'[13]

The question that one may ask, however, is whether *Stranger* is as enigmatic as they suggest. To respond to this question, I will explicate the orchestration of realistic, psychological and archetypal motifs that build several layers of interpretive suggestiveness in the film and turn it into a poem on how the dreams of being and belonging are shattered by nightmares of fear and loss leading to an obsession with the unknown. I will demonstrate how Beyzaie fulfils his self-assigned duty to expose his viewers to emotions, events or relations they have not experienced before[14] by mythologizing the outsider, the marginalized and the outcast's gazes as potential sources of fertility and modernity and by defamiliarizing social dogma and religious certainties about the unknown to reflect their blinding effect on the mind. I will also show that the film's complexity is like his other films, but due to its focus on human relationship with the unknown, it becomes hard to follow for those who only look for simple allegories, political suggestions or regurgitated clichés about life, nature and human psyche.

Analysis: The seer and the rebirth of the fertility agent

Beyzaie's film distances itself from the focus of 1960s and 1970s village films on ideal pastoral life, evil feudal lords and seduced girls, and the emphasis of alternative films on poverty, metamorphosis or rebellion of the little man. Instead, it creates a ritualistically stylized template on human quest for fertility in love and life, subverts the stereotypes of femininity and masculinity by reformulating the archetypes producing them and displays how obsession with the unknown and exclusionist social mores disturb normal lives.

The credits appear in reddish black ink on a white background as the soundtrack plays the percussion music of *nobān* ritual along Baba A'yud's incantatory singing of 'Allah' in Arabic in which the word 'God' and 'my beloved' are prominent.[15] The colour of the credits, thus, signifies the blood sacrifice that occurs in the end while the song signifies human relationship with God, existence and love. A disabled boy playing with the skull of a bull on the coast alerts to a faint sound and notices a stray rowboat approaching through the fog. He informs others, and as villagers rush to the coast following the drumming from their watchtower, the camera frames Qadam Kheir (auspicious), a village elder, Jeirān (deer), a woman of about 60 and Ra'nā (gracious), her young, widowed sister-in-law. A high-angle crane-shot of the village, then, suggests its limitations against the sea and the forest, which become Beyzaie's ideal settings for exhibiting the pantheist elements of Iranian culture.

According to Beyzaie, he had seen similar, semi-circular coastal villages in the Caspian area in 1964, but when he tried to find a village for the film, he found that the construction boom of the 1960s and 1970s had replaced them with modern villas, and with the migration of villagers to mountainous regions, coastal cultures had vanished.[16] Nevertheless, the film is not an anthropological reconstruction of the coastal cultures of the Caspian Sea. Instead, it combines, condenses and traces to their imagined origins practices from several regions to create a microcosm of the neglected sides of Iranian culture. To justify the idea of original forms, he and Raminfar also designed the architecture and the domestic and public costumes, spaces and objects in ways that, though realistic, suggest a timeless setting.

Beyzaie's disabled boy is given centrality in *Stranger*. The circle around him, the skull and his appearance create the image of an outcast seer, whose marginalization makes him be in places or notice things that others neglect. Ra'nā and Jeirān's dialogue, then, reveals that two of the men hauling the boat are Jeirān's brothers, and Jeirān blames Ra'nā's 'ominousness' for her brother's death. It also introduces the idea of waiting, not for a saviour but for the corpse of Ra'nā's husband, Āshub (chaos, turmoil). The succession of news about the boat specifies it contains 'nothing', 'a man' and 'a corpse', that finally, when Ra'nā leaves, is found to be 'alive' and needing treatment which Ra'nā tells her father, an apothecary, to provide when her brother-in-law comes to her house to request it. Thus, from nothing rises a man whose initial framing and the colour of his bruises imply he has risen from the dead or is an effigy that gradually becomes human. The opening, therefore, uses the idea of waiting for a sacrificial saviour to conjure the seasonal rituals of fertility in which human embodiments and later effigies of fertility gods were buried or given to water for future return and were recovered for the planting and harvest season. The focus on Ra'nā, her calm mourning, her baby and her husband having been 'grabbed by the sea a year ago' indicates that she is central to this archetypal aspect and that she represents an earth goddess awaiting her agent of fertility. She, thus, carries the archetypal motifs of Spandārmaz, the Iranian goddess of nature, family devotion, farmers, death and rebirth, the mother earth who chooses her own husband and is celebrated in 'Iranian Farmer's Festival' as she 'endures all' to make fertility possible.[17] The chains of words about the content of the boat, while realistic, are also like the stylized utterances in rituals where the enactment of doubt leading to certainty is used to guarantee divine support in the coming year or for the ritual itself. Thus, like animist shamans talking to natural elements to revive their spirit or gardeners, who perform rituals of fertility on trees by threatening to cut them if they remain fruitless, the first sequence is like a ritual for conjuring the agent of fertility who was given to the sea in the previous year.

For my Western readers, Frazer's analysis of such practices in Europe, which he links to the fertility rites in Western Asia, may provide a more familiar example:

> At the festival of Adonis, which were held in Western Asia and in Greek lands, the death of the god was annually mourned, with a bitter wailing, chiefly by women; images of him, dressed to resemble corpses, were carried out as to burial and then thrown into the sea or into springs; and in some places his revival was celebrated on the following day. [. . .] At Alexandria images of Aphrodite and Adonis were displayed on two couches; beside them were set ripe fruits [. . .], plants growing in flower-pots, and green bowers twined with anise. The marriage of the lovers was celebrated one day, and on the morrow women attired as mourners, with streaming hair and bared breasts, bore the image of the dead Adonis to the sea-shore and committed it to the waves. Yet they sorrowed not without hope, for they sang that the lost one would come back again.[18]

Frazer than discusses such practices in agricultural festivals, links the rituals of sacred marriage and beheading of 'the human representatives of the tree spirit' in Europe to human sacrifice for fertility and explains that the purpose of 'throwing the effigies of Death and the Carnival into water in the corresponding ceremonies of modern Europe' were 'the same'.[19]

Similarly, in Iran, such rituals have continued up to the present. Beyzaie himself provides an example for this in his account of the ritual of beating and washing the shrine rug as an emblem of a martyred saint in Ardahāl, which he compares with the Mesopotamian festival for the fertility god Baal. At their surface, however, such rituals were redefined in pre-Islamic religious rituals of sacrificial heroes Iraj, Siyāvush and Zarir, whose roles were then given to Ashura martyrs after Islam.[20] Beyzaie's work with these motifs, therefore, offers a research-based reconstruction of the archetypal origins of *ta'ziyeh* and several other rituals.

To fulfil this at metatheatrical and archetypal levels, the film uses several *ta'ziyeh*-like circular scenes in which villagers act as audience, but rather than echoing *ta'ziyeh*, these scenes try to conjure the original rituals that gave birth to *ta'ziyeh*. Two of these occur here with a graveyard and a coastal scene focused on Ra'nā and several scenes displaying the stranger's agitation and villager's suspicion in between. In the first, six people sitting inside a circle function like actors under villagers' gaze. Here, chief Nazar (insight), supported by two advisors, Qadam Kheir and the silent man who performs priestly functions, interrogates the stranger who is sitting in front of Ra'nā's brothers-in-law, Zakaria and Esmāeil. The latter two, thus, function like testifiers aware of the conditions of the stranger's arrival. In cinema and theatre, court scenes work like plays within the play/film as the judge, prosecutors, claimants, defendants and lawyers perform for the jury and the audience to prove their case. Beyzaie does the same here but uses a *ta'ziyeh* form. To facilitate the process, Nazar, the lawgiver, first announces the stranger's name, Āyat (sign), as if he is naming him, and then, after the villagers' surprised reaction to the name, asks him what he remembers. The act of naming for the sake of the audience (villagers) and the ritual of remembering mark the desire for controlling the unknown by naming its qualities. Āyat's recalling, however, is like the hazy account of a nightmare performed before a semi-circular gathering near the boat, where he asserts that the 'black boat' is not his and remembers to have been attacked by several people. Thus, brought to the village by winds and waves from beyond the fog, the boat comes to represent a ritual coffin and cradle, and Āyat's arrival implies a journey of rebirth. Villagers, however, are unsure whether this nature-borne entity is a blessing or a curse.

At its realistic level, which is focused on psychology and sociology of marginalization and gender relations and the role of the outsiders' gaze in a progressive cross-fertilization, the film now marks Āyat's anxiety about being chased and not being accepted by the village. Zakaria and Esmāeil, who represent exclusionism and protectionist misogyny, also begin to stress that they 'may be attacked by Āyat's enemies', and he 'may be a thief' or 'a spy' working for invaders. Thus, as in Beyzaie's other works, fear and rivalry are shown to trigger constructive action in the outcast person and exclusionist attitudes in the centre. Āyat now begins to act as a sentinel to protect himself and the village from the unknown, the sea and the fog, while villagers, due to Nazar's emphasis on hospitality, remain kind yet aloof. Placed between the forest (the uncontrolled nature) and the sea (the unconscious or the uncontrollable unknown), the village now embodies the limits of human control over life. The inscrutable nature of this unknown is also implied in that Āshub, who violated the limits of the sea, has not returned, and Āyat, who has arrived from beyond its fog, only remembers menacing presences.

Esmāeil's shouting, Ra'nā's calm face, and Āyat's worried gaze at the sea, then, function, as transitions to close-ups of humanoid and animal-like wooden statues in the graveyard to mark mankind's fear of death. These figures recall West African representations of ancestors and animist forces. However, as always, Beyzaie's backgrounds, which may be foregrounded for scene transitions contain condensed realistic motifs. Thus, these effigies and other unfamiliar objects in the film are, indeed, tokens of Iranian animist practices which though covered under religious layers are still present.[21] Such images suggest Beyzaie's focus on neglected relics of Iranian culture, which the people obsessed with the centre did not even know existed in Iran. Indeed, in the decade following the release of the film, many critics suggested that the film echoes African, Japanese or Chinese films without noticing that Iran itself is a microcosm in which one can find African-like practices and objects in the southwest and Far Eastern ones in the northeast.[22] In other words, one of Beyzaie's themes in his trilogy is how the meaning of Iran has been limited by official and intellectual discourses of the centre (Figure 6.1).

Figure 6.1 Screenshots from *Stranger and the Fog*. Minutes 1′.40″–13′.55″

The sickle, the fertility cycle of death and rebirth and the outcast agent of fertility

The camera, then, follows Ra'nā to the graveyard to register her calm lighting of a candle for Āshub and her contribution to the ritual of feeding the poor, including the disabled boy, for the salvation of the departed. The soundtrack accompanies the scene of mourners in the graveyard with an overwhelming wailing noise to reflect an obsession with the afterlife. A comic relief, then, depicts Āyat being tricked by children telling him some strangers have come after him. This prank intensifies Āyat's agitation and makes an inter-filmic reference to Hekmati's relationship with children and his being a source of their joy either as the butt of their jokes or as their supporter. But Āyat's running to the coast to confront the invaders foreshadows the later invasion sequence as when he arrives, six figures, who, at realistic level, are probably only there to watch the children, are standing near his boat. Number six is relevant here as Āyat's symbiotic bond with the five invaders implies he may be one of them.

The camera, then, frames Ra'nā's wandering near the sea on a foggy day and her discovery of a blood-covered sickle in Āyat's boat. While marking the similarity of Ra'nā's and the disabled boy's powers of perception, this scene links the fog to the uncanny encroachment of the unknown or the subconscious into the known. It also triggers the second assembly where Āyat's answers to Nazar's interrogations about the sickle mark him as an agent of fertility while echoing the scene in which Tāle is interrogated by his would-be father in *The Journey*.

> **Āyat:** I will work. I want to compensate your kindness.
> **Nazar:** How?
> **Āyat:** I know how to harvest the crop. I know how to irrigate the land.
> **Nazar:** What else?
> **Āyat:** I know how to fish.
> **Nazar:** No.
> **Āyat:** I know how to cut trees.
> **Nazar:** No.
> **Āyat:** I know how to build houses.
> **Nazar:** No.
> **Āyat:** Give me the driest of lands, and I will make it fertile in a short time. Give me a dead land, and I will revive it.
> **Nazar:** What else?
> **Āyat:** I don't know anything else.
> **Nazar:** You know how to kill, don't you? This sickle is still covered in blood. See. [Throwing the sickle to him]. Why were you hiding this from us?
> **Āyat:** This isn't mine.
> **Nazar:** It's not? Nonsense, Āyat. That woman has found it in your boat.
> [Āyat remains silent. Ra'nā stands up and leaves.][23]

Āyat's quest for belonging and normal life, which, as Beyzaie states, 'some have by default but some are excluded form' even when serving their communities with unique qualities,[24] highlights mankind's position in Heidegger's conception of fate.[25] Āyat's idea of manliness, his 'disposition' urges him to use his acumen, skills and energy to serve himself by serving the land and its people as an agent of fertility, but the dictates of toxic masculinity and the circumstances of his 'thrownness' require him to enter the nightmarish cycle of violence.

Realistically, Nazar is just checking his honesty, but the scene marks the villagers' desire for having a fishing and fighting hero to replace Āshub rather than a normal hardworking man. Beyzaie uses such situations to depict how the lives of individuals are distorted by social and religious codes. As he states, Āshub was just a good sailor, but the villagers' obsession with heroes pushed him farther into the sea, a task that, as revealed later, forced him to fake his death to survive.[26] Such a hero is, thus, cornered with praise and censure. Like a marginalized person with exceptional physical, mental or working skills, he either accepts the challenge, and his life is distorted by impossible quests that lead to his victimization, or does not, and he is placed in the borders or lower echelons of the hierarchies of belonging. Beyzaie's hero, however, whether an intellectual as in *Downpour* or *The Crow* or an intelligent man or woman of action as in *So Dies Akbar the Hero*, *Stranger* or *Kallat Claimed* always aspires to prove himself or herself by acting as an agent of prosperity and happiness.

The sickle revives Āyat's desire to remember and triggers a quest-like interest in Ra'nā. The film, thus, begins to focus on Ra'nā. In a shot displaying the marginal position of the disabled orphan by framing him with tearful eyes facing his burned house, the boy refers to Ra'nā as a kind woman who gives him food. Holding Ra'nā's new-born baby, her father, then, insists that 'she does not smile at any man', and her younger brother-in-law, Esmāeil, shouts, 'she does not talk to anyone'. The actual encounter between the two in the village charcoal pit is, then, interrupted by Jeirān's firm 'Leave her alone!' and her assertion that Ra'nā's discovery of the sickle was just because sometimes she walks along the beach in memory of her husband who was grabbed by the sea. The camera, then, frames a close-up of Ra'nā's indirect, defiant gaze, which evolved later to form Nāei's direct gaze at the camera in *Bashu*.[27]

Realistically, Ra'nā's position suggests how the lives of widows may be distorted by false conceptions of honouring the husband's memory or people's superstitious belief about their ominousness. Nevertheless, the villagers' commemoration of Āshub as their best fisher and their insistence on Ra'nā's undying love for him implies her function as a living memorial to the myth of Āshub as a sacrificial hero. She is, thus, on a marginalizing pedestal where she is venerated as an inaccessible object of desire in the cult of a dead hero. At an archetypal level, however, her calm strength and the insistence of others on speaking for her make her a silent goddess like the mother in *The Journey*. Here, however, in the absence of the husband, his relatives act as her priests, and the setting associates her with nature and the seasons.

In any case, Ra'nā's ability to notice the sickle and its sign signifies that she has an outsider's vision and can see things that others neglect. Beyzaie, thus, establishes a triangle in which the boy is marginalized by receiving no attention, Ra'nā by receiving too much attention and Āyat by remaining unwanted despite his good qualities. Their link is also seen in that, during Āyat's search for Ra'nā, the only person who does not try to stop him from meeting her is the boy. This link builds on other cases of silent women and orphan boys in Beyzaie's films to augment the implications of Ra'nā's later revolt against control and exclusion.

When Āyat finally finds Ra'nā alone and challenges her for 'her animosity' by stating that he found similar sickles in the market, Ra'nā's words and tone reveal that this defying goddess is a sympathetic seer, and that the elders manipulated her finding to interrogate Āyat. She had noticed an unusual sign on the sickle and assumed it might help Āyat recall his past. Using a quick succession of shots, Beyzaie shows that no one knows the 'sign', 'shape', 'word', or 'name' carved on the sickle. He, then, concludes the search with a nightmarish shot of Jeirān ominously declaring 'it is alarming like a mysterious code' while working on her spinning wheel like a mythical author of fate. People advise Āyat to ditch the sickle which he does by burying it in the forest. The sickle's association with fertility and death, thus, creates an archetypal link between Āyat, as a reincarnated dying god and Ra'nā as an earth goddess. Since natural fertility requires male and female agents of love, Beyzaie highlights Raʿnāʾs interest in Āyat's curiosity and energy by framing her furtive glances through her windows and Āyat's fascination with Raʿnāʾs mysterious charm, perceptiveness and strength which, as he states, has made 'everyone in the village fall in love with her, even women' (28'.30"29').

Beyzaie depicts Raʿnāʾs isolation in a house that echoes Ātefeh's conditions in *Downpour*: she also lives with an old parent and a child. Āyat is also like Hekmati as with love in the air, he also begins to like the village, and, with some assurance from Qadam Kheir, he decides that he may be useful for the village. Qadam Kheir, whose name suggests his positive social role, invites him to help with the construction of a bridge. Like all cultures, however, the village has a combination of inclusive and exclusive elements which, according to Beyzaie, are so distinctly in conflict in Iranian culture that they seem to have come from two different origins and find their manifestations in the dominant discourses that take turn to control life in Iran.[28] Thus, Zakaria and Esmāeil, who suspect Āyat and Raʿnāʾs mutual attraction, act as agents of exclusion and toxic masculinity and use the chief's power to require Āyat to leave. This leads to the third circular gathering prior to which the epic southern (Bushehri) music of *sanj* and *damām* (cymbal and drum) suggests that Āyat is to challenge the village. In the gathering Āyat is given food for a week and advised to leave but Nazar also says that if he finds a wife, he may become one of them. In these gatherings, the people representing Āyat sit or stand behind him and the claimants sit behind Nazar. Thus, here Qadam Kheir, who is initially behind Āyat, moves to Nazar's side after hearing his arguments. The disabled boy, however, is always behind Āyat. While confirming the triangle of the marginalized specified before, this is also because he hopes that Āyat and Raʿnā may replace his lost parents.

Finding a wife proves tough as people consider him odd. As expected, Āyat rebels against this marginalization and although he is set to leave, the people's ridicule urges him to stay and find a wife. His rebellion first appears in iconoclastic actions. He breaks the graveyard candles and effigies, which signify the villagers' obsession with their past, ancestors and inherited culture, the foundations of their exclusionist 'us' which blinds them to his qualities. Exhausted with this breaking, he, then, sits in a rice paddy and fervently strikes the mud with his stick. This muddies his face and turns him into the black-face actor of comic rituals, which, according to Beyzaie, may reflect the evils of slavery in ninth-century Iran and afterwards but empowers the black man by infusing the motifs of rejuvenation and fertility into his depiction.[29] The marginalized loner, thus, becomes like Siyāvush, not only due to his being a migrant but also because he echoes the motifs of the dying god of fertility and rebirth, a blessing, who, like the dark fertile land, replaces the infertile snow-covered land of winter, or the old inflexible culture, embodied in the white-haired Haji of Nowruz comic rituals. In this context, the strikes of his stick, a phallic symbol, imply his virility and the act of ploughing, and his crushing of the bull-headed scarecrow make him a Mithraic hero.

This ritualized spell of madness, then, ends with an encounter with Raʿnā:

Āyat: No one wants me. Do you understand? I am a stranger.
Raʿnā: [She does not recognize him in his black face.] Who are you?
Āyat: Don't you know me? I'm the one who suffers bad luck whenever he sees you.

Ra'nā: What does it have to do with me? What have I got to do with other's bad luck?
Āyat: Oy! You don't need to be afraid of me.
Ra'nā: Who said I was afraid of you. I don't even know you.
Āyat: I'll now make sure you recognize me. [He jumps into the river.]
  [Gently] It's me. You see? Now you know me.
Ra'nā: [Flirting.] Yes. You may not know it yourself, but you are crazy. (35'-37')

The relationship between the two suggests the link between proving one's masculine worth to achieve recognition as the ultimate desire and Ra'nā as the *objet petit a*, the apparent object of the quest for recognition.[30] At the archetypal level, however, she is the earth goddess whose approval is the ultimate desire of the sacrificial agent of fertility (Figure 6.2).

Figure 6.2 Screenshots from *Stranger and the Fog*. Minutes 16'.50"–37'.05"

Religious and social mores, a goddess's dream of emancipation

Significantly, the motifs linking Ra'nā to nature are not of the patriarchal type that turns women into embodiments of nature, an ideal or a nation that a questing man is to confront or win. If anything, she is an archetypal figure or a nation that evolves to speak for herself. Moreover, while the motifs imply that she is stronger than everyone around her, the heroine remains solidly realistic as an individual with sociopolitical agency. She is not the supple nature that is to be controlled and cultivated as a piece of land through a patriarchal training that tames her to follow orders and yield crops, but a nature that has agency and is to be loved, served and obeyed if a man is to become a real agent of prosperity. The idea of true masculinity being not in conquering and controlling but in loving and serving children and hardworking women appears in Beyzaie's oeuvre with motifs that echo the more recent environmentalist and feminist celebrations of nature in which mankind is depicted as part of nature rather than a separate rational subject aspiring to conquer nature.[31]

Beyzaie's trilogy, indeed, subverts the patriarchal association of women with the passive nature because echoing Spandārmaz's act of helping Ārash and Manuchehr to save the land from the demon of draught, Afrāsiyāb, she is an active participant in changing human life.[32] Beginning with Ra'nā's revolt against the dogmas of honour, this continues in Tārā and Nāei, who embody the splendour of nature but display growing levels of assertion in words and deeds that suggest their emotionally charged and inclusive form of rationality.[33] Thus, besides its feminist implications, this approach reformulates Iranian pantheist ideas to extract their modern motifs and suggest they have been more egalitarian in their conception of gender, class, ethnicity and nature than the obsessively patriarchal religions that replaced them.[34]

From this point onwards, the film engages with several cleansing, initiation and marriage rituals which reinforce the idea of the sacred marriage. During a ritual of cleansing in which men are washing their rugs in a scene echoing Beyzaie's description of Ardahāl rug washing ritual,[35] Āyat tells others that he wants to stay and marry Ra'nā. The camera records the impact of the news on everyone, particularly Zakaria, Esmāeil and Jeirān. Ra'nā's reaction, however, signifies despair. She shelters in her house, her space of solitude and power, and starts shaking her baby's cradle while contemplating the situation. Her door and her soot-covered window that opens to the village indicate how the village blocks her desire, but the mirror and the window that opens to the sea reflect the hope of change. As she is looking at herself in the mirror next to the open window, the soundtrack and the camera capture the call and the image of a flying seagull in her mind. Thus, like the scene of Ātefeh's ruminations in Hekmati's room, the bird imagery and the play of light and darkness signify her eagerness to liberate her desire from the dark spaces of her house and her unconscious mind.

The film, then, shows children chasing Ra'nā's father in a carnival procession. Running around with an emblem like a deranged witch doctor or the village fool, he announces that his daughter has finally smiled after a year. The caring rogue, the bitter clown or the wise fool are among the regular characters in works that tap into the grotesque resources of life and carnival. At one level, this is because a transgressive caring rogue is like an intellectual artist who questions or shows the underbelly of dominant discourses, but it is also the case that the irresolvable irony of their being, as people whose positive qualities do not originate in a hypocritical desire for higher ranks, generates a tension that subverts the dictates of social hierarchies. Thus, from Shakespeare's fools and jesters who display intellectual qualities and puncture the arrogance of courtiers to Shane Black's *The Nice Guys* (2016), where two benevolent rogues prove the criminality of the top ranks of social hierarchy, such characters offer emancipatory stances that display the paradoxical nature of human morality.[36]

Iranian folktales and narratives of mystic cults have an abundance of such types. For instance, though reportedly pious in secret, the mystic *malāmatiyeh* (The people of blame), behaved as rogues to punish their ego and escape worldly positions. The reports of such controversial figures as Mansur-e Hallāj (858–922) and Bāyazid Bastāmi (804–874) in Attar's *Lives of Saints*, the picaresque narratives of trickster *ayyārs* and folk anecdotes of foolosophers of Mollā Naserddin's type also suggest the popularity of such types among Iranians.

As discussed in my chapter on *Downpour*, Beyzaie makes ample use of the qualities of such types as major or minor features in his protagonists' behaviours. In *Downpour* and *The Journey*, Hekmati's silly shenanigans or Tāle and Razi's pranks suggest the qualities of the clown and the rogue. Here, however, besides Āyat who displays the qualities of a rebel clown, Ra'nā's father, the village apothecary, functions not only as the gentle priest of the earth goddess, Ra'nā, but also as the foolosopher who makes wise speeches and yet may be stoned by children when he is excited. Like Philoctetes, his skills are vital for people, but he remains underappreciated. At the realistic level, this indicates that Ra'nā, who is dangling between being venerated due to her qualities and ostracized due to her 'ominousness', has an anti-social streak which makes her appreciate the worth of those that society may reject.

Like Beyzaie's other foolosophers, including Navvāb in *Downpour* or Ayuz in *Killing Rabid Dogs*, Ra'nā's father's benevolence and proverb-based wisdom make him a positive figure, but, like them, he also proves to be useless in the protagonists' encounter with oppression. The emphasis on his role as Ra'nā's babysitter shows their independence to highlight how despite their misogynistic protectionism, Āshub's family have had no role in helping Ra'nā and her baby. Taking turns to warn Āyat and Ra'nā, they talk about betrayal, bad omen, Āyat's inevitable leaving and the revenge of Āshub's spirit. Beyzaie's stylized depiction of the attitudes of Āshub's family uses the motifs of (1) patriarchal, divine authority (Zakaria's staff), (2) death (Esmāeil's scythe) and (3) supernatural suffering (the wind and waves that accompany Jeirān's warning), to highlight the challenge that Āyat and Ra'nā face. Repeating the myth of her brother's heroism, Jeirān warns that Āshub 'has merged with the sea', 'the sound of the sea is his voice', and he 'gazes at' Āyat and Ra'nā 'through the fog' and 'ruin your lives'. Zakaria also asserts, 'Āshub went to the sea for everyone; nobody can replace him'. Beyzaie even visualizes the idea of facing the elements by showing Āyat holding on to a tree to avoid being carried away by the wind and shouting, 'No, I won't leave'.

The dark interior of Ra'nā's house now becomes full of light and colours, and Ra'nā wears a forehead pendent signifying her joy and readiness for marriage. Her silent rebellion against being buried alive is now in full force. Thus, when Āyat states that everyone is against her remarriage, she states that she herself is in charge of her life. However, when Āyat construes her response as a confirmation of love, she teases him with 'I didn't say such a thing' as the camera registers in her eyes the signs of a smile hidden under her hijab. Ra'nā's encounter with her in-laws, then, forms one of the scenes that function at several interpretive levels.

> **Zakaria:** [Shouting in a righteous tone.]. For what? Is something missing in your life? Do you need anything? If it is for such things, I'm not yet dead; I'm alive.
> **Ra'nā:** [With her back to him.] Why do you want to help me?
> **Zakaria:** [Continuing his circular movement, he points to objects he is talking about until he stands before Ra'nā] Why? Everything reminding me of my brother is here. This cloak in which he was like a whale. This sword. His child who is dearer than everything to us. We must think of you and this baby.
> **Ra'nā:** Where were you until now?
> **Zakaria:** This is not a court, Ra'nā.
> **Esmāeil:** It's not been long since the sea took your husband. How can you forget him? If you have another man, it is like killing him again.
> **Ra'nā:** I didn't kill him.
> **Zakaria:** He died for all of us. Now that he's dead, we must think about him.
> **Ra'nā:** You should have thought about him when he was alive.
> **Zakaria:** You're judging us as if in a court.
> **Ra'nā:** He hated all of you. He disappeared, died to get rid of you.
> [They are all shocked.]
> **Esmāeil:** [Walking angrily] Ra'nā !!
> **Jeirān:** [Moved by Ra'nā's statement.] Stop torturing her.
> **Zakaria:** You accepted to be with him in everything. You accepted.
> **Ra'nā:** I didn't agree to being sacrificed. You sacrificed him, and now it is my turn. I won't let it happen.
> **Zakaria:** You reply to whatever we say.
> **Jeirān:** [Firmly] Let her be.
> **Zakaria:** What did you say?
> **Jeirān:** Why do you sell a living person to a dead one?
> **Zakaria:** [Pushing her aside.] Be quiet, woman.
> **Jeirān:** [Rising. No, not this time. You wasted my life, isn't that enough? I got old. My hair turned white because of your wrong sense of honour. I rotted. [She bears her chest.] See! But she is young. [Bearing the back of Ra'nā's right shoulder.] See! She is alive. Still alive! Don't listen to them, Ra'nā! Do what you want. Nobody knows your need, except you! Nobody knows what

it means to live alone and raise a child alone. [She puts her head on Ra'nā's lap and cries. The camera captures a still closeup of Ra'nā's determined gaze]. (40′–43′.20″)

During the scene, the camera captures a shadowy presence behind the windows. This is probably Ra'nā's father, but Beyzaie uses such shadows to suggest uncanny presences. This idea is also reinforced by Zakaria's protestations when noticing the onset of the storm and the shadow behind the window: 'The time is out of joint. People have gone mad.' His implicit threat to kill Āyat is then followed by Jeirān's warning that Āyat 'will not be an easy prey'.

The sequence shows how empathy may or must lead to unlikely solidarity between women and makes an emancipatory declaration against the obsessive protectionism of toxic masculinity and its religious codification in Esmāeil's words. Ra'nā's words also indicate how heroes are victims of expectations and condemnations that reduce people to heroes and villains. Zakaria's final words, however, stress Beyzaie's symbolic use of nature imagery, which can be read in light of Northrop Fry's idea that the cycle of quest, fulfilment and frustration in literary genres reflects the cycle of seasons.[37] This is echoed in Ra'nā's stylized acting as she walks with no cover into one of the film's four scenes of rain and exposes her hair, face, chest and hands to the rain as if elevating in a ritual of emancipatory cleansing. Thus, with the coming of spring, the earth goddess is to be reborn into her glory (Figure 6.3).

Figure 6.3 Screenshots from *Stranger and the Fog*. Minutes 38′.50″–44′.50″

Wedding in the Forest, carnival laughter, initiation rites and the invasion of the past

Qadam Kheir's remarks to Āyat about passing tests so that he can be accepted by people opens the path for several initiation and fertility rituals leading to a sacred marriage. The first is a fertility dance, which echoes Manuchehr Sotudeh's account of a spring ritual in Bābudeh near Chālus in March 1944. Known as *Arusi dar Jangal* (Wedding in the Forest), the ritual, which is a diluted form of the ancient *Arus-e Bāo* (Bāo Bride), involves two unkempt bearded men dressed in primitive animal skin fighting over a colourfully dressed woman. With the audience settling after an initial *dohol* and *sorna* playing, the three begin dancing, and soon the young man, who has been curbing his desire for the woman, touches her and kisses his own hand. This infuriates the other man and leads to a fighting dance with sticks and wooden swords, in which the young man kills the old man and takes the joyful bride along.[38]

Beyzaie's rendition of the dance echoes Sotudeh's photo and report. However, he adds details from his own observations of the ritual in Tālesh and Marzanābād (near Chālus) and a similar dance in Arāk in the 1960s to construct his imagined original form in which he uses ritual music and a female dancer, rather than a dressed-up man, as the bride.[39] The bride's dance moves, such as comically pretending to hit herself on the head, suggest her discontent with her marriage and the fight. Beyzaie also enhances the festival aspects by turning the village children into partaking viewers, who rhythmically strike their sticks like clapping along the ploughing and fight dance. He also uses white goat skin for the husband's mask and brown wool for the lover's mask to suggest an infertile old man (winter) being replaced by a young virile lover (spring). The camera focuses as much on the dance as on the viewers' reactions, particularly Āyat, Zakaria and Esmāeil's. Ra'nā's red scarf, smiles and glances also indicate her similarity to the bride in the dance. Thus, while depicting a ritual which survived at least until the 1970s, Beyzaie foreshadows the conflict between Āyat and Āshub. In its carnival motifs, the dance also echoes the school hall scene in *Downpour* as it violates social norms to celebrate youthful work and love over status and age. Thus, the new agent of fertility replaces the old one, and the bride, nature, rejoices in her new source of rejuvenation.

Despite this successful rendition, the archetypal aspects of the dance continued to preoccupy Beyzaie. A few years after his first observation of the dance in 1964, Beyzaie who had remained curious about the presence of a second female character dancing by herself in a corner checked his observations with Sotudeh who also confirmed the presence of another dancer. Both had originally dismissed it as incidental, but Beyzaie has recently argued that the dance is a remnant of a ritual echoing the agricultural origins of the legend of Fereydun (agent of fertility) fighting against Zahhāk (demon of draught) to release Shahrnāz (Spandārmaz/earth goddess) and Arnavāz (Ānāhitā/water goddess) from incarceration.[40]

Āyat's initiation trials include a stick fight, a tug of war and a drinking competition, in all of which he beats a tougher man by using tricks proving the triumph of brain over brawn. His final victory, however, is marred by a Kafkaesque encounter in which five men beat a reeling Āyat after his drinking bout. Thus, the awaited encounter with the unknown finally happens:

> **Voice 1:** You are laughing Āyat! As if you have forgotten everything!
> **Voice 2:** As if you no longer expect us.
> **Āyat:** Who are you?
> [The first person laughs, and they attack the inebriated Āyat with their sticks. Āyat starts shouting in pain. When the tavern's door opens, they vanish.] (51′.48″–52′.40″)

This is the first of several eerie encounters occurring after this point. Thus, as Āyat is achieving recognition, belonging and love, the unknown or his unknowable past begins to catch up with him. He rushes to the forest to dig out the sickle, but it has vanished. Initially, he assumes Zakaria and Esmāeil have taken the sickle and hired people to beat him. This is likely as when in Ra'nā's house Zakaria threatens to kill Āyat, Esmāeil talks about the sickle, but the incursions of the unknown are so intense that Āyat soon discards his suspicions.

Back in the tavern, as Āyat speaks about someone chasing him like his shadow, the camera captures a shadow in the window behind him, which initially seems to be Āyat's but passes as he is standing. Thus, as in *So Dies Akbar the Hero* or *Downpour*, Beyzaie suggests the idea of an unknown force stalking to stifle his hero's dreams. In *Stranger*, these uncanny beings are initially seen only by him, as if they are manifestations of his Jungian shadow, the totality of suppressed tendencies, emotions and experiences behind the individual's mask. This makes sense because 'the less' the shadow 'is embodied in the individual's conscious life, the blacker and denser it is' as every issue if conscious may be corrected and modified by being 'constantly in contact with other interests'. However, 'if it is repressed and isolated from consciousness, it never gets corrected and is liable to burst forth suddenly in a moment of unawareness'. Thus, it forms an ever-present 'unconscious snag, thwarting our most well-meant intentions'.[41] With Āyat's oblivion suppressing the shadows of his past, it is inevitable that they emerge as revengeful demonic projections that darken his life and the lives of his loved ones. As in *So Dies Akbar the Hero*, therefore, the eery coming and going of black-wearing doubles, Āyat's Mr Hydes, suggest that Āyat's dreams of belonging are threatened by nightmarish forms of 'condensation, displacement and secondary revision'[42] (Figure 6.4).

At one level, therefore, like Akbar's shadow, but with multiple delegates, representing his senses and the religions influencing the superegos of Iranians (Zoroastrianism, Judaism, Christianity, Islam and Bahaism), Āyat's shadows also echo his self-resentment for being unwanted and not knowing his place in the world. They, thus, destabilize his potential for happiness and finally emerge as invaders. Thus, as all human beings, his senses betray him and make him unable to be content with life, and the obsession with the afterlife embedded in these religions does not let him live a life of fertility and happiness. This means that though his life force urges him to live, defeat his enemies, help others, work and create to be able to gain recognition, love, breed and enjoy life, the inscrutable forces of his superego subvert his virile desire for life and activate his death wish by attacking him as five invaders.

Figure 6.4 Screenshots from *Stranger and the Fog*. Minutes 45′.00″–55′.30″

The use of the uncanny or the inexplicable in Beyzaie's works echoes some of the stylistic qualities of magic realism, but, as in Kafka's case,[43] his visions are rooted in his experience as a person who suffered marginalization and had regular nightmares of being unjustifiably punished. Its stylistic features also echo his knowledge of folktales and immersion in *One Thousand and One Night*. His focus, therefore, is more on depicting his characters' historical and existential questions about who they are and why they or the people around them do things in the way they do. In other words, such elements construct an emancipatory aesthetics that challenges religious or cultural certainties through defamiliarization. Thus, Āyat's terror is primarily there to question religious or social certainties. However, it also recreates for the spectator the same feeling of confusion that shake the essence of life for marginalized people whose normal life and sense of belonging are undermined by elements that are beyond their control, including, for instance, their birthplace, race, physical appearance, gender or parents' beliefs. This ritualized transgressive aesthetics fulfils the ultimate kind of politics in literature, which, in Rancière's terms, is to 'redistribute the sensible', making visible and audible the presences and voices that have remained hidden and suppressed in society.

From persecution to the sacred union and the call of the unknown

With fear overwhelming the people, he now faces new pressures to leave. Āyat, however, is as adamant to stay as Ra'nā is to marry him. She draws a line over the marks of the weeks she has spent without Āshub and breaks the bowl in which she gave food to the poor for the salvation of his soul. A sequence, then, depicts Āyat's conflicts with Esmāeil, Zakaria and their cohort who harass, torture and cage him to make him leave. Ra'nā formally announces her choice to urge the villagers to accept him, but they accuse him of being a thief. Finally, in scenes that are ritualized by fog, stylized action, symbolic objects and an incantatory noise in the soundtrack signifying the impacts of people's devastating remarks and judgements on the mind of the marginalized, even the wise Nazar and the generous Qadam Kheir change their minds and declare that they 'cannot support a stranger at the expense of their lifelong relatives' (57'–58'). Jeirān's ambivalent attitudes towards Ra'nā also show the pull of the mutually exclusive sides of her character with the obedient sister and serf in her condemning Ra'nā's choice and the rebellious widow and citizen sympathizing with her.

While the motifs in the torture scenes mark Āyat as a sacrificial figure, the sequence in which he escapes challenges the acceptance of suffering as a source of purification. Āyat, thus, escapes and uses an opportunity to ask Ra'nā to elope with him. Ra'nā, however, urges him to abduct her. This leads to a reformulation of the ritual of 'kidnapping the bride'. Though far less widespread in Iran than Central Asia and the Caucasus, this ritual was practised in some of Iran's northern provinces, particularly among the Turkmans and the people who lived near them even until the 1950s, and may, nowadays, be seen as an amusing routine in weddings. The remnants of such mating rituals can also be seen in seasonal competitions.[44] Beyzaie uses the subject to also highlight Āyat's sensitivity to ridicule and Ra'nā's control over her choice which enables her to test or tease Āyat. In any case, the reformulation occurs as Āyat, who is being chased by Esmāeil and Zakaria, sneaks into Ra'nā's house in darkness. The idea of abducting is, thus, transformed into Āyat's stealthy entrance into her space. Thus, once more, Āyat uses his mind instead of his muscles, but, more important, the act turns the abductor into an asylum seeker in the house of his beloved, and the abductee who has absolute power over the abductor's life becomes a saviour who organizes their sacred union.

Thus, at the archetypal level, Ra'nā, the earth goddess initiates her fertilization by sheltering a supplicant of high acumen and energy despite the prohibitions of her spiritual (her father) and military (her brothers-in-law) protectors. Beyzaie even reinforces the motifs of the sacred marriage by allowing her father, her high priest, to become aware of and accept what has happened and by using a religiously charged scene in which Ra'nā becomes the performer and the enforcer of their marriage vows. Thus, the silent goddess now speaks out to utter the performative statement of 'I pronounce us husband and wife' and authorize her union with the agent of fertility. The marriage is also sacredly sealed not only by a vow on the book but also with the music of Ra'nā's father pipe-playing a tune of longing and calm content.

The sequence is significant in how it depicts love, desire and sex while empowering women. As Dabashi states, if Āyat fights against his doubts and later faces 'the invading [. . .] apparitions of' his 'fear of the Unknown', Ra'nā and Jeirān confront the 'ghosts that haunt the village in the form of traditions, habits, and manners'.[45] Thus, while her brothers-in-law are guarding her doors to force her to adhere to their fake sense of honour, Ra'nā discards the burden of these beliefs and defies the taboos that require her to commit to a dead past by sheltering Āyat in her house. The scene implies sex in ways that confront the cliched images of mainstream Iranian films of the 1970s, which depicted women as naïve or rude objects of sex, desire or love for heroic young men and used 'provocative scenes [. . .] with or without narrative justification'.[46] It is far from seduction scenes that appealed to the voyeuristic gaze of sexually deprived men and sex episodes between loose women and young heroes in their path to conquest. Here sex is poetically suggested rather than depicted and is essential in the film's reflection of male and female love and zeal for fulfilment in life. Prior to the scene, Ra'nā's healthy desire is reflected in shots that are juxtaposed with scenes of Āyat's escape. These shots show her combing her hair in the mirror, trying her bridal head ornaments, taking care of her baby, watching her father saying his prayer and worrying about Āyat when she hears the uproar outside. As Shahram Jafarinezhad states, here and elsewhere in Beyzaie's world, 'people appear in mirrors to reflect their desire for joy, beauty and life'.[47] Such shots, of course, are not limited to mirrors as Beyzaie's mirror shots are mixed with close-ups in which women's mentalities are reflected in their gazes, facial features, moves and the objects they handle. Thus, rather than displaying her beauty, Ra'nā's close-ups pull the viewers into a space of empathy where they identify with her desire for happiness to an extent that the voyeuristic gaze becomes irrelevant. The implied sex is, thus, so emotionally charged that their transgression becomes a spiritual defiance of dogmatic conventions. The sequence is also satirically amusing due to the irony of having the embodiments of exclusionist toxic masculinity, Zakaria and Esmāeil, who are to keep Āyat away from Ra'nā, order her to shut her doors and windows when Āyat is actually inside. Beyzaie's irony even has Zakaria advise Ra'nā's father to replace their old dog with a young Saluki and has the brothers and Qadam Kheir engage in a noisy game of *seh qāp* (a gambling game played with sheep knucklebones by tough guys) in a crouching position that implies they are like noisy dogs. Thus, the shrewd divinities of earth and fertility turn the agents of exclusion into guardian dogs of their marriage bed. Then, as Āyat and Ra'nā lie next to each other, with the holy book and Āshub's sword between them signifying his impact on Ra'nā's mind, the second scene of rain celebrates their union while drenching the dogmatic guards.

To clarify the scene's emancipatory aesthetics, its 'redistribution of the sensible', one must inspect it with reference to depictions of female body in Iran's poetic, visual and performing arts after Islam. As Ziba Mir-Hosseini argues, 'Love has always been the main theme in Persian poetry', but since Persian does not have grammatical gender and the body parts that indicate gender are rarely referred to, 'it is seldom clear whether the writer is talking about divine or earthly love', or 'the "beloved" is male or female'. Such an ambiguity, however, 'cannot be maintained in the performative and the visual arts, where both the language and the form demand greater transparency [. . .] in the depiction of women and love'. Mir-Hosseini, then, refers to using male actors for female roles in ta'ziyeh and the early Qajar paintings in which the ambiguity of poetry was reflected in figures that Afsaneh Najmabadi calls 'neuter',[48] and compares such practices with the visual culture that evolved in paintings from the mid-1800s in which the gender distinction moved towards naturalistic depictions.

From a literary perspective, this point is built on the fact that Persian lyricists used ambiguity to augment the applicability of poetic desire without ruining the emotional impact of their poems, and that with the appearance of secular theatre, music and then cinema the presence of visible bodies in the public space required clarity. Though Mir-Hosseini's point has its merits, it is reductive in that she uses the valid example of classical lyric poetry in a context which must be more cognizant of how love and sex are depicted in Persian romances and epics. This is because cinema and theatre are closer to romance and epic poetry than lyric poetry, and whereas lyric poetry can be just about love in the singular, which can be divine, earthly and hetero- or homosexual, love in romance as a genre originating in the myths of fertility and continuity and in epic as one arising from the myths of order and continuity is always earthly and heterosexual. This can be seen in Ferdowsi's *Shahnameh*, Nezami's *Khamseh*, Gorgani's *Veis and Rāmin*, Arrajāni's *Samak-e Ayyār*, the two *Dārābnāmeh* books and many others in which, though patriarchal values are upheld, female agency, bravery, beauty, desire and body parts are cherished, and love between male heroes and militant and non-militant heroines is celebrated with references to sex. Thus, the departure of modern performing and visual arts from indigenous forms was not due to lack of literary depictions of earthly heterosexual love but because such narratives were accessed at less public and visual levels mostly through narration and reading or occasional paintings hidden in books.

Beyzaie extracts the naturalness of romantic and sexual desire in such narratives, increases their gender equality potential, and poeticizes and mythologizes them with motifs borrowed from the lyric tradition of elitist Persian poetry. This reframing also occurs at an archetypal level because according to Biruni and Gardizi, the festival of Spandārmaz (19 or 25 February), which was to celebrate women and earth involved a ceremony called *mardgirān* (getting a man) or *mozhdgiran* (gift receiving) in which women received gifts from men and were entitled to choose their espouse.[49] Ra'na is, thus, the goddess Spandārmaz choosing her own husband despite everyone else. This brings the pre-moment of mythical history into visual history in a way that mythologizes the present and historicizes the past to suggest that modernity, at one level, is the rebirth of the healthy relationships that have been suppressed or distorted due to dogmatic religious and social relations. The scene, thus, suggests how his emancipatory aesthetics engages in a quest for creating an intellectually and physically fertile modern Iranian identity by means of mythical, ritual and literary motifs (Figure 6.5).

Figure 6.5 Screenshots from *Stranger and the Fog*. Minutes 56′.40″–75′.30″

Āyat's encounter with Zakaria and Esmāeil the following morning is given a twist that ridicules superficial religiosity. As Esmāeil is reciting the call for prayer in which the words 'God is great' is repeated, Āyat emerges from the house in Āshub's cloak shocking them. God or nature may be great but not in the way exclusionists assume. Now instead of killing Āyat, they must formalize their marriage. Beyzaie, then, combines motifs depicting Āyat as a temporary king with those of wedding rituals from Iran's north and south in a way that displays their emphasis on public joy and rites and objects linked to resolution (the wedding attire and belt ritual), fending evil eyes (*āviz-e esfand* [wild rue pendants]) and joy (music, mirrors and good-luck trinkets). Ra'nā's emotional worries are also displayed as the camera ritualizes the departure of her father from her house into fog through her window along the villagers' rhythmic clapping as Ra'nā and Āyat are dressed in red and white for the wedding. The use of good-luck charms, mirrors, prayer pendants and extradiegetic southern and diegetic northern music further ritualizes the action and stresses the idea of a sacred marriage.

Beyzaie closes this dreamlike sequence of happiness with a nightmarish intrusion of the unknown followed by Ra'nā's concern about Āyat's restlessness. The disabled boy, whose happiness about the marriage is emphasized, runs in to state that two strangers are looking for Āyat near his boat. Āyat finds no one, but he remains near his boat gazing at the sea. Jeirān, then, ominously comments on Āyat's obsession with the boat, and Ra'nā removes her head ornament as her windowpanes reflect a stylized image of a cloudy sunset. This is, then, trailed by a dialogue in which Āyat says the whole thing may have been another prank played on him. The emphasis on the pull of the unknown amid the rituals of joy reinforces the film's discourse about how human beings' dangling between two unknowns and their awareness of death may reinforce or disrupt their constructive attachment to life (Figure 6.5).

The nightmares of the unknown and the dreams of fulfilment

A new series of uncanny events then follow with the arrival of a wolf in the village the same night. During the hunt for the wolf which realistically echoes the narratives of wolf, lion or boar-hunting expeditions in agricultural myths, Āyat is lost and encounters two shadowy strangers in the foggy forest in a Kafkaesque scene reminiscent of Iranian mystic tales, Macbeth's encounter with the three witches, or Block's encounter with death in Bergman's *The Seventh Seal*. After they stand up and talk in coordination like ghosts, their voices reveal them to be the two people who talked when beating Āyat after the tavern scene.

> **Voice 1:** [Sarcastic] Congratulation for your wedding, Āyat!
> **Voice 2:** Come with us. A boat is waiting for you on the coast. Come with us.
> **Āyat:** Where?
> **Voice 1:** You were summoned but didn't show up. Don't you remember?

Āyat: Who has summoned me?
Voice 1: Don't pretend you don't know! His signs are everywhere.
Āyat: On the sickle?
Voice 1: [Laughing.] He has a lot of land, a lot of trees, a lot of rivers and coasts. The hills are his, the meadows are his, the four seasons are his and the afternoon's nap.
Āyat: What have I done?
Voice 2: Think! Think! You yourself should know.
Āyat: No, I don't remember. I don't know.
Voice 1: We also don't know. We have received orders.
Voice 2: No order is given without a wise reason. If they order, they have a reason.
Voice 1: Mistake! No, it is you who must find the reason. Come!
Āyat: No, I won't. [Brining up his sword.] I want to live.
Voice 1: We'll take this message. [They start walking away.]
Āyat: Do you see that hut? I am no longer alone. A child and a woman are waiting for me in that house.
Voice 1: Your reasons are irrelevant to us. We only convey the message.
   [They walk away.]
Āyat: Listen! Tell the owner of the sign –
[Sound of laughter. They have disappeared in the fog.] (78′.40″–80′.50″)

The idea of being summoned for an unknown reason by an unknown being who possesses everything suggests an existential reading that highlights human status as a being in time. The words used for describing this being is scriptural, but Āyat's position also reminds the viewer of Khayyam's poems about the absurdity of existence: 'The firmaments did not benefit from my arrival**And my departure did not increase its splendour and eminence// And my two ears never heard from anyone**Why I arrived and why I departed.'[50] As in Kafka's *The Trial* or *The Castle*, however, while, at one level, the film may suggest the craving and the failure of the individual to understand God or the meaning of life, at another, it may be associated with a religious or judicial system in which individuals are guilty unless the opposite is proven, a system that uses physical and mental torture along with the drill of 'you must remember and confess' to generate guilt complex and crush the individual or extract information about an unknown guilt or sin. In other words, what happens to Āyat reflects the status of human beings under mutually reinforcing alliance of political systems and religions in which the absolute power of God and the ruler echo each other, and the judicial system is like the absurd system of sin and punishment embedded in the cosmology of such religions.

The forest continues to summon threatening presences depicted with realistic and uncanny motifs with psychological, existential and archetypal connotations. Right after the departure of the two shadowy figures, an imposing man, covered in wool like the man in the ritual of wedding in the forest, appears and accuses Āyat of spying on him. Pressing his scythe-like axe on Āyat's shoulder, he says he must kill Āyat as he has 'seen something that he was not supposed to'. Realistically, this refers to his box of stolen gems that he had come to recover, but the sequence of the two encounters gives an uncanny quality to his words. Nonetheless, when the man realizes that Āyat does not know him, he asks him to act as his messenger and tell Ra'nā to meet him near the old bridge. The dialogue, thus, uses dramatic irony to imply that he is Ra'nā's husband. Furious at the man's assertions that Ra'nā would definitely want him, Āyat states that he has just married Ra'nā. The man attacks Āyat, but Āyat's agility enables him to dodge and mortally injure his stronger opponent who falls into the river.

The encounter is a point of anagnorisis that changes the imports of earlier events. It clarifies that fed up with playing the providing hero and risking his life by going farther into the sea, Āshub feigned his own death and now intends to take Ra'nā away. From a psychological perspective, however, if one takes the whole film as a nightmare, the encounters in the forest as a space of the unconscious, suggests Āyat's desire to destroy the myth of the man whose memory has prevented him from having Ra'nā's heart to himself. Thus, he wishes to destroy Āshub's memory by proving he has been a coward. At an archetypal level, the same conflict also signifies that the villagers' myth of Āshub as a sacrificial hero has been a lie and that Āyat's arrival as an agent of fertility has occurred because the villagers' hero or dying god failed to fulfil the ritual death, and Āyat's role is to end Āshub's life to complete the cycle.

Having slayed his so-far-invisible rival in the battle for recognition, Āyat finds the other villagers who are torturing the captured wolf. The idea of villagers always acting together and inflicting sadomasochistic punishment on the animal suggests a form of 'we' formed out of fear rather than collaborating citizenship. This defines them not only against strangers and outcasts but also against their own heroes who are expected to act individually. This idea, which is properly established later in the sequence of the battle with the five intruders, echoes Kurosawa's discourse in *Seven Samurais* in which the samurais learn about the pressures that their cast has been imposing on the villagers and become real heroes, and the villagers learn to become citizens and act instead of just waiting for saviours to act on their behalf.

In any case, Āyat, who originally suspects Ra'nā due to the man's words about Ra'nā's love for him, realizes the truth when the man's body is washed ashore, and he finds that the man was Āshub. The film, then, registers the villagers' mourning rituals. This emphasis on rituals highlights how human life is shaped by secular and religious rituals inculcated in the mind before one is capable of thinking and how this inculcation determines the way one perceives actions, relations, events and objects or associates them with happiness and misery. Being aware of this, Beyzaie presents his emancipatory modes of seeing and doing by reframing rituals and the beliefs associated with them. For him, rituals and the myths that have evolved with them for mutual validation contain a path to the unconscious, and their templates reflect the impacts of exigencies of the time on both, those who believe in them and those who claim to have transcended them. Thus, he argues that every society must either find their potential senses and modernize them by reframing their progressive, egalitarian qualities or suffer the consequences of their superstitious obsessions and distortions on our daily lives.[51]

Sitting around a fire in a ceremony which echoes typical Ashura wakes without their religious sides, the villagers perform their grief through tearful wailing, chest-beating and stereotypic rhythmic movements accompanied by the pulsing sound of stick beating performed by men who sway like others while performing. Associating the marriage with the return of the corpse and interpreting both as signs of impending disaster, the villagers now ostracize Ra'nā and Āyat. Ra'nā's father's happiness for being allowed to join the mourning implies the intensity of this ostracization. His comments on having a good time and a good cry also emphasize how people use such rituals as judgement-free, carnival-like communal zones where they can release their stress and pent-up emotions through ritual mourning. Once more, the old man also plays the foolosopher by giving two contradictory pieces of advice. Both sound compassionate, but whereas the first is life-affirming and specifies that Āyat should ignore the villagers' ostracization as a temporary aberration, the second 'avoid attachments as it makes letting go hard' has religious overtones and implies that Āyat may have to leave.

Beyzaie's marking of mourning rituals as a space of catharsis and abreaction for communal healing automatically turns them into purification rituals and performances analogous to ancient Greek tragedies or European, Iranian and Indian passion plays. As Stanely Jackson states, all cultures have historically had 'ways of stimulating, intensifying, and, eventually, releasing emotions' and 'although often interwoven with other techniques such as suggestion, persuasion, confession, or elements of a mourning ritual, catharsis frequently can be detected in [. . .] healing practices'. Since the 1890s, with the rise of psychoanalytical approaches to healing, catharsis began to denote the recalling of disturbing memories in settings that led to emotional release, and 'abreaction' began to mean emotional release.[52] Thus, recalling traumatic memories in a conscious process that led to emotional discharge and integrated these memories into the patient's narratives of selfhood as moments of crises leading to redemption became essential in modern approaches to psychological healing.[53]

Thus, at one level, Beyzaie's use of narratives echoing the reports of individual and collective traumas in Iranian myths, literature and history through methods that highlight the experience of common people rather than the elite displays the impacts of such events on contemporary mentalities and practices by suggesting the way the traumatic baggage of such experiences continue to programme our minds. Thus, his ritualistic films – *The Journey*, his village trilogy, *Death of Yazdgerd*, *Maybe Some Other Time* and *Travellers* – function like rituals of purification and exorcism intended to purge the filmmaker's and his spectator's minds of such mentalities. It is in this context and due to his focus on the origins, transformations and consequences of exclusionist and oppressive mentalities and practices that he has managed to sublimate his own traumatic memories of marginalization to epistemic authority. He, thus, uses his experiments with rituals, legends and myths to hold a mirror to current practices.

The film then focuses on the outcasts. Unaware of Āshub's betrayal, Ra'nā bewails her fate before a fire in solitude with crying, stereotypic movements and incantatory sounds implying her feelings of loss and guilt. These motifs echo the communal mourning outside, but her ritual placing of a horn on her forehead, a symbol of phallus and virility, and her hysteric shaking and sweating as if trying to sever it from her forehead suggest an act of exorcism for failing to remain faithful to a virile agent of fertility. Her beating of Āyat's cloak also implies her feeling of guilt for remarrying when her husband was alive. Worried about her intense wailing, Āyat, who has been brooding outside, enters the house and confronts her with the account of his encounter with Āshub and adding that her 'beloved husband' was not a loving hero but a coward who left her to fend for herself and a baby and suffer the allegations of being ominous. Being an iconoclastic, Āyat adds that Āshub was a bandit who had probably killed many people to fill his box of pearls and coins. Ra'nā's rejection of Āyat's account and assertions about Āshub's spirit making them miserable show how the burden of centuries distorts perception. Āyat's emotional response is to tear the black dress from her body and make love to her to prove his love and cleanse her of Āshub's spirit. At realistic level, this means that they both transcend their guilt complex but must keep silent about what has happened. Thus, Āyat overcomes his feeling of guilt by enumerating the reasons for the fight, and Ra'nā by realizing that the guilt has been Āshub's not hers. For Āyat, the situation is, indeed, Oedipal because if one considers Ra'nā his *objet petite a*, the replacement for the unattainable mother, Āyat has inadvertently killed his father figure, an epitome of patriarchal heroism, and married his wife. However, knowing that he and Ra'nā have not done anything wrong, he engages in lovemaking as a last resort for rechannelling the pent-up emotions that have led to her hysteria. Thus, Beyzaie creates a situation in which viewers feel that acts of iconoclasm like Āyat's and Ra'nā's are essential for creating a better future as they entail breaking the outdated laws and constructs of our suppressive superegos. The sequence also means that Āyat's acumen and propensity to act bravely under duress, once more, saves the day and allows him to turn his nightmare into a dream. The theme of mutual saving in love, thus, fulfils a full circle: Ra'nā saves Āyat from rejection; Āyat saves Ra'nā from her past.

The implied sex scene marks lovemaking as an exorcizing ritual by placing the second scene of communal mourning between the two scenes that suggest the beginning and end of Āyat and Ra'nā's lovemaking. The mourning wake also becomes more like a purification ritual. As the corpse of the wolf is put on the fire, the villagers fall silent and engage in self-flagellation with chain as Nazar delivers a formal sermon about the ominous events. The juxtaposition of the scenes, thus, contrasts lovemaking with acts of burning and self-flagellation. Both purify, release pent-up emotions and achieve a catharsis of hysteria triggered by traumatic events and fear, but one works with mutually pleasing action and spiritually charged physical compassion in a process that is associated with fertility and the other with inflicting pain on oneself and burning the effigies or bodies of unwanted presences. Beyzaie further celebrates this love and its link with fertility and happiness by showing Ra'nā rise with a white underdress from her bed with a smiling face to gently rock her baby's cradle (Figure 6.6).

Figure 6.6 Screenshots from *Stranger and the Fog*. Minutes 78′.45″–84′.40″

Facing ostracization and the reconnaissance agent and contentment in love

Having overcome her guilt, she now takes measures to keep Āyat. While everyone is asleep, she digs a hole in the sand and buries the boat in it. The only person who appears towards the end to witness this is a silent Jeirān. Ra'nā's burying of the boat marks her agency and resolve to bury a false idea of heroism. She knows that either the boat, which stands for birth (cradle), death (coffin) and transcending human limits to face the unknown (like Hercules going to the underworld in Charon's boat), must be buried or it will reclaim her man. Thus, Beyzaie shows that true heroism is not achieved by feats of fighting, hunting and killing, or questing to tame the unknown but by building a better life for oneself and others by simple means, expanding the borders of belonging and improving the way humans see and do things.

The villagers, who remain attached to the myth of sacrificial Āshub now become like the automatons in *The Journey*, yet whereas in *The Journey*, the bee-like workers are trapped in mechanical work and illusions, the villagers are drowning in their obsession with the afterlife. Beyzaie implies Āyat and Ra'nā's emancipation by showing them with normal clothes going to work and being surprised by the villagers' robotic murmuring, walking and apathy. The boycotting attitudes of the women in the graveyard are also reflective of their obsession with the dead. This attitude continues even after the mourning period. In a typical Beyzaiean scene about the absurdity of people's exclusionist attitudes, Āyat joins a circle of villagers watching a cockfight, but the moment he arrives, they rise and go, leaving Āyat with a dying cock in the centre of an empty circle signifying the feelings of those who suffer such attitudes.

Āyat, who is ostracized because the villagers think his presence 'has disturbed the tranquillity of the village', now resorts to solitude, but while watching the sea on the coast, he is accosted by the disabled boy. Their dialogue creates a significant moment of human connection while reflecting Beyzaie's concern with a society's failure to care for the underprivileged.

Disabled Boy: At least, you have each other.
Āyat: Yea, you have no one. I know you are unhappy. Let's do something. What should I do to make you happy? [He summersaults.]
Disabled Boy: [He laughs.] I don't want anything.
Āyat: If I stay here, we'll be friends. Let's shake hands. What do you want from god?
Disabled Boy: I don't know. Just a shelter.
Āyat: Just that. So, let's build it together.
Disabled Boy: Will you really build me a shelter, Āyat?
Āyat: It's nothing; takes a day or two, we will do it before the rain season.
Disabled Boy: Promise, Āyat, will you build me the shelter?
Āyat: Yes, yes. We'll build it if they allow us.
Disabled Boy: They? Who, Āyat?
Āyat: [Looking and running around, agitated.] My boat is not there. (100′–101′.36″)

The pronoun 'they' here refers to both the villagers and the intrusive agents of the unknown. The villagers because of their crass, exclusionist attitudes and obsessions with the dead, and the intruders because of their power to disrupt life. As an individual with high emancipatory potential, Āyat, like Hekmati in *Downpour*, is concerned about the conditions of the outcasts and the poor while everyone else is concerned with dead heroes and superstitious practices. Indeed, Beyzaie demonstrates that the only thing that the villagers, like all religion-obsessed people, occasionally do for the poor is to feed them to buy salvation for the soul of their dead ones. The discourse on the conditions of the underprivileged now becomes central to the film as the boy's fate becomes as important to Āyat as his own or Ra'nā's happiness.

This positive attention, however, is disrupted by Āyat's guard against the unknown, reflected in his concern about the vanishing of the boat. Others insist that the boat has been lost due to the tides, but Āyat is worried that its disappearance means his harassers will return. Ra'nā's silence about the boat shows that she loves Āyat as much as Āyat loves her. Significantly, this expressive silence is highlighted by the cinematography which places Ra'nā with green, blue and white costumes at the centre of shots of natural beauty to associate her with nature while setting her apart from the villagers to reflect the similarity of the three. Thus, whereas the nature and the downtrodden are adamant to keep Āyat, the potential agent of fertility, modernity and emancipation, the villagers' obsessions with the afterlife as the ultimate unknown and Āyat's final decision to confront the unknown disrupts their plans.

The next sequence begins with the disabled boy, the marginalized seer, noticing the arrival of a boat when standing in his fish-like circle on the coast, which depicts him as a forgotten Juna in the belly of time. He warns others by a bell as the camera displays a market with plenty of mirrors, an old folk singer, a puppeteer whose presence comments on human lack of control over life and Ra'nā trying a new scarf before a full-length mirror that frames her happiness. The threat makes Nazar and a few other villagers show some sympathy. Nazar tells Āyat and Ra'nā to hide in the crowd and goes to talk to the man, but the tall stranger ignores everyone. Ra'nā and then Āyat stand before him, but he just walks towards the market. The plot marks him as a scouting agent, but Beyzaie's use of mirrors to trace his path in the market and his odd hat with its ladder-like top imply an otherworldly threat. He trades a fish with a mat, touches the sickles in the shop, walks back to his boat, ignores Āyat's attempt to question him and stands in his boat which moves away as if propelled by an invisible force.

The villagers insist that the man had just come to shop in their market and find Āyat's anxiety about his boat and the man weirder than the man's appearance. Āyat, however, insists that he never fantasizes and that he has been draining a wetland to build a house for the boy. In a dazzling shot of nature with Ra'nā at the centre and the third scene of rain setting the mood, Ra'nā feels the depth of Āyat's anxiety and finally tells him in a gathering that she has buried the boat to keep him. This revelation astonishes and charms Āyat. Elevated with the ultimate sign of Ra'nā's love, he promises to build the boy's house the following day. A stylized transition, here, has the folksinger sing a Turcoman song which continues extra-dietetically. Along Āyat's assurance to Ra'nā about the end of their troubles, Ra'nā's smile and tears of joy and the parallel shots of nature, the song implies a moment of fulfilment in their quest for happiness, but, as in *The Journey*, its sad melody foreshadows a tragic end (Figure 6.7).

Figure 6.7 Screenshots from *Stranger and the Fog*. Minutes 85′.30″–112′.40″

The completion of the cycle with the rituals of self-flagellation and bloodletting

With the circle of love complete, Āyat now feels belonged, particularly because like Hekmati, he sets himself the task of helping deprived children. As in Hekmati's case, however, the unknown disrupts his life. Thus, as he and the boy set off in the morning to finish the boy's hut, a long shot displays five boats approaching the coast. Āyat's first reaction is to escape. Thus, as the boy pulls himself up the tower to inform others by drumming, Āyat urges Ra'nā to escape, and when Ra'nā refuses to leave, he sets fire to her house. At one level, this shows how war changes fertility agents into tools of destruction. Beyzaie reinforces this by having the battle concurrent with the fourth rain, a torrential one, which sets the mood of chaos to mark how a season of joy, fertility and harvest is distorted into one of burning, death and devastation. Realizing that Āyat has been telling the truth, Zakaria catches up with them and reconciles by giving him the sickle, revealing that, indeed, he and Esmāeil had taken it.

The actions of the five invaders display a calm approach to inflicting violence implying that, unlike the villager, they are warriors or unearthly beings. The surreal motifs of the sequence reinforce the film's archetypal suggestions. The invaders' weapons reframe the use of sickle to suggest death in Persian poetry and the idea of harvest season as when Āyat must leave. Ra'nā's refusal to leave again associates her with the earth, and the burning of the house suggests the burning of a land to make it fertile in the slash-and-burn approach to agriculture.

In any case, the invaders catch up with Āyat. In a typical Beyzaiean scene of encounter, Āyat and Ra'nā face their tall persecutors, who demand that Āyat must go with them 'into the fog' as he has been summoned. The men's assertion that Āyat himself must recall where and why he must go underpins the inscrutability of human condition, yet the reality of their presence upholds the sociopolitical and religious idea of a suppressive system of divine and earthly authority and judgement. A bloody battle ensues in which Āyat and Ra'nā are the only people who really fight against the invaders while the villagers distract them, attack their corpses, wail, shout, perform Islamic prayers or ritual mourning, or push the invaders' boats into the sea. Thus, while the two role models of citizenship defend themselves and the village and some villagers help by distracting the invaders, most men continue with their useless rituals. Ra'nā's rising agency even transforms her into a warrior. Where even Zakaria and Esmāeil look like helpless children, Ra'nā's slaying of one of the invaders reflects the type of calm bravery seen in Iranian legends but rarely seen in Iranian cinema. Subverting the stereotypes of docile motherhood or shrill female audacity, she quietly passes her child to Jeirān and kills one of the invaders with Jeirān's spear. The invaders' role as personifications of death is also implied by their unscrupulous killing of a helpless woman and the disabled boy. When the battle finally ends, Ra'nā's face reflects relief, and Āyat is framed from Ra'nā's perspective sitting near the body of the disabled boy whose corpse does not show any wound.

The surrealistic motifs of the battle sequence reinforce the archetypal aspects of the film. In addition to the rituals initiated by the silent priest who engages in dice divination and then leads the villagers in their self-flagellation, prayer and rhythmic stick and chest-beating, these motifs include the way the corpse of the invaders are submerged as if to fertilize the land, and the way the invaders, particularly the last one, die. In each case, when Āyat or Ra'nā wound an invader, Āyat bleeds as if injured on the same spot and loses an item of clothing as if shedding his masks or belongings to prepare for afterlife. Moreover, when the villagers attack the invaders' corpses with their sticks, his pain intensifies. These motifs support the idea that Āyat is an agent of fertility inherently related to the five invaders. Thus, if they embody pure water and fog, Āyat embodies the water that has chosen to mingle with earth. As the last invader attacks Āyat to kill him, Ra'nā shouts and runs towards him with her spear, and Āyat splashes his face with mud, which seems to shake and metamorphose the man as if the soil has captured his soul and turned him into mud. He frightens the villagers by brandishing his sickle and then hits himself on the head with the sickle. Once more, instead of the man, Āyat bleeds and suffers pain, but he continues hitting the man until he sinks into the mud and is submerged by the villagers. Thus, with Āyat being the only person who bleeds, the whole sequence suggests the idea of bloodletting and sacrifice as a fertility rite whose ritual essence echoes the cycle of female fertility with menstruation and purification making fertility possible. Āyat's blood, therefore, makes the fertility of the mother earth possible by a cycle of initiation, bloodletting and purification which may prepare her for the following year.

In answer to Qukasiyan's question about Āyat being injured each time he strikes his enemies, Beyzaie states that the film is a poetic reflection on human birth, life and death and that he thought of the events in accordance with his creative impulses during writing or filming. Yet, he adds that later he heard about similar images in Iranian mystic narratives and paintings.

> The five black-wearing men may be multiplications of the face of death, so with each strike Āyat is hurting himself. The idea occurred to me when cutting the scenes, not when I was writing the script. A few years later, someone told me he had seen a similar image in a mural in [. . .] Shiraz, and later gave me a photo of the mural. An old man in the middle with five or six wounds inflicted on him with five or six different blades by five or six people who were bleeding themselves. I was surprized. The script of the mural suggested the man was the King of Mystics, Bāyazid Bastāmi [804–874]. In [Attar's] *Biographies of the Saints*, there is an account that says; 'Once, [in ecstasy] he said "God, is anyone higher than I?". When he regained awareness, his displaces asked him about this. "God be your enemy if you do not tear me into pieces if you hear me say that again." Then, he gave a knife to each, but when it happened again, they saw the house full of Bāyazid, so that all the four corners were full of him. They stabbed and stabbed, but it was as if they stabbed water.' You see, this is different yet similar. [. . .] The injury of the disciples is not mentioned. Instead, the idea of Bāyazid becoming huge is present as Bāyazid is huge and the disciples small [. . .] which may have been taken from another account that I don't know about.[54]

At the philosophical level, therefore, Beyzaie had subconsciously reframed the magical world of Persian mystic tales in which the reports of uncanny events and beings, encounters with the unknown, or facing incarnations of death are frequent[55] (Figure 6.8).

In this context, Āyat's resistance against the summon is finally overcome by the symbolic deaths of the delegates of the unknown who also echo the relationship of his senses with death. Thus, the conflict which leads to the deaths of the old and the weak

Figure 6.8 Screenshots from *Stranger and the Fog*. Minutes 114′.10″–139′.20″

including the disabled boy, burdens his conscience and prepares him for the journey. The embodiments of the unknown, therefore, fulfil their mission and make him leave the village by imposing a war on Āyat that leads to their own deaths and that of some villagers. Despite these surrealistically archetypal overtones, Beyzaie demonstrates that his journey is primarily due to the death of the disabled boy. Thus, he resigns to his destiny not to quench his curiosity for knowing the nature of this violent unknown but to avoid putting others in danger.

Ra'nā's content face at the end of the battle and her gaze at the trees, the rainy sky and Āyat's naked torso as he is covering the disabled boy's body with his shirt, are reinforced by the calls of seagulls implying her feeling of freedom. After framing her happiness, the camera provides a close-up of Āyat's hand as he takes a handful of mud to take in its scent. Āyat then rises and walks towards a boat. With no shirt and wounds and bruises all over his torso, he looks like when his boat arrived in the village. Ra'nā greets him with 'it is finished', but as if mesmerized by the boat, he states, 'No, not like this. They may come again. I must know what is there, on the other side.' As he walks towards the boat, Ra'nā's screams are juxtaposed with the villagers' ceremonial self-flagellation and stick and stone beating, and the priest's dressing of Āyat's torso with a shroud-like cloth. Āyat, then, falls into the boat as if exhausted. As the boat is carried away by the waves, Ra'nā's father states, 'Why did he come? Why did he leave?' Women begin to walk in a circle and ululate around Ra'nā, who takes off her white dress to reveal a black dress underneath. Her white dress seems to appear on Āyat's boat like a guiding flag as it vanishes in the fog. Ra'nā, the goddess of earth, then covers her face with mud, a sign of mourning, as the chest-beating and ululating reaches a final high. The film then closes with a shot of the fog and a final click sound of sticks.

Reception and concluding remarks

Beyzaie's films, like all films, have flaws. Beyzaie's selected folk music pieces which were to be added to the soundtrack for the fighting and initiation scenes were ruined by the people in charge of dubbing, and since everyone, except Beyzaie, insisted on rushing the job to get the film ready for Tehran's International Film Festival of 1974, the soundtrack is by no means what it could have been. The acting of some secondary characters is also occasionally stilted. *Stranger* was the first Iranian film that engaged with large-scale costume and scenic design without artificial pageantry, and Beyzaie's use of make-up and colour symbolism was unique, but the costume of the invaders remained unconvincing at realistic level. Though the length is arguably justified by the scale, another issue that some critics insisted on was the length of the film. In fact, David Robinson's comments, 'marvellous, fatally over-long, but (even without translation) hypnotic', sum up the reaction of most critics to the film.[56] To sum up, as the reports of Peter Cowie, John Gillett, Javad Mojabi, Behnam Nateqi and several other critics suggest, they knew that the film was extraordinary in its technical qualities, poetic power and scale,[57] yet many also found the length problematic.[58] However, considering the limitations of Iranian cinema in the 1970s and the difficulties Beyzaie went through while making the film, it is definitely one of the greatest poetically sublime films ever made in Iran.

Due to the economic, intellectual and political rivalries of the 1970s, the film did not achieve the box-office success it deserved. Due to the failure of Rex Cinema and Theatre Company to fulfil its commitments as the producer, Beyzaie had been forced to secure a loan from the Ministry of Culture to complete the film. To some leftist intellectuals this was like a betrayal of their distorted ideals of committed writers which they wished to impose on everyone. Thus, some of the pseudo-intellectuals of the time used an Islamist fearmongering technique to ruin Beyzaie's reputation by linking the film to Bahaism. Equally disruptive, however, was the attitudes of the West-obsessed intelligentsia who wished Iran to be depicted like a European country and saw Beyzaie's indigenous-style forms and concerns with rituals and regional music as backward. Exemplifying the pressures imposed by non-governmental right, left and Islamist groups, such attitudes led to a situation in which during the first festival screening, some critics left the cinema when the initial credits appeared along a regional music. The film, therefore, did not receive the favourable reviews that urge people to see it.

Nevertheless, its merits were immediately recognized by fairer critics. Mojabi called it an 'authentically indigenous document', 'a masterpiece that saved the festival' by presenting 'a symbolic story about existence, coming from the unknown, living with anxiety and departing for the unknown'.[59] Jamshid Akrami, who rightly identified Āyat as 'a rebel who thinks out of the box and changes the rules', decided that his final departure means resigning to the rules, and emphasized that the film 'is an instance of incredibly powerful cinema, which we have never had in Iran before. [. . .] It is pure cinema with unadulterated imagery'. He, then, highlighted some of the film's magical scenes, such as the world of the graveyard or Ra'nā's purification rite under the rain. The film's detailed mis en scene, scenic design, background and costume which generated the archetypal suggestiveness and nightmarish ambiance of the film's poetic realism dazzled the British film critic, Cowie, who praised Beyzaie's stunning technique and concluded that 'no country in the Middle East has ever been able to produce such a film'.[60] Mehrdad Fakhimi's captivating cinematography also gained the film a top prize at the first Cairo International Film Festival in 1976. With time the film also proved its significance to those who had refused to accept its significance, and several generations of viewers have come to admire the scope, the vision and the cinematography that contribute to the creation of a ritually charged, philosophical film about life.

As observed in my analysis, *Stranger* is rich in its poetic suggestiveness. This aspect was not different from Beyzaie's other works, but since the film's primary subject is human existence and it avoids motifs that may have been used to reduce it to its political propositions, it was declared too enigmatic. In my analysis, I examined the film's motifs at realistic, existential, psychological and archetypal levels to show how they conclude with clear ideas wherever human limits allow clarity without claiming to have access to truth. Existentially, Āyat's arrival, like the journey of life, begins with being 'thrown' into a place with the boat standing for a womb, a cradle and a coffin carrying the gift of the unknown. Like a child, he is circled by people's gazes in ways that form his destiny. He, then, tries to achieve fulfilment in love and recognition by contributing to the prosperity of the village but is forced to leave just when he attains both. Psychologically, the plot echoes Āyat or Ra'nā's dream of fulfilment and stability disturbed by the nightmarish motifs of their subconscious fears and prohibitions. Thus, the invaders who are originally shadow-like and immaterial gradually materialize until they emerge like revengeful gods or demons to turn their dream into a nightmare of death and loss. Both face their demons to exorcise them, but the intensity of the experience is so that Āyat sinks back into the unknown. Like the realistic level, this level is also concerned with the position of the marginalized as most of the fears are about the individual's failure to achieve recognition and be able to have a feeling of belonging and a normal life.

Yet, these nightmare motifs can also be studied by using Freud's theories about displacement and replacement to establish a link between the film's psychological suggestions and its realistic discourse about human existence. Like all human beings, Āyat comes from the unknown and returns to the unknown and is surrounded by the gaze of a social other that reconfigures his life at every step by placing him in the middle of or outside questioning circles of people. He then undergoes initiation rites in the competition, torture and spiritually and sexually charged unification episodes. As in the ritual dance of 'Wedding in the Forest' reconstructed in the film, he must also fight with his rival to gain his beloved. He even has a social quest for helping the poor which contributes to the formation of his identity.

The film's realistic discourse builds on Āyat's amnesia due to an unknown conflict and his desire to settle and have a normal life in the village in which he has regained consciousness. He goes through a series of encounters which comments on the position of marginalized people in exclusionist societies and the impact of the past on the present, but, in the end, exhausted by being constantly worried about invasions and causing the village more harm, he leaves. At this level, the film's juxtaposition of Āshub and Āyat subverts the cliché of heroic masculinity as Āshub, the epitome of masculine bravado, proves to be a bullying fraud.

Āyat, however, evolves from this realistic aspect to become an unwilling sacrificial hero. He loves life and helping others as he himself has been denied the chance of having a normal life, but he eventually tries to save people by embarking on a quest to confront the unknown. However, both Āshub and Āyat are shown to be victims of cultural templates that trap them and distort their lives. As in his other works, Beyzaie enriches his poetic realism with ritual *ta'ziyeh* motifs which suggest how his heroes, a common man and woman are forced by circumstances to resist existential, religious, social, cultural or political injustice. These ritual motifs, in turn, enhance the emotional impact of the film and give archetypal depth to the sacrificial/tragic routine, but they also subvert the exclusionist content of their contemporary forms and make them more inclusive by reimagining their original nature-related forms. In the first archetypal level, therefore, like Iraj, Siyāvush, Jesus or Hossein, the two reveal their constructive qualities and suffer for the sins of others, but unlike them, they are not aware of their destiny or willing to be sacrificed. Indeed, in Āyat's case, rather like Oedipus, it is his quest for awareness and his reluctance to endanger others that turn him into a sacrificial hero. At their pre-legendary, animist level, however, the archetypes turn the *ta'ziyeh* of common people into an animist fertility rite in which nature, embodied in Ra'nā's desire for happiness, is the main character, and Āyat is an agent of fertility, a dying god who is caught from the sea, kills Āshub, the cheating dying hero, contributes to the fertility of the land by his sacred marriage, blood and toil and is finally given to the sea for a later return. Thus, Beyzaie uses these rituals to subvert the stereotypes of violent, exclusionist patriarchy and religiosity and introduce ritually configured ideals of masculinity and femininity. In the process, he also joins the pre-religion rituals of fertility with modern ideas to suggest the latter's 'naturalness' in comparison to the patriarchal obsessions of Abrahamic religions. In *Stranger*, Beyzaie still has a male protagonist who, as in his 1960s plays, has sprung from the marginalized to embody a form of citizenship that creates prosperity for others and sacrifices his own desires and interests to save others, but Ra'nā and even Jeirān and the disabled boy achieve a level of centrality that is unique in Iranian cinema. Thus, Beyzaie's emancipatory form suggests how regardless of gender or physical limitations, everyone can act heroically and become an ideal citizen without being obsessed with the inherited ideals of heroism.

With *Stranger*, Beyzaie's position as a leading experimental filmmaker with a multifaceted talent was firmly established. His next film, however, did not copy the vision he had created in *Stranger*. Instead, he reformulated the thriller genre to create a new template.

7

The Crow (1977)

City, home and the pitfalls of Iranian modernity

The zeitgeist of the 1970s and the rise of female protagonists in Beyzaie's cinema

Following *Stranger*, Beyzaie tried to make *Ayyār-e Tanhā* (Lonely Warrior), which examines the pitfalls and ideals of heroism, the illusion of waiting for saviours and the transformation of human identity under pressure in a plot that focuses on the conflicts of trickster partisan warriors, *ayyārs*, during the Mongol invasion. However, as Manuchehr Farid, who had undergone rigorous physical training for the lead role, states, the producers ruined Beyzaie's plans by insisting that the lead role must be a superstar.[1] Beyzaie wanted a man dangling between being a villain and a hero, a man who could display the conflicting sides of human identity, but using a superstar would have turned the role into a good bad tough guy, triggered cliché expectations in viewers and reinforced the tough guy cult of mainstream cinema. In *Ayyār-e Tanhā*, the would-be saviour who is to defeat the Mongols is shown to have become a penniless drunkard, but a traumatized *ayyār*, who robs and kills a man of letters, is transformed into a hero by the man's daughter whom he has raped earlier. What is ironic and reflective of the role of authors and women in continuing the idea of Iran is that the writer who insists that the Mongols cannot defeat Iranians is killed by an Iranian warrior but ends up being right in an unexpected process in which his daughter, whose role is suggestive of all Iranian women, plays the central role. Like most of Beyzaie's works, the film could have introduced a new template to the Iranian New Wave while generating commercial success.

Beyzaie's next project, *Truths about Leila the Daughter of Edris*, which was to be produced by Bahman Farmanara's *Sherkat-e Gostaresh-e Sanāye-e Sinemāei-ye Irān* (Corporation for Expanding Iranian Cinema Industry), was similar in its emancipatory aesthetics. The script focuses on how the patriarchal obsession with sex and using violence to control others violates women's dreams by setting them on the pedestals of coy girlhood and sacrificial motherhood and demonizing free-spirited women. In the script, Leila, a lower-class girl of Ātefeh type, aspires to live by herself and change her life by working as a typist. Beyzaie, thus, focuses on a new neglected type, a woman, whose gender, simple aspirations and lower-class origins lead to her marginalization in her own country. Thus, whereas in *Downpour*, an educated middle-class man is placed in a lower-class district, in *Truths*, an aspiring, lower-class woman who has managed to obtain her high school diploma tries to live independently in a society in which women who live alone are demonized as loose. To make matters worse, the flat she has rented with her limited means was formerly occupied by a sex worker. Thus, while the realistic level displays how she is harassed by the latter's customers, the metaphoric level highlights the obstacles to the social mobility of working-class women in Iran and shows how hard it is for them to carve a new place in a sex-obsessed public space. Beyzaie, thus, shows how suppressive religious and patriarchal beliefs from below and the mass media's imitative idea of modernity, which inadvertently advertised the dolled-up American housewife or secretary as 'the modern woman', distort the lives of women who aspire to achieve social mobility through education and work. Rather than return to a future of closed doors in her old district to avoid the oppressive role that sex-obsessed men try to impose on her, she picks up her grandfather's sword to confront her harassers. Thus, unlike *Ayyār-e Tanhā*, in which a young woman turns a deranged *ayyār* into a hero and joins him to confront invading embodiments of toxic masculinity, in *Truths*, she does the job herself. Beyzaie's position in this 1975 script predicted the feminist discourses that evolved in the 1980s to argue for an epistemology of survival and resistance rather than victimization.[2] The similarity of such discourses to Beyzaie's lifelong focus on marginalization becomes clearer if one traces the way this discourse evolved in the 1990s when bell hooks stated,

> Understanding marginality as position and place of resistance is crucial for oppressed, exploited, colonized people. If we only view the margin as sign marking the despair, a deep nihilism penetrates in a destructive way the very ground of our being. It is there in that space of collective despair that one's creativity, one's imagination is at risk, there that one's mind is fully colonized, there that the freedom one longs for is lost.[3]

Beyzaie noticed this resistance space prior to feminist theorists and evolved it to produce his emancipatory aesthetics due to his own marginalization which he had sublimated into epistemic authority. Thus, he promoted his ideals of modernity and its manifestations in modern Iranian identities by critiquing the marginalization of people due to their age, gender, ethnicity, race, religion, class origins, disability, facial feature and other imposed categories. In other words, *Truths* predicts the later directions of feminist discourses by concentrating on a blind spot, one of the silently sanctioned spaces of cultural marginalization, which feminists neglected by not paying attention to the struggles of women from underprivileged backgrounds or by focusing on victimization of women rather than celebrating and promoting their ways of survival, self-empowerment and resistance. Centralizing what was already present in his earlier work, he replaced the marginalized creative intellectual and neglected children with modern working women from lower-class backgrounds. This was important as these categories of women have always had a daily battle with the oversexualization of female body in the popular culture. As stated previously, in the 1970s, such women suffered ostracization due to dogmatic religious beliefs and the overbearing dictates of toxic femininity and masculinity from below, and a superficial conception of modernity which created reactions among the conservative layers of society from above. The condition did not improve after the revolution because although the revolution itself led to major changes in the public space and enhanced the possibilities of grassroots emancipation, from the early 1980s, the new state imposed a religiously dogmatic conception of womanhood from above. Beyzaie, therefore, continued to have female protagonists because they enabled him to hold a mirror to the exclusionist culture of toxic masculinity and religiosity.

In *Truths*, he also uses surrealistic stylization to suggest the possibility of extracting modern identities from indigenous roots. Leila's late grandfather, for instance, appears to embody the existence of positive tendencies in Iran's pre-modern conceptions of masculinity and femininity. Yet, her grandfather is ultimately unable to help her because as Iranian history shows, until the 1850s the power of religious dogma and its tactical trades with tribal, feudal and economic poles of power in Iran stymied the centrality of the secular mentalities and practices that could have led to emancipatory modernity. However, just like what Beyzaie does, Leila's conjuring of her kind grandfather, the emancipatory elements of Iranian culture, in moments of despair, enables her to reread her narrative of selfhood to gain strength or a sense of direction. Conjuring a spirit to represent the continuity of the past was also a stylistic novelty that was given more centrality in his *Ballad of Tārā*.

However, the idea of a girl saving herself in a film that used Kafkaesque and noir motifs to reflect the obstacles to the rise of the new woman seemed too risky to producers. Average producers remained conservative in their understanding of popular taste and understood women in the context of Western mainstream films, in which they were often damsels in distress. Yet even to Bahman Farmanara, whose company aspired to expand the stylistic and thematic resources of Iranian cinema, the film remained unpalatable. Though Farmanara states that the disagreement was over Beyzaie's determination to have Parvaneh Masoumui in the lead role,[4] a more likely reason was because Beyzaie's emancipatory vision was not aligned with that of the state, or its leftist and Islamist alter egos. Yet even when the state found his vision supportable due to its potential to win international attention for Iranian cinema, some of Beyzaie's rivals used unscrupulous methods to derail his projects and redirect the limited resources to their own projects. Thus, they either argued that his films are beyond public understanding or used his family background to reduce his works to Bahai ideas, a distortion whose aftershocks are still observed in the writings of his post-revolutionary detractors, including Shi'i fundamentalists and critics who find him odd or resent the emancipatory worldliness of his works.[5] Beyzaie's awareness of Bahai myths and ideology has clearly enriched his views as one of many Iranian sources and more as reinforcement for his archetypally charged depictions of distortions of life in Iran. His direct experience of the pressures that the Bahais and other marginalized groups suffered also meant that he realized such people must be protected against extremists. However, associating him with Bahai ideas is like linking Hedayat or Shamlou with Shi'ism. Beyzaie continued to have such problems during his career and often had to use his own resources or those of his actors or film-loving friends to complete his films. For *The Crow*, for example, renting a proper house for the setting was beyond his budget, but Shahro Kheradmand (1941–), a renowned actress, convinced one of her friends to let them use their house which was to be demolished. In any case, as Beyzaie states, in 1975 everyone working in any capacity relevant or not relevant to making films found a way to prevent the making of *Truths*.[6] These barriers urged Beyzaie to approach the question from another angle, which, though lighter in its depiction of class contingencies and female resistance against symbolic and physical violence, is even more focused on memory, cultural history and sociopolitical inhibitions for the rise of the new woman. *The Crow*, therefore, is the result of three years of negotiation with a cinematic culture beleaguered by undue rivalries over limited resources, obsessed with superstars, and concerned about royalist, leftist and religious demonization.

In my analysis of *The Crow*, I argue that the film constructs multiple axes of referencing to comment on the history, pitfalls and potential directions of Iranian modernity in a context in which Tehran as the first site of Iranian modernity and the modern family as its building block are placed in a space of negotiation where the givens of the past are reread to replace artificial derivative modernity and subjecthood with emancipatory modernity and citizenship. As Hamid Reza Sadr argues, the film's focus on the 'search for a young woman' may be read as 'a symbolic yearning for lost youth and an intuitive demonstration that a particular historical phase was coming to an end' and that it may seem 'impossible not to read this parable as a political critique of a regime that had had its day'.[7] Yet, in my reading, I argue that the film's focus is emancipation rather than revolutionary politics. The film has also been described as a nostalgic remembrance of the past,[8] but my analysis demonstrates that it uses nostalgia, recollection of the past and expressionistic journeys in time to study the meaning of time, revive the memory of a lost opportunity and display Āsiyeh's divergent perceptiveness as a more authentic and historically conscious path to modernity. In several cases, Beyzaie also uses limited third person POV with expressionistic elements to display the absurdity and violence of life in a commercialized world where medieval superstitions and superficially modern consumerism live side by side. While this line of inquiry bears similarities to my own former writing on city and home in *The Crow*, Sheibani's on *The Crow* and Pak-Shiraz's on Beyzaie's city films, it diverges from my own in its depth and from the latter two in its arguments and focus.[9] I use scene-by-scene explication to trace the evolution of Āsiyeh's character as an ideal citizen, engage with theory to analyse the film's take on emancipation and on the roles marginalized people can play in modernizing a culture by revealing its exclusionist fixations. To set the stage for this analysis, I first discuss the status of cultural production in a world of consumerism and the value of rereading the past and mourning the lost for cultural exorcism and rejuvenation where even memory is being commodified. I also analyse Iran's encounter with authoritarian modernity, capitalist consumerism and Islamist market ideology as the contexts in which the new approaches to cultural production evolved and show how and why Beyzaie's approaches to cultural production in the pre-revolutionary era functioned as models for the approaches that gained centrality in Iran in the 1990s.

Authoritarianism, memory and emancipatory reframing

In his writings on the role of literature in rereading the history of Latin America, Idelber Avelar argues that 'the dictatorships' raison d'être was the physical and symbolic elimination of all resistance to the implementation of market logic' which, in turn, led to a 'dissociation between literature and experience' and a situation in which 'literature no longer occupies the privileged position that it once did'.[10] He also quotes Jose Joaquin Brunner to argue that the function of modern authoritarianism in Latin America was to create 'the order adequate to the new model of capitalist development' in which 'the three components of the authoritarian conception of the world' – market ideology, religious traditionalism and military control – produce an ideology that guarantees the dominance of consumerist oblivion in all aspects of life including memory.[11] Thus, memory becomes immaterial as 'new commodities always replace previous commodities' and make recollection unnecessary.[12] The process brought dissenting cultural and political activists, leftists and liberals, face to face with a terrorized, fragmented, consumerist society in which any plan for cultural or political emancipation seemed futile. Avelar then uses Fernando Reati's analysis of narratives produced during the dictatorships to argue that 'the need to represent what appears unpresentable, coupled with the subsequent imperative to mourn the dead', led to 'a deep crisis in the very structure of mimesis'.[13] This crisis, then, continued in new ways in the post-dictatorial era as with the turning of memory and history into a commodity, the task of mourning and remembering the barbarian origins of the capitalist democracy of the present created a contradictory situation in which mourning the past in some cultural products neutralizes the memories of violence and obscures the ties between the dictatorships and the ensuing democracies, while in others it contradicts the appeasing account of the past and the consumerist forms of remembrance.[14]

Using the example of Latin America, one can argue that where this authoritarian triangle is not complete, cultural production maintains its emancipatory role as a space for alternative views about life. However, where it is fully formed, the three forms of censor emanating from consumerist capitalism, military control and religious dogma make cultural production either over-politicized, militant and radical or too depoliticized, morally simplistic, sentimental or merely entertaining and playful which makes cultural production even more irrelevant.[15]

To offer a simplified yet still relevant account of a similar process in Iran, one can argue that the first Pahlavi period (1921/25–41) fulfilled some of the tasks associated with aligning Iran with the still-in-rising ideology of Western capitalism to protect Iran against the equally distorting rise of communism. This continued with the direct influence of the allies during the occupation era (1941–7) and the democratization attempts of the post-occupation era (1947–53). The systematic process of founding a militarily enforced capitalist ideology, then, began with the 1953 coup in which the clergy sided with the Shah against the constitutionalists headed by Mosaddeq. However, when the marathon of moving from feudalism and outdated bazaar relations to modern capitalism and capitalist democracy intensified with the Shah's reforms in 1963, the state's pact with Iran's religious establishment crumbled, and Khomeini and his militant, fundamentalist cohorts launched a fierce campaign against the reforms. Apart from other aspects discussed in Chapters 1 and 2, this was because the socialist aspects of the reforms, which aspired to control the influence of communism, worked with the bid for industrialization and the capitalist emphasis on modern entrepreneurial market relations, to diminish the power of the clergy and landlords and create a new basis of legitimization for the Shah among peasants and workers. This power transfer was both economic and cultural. Economically, the process would redirect to modern channels of investment and taxation the financial resources of landlords and traditional bazaar traders whose religious taxes were the main source of funding the independence of the clergy from the state. Culturally, the idea of vote for women and employing male and female high school and university graduates in the literacy, hygiene and reconstruction and development corps and sending them to remote villages would also mean that the clergy's control over people's lives diminished.

Thus, the tringle of religiously and militarily backed capitalist authoritarianism was briefly established in Iran between 1953 and 1963 but began to collapse in 1963. With the 1953 coup having antagonized and weakened liberal constitutionalists who could have been the Shah's best allies for modernizing the country by providing corrective angles, the situation approached a dead-end. Consequently, the Shah's plan for pushing Iran into modern capitalism by suppressing all political opposition and then imposing a single-party rule with his Rastākhiz (Resurrection) party in 1975 backfired and led to the 1979 revolution.

Despite the country's surface stability, these volatile undercurrents and the contradictory outcomes of the 1963 reforms also meant that cultural products remained relevant in their emancipatory potential until the 1979 revolution. SAVAK interferences, state censor and the Islamists' and leftists' ostracization of authors who did not support their radical ideals made the underlying clashes of cultural production more intense. However, the Iranian queen, Farah Diba (1938–), an art graduate with liberal ideas about arts, had several of her supporters in charge of key cultural initiatives. Thus, authors whose works had democratic potential but did not directly criticize the regime or support communism used the space between Marxist, Islamist and capitalist discourses to open an emancipatory dialogue with the state and the people. With the rise of the Islamist state after the 1979 revolution, however, the path for the rise of a unique kind of market-religion-military authoritarianism was set. Thus, despite the attempts of socialist Islamists for creating their own version of 'classless society' in the 1980s and the incessant rhetoric against Western capitalism, a predatory and militarized form of capitalism, which had all the negative but only a few of the positive aspects of capitalism, evolved and completed the triangle of authoritarianism by the early 1990s. This form of religion-backed capitalism, which has continued to control Iran's economic, political and cultural resources until now (2022), is even worse than its Russian and Chinese foils, as apart from political violence and state-distributed economic opportunism, it levies Islamist limits on people's lives and cultural production and has already derailed its democratic potential.[16]

However, the heavily stifled post-revolutionary cultural production, which suffered a crisis of irrelevance in the 1980s and further twists due to the postmodern crisis of representation triggered by authors' resorts to formalist games to avoid persecution in the 1990s, continued to display emancipatory trends that 'redistributed the sensible' with little engagement with daily politics. Thus, whereas 'the committed' art of the 1960s and 1970s was chiefly concerned with criticizing the state with allegorical motifs, emancipatory cultural production, which began to recreate itself from the late 1980s, promotes the rights of those in the lower echelons of the pyramid of power, which has since the 1979 revolution included not only women, children, lower-class men, ethnic and religious minorities and other types of marginalized people but also the secular intelligentsia. Since the mid-1990s, it has even included some religious people who sacrificed their health or loved ones during the revolution or Iran-Iraq war but feel betrayed by the results. This emancipatory trend which expanded in the reform era of Khatami's presidency (1997–2005) and has so far undergone several eras of contraction and expansion, remains committed to improving the status of the marginalized by influencing the religious sensibility of the people and the state rather than changing the state.

Let me rearrange my argument from another outlook. A major function of cultural production since the early 1800s has been to reformulate myth, history and memory to promote, resist or transform the rivalling discourses of being, belonging, identity and nationhood. Although this function continues everywhere, including Iran through state-sponsored cultural products, the crisis emanating from the success of capitalism in derailing its rivalling ideologies in the 1990s led to a situation in which this revisionist role which had already lost its momentum in Iran gave its place to the primacy of individual fulfilment or types of artistic playfulness which twist literary, cinematic or dramatic forms to shock and entertain without invigorating the work's expressive power. Thus, as the ideology of consumerism promotes an excessive discarding of old commodities and replacing them with their latest models and minimizes the desire for holding on to memories of places and objects, in consumerist cultural production topical excitement, visual or verbal playfulness and intriguing plotlines have become more vital, and the past has become a commodity that has no customer unless it is presented in ever new and attractive packaging. Nevertheless, the need for rereading the past to achieve closure for traumatic experiences and turning them into points of redemption for understanding the present has resulted in works that though using intriguing forms and focusing on individual memory and experience, extract from the past emancipatory discourses that redistribute the sensible and make people conscious of the need to support the marginalized.

This approach to cultural production is not new as the greatest artists have always been those who have arisen from temporarily or permanently marginalized backgrounds and turned their marginalization into means for defamiliarizing their subjects through forms that allow for new ways of seeing. However, in the past few decades, the ability to strike a balance between being entertaining and playful and creating emancipatory artistic spaces for more inclusive and compassionate ways of seeing and doing things has become even more important.

As reflected in this book, Beyzaie's forms have always been intriguing. Moreover, since he had suffered the pressures of religious marginalization, from the start his concern was not just the failures of the state or the status of the lower classes or dissenting individuals but the whole machination of cultural exclusion in its economic, religious, cultural, ethnic and political aspects. Thus, whereas the focus on the marginalized, including women, divergent intellectuals, minorities and children, became central in the cultural products of the 1990s, such characters were essential in Beyzaie's work from the beginning. Another element that makes this attention to the personal and collective histories of the marginalized interesting is that they highlight the problems of the present. For instance, *Arash* and *Death of Yazdegerd* use myth and history to critique the royalist nationalism of the Pahlavi era, and *The Crow* and *Ballad of Tara* use expressionistic journeys in time to display the results of past failures.

Some of Beyzaie's historical works link the events of Iran's occupation during the 1940s to the history of modernity and the lives of middle-class families. These include two films, *The Crow* and *Maybe Some Other Time*, and a screenplay *Occupation*, which link the idea of getting lost, vanishing or dying in an era in which human life is of no value to the loss of the normal paths of progress to reveal how during conflicts, individuals' lives are crushed and memories that contradict dominant discourses are hushed. By focusing on the experiences of women, these works offer emancipatory views on the impacts of the past on the present and create forms of 'cinematic performativity', in which self-reflexive playfulness, incongruent motifs and characters' uncanny memories or perceptions defamiliarize the action and expose the viewers to the pressures that marginalized people undergo, but others accept as their sociopolitical, religious, gender or artistic biases normalize them. In this way, Beyzaie displays various layers of people's history to show how sociopolitical and religious suppression and judgemental or ostracizing surveillance distort the lives of individuals.

Originating in J. L. Austin's linguistic theory, the concept of 'performativity' was first used to denote those expressions that at the time of utterance performed an action or had direct impacts on other people's lives. For instance, when a priest states, 'I pronounce you husband and wife'. In cultural theory, particularly in Judith Butler and Jacques Derrida's writings, this concept refers to a process that uses the expressive tools of artistic, political, class or gender discourses to instate specific identity templates in people or deconstructs these discourses by breaching their expressive or behavioural markers.[17] In cinema, this is mostly reflected in stylized shots registering a character's subjective outlook or that of an independent roving camera which challenges naturalized, retrogressive sociopolitical and cultural ways of behaving, doing and seeing things through form, often with minimum verbal referencing. Thus, though well-versed in the grammar of classical or realist narrative cinema, the filmmaker may distort the narrative to break the illusion of reality and enable the viewer to have a heightened vision of a situation to, for instance, notice that what seems to be an unalterable reality is just like a cinematic arrangement that can be transformed. In Beyzaie, the scenes highlighting the psychosocial distortion of perception are playfully placed in justifiable narrative locations in ways that create the assumption of self-reflexive or odd forms of expression before reframing them as part of the narrative. Previously analysed examples include the disembodied noise of toddlers' crying over an eerie scene of violence or neglect in *Uncle Moustache* and *The Journey* and then returning to the usual narrative by showing that a toddler is present. As stated before, Beyzaie's stylized, expressionistic, surrealistic or uncanny scenes echo indigenous forms, which, as in *goriz* (diversion) technique in *ta'ziyeh*, may also include free-floating uses of time and space like the ones in *The Crow*. Nonetheless, whereas in his village trilogy, his sources of inspiration are Iranian folktales, rituals, epics, material culture and artistic forms reworked with attention to Asian performing traditions and Japanese films, especially Kurosawa's; in his city films, he reformulates them with cinematic devices that echo the works of leading Western directors, particularly Lang, Ophüls, Hitchcock, Welles and Bergman, whose works, he argues, are closer to his taste in depicting the vicissitudes of modern urban life.[18] In the process, in both cases, he creates unique forms that are ideal for registering the violence, neglect, fear, sorrow and mental pressures that individuals may suffer due to exclusionist attitudes.

In the context of the 1970s, this indicates that, unlike revolutionary leftists and Islamists who assumed that by grabbing the absolute power of the king and launching their utopian ideas, they can resolve all social ills according to their own version of reality, the emancipatory vision of Beyzaie and some other creative artists, including Farrokhzad, Kiarostami, Naderi, Radi, Mofid or Mehrjui, implied that the real impediment in Iran's path to progress is the obsession with controlling and excluding those who do not follow one's views. In *The Crow*, such a discourse is also aligned with Beyzaie's use of noir motifs to turn women's memories and experiences into a crucible for displaying the triumphs and failures of modernization in Iran. While continuing the toned-down use of similar motifs in *Downpour* and *The Journey*, and their ritualization in *Stranger*, the dominance of noir and thriller elements in *The Crow* also suggests it as the first film in Beyzaie's city tetralogy, which includes *Maybe Some Other Time*, *Killing Rabid Dogs* and *When We Are All Sleeping*. Interestingly, in all these films, a major aspect is a panoramic display of discordant objects and alienated people in various occupations, which constructs the metaphor of an alienated city.[19] The protagonists are also all women, who, except in *Maybe Some Other Time*, evolve to become perceptive detectives. Thus, as in his village trilogy, these films build an inter-filmic link in which the heroine's rise to a more creative identity is linked to the vicissitudes of family and city life in the junctions of modern history such as the occupation era in the 1940s, the reign of terror and Iran-Iraq war in the 1980s, and the betrayal of people's dreams in the reform era of the 1990s.[20]

Analysis:[21] From home, work and technologies of communication and clairvoyance to flashy consumerism, subjecthood and citizenship

The film opens with the image of a newspaper announcement reporting the loss of a girl with the picture of a girl of about 18. This is then juxtaposed with a flashily dressed man, Deimkār (dryland farmer),[22] reading adverts by an 18-year-old girl looking for a husband, a rich 30-year-old man looking for people who may want to be his parents and finally the one about the missing girl. The reading, which is done to find exciting news for their newsreels, occurs as Amān Esālat, a news anchor, whose name suggests 'shelter in authenticity', is powdering his face for his news programme. Despite the frivolity of their discussions, the final advert attracts Esālat as the picture looks disturbingly familiar to him. This self-reflexive scene draws the viewer to the world of pseudo-modern capitalist representation in which everything is turned into an advert and surface has priority over essence. Esālat and his friends' superficial chasing of information do not serve the ideal of raising awareness but is only to entertain or fulfil a financial purpose. However, the adverts also highlight the film's subjects: the idea of missing or loss, quest for love, and craving for recognition and recovering a lost sense of identity and belonging. These subjects are also found later to be relevant to the lives of the protagonists: Āsiyeh, Ālam and Esālat.

Esālat's TV programme is then used as a transition to a home in which Esālat's mother, Ālam (the universe), is amusing herself with cartomancy. Noticing Esālat's faltering, Ālam turns to a young woman, Āsiyeh, who is reading a newspaper, to ask why Esālat sounds confused. Thus, Beyzaie uses the technologies of recording light and sound to signify his central idea of presence in absence and link the two generations and the worlds of work and home. Esālat's report, itself, stresses the modern technologies of communicating across the globe, which Beyzaie uses to propose that although his own work is associated with the mass media and communication technologies, he fails to communicate with his mother or understand his own past or the codes of his culture. Ālam's cardplaying displays her sense of ennui, but it also shows her resolve to create the intrigue that forms the plot by linking the past to the future. Two close-ups frame her handling of the queen of Clover and the queen of Spade, which in Persian cartomancy respectively imply a self-effacing girl and a bitter widow. Thus, the shots imply that her young and old selves are to play major roles in the film. Āsiyeh's newspaper reading is also used to indicate that, unlike Esālat and Deimkār, she reads for awareness rather than finding subjects for newsreels. In *The Crow*, Beyzaie's usual inclusion of two generations of women becomes more focused on analysing the rise of the new woman. In *Downpour*, four young and four old women mark the range of shallow and authentic approaches to modernity, the potential of lower and middle-class women for growth and the impacts of crushed dreams on women's lives. In *Stranger*, Ra'nā and Jeirān's relationship generates an undercurrent of shattered dreams, unlikely solidarities, moving from resentment to empathy, and desire for independence, love and productivity. In *The Crow*, however, the sympathy between Ālam and Āsiyeh reflects on the meaning of memory and intergenerational continuity and creates the context for rereading the history of modernity and the position of women in society.

The ringing of the phone marks another use of technology for linking the worlds of work and home and introduces Esālat and Āsiyeh's dispute to reflect the structure of the modern family. Whereas Āsiyeh resents the pretentious parties of Esālat's colleagues, Esālat insists that her presence at these parties is essential for his reputation. Āsiyeh's silent resistance and leafing of the calendar and Esālat's garrulity suggest the gap between their conceptions of reality and time. For her, the phoney relations, attitudes and jokes characterizing such parties are simply unbearable. The dialogue between Ālam and Āsiyeh and the party display Āsiyeh's caring self and moral integrity, and the discrepancy between her and the superficial conceptions of modernity in 1970s Iran. Esālat wants Āsiyeh to dress like his female colleagues and become like them, but her taste, worries and hobbies are different from Esālat and his colleagues. The party, thus, becomes a locus for revealing the pitfalls of authoritarian, capitalist modernity in which obsessive policing and the consumerist copying of latest fashions distort the possibility of genuine citizenship and turns individuals into frivolous, submissive and imitative subjects who bend to any degradation. Here, while drinking, laughing and listening and dancing to Western music, colleagues speak behind each other's back, make jokes about the missing girl and search the guests' pockets when the gem of a ring goes missing. The use of Western music over shots of unheard dialogue creates the typical mood of such parties. Āsiyeh loves music, dancing and engaging in pleasant discussions but cannot tolerate their hypocritical attitudes, seemingly innocent yet deeply insulting jokes and general lack of moral integrity.

Using silence and pauses in the action, Beyzaie turns two events – Āsiyeh's encounter with one of Esālat's female colleagues who has been vilifying Esālat behind his back and that of searching the guests – into Bakhtinian chronotopes for exposing the guests' frivolity.

> [Sound of a glass breaking. The music stops, and the room goes quiet as Esālat goes forward. Everyone's gaze is directed towards Āsiyeh who looks determined.]
> **Āsiyeh:** One does not need enemies when friends are like you.
> **The woman:** How could I know that you're –
> **Āsiyeh:** He is your colleague. If there is an issue, talk to him about it, not others.
> **Esālat:** [Comes forward. To the woman.] Please accept my sincere apology.
> **Āsiyeh:** What for?
> [Esālat sits down to pick up the pieces of the glass that has fallen from the woman's hand. Āsiyeh bends to help.]
> **Esālat:** [Whispering] The reality is that –.
> **Āsiyeh:** [Whispering] What is the truth?
> **Esālat:** [Whispering] You don't follow the appropriate codes. You are ruining my reputation before my colleagues.
> **Āsiyeh:** I'm defending your reputation. [Āsiyeh leaves the reception room. In the quiet sitting room, she picks up a newspaper and notices the lot girl's advert.]²³

Her dialogue with Deimkār, then, exemplifies Beyzaie's usual use of irony as Deimkār's comment about Esālat's mistake turns out to be about the missing girl not his reaction to Āsiyeh's dispute with the woman. It also displays the happy-go-lucky mentality of accepting things as they are, suggested in Deimkār's name and attitudes, which embody the fun-loving, West-obsessed men of the 1970s. As he is trying to exonerate Esālat by explaining Esālat's outlook and stating that she must not 'take things so seriously', a clam police-like voice in the reception announces that no one can leave until the contents of their pockets are checked.

> **Deimkār:** [Appeasing.] If it weren't for social codes, he would join you. He is upset that you don't consider his reputation –
> **Āsiyeh:** [Concerned about the voice.] Hiss!
> **Voice 1:** Gentlemen, we do not say that the person who has found it [Deimkār opens the door.] intended to take it. So, if any of you has the ring

[compassionate laughing], please, inform us without any concerns! [Silence. The camera pauses on Āsiyeh's concerned face.] Gentlemen, unfortunately, we must search you!

[Āsiyeh walks towards the door. The camera now registers an out-of-focus longshot of the silent crowd in the reception room from behind the closeup of Āsiyeh's head.]

You appreciate that I've been asked to fulfil a difficult task, but I cannot do anything else. First gentlemen, and if it is not found, ladies.

Voice 2: I won't allow anyone to search my pockets.

Voice 1: It is a pity as this makes all of us suspect you. Hands up! Up! Up! Fully up!

Āsiyeh: [To Deimkār.] We are nothing. I want to leave.

Deimkār: That is the worst time to leave. Everyone notices.

Āsiyeh: [Ashamed that people are being searched.] I have stolen it.

Voice 1: [Now a middle-aged man, speaking, out of focus, in a patronizing voice as if humouring her!]: You did!? What kind of a thing was it?

Āsiyeh: It was just a piece of stone.

Voice 1 (The Man): [Out of focus.] We said that ourselves.

Āsiyeh: It was very ugly and badly shaped.

The Man: [Out of focus.] I am sorry, but it was still passing from hand to hand when you left the room. No one suspects you. [He turns to others.] Hands up! Upper!

[Esālat calmly goes froward to be searched and Āsiyeh, unable to accept such a degradation turns her head towards the camera.]

Deimkār: We must be patient.

[The camera focuses on the crowd and the smoke-covered room. Almost all the men are smoking. Some are drying their forehead and face. Putting back his handkerchief after drying his forehead, the policelike man notices the gem in his own pocket.]

The Man: I am sorry. It was in my own pocket, but I did not notice it at all. Drinks for everyone. Have fun, guys!

[The music resumes. Guests start laughing, drinking and speaking of what happened as funny. Esālat, who looks furious, tells Āsiyeh they must leave.] (12′.00″–15′.12″)

Up to this point, Beyzaie has depicted two houses: (1) the palimpsestic space of memory and home reflecting the spirit of Iran as an old culture trapped in unending cycles of transitional eras, whose manifestations include (2) the partying world of borrowed modernity which is alienated from this spirit. The two performative scenes use expressions such as 'reputation', 'hands up!' or 'No one can leave' to signify the sociopolitical policing of the public space under authoritarian capitalism and the contrast between the real and false conceptions of 'reputation'. Where everyone is easily accused of theft, Esālat is worried about his wife's objection to the hypocrisy of his colleagues. The synecdochic attention to movements in the searching scene and its multi-layered dialogue portray how citizens are metamorphosed into obedient subjects in surveillance societies. Using smoking, drinking and flashy suits, dresses and hair styles as typical motifs of the feigned modernity of the 1970s, Beyzaie reveals how these people function like automatons who obey orders due to the machination of shaming, blaming, ostracization and exclusion which makes them accept the hierarchies and games of new forms of power. With Deimkār functioning as the apologist of social ills and the clueless observer of Āsiyeh's complex processing of events, the film uses in-focus and out-of-focus cinematography to contrast individual awareness with mass mentality. Though originally several women are present in the crowd, in the searching scene women are placed out of the camera frame which is limited by the double door. This is realistic as men are searched first, but it also suggests how the public space is dominated by men. The men are, thus, either automatons who facilitate the enforcement of the same forms of obedience on women or, as observed later, official and non-official violators of other people's rights. The ending of the scene also shows that the ones who must be interrogated are the officials who shout 'catch the thief' or violate other people's rights without any proof. This reading is also reinforced by the following scene in which Āsiyeh jumps from a nightmare as Esālat is walking nervously around their bedroom trying to remember where he has seen the missing girl. Āsiyeh's emphasis on being in a large room where she did not recognize anyone suggests the alienation that she has observed in the attitudes of the so-called modern Iranians. Thus, she seems to be lost as much as the missing girl that Esālat is worried about (Figure 7.1).

Spaces of belonging and communication: The past, the present and the metaphoric

The next scene marks Āsiyeh's happiness at work where, as a teacher of deaf children, she belongs and shines. In a self-reflexive scene displaying the truth-focused nature of her world, a boy, Qorbān (victim/sacrifice), is at the board conjugating the positive form of 'to go to cinema with one's father' with Āsiyeh and her pupils' supportive comments and laughter setting the mood. Āsiyeh then recounts the story of a crow and a woodpecker by articulating each word and performing some scenes with her hands. In the story which reflects Āsiyeh's conception of modernity, the woodpecker tells the crow that she tolerates the pain of drilling the crusts with her beak to find what lies behind the surfaces: 'what I find is worth the pain; whoever is looking for something must endure the hardship of finding it' (18'.00"–21'.30"). Sheida Qarachehdāghi's music with its flute-based tranquillity completes the dialogue and gestures to show how dedication, love, narration, performance and fun enhance learning. As Āsiyeh moves her hands to copy the crow and the woodpecker's actions, the camera records the children's joy and longing to express themselves. When Āsiyeh asks for volunteers to retell the story, Qorbān volunteers, but he only writes, 'Last night I did not go to cinema with my father'. As the class leaves for their break, Āsiyeh remains astounded by what Qorbān has written, and Qorbān is upset that she did not understand him. Beyzaie, thus, implies that for Qorbān the story's point is the need to find and tell the

Figure 7.1 Screenshots from *The Crow*. Minutes 2′.10″–13′.55″

truth and that Qorbān had issues in writing the sentence because being an orphan, he could not go to cinema with his father.

Beyzaie's attention to disabled children expands in *The Crow*. In *Downpour*, Hekmati evolves into a constructive intellectual by dedicating his energy to the growth and happiness of his pupils including a disabled boy who plays the main role in Hekmati's temporary ascendance in the school hall scene. In *Stranger*, Āyat is determined to help the disabled boy that he loves and feels responsible for. In both cases, however, due to external impositions, the protagonists fail to fulfil their self-assigned responsibilities towards the next generation. In *The Crow*, however, with Āsiyeh settled in her role as a teacher dedicated to educating disadvantaged children, the film focuses on how her identity has evolved due to her dedication to her intelligent pupils, who, in turn, adore her innovative and compassionate approach to teaching. Beyzaie also shows how this constructive identity helps her understand the past and the present and prepares her for having her own child. The film, thus, highlights dedicated work for expanding the intellectual resources of the underprivileged as the best path to progress at collective level and an ideal form of giving significance to one's life. This also allows Beyzaie to introduce the first female intellectual of Iranian cinema, who, like Beyzaie, grasps, records and reinterprets the fleeting time and its marginalized accounts to cast light on what went wrong and how it can be avoided in the future.

To expand my arguments about creativity in the first chapter, I contend that those who have powerful memories, which may itself originate in and enhance epistemic privilege, have an acute concern with the fleeing time, which is intensified by their capacity for vivid recalling to disrupt the process of automatic forgetting and reconstructing required for the formation of a coherent future-directed narrative of selfhood. Thus, the time lost and its memories become like a burden, and the act of creativity functions like a healing process that provides temporary solace by projecting parallel visions that may achieve concord with imagined addressees and enable the individual to have a feeling of having control over time and the past. In Beyzaie's case, this process is also linked to his concern with the roots, identity and 'being in time' of Iranians. As evident from his discussion with Amjad about how the 'faded photo' problematizes the concepts of waiting, transition and being in time in *Afrā, or the Day Is Passing*, from an early age he has had a philosophical concern with being and time.

Beyzaie: I have, unfortunately, had this concern with time since my earliest works.
Amjad: Why unfortunately?
Beyzaie: Because sometimes you literally see time escaping your grasp, but you cannot do anything about it. As with the pollution of air [in Tehran] which, at times, becomes so tangible, so thick that you think you can take a knife and cut a portion out, I continuously see the passage of time. And the reason I say, unfortunately, is that the constant seeing of the passage of time is by no means pleasant; it breeds suffering.
Amjad: Well, of course, the modern perceptivity breeds suffering, anxiety, and stress.
Beyzaie: I think anyone in any period, even far in the past, would suffer when having such a feeling. As creatures passing in time, such feelings have always been part of our lives, although maybe not for all of us. Those who accept coming, being alive for a time, and then going as a law or habit of nature, may not see it as a concern, so they may not experience this suffering. But for those who are not able to accept this law or get accustomed to it, it remains painful. It is also likely that the idea of the circularity of time and the final return have been originated in a desire to eliminate this anxiety.[24]

If one ignores the verdicts given by others after a person's death, one may argue that a person's identity in its existential, psychological, religious, gender, ethnic and national scopes is a process that ends only when the person dies. Thus, every moment of life harbours the prospect of change in one's identity. Beyzaie is preoccupied with recording the changing forms of our individual and collective identities in an age of rapid transition. He depicts the looming presence of death as a force that may activate or paralyse our constructive curiosity about being or distort it into vicious or distracting habits. He urges his viewers, the potential citizens of his ideal form of togetherness, to activate their positive curiosity and transcend the constructs that discourage them from trying to reshape their lives. His works, therefore, also depict people whose emancipatory curiosity has been (1) disrupted – creating in them reactionary anger – (2) muzzled – making them obedient – or (3) reduced to masochistic, hypocritical and sycophantic attitudes that fuel the engines of arbitrary power and its claims of divine origin. These people fail to be citizens as they shun their social duties, obey instead of thinking, cooperate with the cruel 'others' of their lives to destroy what they do not understand or wait for saviours whom they abandon when the critical moment arrives.[25]

Āsiyeh, therefore, becomes like Beyzaie's spokesperson, a woman whose concerns with origins, time and communicating truth are juxtaposed with the superficial and mediocre mentalities and practices that distort the growth of Iranian culture. Her authenticity is, indeed, reflected in all her encounters. For instance, the scene immediately after the classroom scene highlights how she manages the flirting comments of her colleague, Ebtekār, with politeness and collegial compassion, but with a firm reference to his wife which makes him back off.

Once she is home, the spectator realizes that Deimkār has arranged a TV broadcast of the missing person advert. Āsiyeh and Esālat's disputes – about Esālat's fixation with the missing girl and his acceptance to be searched in the party or Āsiyeh's job, her obstinate ways and dress code which Esālat considers plain – display their differences, but their manners also imply their equality and mutual attraction. The dialogue, here, clarifies that Āsiyeh is writing Ālam's memories, that Āsiyeh and Esālat first met when he was reporting a fund-raising event at her school and that Esālat has a truth-finding side which, though superficial, has potential for growth. Then, when Ālam suggests that it may be better if they have a child, Āsiyeh states, 'she is scared that the child may have hearing disability' (25′–26′). Though realistic, the relationship between the three characters reflects the problematics of individual and familial identity and two clashing ideas of modernity and their corresponding historical and national modalities. As implied by their jobs, Āsiyeh is concerned with mutual communication and enabling her students to speak and use their eyes to hear and read, and Esālat with one-sided communication and top-down provision of ideas through modern technology. While implying a self-reflexive aspect in which Beyzaie urges his viewers to hear his voice by seeing his coded mise en scene and background, her role also makes her represent the desire for finding the origins, qualities and possibilities of grassroots modernity and for genuinely modern people who can see, hear and speak like free citizens and can modernize themselves and produce new forms of being due to their modernity. Āsiyeh and Esālat's attitudes in the party also show that she believes in creating true modernity by curbing the mimicry embedded in consumerist modernization, but he believes in obeying the new social norms and dominant discourses to one's advantage. Symbolically, therefore, Āsiyeh's fear of having a child that cannot hear and speak signifies that Iran's borrowed, top-down modernization is like one-sided communication as it does not produce perceptive citizens who can express their views and become modern by contributing to their own modernization but subjects who cannot hear and talk. Thus, Āsiyeh's role echoes the task that Beyzaie set for himself in a press conference about *The Crow* in 1977: enabling people to experience, see, hear and speak about what they are not used to seeing, hearing and speaking about.[26] This is the same emancipatory trend that Rancière finds in transgressive artists when he suggests his idea of 'redistributing the sensible' and specifies that 'politics revolves around what can be seen and what can be said about it, around who has the ability to see and the talent to speak, around the properties of spaces and the possibilities of time'.[27] In this context, Āsiyeh's role is shown to be like the emancipatory role of an ethically sublime transgressive artist, and her tale and Qorbān's urge to speak the truth about 'not going to cinema with his father' become even more momentous. Āsiyeh trains her students, to find and speak the truth to themselves, to others and to the holders of power, and Qorbān, despite Āsiyeh's original assumptions about his naughtiness, is her best student.

Āsiyeh's writing of Ālam's memories and her participation in Ālam's family gatherings indicate her ability to communicate with the past and desire to write the history of people. As argued in Chapter 1, Beyzaie shares this concern with those who argue for using memory, multiple perspectives and oral history in histography as in *histoire des mentalités*, *annales*, and their micro-cultural forms in *Alltagsgeschichte* or other similar methods of studying lived experience.[28] The slow-paced scene in which Ālam tells her memories to Āsiyeh right after Āsiyeh's dispute with Esālat highlights the intellectual satisfaction Āsiyeh gets from her communion with the past and its importance. Sitting in an armchair with the camera slowly moving in a semi-circle from her left to her right profile, Ālam leaves through her photo albums to open the film's path to historical probing by recounting the stories of her youth. The use of photos for recollection indicates how the new technologies of recording have created new forms of continuity which have changed the philosophical meaning of time and perception. Beyzaie juxtaposes Ālam's shots with shots of Āsiyeh's content face to suggest how these new technologies may boost the work of the historians of lost times. As always, Āsiyeh is associated with illumination by her medium and long shots being framed with a lamp. The spectator finds that Ālam is from a well-established family, and her memories mark the era immediately after the compulsory removal of women's hijab (1936–41), one of the turning points of Iran's history. She talks about women with sun umbrellas, going to cinema with her fiancé who was a colonel, horse carriages, charity events in the national park, listening to a beautiful waltz performed in their honour by the garden party military orchestra and then the war that robbed her of her beloved and gave her a son. While reflecting the era in which the bid for rapid modernization and beautifying the country with the relics of Western modernity took precedence over creating modern citizens, the dialogue signifies that even this faulty approach had a potential for growth that was lost due to the war.

At the school event, as the camera marks Esālat's boredom and Āsiyeh's joy, the first game displays shackled pupils trying to bite into hanging apples, which implies the challenges that voiceless people face when trying to have a proper life in exclusionist societies. Dominated by unintelligible sounds made by the pupils, the soundtrack reinforces this reading. Instead of footballs, they have chains and metal balls, and instead of voice, they produce sounds that while understandable to Āsiyeh are like noise to unequipped ears. A self-reflexive scene, then, offers a play which reflects the nature of policing in Iran and the way official and non-official censor forces authors to say things as if in a sign language. In the play, while a soldier (the police) is arbitrating between two men, he is slapped by a sneaky bystander, but he grabs one of the claimants, assuming he slapped him. Esālat's boredom, here, characterizes him as a man who understands the surface and has no patience for signs and deep structures.

When Esālat leaves 'to waste time somewhere else', Beyzaie introduces a new mystery with a red rose thrown to Āsiyeh lap. The motif of Āsiyeh receiving flowers from a secret admirer is repeated a few times until it is resolved near the end, but each time it is also contrasted with a scene reporting the violence of Tehran's streets to highlight the beauty of Āsiyeh's approach to life, her upbringing as a gardener's daughter and her role

Figure 7.2 Screenshots from *The Crow*. Minutes 14'.50"–28'.40"

as a carrier and creator of beauty.[29] The scene of Āsiyeh's confusion is, then, contrasted with a high-angle long shot of Esālat standing with an open newspaper on the junction of two footpaths in the middle of a park. The two forms of confusion represent their approach to life. Hers is due to a red flower, a symbol of beauty and fertility, a mystery that she must resolve as in a quest. His is due to changes in the appearances of the city which has turned the address of the missing girl into a park. Reinforced by the leafless autumn trees and the crows' cawing, Esālat's confusion is then intensified when he goes to the office of the newspaper to recheck the girl's address but finds that the photo, the letter and the money for the ad arrived in post (Figure 7.2).

Toxic masculinity, fear and the vestiges of medieval and pseudo-modern alienation

This moment of confusion is, then, used as a turning point to reflect the dark aspects of the new city that has replaced the one in which the address still existed. This violent world of kidnapping, rape and death is projected in a nightmarish sequence like the one in *The Journey* when Tāle and Razi are chased by a paedophile tough guy. Waiting for Ebtekār to give her a lift, Āsiyeh mistakenly gets on a car whose knife-holding driver decides to kidnap her when he finds she is not interested in him. Āsiyeh uses an opportunity to hit the man with her shoe, jump out of the car and run. Thus, the film breaks the glittery façade of the new city by taking its heroine out of her socially stable life to the terrors of the city. While implying the type of policing that always arrests those who think differently but fails to do so with those who destroy people's lives, the expressionistic use of camera enhances the noir elements. This is first done by directing the camera's gaze at Āsiyeh's moving body from the driver's view and then showing his hands on the gear and the steering wheel which suggests how an incarnation of toxic masculinity uses a modern vehicle to chase women like preys. It, then, displays images of the city's past and present from Āsiyeh's terrified viewpoint. This use of objects turns them into 'crystal' images, the cornerstones of Gilles Deleuze's theory of 'time-image' in cinema. They, thus, become two-way mirrors which reveal the division of the present into two opposite directions, one 'launched towards the future' and 'the other falling into the past'.[30] While revealing the two directions of time in his 'crystal' images, Beyzaie also splits the camera's perception into the objective, what is seen at the surface, and the subjective, what is felt by Āsiyeh. For Āsiyeh, who is escaping from rape through noisy streets, the billboard of the happy 7-UP woman (who seems to be biting Āsiyeh's head off) and the gaze of the middle-aged man (who looks at her like a commodity and is amused by rather than worried about her running) highlight the absurdity of the present. In a metaphoric turning point, a panting Āsiyeh temporarily shelters in a clocks repair shop where the discrepancy of the hours and minutes displayed on the clocks makes time meaningless. The curious gaze of the frowning owner through his dark glasses makes her give him her watch for inspection. While she is checking outside to see if the driver has chased her, the man inspects the watch. Then, without taking his magnifying loupe, which makes him look hostile, he bends forward to return her watch and states, 'There is nothing wrong with this watch' (31'–34'.30"). The sentence implies that Āsiyeh's conception of the present is correct, but her escape without her watch implies that her experience of the violent present has enhanced her already profound idea of time and that sheltering in this space of timelessness cannot resolve her problems.

The juxtaposition of silence with the chiming of the clocks and the thriller music that plays again after she exits the shop prepares the viewer for a second bout of running which is juxtaposed with 'crystal images' to imply escaping from the infertile litters of old ideas and medieval and modern poles of patriarchal femininity. Thus, a high-angle long shot marks her running along a pavement littered with winter leaves and passing through a gigantic pair of glasses which, though realistic in that such frames are used for marking optician shops, highlight the formation of identity under the gaze of powerful others. Another shot uses a Judaeo-Islamic symbol of divine intervention, *panjeh* (hand/hamsa), as a focal transition to display several full-length mirrors reflecting Āsiyeh's images in contrast with fully covered religious women whose face covers make them like faceless automatons. She, then, passes a cannon of Nader Shah's era (the 1740s), which marks the last of Iran's military victories against Europeans before the Russian and British routing of the Qajars in the 1800s catapulted Iran into several periods of jumbled modernization. Then follows modern motifs of alienation, with heavily made-up faces of female hairpiece mannequins implying how pseudo-modernity turns women into automatons who are as alienated from reality as their religious prototypes in the previous scene. Āsiyeh's fear of the heads is reflected in the flight of terrified pigeons, her gaze at the gigantic steel skeletons of half-finished skyscrapers next to old buildings and her descent from more than sixty steps. The step scene is in dialogue with Golestan's *Brick and Mirror*, in which in one scene, Hāshem, an antihero, is shocked by a similar set of steps, but instead of going down (to the past), he goes up as if escaping into a half-finished building signifying the incomplete business of Iran's modernization.[31] Āsiyeh, however, descends the steps, which foreshadows the intensification of her quest, for finding the origins of the present by investigating the past. Together, these expressionistic shots represent the alienating impact of living with fear under multisided surveillance in a city whose residents are dangling between medieval and pseudo-modern forms of alienation. When Āsiyeh arrives home, the camera registers how she has been shaken by the experience. As thunder strikes, she goes under the shower with her raincoat in a shot that echoes Hekmati or Ra'nā's moments of cleansing and rebirth by walking under the rain. The camera, however, extends the game of fear by creating a shot like Hiscock's shower scene in *Psycho*, but in the absence of actual stabbing, the shot implies metaphorical death, cleansing and rebirth (Figure 7.3).

The film, then, switches to Esālat's conversation with Deimkār about the address of the advert being in the middle of a park. This motif later evolves to display the nature of life in a 'short-term society' where, as Homa Katouzian states, the 'pickaxe' approach to politics and modernization leads to constant demolishing and rebuilding rather than refurbishing and reforming.[32] At political levels, this tendency involves denying the achievements of previous regimes or managers, focusing only on their failures, ruining the signs of their success and suppressing independent systems of

Figure 7.3 Screenshots from *The Crow*. Minutes 30′.40″–34′.35″

transferring and assessing the knowledge of the past in fear of losing legitimacy. It also suggests a tendency to engage in revolution and regime change rather than reform. In Beyzaie's vision, this phenomenon is highlighted to signify that in Iran the past, like the country's 30-year-old buildings, is demolished rather than recreated for awareness. The film plays with absence, presence, nostalgia and contentment to highlight this. The girl's alley, Gozar-e Delgoshā (Heart-warming Alley), and the gardened mansion that it led to, Bāgh-e Delgoshā (Heart-warming Garden), imply a cure for nostalgia. However, while the alley and the mansion were turned into a park thirty years ago, their names are repeated on the TV screen as no one seems to know about the past of the city and its people.

The hallucinatory present, the house of the past and the home of fertility and love

Āsiyeh does not mention anything about her experience, but having suffered a kidnapping trauma, she now identifies with the missing girl. This is first reflected in the next scene in which a dazed Āsiyeh, sitting next to a Valor heater, murmurs to Ālam about being unwell and having joint pain, like her. The metaphorical mis en scene and dialogue, here, place the references to Āsiyeh and Ālam's painful joints next to the image of the missing girl on the TV to suggest how the joints of time are flawed (37'–38') and link the two eras by linking the two women. Āsiyeh now insists that rather than broadcasting a TV report, one must search for a missing person. Thus, when the newspaper editor, Dabiri, informs them about finding a girl's corpse, she asks Esālat that they go to the scene. This leads to the second noir encounter with the city around a corpse that Dabiri has already identified as not related to Esālat's case. The noir motifs are enhanced by the rainy night, the presence of the police and Dabiri's references to fingerprints. The use of dramatic irony allows the viewer to trace the feelings that overwhelm Āsiyeh as she kneels, gazes at the corpse and faints just when the corpse is lifted to be carried away. Though realistically justifiable, the presence of five observers with mask-like hats watching Āsiyeh as she faints creates an inter-filmic link with Beyzaie's *Stranger* in which the protagonists encounter five tall men in situations in which their uncanny presence surrealistically represents the forces of death and destruction.

Āsiyeh, who has fallen ill and is cared for by Ālam and their young housemaid, hallucinates about her pupils cheering and Ebtekār calming them in her room, someone throwing her a red rose, a door opening by itself and a crow cawing a few times as the change of light indicate the passing of time. She finally wakes up during one of Ālam's family gatherings and realizes that she has been sleeping in front of the guests. She watches a guest moving his glasses back and forth to inspect a photo in a newspaper, Ālam playing cartomancy, the maid turning on a kerosene lamp and the guests who are mostly old and have seeing or hearing issues, chatting, playing games, napping, having fruit or tea. Esālat, then, waves to her, and she jumps when a child runs in to comment on their beautiful flowers. The sequence is one of Beyzaie's typical forms of linking everyday activities to his protagonist's mental processes and worries. While in dialogue with Sohrab Shaid Saless's *Still Life* (1974), the focus on the manners, facial features and hobbies of old people and Ālam's recollections of being a nurse during the Second World War and caring for her husband for three years also reveal Beyzaie's artistic attention to neglected individuals and their histories. Thus, displaying the people of the past in present becomes Beyzaie's second way of constructing a 'crystal image'. These people share Ālam's memories and their presence points to hidden pasts and unknown futures, a point that Beyzaie later expands to construct an idea of memory which I call the nostalgic burden of the past. This form of memory, which Henri Bergson only hints at in his writings, diverges from his idea of habitual, automatic memory, which replicates past action as if engraved in the mind and body, or that of pure image remembrance, which signifies and is recognized as the past. As David Gross argues, this third type, which may be triggered by sensory inputs, overwhelms the mind with 'unsolicited' floods of images which are so intensely detached from the individual's immediate situation that they disrupt his or her ability to deal with reality.[33]

Beyzaie had already experimented with such forms of memory in *So Dies Akbar the Hero* in a style that echoed Shakespeare's use of soliloquies and asides in his tragedies and O'Neill's *Long Day's Journey into Night*. Here, however, he made it more tangible by focusing on how Āsiyeh's writing of Ālam's memories triggers in Ālam the memories of hope and love and then the 'unsolicited' recollections of loss, which disrupt her ability to cope with her present reality. At an allegorical level, for what it is worth, I also argue that the references to Ālam's fiancé, a colonel, who died in the war, her husband, a judge, who died after three years of illness following the war and Esālat's adoption in the 1940s, mark Ālam as an embodiment of Iran's encounter with the hopes and failures of rapid modernization. Thus, the colonel and the judge as well as Esālat, who shares an interest in modern technology with the colonel, represent the dominant discourses of their eras: the militarily defined, yet still hopeful modernization of the 1920s and 1930s, the paralysed and chaotic democracy of the 1940s and early 1950s, and the consumerism of the 1960s and 1970s. As to the two women, both are intelligent, educated and caring, but Āsiyeh transcends Ālam. Whereas Ālam is stock in a lost past, Āsiyeh's job, quest for knowledge and divergent thinking enable her to sublimate her marginalized origin as a woman from a lower-class background and behave in ways that suggest her as an ideal role model for modernity. This level may also contain an allegorical aspect in that Āsiyeh's name echoes that of Pharaoh's sympathetic wife in the Quranic tale of Moses. Thus, Āsiyeh's enlightened visions may echo Farah Diba's views, which were more constructive than the Shah who was more like Esālat.

Beyzaie builds on Āsiyeh's hysteric concern with the missing girl to list the fears of women in a world in which toxic masculinity is still accepted, if not celebrated. Āsiyeh's heightened sensibility now works like Hitchcock's protagonists for whom, as in Ben and Jo McKenna's case in *The Man Who Knew Too Much* (1956) every corner may hold a sinister presence. She enumerates that the girl may have been kidnapped, beaten, seduced, raped, killed or forced into prostitution. Esālat's matter-of-fact approach to life, however, makes him brush away such events as inevitable in large cities. Completing the discourse that he initiated in *The Journey*, Beyzaie, here, questions this acceptance and suggests that curbing violence, including the hushed forms against women, children and the marginalized must be the main goal of a modern society as it enables them to contribute to the life of the country.

The conflict between Esālat's centrist practicality and Āsiyeh's outsider perceptiveness is further illustrated with a display of her class origins. When Āsiyeh's parents come to visit her during Ālam's family party, Āsiyeh's father, who is anxious that their lower-class appearance may damage Āsiyeh's standing in the family, chooses to meet her in the greenhouse. He examines the flowers as Āsiyeh and her mother talk.

Figure 7.4 Screenshots from *The Crow*. Minutes 35′.30″–44′.45″

Then, in response to Āsiyeh's insistence that they go inside, he talks about how she can improve her already remarkable greenhouse.

While implying the impact of class boundaries and the remnants of feudal relations on human identity, the dialogue reveals that their compassion towards and concern for creating natural beauty have been influential in shaping Āsiyeh's character. Moreover, unlike the old men and women in the house, who are sedentary and busy eating, smoking or playing backgammon and bingo, Āsiyeh's parents look active and are probably still working. Thus, the third house of the film is a greenhouse teeming with compassion, fertility and flowers in which the camera associates the three characters with the beauty of nature. This is a green oasis in the world of violent streets where no green trees can be seen. This oasis is free from class pretentions and boundaries, and Āsiyeh's father who is still anxious about such boundaries feels comfortable in it. Unlike her parents, Āsiyeh has transcended class boundaries.[34] Because she gains satisfaction from her dedication to growing flowers and educating deprived children, her sense of belonging is not linked to origins and class recognitions. As her sleeping in presence of Ālam's relatives suggests, she is as comfortable with them in the house as with her parents in the greenhouse. The city, however, is not safe enough for this new woman whose potential for growth and contribution to life transcends the people around her. Her class mobility and her awareness of the strength and failures of both classes have intensified her ability to identify with her others, which is the source of true morality, but the greenhouse and the school are her real homes as they contain the possibility of fertility, care and growth (Figure 7.4).

Performative depictions of alienation and the intrusion of the city into the house

The third meeting with the city, then, occurs in a space dedicated to unidentified corpses, a morgue, which, as a locus of the dead, is contrasted with the greenhouse. Esālat, Deimkār and Dabiri discuss a girl who committed suicide by potassium cyanide. This suggests she was either a leftist rebel or a victim of seduction or rape. Though different in their implications, the three causes reflect the violence and opportunism embedded in the hierarchy of power relations. Dabiri's joyful references to the sociological and psychological studies on sadism and sexual violence and the possibility that the girl's murderer himself may have sent the advert for fun highlight how detached reporting of such events neutralizes one's sensitivity to their import. Determined to make Āsiyeh happy, Esālat now offers to pay for a new advert with his own address and promise of payment for information. The next scene, then, depicts Āsiyeh explaining to her colleagues that the sedatives made her 'jump from Sunday to Tuesday' and that she does not remember the day in between. Then, in response to Ebtekār's friendly complaint about standing him up when he was to give her a lift, she says, 'I am not a trained woman, Mr Ebtekār. I won't stand you up next time' (46'–48'). These dialogues are realistic, but their juxtaposition defamiliarizes their content to imply how trauma disrupts one's perception of time and history, how violence is accepted as normal and how the performative extremes of gender roles dictated through education may disrupt growth.

The next sequence offers another noir encounter with the city, this time in a self-reflexive setting to show how perception can be manipulated by cinematography. A man contacts Esālat and tells him to come to a local scrapyard to get the missing girl, alone, with money and without informing the police. The mise en scene and action combine eerie, performative motifs with realistic ones as a woman with a white lace on her face emerges from within the ominous smoke of burning wastes. The anxiety created by Esālat's cautious steps through the smoke and the broken oil barrels as he follows this ghost-like idea of the past is intensified by the thriller music creating an ambiance of sinister mystery. Suddenly, however, Esālat notices a camera on a tripod and his friends appear from behind piles of broken tins to laugh and state that they are directing a newsreel about pollution and could not think of a better way to bring him here as their reporter. Beyzaie's use of terror to create a moment of sublime and meta-cinema to reveal its mundanity transcends his self-reflexive motifs in *Downpour* and *The Journey* and becomes the foremost example of playful engagement with meta-cinema in Iran. Thus, while maintaining the narrative function of the scene, Beyzaie creates a different form of sublime which uses comic relief and parodic framing to defamiliarize reality by showing the constructed nature of what may be assumed to be objective reality. Such forms of framing are among his most striking tools of expression and thus deserve theoretical examination.

In his writing on aesthetics, Rancière argues that though it may embed mimesis, the aesthetic regime is often anti-representational. Thus, rather than being limited to mimesis, it assembles images to create new orders which redistribute the sensible.[35] Considering the chaos created by consumerist advertising, which uses such forms of reassembling to manipulate the sensible without redistributing it for emancipation, this means that emancipatory art occurs only when its aesthetic reframing shocks the viewers into seeing or hearing what they are indoctrinated to ignore as useless noise, trivial or inevitable. This interruption in the customary ways of seeing and hearing has the potential to create alternative orders and trigger moments of emancipation when the viewers may step out of their normal roles as cogs in the scheme of distribution and perceive things, including their own lives and functions, differently. Thus, great art, whether directly political or not, is always political in the cultural sense of the term. It is a transgressive deviation that displays the possibility of another sphere by new forms of framing. As argued before, framing has always been the foremost factor in producing meaning in society, especially in beatifying rituals. With the aesthetic regime of art, however, framing became more radical in the way it yoked together motifs from conflicting ends of the pyramid of power relations and from the new forms of intercultural and inter-paradigmatic cross-fertilization and reformulation. The process always involves changing and repositioning the motifs of a frame or combining them with motifs and processes from others to initiate 'key change', in which an activity, 'already meaningful in terms of some primary framework, is transformed into something patterned on this activity but seen by the participants to be something quite else'.[36] The example of *The Crow*, therefore, demonstrates that Beyzaie's use of noir or Hitchcockian motifs and techniques, which critics refer to as 'influence',[37] transcends the limits of this term as instead of acquiring and expanding the grammar of the genre, it achieves a level of reframing and key change which subvert the genre to comment on cinematic and social reality.

The newsreel itself suggests Beyzaie's concern with the environment at a time when it was rarely a subject of inquiry in feature films. The two interviews with the repairmen who own the scrapyard exemplify Beyzaie's dark satire. The concocted appearance of the repairmen, the smoke that blinds the view of the camera and the dialogue mock the bureaucratic nature of such programmes. One of them states that since their film is about pollution in Tehran and their scrapyard is outside Tehran, the crew should go to find the causes of the pollution inside Tehran. The other, whose malapropic use of technical words and conjunctions suggests his ignorant attempts to exonerate himself, makes boastful claims about solving the problem at the global level if he is given facilities. As part of Beyzaie's panoramic display of rootless people and odd locations representing the alienated city, the scene reinforces the idea of how obsession with the surface has made people unaware of their roots and obsessed with trivial forms of contentment, as in the parties, or absurd appearances and comments, as in the interviews or Deimkār's suggestion that Esālat may change the news if he does not like it. This dark comedy continues with people calling their home number to give fake information in hope of receiving the prize. Then, two policemen – a sergeant and a clerk – show up at their door. Beyzaie uses their difference in heights, hats and moustaches and their confusion over Āsiyeh's responses to turn them into copies of Franco and Ciccio and suggest the essential absurdity of the way they interrogate Āsiyeh when the city is overwhelmed by crime.

> **Sergeant**: We want to ask you some questions about this missing person.
> **Āsiyeh**: Me? I don't know anything about her.
> **Sergeant**: Isn't this your address?
> **Āsiyeh**: Yes.
> **Sergeant**: The advert was given by you, so tell us more about the girl.
> **Āsiyeh**: We don't know.
> **Sergeant**: How come? Isn't it odd? Maybe you are hiding something. Did she go missing from this house?
> **Āsiyeh**: No, she wasn't here before. She appeared amongst us only when she got lost.
> [The clerk smiles. The sergeant looks up unable to process.] We are helping you. My husband is trying to find her [pause], so am I, in a way. You know searching is a contagious disease. [The sergeant looks at the clerk.]
> **Clerk**: I don't get it.
> **Āsiyeh**: Maybe my husband can explain it better.
> **Sergeant**: Please, tell him to pay us a visit. The police station near the post office.
> **Āsiyeh**: Yes, sure.
> **Sergeant**: [Sizing the house and Āsiyeh.] You have a pretty house, ma'am. (53′–55′)

Āsiyeh's confusion is due to their unjustifiable involvement with the case and the unexpected nature of the call. Beyzaie's performative rendering, however, uses this confusion to generate poetically charged statements about being and not being and appearing only after getting lost. This poetic comment suggests the nature of human attention which may only realize the importance of something when it is lost. Āsiyeh's encounter with the policemen also displays the discrepancy between the house and its greenhouse and the infertile world of violence and practical policing which is incapable of understanding the situation. Failing to understand Āsiyeh's account, the tall sergeant, who has an armband of judo and a handlebar moustache, comments on the beauty of the house as if he is referring to Āsiyeh. The implied equating of a house with a woman further reinforces the idea of the outside world

Figure 7.5 Screenshots from *The Crow*. Minutes 49'.30"–64'.40"

invading the house and exemplifies the objectifying gaze directed towards women in toxic masculinity (Figure 7.5).

Magic or enlightenment: Voyage to the past and the army of alienation in the present

Āsiyeh's anger shows her frustration with this gaze and the sergeant's interrogation-like approach and insinuations. When she enters the house, initially she picks up a cigarette, but she immediately puts it away, moves to her desk which has an antique lamp, picks up her pen and says, 'Okay, let's continue. You were talking about springtime and decorative lighting' (55′–56′). The motifs of the mise en scene and the scenic design, here, signify how intellectual curiosity and creativity may protect individuals from frustration and addiction. While the light on Āsiyeh's desk associates her with enlightenment and producing and transferring knowledge, Ālam's appearance, her shuffling of her cartomancy set and the armillary sphere which conjures the idea of the universe or an orbuculum associate her with magic and ritual divination. This also echoes Ālam and Āsiyeh's metaphoric roles because whereas Ālam's era sought to conjure modernity from nothing, Āsiyeh wants to construct it by knowledge.

Ālam talks about her engagement with the colonel, his large format camera that someone had brought for him from Europe, people pointing at them in admiration and her father who had not yet gone bankrupt. Āsiyeh comments that in her family memories are luxuries and that no one seems to have a memory worth recounting. While apparently a comment on class, this is more about how poverty and lack of education rob people of their potential for citizenship. For her, having and recording memories for the posterity is like having a voice to oppose the dominant discourses which brush away unwanted details to reduce the past to a disaster zone or an anticipation of a present that they, the saviours, have created. Āsiyeh's contradictory attitudes towards the newspaper advert – tearing one and gazing at the one used for wrapping their laundry – marks forgetting as a cultural failure. She softens the advert photo and states: 'How soon they threw it away!' and tells the maid to 'keep all the newspaper copies'. Her dialogue with Ālam reflects on the difficulty of finding the girl, the threatening size of the city and the prospects of Ālam joining her to see the city. Ālam responds that her city was the old Tehran but finally agrees and says, 'Let's look for the old Tehran!' (57′–59′). The points about the old and the new Tehran juxtapose the promise of modernity and its derailment into consumerism and authoritarianism. Thus, here, the dialogue switches to the Second World War as Ālam talks of typhus, rationing of bread and yellow sugar, becoming a nurse, polish immigrants, heavy snow reaching the knees, a hospital flooded by patients and a little boy crying as if asking for *amān* (mercy/shelter/respite). Esālat's arrival, then, becomes a transition suggesting the connection between the little boy's status and his first name. Beyzaie, thus, turns Esālat into the grown version of one of his lost boys who has, nevertheless, been lost at another level despite being adopted. Esālat's excited report of his detective work on a magnified version of the photo displays this loss while echoing what Ālam has been saying about her youth. His technology, however, has only given him the surface: smiling, happiness, spring, earrings, a necklace and a flower pergola. The actual links are beyond his idea of reality as his curiosity is skin-deep. A satiric scene, then, implies how the police's approach is even worse than Esālat's as they now suspect him and want to send him to the Criminal Investigation Office.

The film, then, creates a unique expressionistic scene with Ālam and Āsiyeh dressed in the 1930s' style walking near Hasan Ābād Square, National Garden Gate and Office of Birth Certificates, where the first vestiges of Iranian architectural modernity appeared in the 1900s. Her plan is to find the districts, images and people that have been lost to time, the city of the mother, the pre-war Tehran of the years of authoritarian modernity which was to rebuild Tehran like a European capital. The soundtrack which has, up to here, been dominated by noise, voice and thriller music becomes nostalgic and calm. First, the sounds and images of cars are replaced with the sound of the wind and horses' hooves on cobblestone, and then, the carriages, buildings, a bike moving in slow motion and photo-like soldiers and people in the 1930s costume start moving to conjure up the past as Ālam's voice completes the magic.

> **Ālam:** Look at this. It is old, crumbling. The tram is no longer there. *La cantine* is no longer there. Where is the wheat silo? Who will believe that one day all the streets were cobblestoned? I told him, 'Qāzi (judge). His is an indelible memory. I can't forget my beloved who died so young. I will marry you, but not because of love. Qāzi, I will remain loyal to him.' He ruined his life with me. He said, 'Ālam, you don't love me. Why should we live together?' That was why he left, but he never married until he fell ill, and I nursed him for three years. (59′.45″–61′.10″)

The two failed love stories, thus, form the narrative of desire for belonging, freedom, growth and joy and its failure which echoes how in the 1920s, the intelligentsia gave up the dreams of freedom and democracy for stability and rapid progress under the first Pahlavi, hoping that democracy will be attained later, and how this hope was derailed by authoritarian capitalism and consumerist modernization. The music which is made diegetic with the unreal orchestra in the background evolves with the melodies of Javad Maroufi's *Golden Dreams* and *Zhila* (1950) to combine nostalgia and hope and reinforce the idea of a forgone life with children playing and box cameras taking people's photos in lively streets with food stalls, people on bikes, soldiers and carriages. The slowing of the action turns this forgone land into the film's second chronotope where the present pauses to embrace the past. The camera, then, zooms out to focus on Āsiyeh and Ālam with the images of the past in a blurred background and the melody of Maroufi's *Golden Dreams* on accordion conjuring the idea of recovering the lost time.

> **Āsiyeh:** Your childhood neighbourhood [...]. Why don't we go there?
> **Ālam:** How can you know where it is? My neighbourhood has been lost for years. A few years ago, once my late brother and I went to find it, but we ended up in an unreal world, where all people were like strangers. (61′.10″–64′.30″)

The music of *tār*, here, reinforces the slowing of the action to enhance the poetic impact of Ālam's lines which create an emotion like Sohrab Sepehri's 'I am from Kashan, but my city is not Kashan//My city has been lost//With fever and ardour I have made a home on the other side of the night'. Musing about the past, reactions to it and nostalgia are, of course, central to many literary works. In Proust, it marks the vicissitudes of human sensory experience, thoughts and emotions and the process of coming to terms with one's conflicting impulses. In Sepheri, it leads to transcendence by embracing solitude. In Shakespeare, it evokes the 'sweet silent thought' and 'remembrance of things past', but it also triggers a realization of how the memory of love wash away the pain of 'old woes'. In Edwin Arlington Robinson, it makes a drunken Mr Flood get drunk in memory of the past, but it also makes him realize that 'There was nothing in the town below – Where strangers would have shut the many doors//That many friends had opened long ago'.[38] In Beyzaie, however, poetic nostalgia is not conjured for transcendence or wallowing in self-pity and feelings of loss or desire for returning to the past. He loves its poetry but is adamant to show how the loss or the mistakes of this past affected the present or how the absence of proper preservation destroys its treasures.

Thus, the smoke that implies the vanishing of this past functions as a transition to the present and images of dust- or cloth-covered workers with pickaxe and shovels in a lime factory. Thus, the army of the present is shown to be preparing for a mission to destroy the vestiges of the past in a self-reflexive scene in which Esālat is a reporter in a documentary about Tehran.

> [A construction worker picks up his shovel like a rifle. The camera turns right where a smiling Esālat is standing with a worker. In the background workers are marching.]
> **Esālat**: It seems as if the real face of all of us will be forgotten soon. [Turning the microphone to the head worker.] Don't you agree?
> **Worker**: What can I say? To be honest, although we're working together, we rarely see each other's face.
> **Esālat**: What do you do if you want to find a co-worker between these people?
> **Worker**: I will call his name, loudly. If he doesn't hear me, I will call him louder. If he still doesn't hear me, then, I'll shout. (64'.30"–6'.30")

The robotic military imagery which echoes similar scenes in Beyzaie's earlier films conjures the idea of an unthinking army dedicated to destroying the past. This is a world in which no one knows others, voices remain unheard due to the noise of demolishing and building, and everything is changing with such an astronomical speed that uprooting has become a natural part of life.[39] Rather than being anti-modern, however, such scenes in Beyzaie's city films reflect his preservationist and conservationist views about nature and art forms, including the architectural achievements of the nineteenth and early twentieth centuries. Thus, he promotes a kind of modernization which, though hybrid and cosmopolitan, is not alienating because it works by reformulating culture for emancipatory and democratic purposes (Figure 7.5).

A room of one's own against the fake present and its worlds of fiction and mimicry

Beyzaie's emphasis on the occupation era is not limited to sociopolitical aspects. As in *Occupation*, he links the loss of people to the loss of potential for growth. Thus, at one level, the film highlights the forgotten tales of human suffering in the era and the disastrous impacts of imposed wars and political suppression on people's lives. However, since the film's setting is the mid-1970s, and it marks the loose foundations of the tower of Iranian modernity, the interaction between the past and present suggests the occupation era as a turning point in the journey of Iranian modernity and like Beyzaie's earlier films or Golestan's *The Ghost Valley's Treasure Mysteries* (1974) predicts a disaster lurking in the corner.

Undergoing a nervous breakdown due to being overwhelmed by her memories and people calling with fake news about the girl, Ālam tears the notebook in which Āsiyeh has been writing her memories. She complains of having nightmares about the girl and insists that they must find her. Collecting the torn papers, the maid nags about Ālam calling her nosy when she wanted to clean her room, and Āsiyeh goes to her own centre of gravity, the greenhouse to water her plants while watching the maid taking the torn papers out under a downpour. With her desire for registering the past shattered like the petals of a flower, Āsiyeh resorts to caring for her greenhouse present, a room of her own. As the first time Ālam's sensitivity to her room is mentioned, the scene foreshadows the final revelation while implicitly comparing the room with Āsiyeh's greenhouse. The two women, thus, are suggested to have their own rooms, which like Virginia Woolf's 'A Room of One's Own' function like places for contemplation, regeneration and productivity. It is doubtful if Beyzaie had access to Woolf's essay, but the ideas are similar. Both Ālam and Āsiyeh are outsiders to the world around them and have rooms that reflect their inner space, but whereas Ālam uses her inner space to create an intrigue to test her son and make him aware of who she is and what is being lost, Āsiyeh uses hers to create beauty and contemplate the givens to create resolutions.

A dialogue then reflects Esālat's failure to grow. He enters the greenhouse and compares it to paradise, yet he does not see that care is the component that has enabled Āsiyeh to create this paradise. His inauthenticity is, thus, re-established as he declares that he no longer wants to look for the girl and does not care if Ālam is anxious as she is not really his mother. Thus, although Esālat's abilities and relations remain realistic and suggest his positive qualities, his attitudes, background and occupation suggest the alienation of pseudo-modern intelligentsia. The greenhouse scene ends with Āsiyeh stating that Ālam is so obsessed with the girl that she seems to assume that finding her will delay her own death and oblivion. Her comment on death, then, functions as a transition to the third reflexive scene, a TV newsreel in which five men are crying over a woman's corpse, while people are watching from roofs and windows. While its embedding in the film comments on the play of reality and fiction by referring to an earlier scene in which a real corpse was not mourned, the newsreel itself highlights the theme of loss and violence against women. Due to Deimkār and Dabiri's presence, wherever Esālat is, and their three-musketeers-like quest for finding the girl, the scene also reflects on pseudo-modern masculinity. This theme is reinforced by their dandified looks, detective gestures, constant smoking and drinking, cheery attitudes when listing the fates of missing girls and finally their drunken decision to calm Āsiyeh and Ālam by lying about the girl (77′–78′).

Once more, Beyzaie's approach to breaking the film's narrative illusion deserves attention. The scene is seamlessly sutured to the narrative until children start throwing rocks at the corpse causing the actress to jump up and curse them until the director persuades her to retake the shot. She then lies down and covers herself with a chador, the five men pretend crying and Esālat talks to the camera about negligence and disaster. Finally, the actress gets up and removes her chador and her dark brown wig to reveal her Farrah Fawcett style, permed and dyed blond, hair. Besides their film-on-film reflexive aspects, the three 'newsreel' scenes use dark comedy, Juvenalian social satire and a juxtaposition of poor people with pseudo-modern intelligentsia to comment on the prevalence of mimicry and borrowed identities among the latter, particularly those involved in cinema industry. This final reflexive scene also reframes Shakespeare's use of comic relief and Hitchcock's use of sequences of frightening and comic scenes. Both use the technique to joke with death and suggest the apathy of life to human suffering or the normality of death to those dealing with it, like a gravedigger who may even joke about it. *The Crow* evokes the same feelings but by contrasting a serious reflection on death with a performance which becomes comic due to children's meddling, it also displays the constructed nature of reality in cinema, the interplay of reality, illusion and fiction in identity formation and the difficulty of filming in actual locations. The momentary puncturing of cinematic illusion, thus, reinforces the tragedy of Ālam's life and the dark comedy of our apathy to other people's suffering while displaying how cinema communicates truth through deception or distorts truth by reconstructing or editing recorded images.

The next sequence then resolves the mystery of the flowers and implies the need to support the marginalized by celebrating Qorbān's love for Āsiyeh. Āsiyeh, who has been helping Ebtekār to make his 'craft classes' innovative, criticizes Ebtekār about the flowers, which urges Ebtekār to find the real culprit. This leads to a key scene in which Ebtekār, Āsiyeh and their students watch Qorbān through the glass door of the class as he leaves a flower for Āsiyeh. Here, as the mise en scene suggests Ebtekār and Āsiyeh's similarity, the statement in which Ebtekār reminds Āsiyeh that Qorbān 'does not have anyone' elevates his position from an infatuated idiot to an intellectual admirer. Thus, Ebtekār's role, played by Jamshid Layegh who also played Navvāb in *Downpour*, allows Beyzaie to make an inter-filmic reference to a type of middle ground, passive intellectuality that lacks Hekmati or Āsiyeh's divergent thinking and innovative probing but is sympathetic towards the marginalized and influential in raising the protagonists' awareness. The scene also compares Ebtekār's love for Āsiyeh with Qorbān's as he is trapped in a loveless marriage in which he 'does not have anyone' to talk to.

By juxtaposing the children's reactions with Āsiyeh and Ebtekār's, the scene also implies the need for a form of surveillance that promotes support rather than punishment. Learning that Qorbān has been leaving the flowers for Āsiyeh, his classmates ridicule him, and they fight, but Ebtekār separates them, and Āsiyeh embraces the bruised Qorbān under the blossoming tree in the school yard which signifies the change of season and the beauty of reclaiming the marginalized. Thus, the emotional attachment between an orphan and a caring adult, which was disrupted in *Downpour* and *Stranger* and crushed in *The Journey* reaches fulfilment in *The Crow*. Between the two flower-related school scenes, a shot displays Esālat and Dabiri in the bleak Office of Criminal Investigation where after they fail to answer any questions about the girl, the inspector says, 'Our duty is not to search for *something* about which we don't know anything'. Then, a scene reflecting Āsiyeh's thoughts compares Qorbān's love for her with her parents' love as her father gives her a white rose. Both represent the downtrodden, implying that Āsiyeh embodies an Iran that appreciates and silently

Figure 7.6 Screenshots from *The Crow*. Minutes 66′.50″–77′.25″

communicates with them. Thus, the unknown *something* in the inspector's statement is revealed to be the feelings of belonging and being loved, as the ultimate sources of happiness for all people. Āsiyeh has the potential to give and receive these feelings due to her ties with her marginalized parents and pupils, but these are missing in Ālam's life. Like Iran's chance of having an authentic form of modernity, she has lost the chance of having these sources of happiness (Figure 7.6).

The people of the past and present in the city of the present

Beyzaie, then, uses the flower in Āsiyeh's father's hand and the one on Ālam's dress in a family party to suggest fertility as the source of his content, and its lack as that of Ālam's discontent. Ālam talks about the pain in her fingers being due to working with cold water during the Second World War and dismisses the nursing award she received for it. While the focus on her hands marks her agency, the pain and the term 'worthless award' signify the absence of outcomes, darkening the present like her 'unsolicited' memories of lost dreams. As Ālam is stating that Āsiyeh needs a hat to resemble her youth, Āsiyeh arrives and tries to cheer her up with a record of one of Qamar's 1930s love songs. Assuming that she has taken the record from her room, Ālam furiously goes to check, but even after being reassured, she remains troubled. When the guests praise Āsiyeh's beauty in her wedding photo, she insists Ālam looked prettier in hers. Yet, when she shows them Ālam's photo, they cannot see properly. Their failure to recognize Ālam justifies her feelings of being confined in memories that no one else has. This, in turn, makes Āsiyeh identify with her. Marking how self-identification enables us to transcend the self-obsessed limits of seeing, a mirror shot, then, captures Āsiyeh ordering her hair like a young Ālam. Thus, Āsiyeh's sensitivity to signs as a teacher of deaf children and her empathy with Ālam's narrative of selfhood enable her to transcend Esālat's detective games. The focus on the record and photo as technological products signifies how technology may help reread the past at personal and collective levels and give depth to our conception of modernity rather than making it shallow. It also shows that without rereading the past, one cannot understand or improve the present, particularly because recording microhistories that contradict official histories is a democratic and emancipatory practice.

Āsiyeh's ability to surpass superficial objectivity enables her to discover Ālam's microhistory which is mourning its loss due to her son's superficiality and people's oblivion or apathy. This ability is also marked when Esālat's white lie about finding the girl infuriates Ālam. Beyzaie places these debates in the family reunion to display the inability of others, even those born in the same era, to penetrate the surface of events. Working with the interplay of shadows and light as Āsiyeh follows Ālam up the staircase, the camera reflects her gaze at Ālam entering her room and Esālat seeing off the guests. With the camera framing the back of her head and torso in-focus and the out-of-focus image of guests leaving, Beyzaie creates a shot like the earlier pocket searching party scene to imply Āsiyeh's sublimated vision and reinforces it by having Āsiyeh criticize Esālat for not showing Ālam any gratitude or love and for giving her alcoholic drinks. When everyone has left, Ālam, who seems to have realized the depth of her character, emerges from her room to share another of her guarded relics with her.

> Ālam: [Descending the steps.] Did they leave? [Āsiyeh, who has lighted a cigarette, looks up, puts it out and gets up to help her.] You have not seen their youths. We were a large family. Today, my family invites you to see them as they were.
> Āsiyeh: This album, hmm?
> Ālam: [The camera zooms in from behind Āsiyeh to show her focus on the photos.] He took great photos. He had a large format camera that someone had bought for him from abroad. [As the camera pans from Āsiyeh's left to her face and right.] Look at them! You're a little girl, and they're grownups. The fairy-tale titans of your dreams. [The camera focuses on Āsiyeh's hand touching the empty spaces and stickers of numerous small photos missing from the album.] Strong and immortal heroes. [The arc shot of Āsiyeh gazing at the photos and listening to Ālam brings the camera to its initial position behind her head.] Then, you gradually become bigger, and they become smaller until they die one by one, and you have to bury them. (86′.30″–88′)

The camera's circling around Āsiyeh marks how her vision is sublimated by the experience. The close-up of her hand touching the stickers of the missing small photos as she briefly gazes at the large ones reflects how she, like an epistemically perceptive genealogist of knowledge, pays as much attention to what is missing as to what is present. The large photos, the reports of dominant discourses are there, but the small ones, the people's accounts, are missing.

The next scene features Āsiyeh's journey to the old Tehran to fill these metaphoric gaps. The camera follows her mind as she leaves a half-lit tunnel and is embraced by the accordion music and the images of old Tehran. While exiting the tunnel implies Āsiyeh's journey from a subconscious hunch to conscious discovery, the repetition of the shot of a girl pulling a face echoes Ālam's youthful mischief in her old body. The focus on a camera and a wheel also marks Āsiyeh's attention to Ālam's words about her fiancé's camera and how the past rolled to the present. The occupation era is, thus, marked as the advent of a neo-colonial era leading to the escalation of the distorting changes in Iran's modernization. Wearing a hat like those worn in the era of hijab removal, Āsiyeh visits one of Ālam's relatives, a colonel. He recalls the names of soldiers serving under him, but the name of Ālam's alley escapes him. Āsiyeh, then, accompanies Ālam to a cemetery, where even the stones can no longer be read. This is, then, contrasted with a lively morning scene in which while Esālat is doing Swedish exercises, shaving and dressing and Āsiyeh is brushing her hair and teeth, Āsiyeh states that Ālam's reaction to the news about finding the girl shows she knows something. The sequence highlights the couple's contrast. Esālat is technologically adept and objective but superficial and obsessed with the present. Though open to technology, Āsiyeh is not fascinated by it and her apparent subjectivity is only because she sees a subject of inquiry in every object. Esālat is trapped in instrumental reasoning, synchronic inspection and surface structures; Āsiyeh is a genealogist of knowledge whose emotional intelligence, communicative reasoning and diachronic scrutiny of roots make her alert. Prompted by what one of Ālam's relatives says about getting lost to make others look for him, her hunch is now reinforced by details. Thus, she now talks about Ālam's relatives having a secret. Obsessed with instrumental reasoning, Esālat assumes she suspects them. He, thus, misinterprets Āsiyeh's words and even jokes about their being involved in killing and burying the girl in the storage room in their yard. He also compares Ālam's parties to the feast of phantoms which implies his passion for fun. Āsiyeh's passion, however, is knowledge and care. Thus, she sees Ālam's family reunions as loci where a whole generation share their secrets and mourn their lost dreams and youths.

To Āsiyeh, this secret is a neglected history that needs uncovering. Thus, when Esālat states that he cannot accompany her, she gets out near a traffic sign featuring an adult taking the hand of a child for crossing the street and a direction hand which implies the city is now a caring entity ready to guide her. Thus, rather than paralysed by fear and trauma and become housebound, Beyzaie's ideal woman is one that aspires to get under the skin of the city's past and present to understand where she stands and how the aspirations of the previous generation failed. Having completed two voyages to the city's past, she now embarks on a new voyage to its present to visit the park that used to be Ālam's district. Here, the cawing of the crows flying around naked trees creates the ambiance as Āsiyeh walks in the park. The camera records her gaze at the trees and her pause on an old park attendant sweeping the footpath and then sitting on a bench to smoke his chibouk. She gazes at him, and he gazes back calmly, and the close-ups of their gazes imply how, as in Āsiyeh's parents' case, the old man's lived experience remains unseen. Thus, while placing Āsiyeh on her path to recovering the truth, Beyzaie shows that Ālam's story of lost opportunities is only one among many, and that while her story is heard due to her agency and Āsiyeh's skill in reading signs, those of others, including Āsiyeh's parents, the park attendant and Qorbān, remain unheard (Figure 7.7).

Hope for the future and reconnecting the past and present

Āsiyeh's visit to their local post office is, then, set against Dabiri's phone call to Esālat about finding the original advert letter, a school birthday party in which a pensive Āsiyeh and her pupils are photographed by Ebtekār whose camera attracts Āsiyeh's attention, and Āsiyeh's anxious entry into their storage room. The quick scenes, thus, lead to a slow focus on objects in a room embodying the derelict world of Ālam's subconscious. As in other scenes in which Beyzaie places a perceptive woman alone in a room, the play of light and shadows conjures intense emotions, but instead of love and doubt as in *Downpour* or *Stranger*, here, he evokes fear and mystery. As she walks among old baskets, cobwebs, net-like sieves, hanging bags and carriage wheels, something scares her just when Esālat arrives to say the letter has been found. While the scene, in general, implies the undetectable world of Ālam's mind, the net motif signifies entrapment in time and the broken wheels the torpor of the movement of life in old age and the apathy of the wheel of fortune to human desire. Esālat, who knows that Āsiyeh suspects Ālam, orders her to stop chasing the matter, which implies the authoritarian regimes' patriarchal desire to treat their citizens as subjects and control even their curiosity.

Figure 7.7 Screenshots from *The Crow*. Minutes 77′.25″–94′.30″

Beyzaie's placing of his protagonists in rooms alone with objects triggering memories and ideas is a technique that echoes O'Neill's *Long Day's Journey into Night*. In his films, however, instead of using soliloquies or asides, Beyzaie uses point-of-view shots which echo Hitchcock's and Ophüls's methods for reflecting their characters' isolation or fear. Beyzaie, however, reframes both to display the sublimated inner worlds of his characters and invite the viewers to see the world as they do. Thus, as Sheibani states, whereas most leading Iranian directors have been concerned with verisimilitude in its realist and neo-realist senses, Beyzaie initiated in Iranian cinema 'a highly polished and understated drama of peoples' interior worlds'.[40] Evidence of this can be found for both women and men in his earlier works, but since Āsiyeh is the first fully developed female protagonist of resistance in Iranian cinema, and the film even reflects Ālam's inner world, his achievement becomes more significant.

The plot evolves by marking Ālam's annoyance with Esālat's patronizing gestures, her love for Āsiyeh and her joyful reference to Āsiyeh's pregnancy by 'it will revive us'. Esālat's joy in watching his TV interview with six heavily made-up 'formerly missing' 'found' girls once more illustrates how subjects are trivialized in superficial modernity. The girls' words and looks indicate their metamorphosis by exposure to pseudo-modern obsessions, and the report implies that whereas in the past 'finding oneself' meant becoming religious and marrying, in its pseudo-modern context 'being found' means mutating into noisy dolls. Thus, in both cases, finding oneself means bending to a dominant discourse. Overwhelmed by their noise and Esālat's childish attempt to calm her by saying his team is to make a newsreel about the old Tehran, Ālam moves her hand in dismissal of Esālat's way of thinking. Such codes, however, are beyond the comprehension or concern of the people of Esālat's type. Āsiyeh uses this moment of crisis to climb the steps and enter Ālam's room. Juxtaposed with the storage, which represents the chaos of Ālam's subconscious mind, the room embodies her conscious mind. Old photos, picture frames, candlesticks, lamps, an hourglass that Āsiyeh sets running, clocks, mirrors, bedding, curtains, her fiancé's suit, a Pahlavi cap and a fedora hat, her dusty wedding dress, a gramophone, a camera, a trumpet and finally the photo of the missing girl which features Ālam at 18. Āsiyeh's archaeological probing and finding is, then, juxtaposed with Esālat's attempts to drill his 'reality' – murder, suicide, hiding, playing a game and no hope for finding – into Ālam's mind. Then comes Āsiyeh's revelation. Ālam's longed to find her lost youth, so in an act of artistic framing, she 'reframed' a photo taken by her fiancé as a subject of inquiry. The film closes with the two fulfilling Ālam's wish to see her childhood alley. In the park, Ālam states, 'He had a camera which had been brought for him from Europe. We were happy; who could have known he would die soon? It was here he took the photo, and I was only 18.' The bases of her four sentences 'happy', 'die', 'here' and '18', thus, suggest the death of her happy self at 18 while problematizing the meaning of time and space with 'here' as this 'here' is now in the middle of a park. Āsiyeh, then, gazes at the crows cawing in the sky with Esālat in the background watching (Figure 7.8).

Figure 7.8 Screenshots from *The Crow*. Minutes 95′.40″–108′.05″

Conclusion and reception: A mystery thriller about what happened to modernity

Using the diachronic space of a micronarrative to examine the lives of middle-class Iranians, *The Crow* examines the pitfalls of Iranian modernity in the 1970s. In this narrative of loss and longing, the philosophical meaning of time as a succession of changing spaces is set against the mind as a space of relative stability. Displaying the people of the past in the present and metaphoric voyages in time are the two methods

Beyzaie uses for his diachronic examination of Iran's journey. In both cases, he proposes a rethinking of the roots as the way forward. For Ālam, time and space are of the same material, and the Tehran of her memories has nothing to do with the current Tehran. For Āsiyeh, however, time is time, and space is space. She visits whatever remains of the old Tehran and imagines the experience of living in them by animating Ālam's words, photos and recorded sounds. She, thus, finds that the new Tehran is the same as the 1930s' Tehran that embodied the European-inspired Iranian modernity. This search for the forgotten origins, places, events and human beings, however, also reveals the breach between old dreams and new realities. She, thus, acts like an intellectual bridge between two spaces, the illusions of the ideal modernity in the pre-war era and the dizzying outcomes of its imitative origins and its switch from obsession with Europe to obsession with the United States. In this context, she is the only one who rereads the past to perceive the present, the only one who discovers that the girl in the photo is the old woman mourning her youth.

The Crow is the first film in which Beyzaie's critique of contemporary life appears in a template akin to mystery thrillers. Detective elements have always existed in literature. In the legend of Siyāvush, Keykāvus corroborates Siyāvush's account of what happened between him and Sudābeh by smelling his clothes and realizing that he has not tried to embrace her. Or in *Hamlet*, the eponymous hero uses a play to validate his suspicion of his uncle. As a modern literary genre, however, the detective's experimentation and divergent thinking find centrality. In its literary origins, therefore, the genre combined the trial-and-error method of scientific analysis with the archetypes of initiation and quest in a process that transformed the physical hero of the latter into a scientist detective, their vicious witches into femme fatales and their object of desire into damsels in distress. Since this genre inherited the worlds of gothic novels and Edgar Alan Poe's writings and evolved along with the rise of naturalism in literature, its literary and cinematic products combine gothic mystery, symbolism and fear with scientifically and sociologically charged dark realism. The Freytag's Pyramid of their plot often begins with the calm world of home, family or city being disturbed by an external force representing the outside world of violence and fear. Then, after a series of frightening encounters, the plot is resolved by the hero's unexpected yet scientifically explicable resolution which leads to his victory and the return of life to a new equilibrium.

In Beyzaie's reframing, the external force that disturbs the family's calm is a picture, a voice from the past, which heightens the heroine's awareness of the violence of the city and the time's violation of life and dreams. The plot and the conception of home, family and city are like detective films, but the ones playing the detective, Esālat and his sidekicks, are too concerned with surface structures to achieve divergent thinking. They, thus, function like dutiful, inefficient police officers who can only be dazzled when the real detective, Āsiyeh, unravels a plot that is beyond their imagination. Thus, a woman whose education and job have helped her sublimate her marginalized background and gender into epistemic privilege becomes Beyzaie's detective. Truth has been distorted or buried and dominant discourses use peer pressure, authoritarian gaze and patriarchal rhetoric to impose a superficial and imitative identity on her. Yet, she uses the clues to reread her own identity and that of the missing girl to find out why she is not where she must be. Āsiyeh's divergent gaze intensifies her deductive precision in analysing details, and her ethical integrity, compassion and self-control make her care for the weak and react against the impositions that others may bend to. The film begins with Esālat's curiosity about the missing girl, but Āsiyeh's desire for knowing Ālam, herself and the missing girl places her at the film's moral centre so that her resistance against patriarchal social conventions and the fake relations of pseudo-modern intelligentsia displays their absurdity. By placing her in difficult situations and comparing her behaviours with others, Beyzaie highlights the typical problems women face in society and suggests that the salvation of a society depends on how it treats women, children and the marginalized. This does not mean giving a privileged space to these groups of people, but that if a society grants human rights and the chance for success only to those who bend to dominant discourses, instead of citizens it will have subjects and will never be modern in the true sense of the term.

Unlike Esālat, who is obsessed with sensational news and has a consumerist desire for new surfaces, Āsiyeh's involvement in teaching deaf children enables her to interpret signs and link them to feelings and thoughts. These abilities enable her to identify with and read Ālam's silent cry for recognition, but the two are also similar in their lives. Her husband, like the colonel, embodies the discourse of his time and has expertise in technologies of image and voice. Thus, if one sets aside the film's ontological discourse on the meaning of youth, love, parenthood, old age and death and the changes in a person's idea of the self as he or she goes through these stages, the question that Beyzaie raises is: Can Āsiyeh and her generation, including Beyzaie himself who is like Āsiyeh, fulfil their potential and create a better present and future by rereading the past, or are their lives also caught in the vortices of internal and external conflicts, historical oblivion, consumerism and pseudo-modernity? Ālam's city, home and family were lost to the inevitable bending of history to these forces, so nothing remained of them but a memory, some photos and two rooms full of objects, so what is going to happen to Āsiyeh's home, family and city? Āsiyeh's pregnancy implies a degree of optimism about the generational continuity of her woodpecker-like personality, but her fear that the child will be voiceless, and the sorrow displayed in the final scene, shows his doubts.

Reflecting Āsiyeh's feeling that her fate will be like Ālam's, this sorrow was so central to the film that it led to a dispute between Beyzaie and her lead actress Parvaneh Massoumi. Beyzaie's ideal in his city films was to let Massoumi find the role herself. He, thus, expected her to feel the implications of the plot, but Massoumi was probably more preoccupied with Āsiyeh's success in resolving the case.[41] Beyzaie returned to this subject in *Maybe Some Other Time* (1987) which may be read as a sequel to *The Crow* in its analysis of the impacts of another historical breach on the lives of people of Āsiyeh's type. The breach which had great impacts on Iranian modernity and the people's private and public lives was the 1979 revolution and the war that shook the country in the 1980s. I will, thus, return to the subject of historical breach and its impacts on society when examining *Maybe Some Other Time*.

Ironically, however, the revolution also had a great impact on the reception of *The Crow*, which could have been Beyzaie's bestselling pre-revolutionary film if the burning of the cinemas had not led to their closures after only three days of very successful screening in November 1978. The film had already been praised during and after

Tehran's Sixth International Film Festival in October 1977. Writing for *International Film Guide 1978*, Daryoush compared the film with Proust's *In Search of Lost Time* and praised Beyzaie's success in giving 'universal validity' to a film focused on 'identity, the passage of time and the search for one's roots' in the context of 'the recent past of his homeland'. He also praised its innovative form but misread its celebration of divergent thinking by linking it to what he construed as mysticism in Kiarostami and Shahid-Saless's works.[42] Ramin Molaei praised the film for transcending the obsession of third world intellectuals with poverty, hunger and sex to win prizes in the West for displaying what Westerners want to see.[43] While criticizing Beyzaie for using vice and virtue names, Abdollāh Bākideh praised the film's success in dealing with human memories and emotions and its technical success in evoking the idea of old Tehran.[44] In any case, though the film did not generate the international praise and the box-office sale it deserved, it remained a prime example of combining commercial success and cultural significance, and in time inspired some of the greatest films of the same genre, including most of Asghar Farhadi's films, particularly *Nader and Simin: A Separation* (2011) and *The Salesman* (2016), or such successful TV series as Naghmeh Samini and Hasan Fathi's *Shahrzād* (2015–18). Beyzaie, however, did not repeat the template in his next film and instead moved back to his village trilogy with a film that, like *Stranger*, offered a unique perspective about excavating the past not for glorifying it but for understanding the modalities of Iran's historical identity and producing a productive present.

8

Conclusion

In dialogue with time

The history of artistic production in a country does not follow its political history. It has its own trajectory of cultural and aesthetic transformation which is in dialogue with its own origins and the global trends that evolve in dialogue with one another. Thus, even at its political levels, artistic works have their own emancipatory or reactionary aesthetics and ideals that promote or resist dominant discourses that go beyond party politics and rivalries. Nevertheless, the impacts of events such as the 1979 Iranian revolution on the transformation of dominant discourses and on the range of images and voices that are permitted in the public space force creative writers and artists to initiate new expressive strategies in their works. Thus, although there is clear continuity in all aesthetic and sociopolitical aspects of cultural production before and after the 1979 revolution, the year 1979 marks a turning point that resulted in numerous shifts in the regulations that determined the nature of cultural production in Iran. Beyzaie's work was not an exception, and as a result, I have used *The Crow*, the last film that Beyzaie completed before the revolution, to close this book.

As reflected in this book, between 1959 and 1979, Beyzaie relentlessly researched and published his findings on Iranian and Asian performing traditions, folktale and myths. He also completed several films and screenplays and wrote and directed several influential plays that reformulated Iranian artistic forms and rituals to initiate the dramatic tradition that evolved to become modern indigenous-style Iranian drama. This initiative was also important as the new forms that evolved in Beyzaie's works also introduced new ways of seeing and doing into Iran's public space and deconstructed the dominant discourses on identity, politics, arts and many character types and culturally significant narratives. In my introduction, I examined the origins of this deconstructive gaze and outlined a theory of creativity which argued that the initiator of his creative impulse was his ability to sublimate his traumatic experiences of marginalization. The key terms in my theory were 'trauma', 'marginalization', 'sublimation', 'outsider gaze' and 'epistemic privilege and authority'. I also highlighted his focus on displaying the failures of the centre, on the origins and rise of cultural practices and beliefs and on working with Iranian, Asian and Euro-American literary, dramatic and cinematic traditions as the most significant building blocks in the evolution of his vision.

My main chapters focused on demonstrating how his type of creativity almost always involves transgressive and emancipatory framing and reframing and redistributing the sensible by introducing new ways of seeing, hearing and doing things. Having suffered marginalization and discrimination in his school years and later, Beyzaie was also always concerned with the conditions of the marginalized and disenfranchised and how human identity evolved in response to sociopolitical and cultural pressures. Beyzaie, thus, continued to reflect on how the proponents of dominant discourses function like criminals or foreign invaders by unscrupulously marginalizing, ostracizing or punishing some groups of people to fulfil their opportunistic purposes and how the marginalized people's desire for belonging may lead to quests for recognition and assertion in positive or negative ways.

Using some of these key concerns, I analysed Beyzaie's *Puppet Trilogy* as an example of how he reformulates Iranian dramatic forms to extract an emancipatory aesthetics from the self-reflexive aspects of this theatre tradition. I argued that he subverted the stereotypes of Narrator, Wiseman, Hero, Black and Girl in Iranian puppet plays by creating a narrator who forces the puppets to repeat cliché roles, a wiseman who realizes that his insistence on showing off his knowledge is like parroting inherited ideas and repeating the vicious cycles that endanger the lives of those who want to transcend them. I also analysed the way puppets evolve to act like free human beings as Hero realizes the absurdity of the games of power he has been forced to play, and Black and Girl confront the narrator/puppeteer and become capable of making their own wrong or right decisions. Beyzaie's focus on unlikely heroes also allowed him to deconstruct the hero/demon, hero/girl, hero/black and black/wiseman binaries to show that these stereotypes are victims of a system that pushes individuals into absurd or extreme roles. The hero must fight unending wars that ruin his personal potential for happiness, the girl must just wait to be saved and loved, the black man must just be a servant or a jester and the demon is a black man or physically different individual who has failed to be a jester or servant and has, therefore, been ostracized as a demon so that he can be used as a source of fear for taming others.

While analysing Beyzaie's early works, I argued that Beyzaie's priority in the 1960s was to confront the obsession with tough guys and toxic masculinity in Iranian cinema by focusing on underrepresented character types (Black and Girl in *The Puppet Trilogy*) or examining central types from new perspectives (*Ārash* and *So Dies Akbar the Hero*). Thus, one can observe the rise of wronged heroes, intellectuals, creative individuals, children and women as protagonists in Beyzaie's oeuvre and the depiction of heroes as victims of marginalization. I also examined these new types in *Uncle Moustache*, *Downpour* and *The Journey* in which in addition to the numerous subjects that the films handle at sociopolitical, archetypal and metaphoric levels, they also construct meta-cinematic critiques of Iranian cinema and establish a dialogue with Iranian cinema by introducing a variety of new character types.

The chapters, therefore, demonstrated how Beyzaie's pre-revolutionary works always offered revisionist readings of mythical and historical narratives or contemporary situations and subverted the dominant discourses of gender relations, heroism, intellectuality, nationalism and collective identity. As a thinker voicing the concerns of the silenced and the unseen victimization of those who are goaded into sacrificial acts by deceptive discourses and superficial celebration, in these early works, Beyzaie also questions the inherited violence that is used to maintain the hierarchies of power and belonging. He also depicts individuals as victims of distorted cultural, religious and political narratives and redefines the ideals of citizenship, leadership and gender relations. At their political levels, these works also comment on modernity, modernization, democracy and social and political surveillance and control. Thus, in *Uncle Moustache*, the conflict between a retired man and the boys who have turned the deserted field in front of his house into a dusty football pitch allows Beyzaie to turn the boys into agents of emancipation and democratic change in their relationship with the old man as a figure of patriarchal authority who learns to become more flexible and open to new ways of seeing and doing. Or in *Downpour*, the Bespectacled Man and the Headmaster represent the agents of cultural, religious and political surveillance and suppression who suffocate constructive innovation when it does not contribute to their opportunistic goals.

Inherent in all these works is also a constant questioning of exclusionist and suppressive discourses on life, art, human identity, belonging, power, heroism, masculinity, intellectuals, women and children. In *The Journey*, for instance, the twelve stages that the two boys go through in their archetypal quest for finding a home and a sense of belonging bring them face to face with the major failures of Iranian culture. The same critical gaze is also observed in *Stranger and the Fog* and *The Crow*. Yet, whereas the former focuses on a timeless mythical land, the latter focuses on the here and now. *Stranger* establishes a dialogue with Iranian and Asian dramatic traditions and uses explicit rituals and archetypes of birth, death, purgation and fertility to go to the pre-history of Iranian culture and reflect on the obsessions of a religion-obsessed society with afterlife. *The Crow*, on the other hand, establishes a dialogue with Noire films to focus on the lived experience of the mid-1970s but functions as a ritual of purgation and a quest for awareness that releases a woman's potential to introduce her as the first female intellectual of Iranian cinema. Simultaneously, however, it comments on the absence of cultural authenticity due to a superficial understanding of modernity and a city characterized by unbridled demolition and modernization, an ignorance of the past and extreme forms of medieval and modern forms of opportunism, surveillance and punishment.

By 1978, therefore, Beyzaie had already established numerous templates that reformulated Iranian, Asian and Euro-American artistic forms to create works that expanded the aesthetics of cultural, mythical, historical, political and everyday representation. In other words, these works fulfilled what Jacques Rancière celebrates as the main political function of arts, artistically redistributing the sensible by expanding the range of what is considered voice rather than noise or is permitted as visually acceptable in the public space.[1] The revolution, however, initiated new forms of policing that led to the ban on Beyzaie's first two post-revolutionary films, *Ballad of Tārā* (1978–80) and *Death of Yazdegerd* (play 1979, film 1981) and postponed the release of his third film, *Bashu the Little Stranger* by more than three years. Nevertheless, his incessant attempt to recreate himself despite all the odds gave birth to some of Iran's greatest dramatic and cinematic masterpieces including the earlier mentioned works as well as such great screenplays such as *Parchment of Master Sharzin* (1986) and *New Preface to the Shahnameh* (1986) or plays such as *Kallāt Claimed* (1982), *Reed Panel* (1992), *Afrā or the Day Is Passing* (1997) and *The One Thousand and First Night* (2002).

As specified in my introduction to this book, my approach to analysis is characterized by scene-by-scene explication and thick interdisciplinary description informed by aesthetic, political and cultural histories of Iranian cinema and theatre as well as theories of performance, reception, psychoanalysis, gender relations, translation, post-colonialism and cultural semiotics. To analyse Beyzaie's dialogue with Iranian culture, in my thick descriptions I also investigate the origins of the ideas, characters and forms that appeared in Beyzaie's works. I will continue the same approach in my second monograph on Beyzaie, *Bahram Beyzaie's Cinematic and Dramatic Worlds: In Dialogue with Time 1979–2021*, in which I will focus on his post-revolutionary oeuvre in general and his films in particular.

Aware of the suppressive tendencies of the proponents of militant Marxist and Islamic groups,[2] Beyzaie faced the revolution with a unique knowledge of the violently exclusionist undercurrents of the utopian claims of those who were competing for power during and after the 1979 revolution. As a result, he was not consumed by the euphoria of new beginnings and had no illusions about what was to come. Towards the end of his *Death of Yazdegerd*, therefore, he had the Miller's wife state, 'Yours were white banners and this was your ruling. Time now to behold the ruling of their black banners!' With the white banners of the king's White Revolution gone, Beyzaie was now awaiting the ruling of the black banners of the Islamic revolutionaries who made his life harder than it was before the revolution.

Like many other creative artists and intellectuals of the era, however, he hoped for the best and continued to work despite the new obstacles. After a major halt that occurred due to the uncertainties of filmmakers about the ever-increasing limitations, from 1984 onwards Iranian cinema began to find a new space because of the activities of the more open-minded members of the cultural institutes of the Islamic Republic. This limited space enabled a few leading filmmakers to adapt themselves to the new regulations by addressing less controversial subjects and creating new forms of cinematic expression. The chasteness of the post-revolutionary cinema also allowed the leading filmmakers of the Iranian New Wave to be noticed more as their works were, in general, chaster than the mainstream pre-revolutionary films. In any case, the state-imposed limitations meant that in the 1980s, most outstanding films focused on children to avoid censorship, but this strategic choice revolutionized Iranian cinema as it built on Beyzaie's and Kiarostami's child-centred films of the 1970s to create a great filmic tradition, which, in turn, made Iranian cinema more visible in the world.

Like others, Beyzaie used the new space to make a few films in the 1980s. Nevertheless, his insistence on undermining dominant discourses and depicting marginalized characters, including independent, artistic or intellectual women, as his protagonists was not welcomed by the Islamic state. Beyzaie, therefore, continued to have problems, particularly from 1991 onwards when the capitalist rivalries of the pre-revolution era returned to Iranian cinema and joined the state restrictions to make it harder for him to make films. The issue becomes clearer if one notices that despite all the problems that he faced in the 1970s, in the relatively short span of eight years Beyzaie made six films,[3] but in the next thirty years of his residence in post-revolutionary Iran (1979–2009), he could only make seven films. Nevertheless, his films and the plays and screenplays that he wrote during the periods in which he could not make films or direct plays continued to leave great impacts on Iranian drama, cinema and literature.

This ceaseless creativity has been in line with what Beyzaie considers the task of all creative individuals: to generate ideas, images, stories or products that share human experience to raise awareness, civilize the people obsessed with power or contribute to the survival of the best aspects of the culture. This is the task that the two intellectuals, Ermāeil and Germāeil, fulfil by using their cooking skills to save one young man every night from Zahhāk's snakes while setting the stage for the revolution against him. It is the feat that Shahrzād and Dināzād achieve in the lost Iranian book *Hezār Afsān* (*A Thousand Tales*) and its extant Arabic version *One Thousand and One Nights* by an extended storytelling performance which saves one girl every night and gradually turns the dragon king Shahriar into a good king.[4]

I close this book with reference to these aesthetically emancipatory visions because they have influenced Beyzaie's vision about the sociopolitical function of the arts and they represent the best expressions of the Iranian idea of how emancipatory art can pave the way for a revolution (the myth of Zahhāk) or gradual reform (the framing story of *One Thousand and One Nights*). Beyzaie's whole oeuvre from *Ārash* to *The Crossroads* is characterized by this emancipatory vision but his post-revolutionary works are even more emancipatory in their visions than his pre-revolutionary works. Therefore, my second book on Beyzaie will pay more attention to the modalities of this emancipatory vision in his seven post-revolutionary films and the numerous pre- and post-revolutionary plays that are in dialogue with these films.

Notes

Chapter 1

1 Basij is a paramilitary group active at local levels and supervised by the Islamic Revolutionary Guard Corps.
2 Farhang, 'Nāgofteh', Video Clip.
3 Raminfar and Rastin, 'Bahram Beyzaie', podcasts 113, 114, 115, 116 and 117.
4 For a general study, see Naficy's four-volume book, *A Social History of Iranian Cinema*.
5 Ashoori and Sarrafinezhad, 'Bahram Beyzaie', podcast 90.
6 See Raminfar and Rastin, 'Bahram Beyzaie', podcast 113; and Rafi Jam, 'Bahram'.
7 Beyzaie, 'Tark-e', 36.
8 Dabashi, *Close-up*, 84.
9 Benjamin, 'Theses', 257–61.
10 Rancière, *Politics of Aesthetics*, 21–41. See below.
11 Lipp, 'Writing History', 66–100.
12 Beyzaie, 'Interview with National TV', 26.
13 Hall, 'Cultural Studies', 280.
14 Ibid., 286.
15 Rancière, *Politics of Aesthetics*, 12–13.
16 Bourdieu, *Outline of a Theory*, 85.
17 Lawrence and Karim, 'Pierre Bourdieu', 188.
18 Foucault, 'Truth and Power', 131–2.
19 Ibid., 133.
20 Rockhill, 'Glossary', 91.
21 Ibid., 86.
22 Ibid., 91.
23 Rancière, *Politics of Aesthetics*, 27.
24 Rockhill, 'Glossary', 81. The italics are mine.
25 Rancière, *Film Fables*, 107–22. The direct quotation is from page 5.
26 Sophocles, 'Philoctetes', 563.
27 Rich, 'Twenty-One', VII. Though it sets the stage for the following poem which reflects the desire to transform suffering into emancipatory love, this poem is more concerned about transforming guilt and self-loathing into creativity, the type that is Ian McEwan's metafictional concern in his novel, *Atonement*.
28 Rich, 'Twenty-One', VII and VIII, 28–9.
29 See above. Lawrence and Karim, 'Pierre Bourdieu', 188.
30 See below for a discussion of epistemic privilege.
31 Said, 'Professionals and Amateurs', 72.
32 For definitions of culture, see also Eagleton, *Culture*, 1–29, and Williams, *Key Words*, 49–54.
33 Williams, *Culture and Society*, 354.

34 McAdams, 'Narrative Identity', 99–116; and McAdams and Logan, 'Creative Work'.
35 The song is called Ali Concouri, and the line is:

سرت و خم کن که درا وا می‌شن، تا بگی نه پشت کنکور می‌مونی.

36 See also Bar On, 'Marginality and Epistemic' and Janack, 'Standpoint Epistemology'. Though similar, my use of the term departs from these in how I focus on the psychosocial processes leading to epistemic privilege and emphasize the need to transcend the minority and majority binary to be able to achieve epistemic authority.
37 For theories of creativity, see Kaufman & Sternberg, *Cambridge Handbook*. Though my theory is based on my personal experience and studies on how traumatic marginalization changes human beings, empirical studies have also identified links between creativity and 'posttraumatic growth' or 'growth through adversity'. See, Simonton, *Greatness: Who*, or Forgeard, 'Perceiving Benefits' and 'Creativity and Healing'.
38 Said, 'Professionals and Amateurs', 72.
39 See above for Rancière's discussion of emancipatory art.
40 For articles numerating Said's misconceptions, for instance, see Macfie, *Orientalism: A Reader*.
41 See also Fischer, *Iran*, 187; and Alam, *Yāddāshthā*, Vol. 1, 160.
42 Talajooy, *Interview*, 1 December 2020.
43 See Talajooy, 'Beyzaie's Formation'.
44 Ibid., 689; and Talajooy, 'Shahr, Khāneh', 148–51.
45 Hashemi, 'Marg-e Yazdegerd' and 'Bahram Beyzaie', podcast 171.
46 Amjad and Sarrafizadeh, 'Bahram Beyzaie', podcast 97.
47 For an analysis, see Talajooy, 'Intellectuals', 399–405.
48 In my translations of Beyzaie's play, I have tried to strike a balance between keeping the play's poetic qualities and their performablity. Other translations of Beyzaie's plays include 'The Puppets', 'Evening in a Strange Land' and 'The Story of the Hidden Moon', in Kapuscinski, *Modern*; Anvar, *Death of Yazdegerd*; Ghanoonparavar, 'Four Boxes'; Parsa, 'Peter Farbridge and Brian Quirt's 'Aurash' and 'Death of the King''; and Ghanoonparvar, *Memoirs of the Actor in a Supporting Role*.
49 For taʿziyeh, taqlid and other Iranian performing traditions, see Beyzaie, *Namayesh*. See also Talajooy, *Mythologizing*, 6–22 and 101–7; and 'Indigenous Performing', 497–519.
50 Talajooy, 'Beyzaie's Formation', 691.
51 Ibid., 691–2.
52 Bassan, 'Cinemagari', 113–27.
53 Parham, 'Kudak, Zan', 12–43.
54 Azadivar, 'Bahram Beyzaie', 85–105.
55 Arjomand, 'Talāsh-e Nābasandeh', 105–13.
56 For Iran's modern history, see Amanat, *Iran a Modern* and Keddie, *Modern Iran*. See also Ansari's books, *Iran under Ahmadinejad*, *Crisis of Authority*, *Politics of Nationalism* and (ed.) *Perceptions of Iran*.
57 For another review of Beyzaie's works with charts on his works until 1982, see Kuban, 'Zamān', 45–84.
58 The term refers to a series of assassinations occurring mostly between 1988 and 1998 in which more than eighty intellectuals, politicians and human right activists were targeted, inside and outside the country, by unknown groups which were later revealed to have been operatives working with Iranian Security Offices.
59 Beyzaie and Amjad, 'From the Land', 721–36.

60 See Ghanoonparvar, 'Collective Identity', 753–64; and Hashemi, 'Chāhār Sanduq', 99–118.
61 See Talajooy, 'Bahram Beyzaie va Jang-e'.
62 The sheer number of books, articles and theses written on Beyzaie in Iran is an indication of this significance.

Chapter 2

1 Abdi, *Gharibeh-ye*, 22–4.
2 For these techniques, see Beyzaie, *Namāyesh*; Talajooy, 'Indigenous'; and Beeman, *Iranian*.
3 Javanmard, *Didār*, 219–20.
4 Beyzaie, *Divān*, 6.
5 See, for instance, Yarshater, 'Modern', 59; or Aliabadi, 'Ghorub', 548.
6 Beyzaie, 'Interview', 16 November 2021.
7 Beyzaie, 'Sāyehbāzi', 24.
8 Leiter, *Kabuki Reader*, 3–32. See also Beyzaie, 'Namāyesh dar Zhāpon 3', 38–40.
9 See, for instance, 26'–29'.20" and 73'–77' at https://www.youtube.com/watch?v=giABfnfy9R0.
10 Al-e Ahmad, 'Darbāreh-ye Pahlevān' (1965), 1976–7.
11 Ghaffary, 'Iranian', 63, compares the puppeteer's breaking of the puppets with a similar act by the puppeteer who destroys his puppets in Attar's *Oshtornāmeh*. Beyzaie, *Namāyesh*, 89–90, quotes 'Hekāyat-e Ostād-e Tork va Pardeh-bāzi Uo' from the *Oshtornāmeh* to reflect on puppet shows in Iran. He may have, thus, been inspired by the idea of a puppeteer destroying his puppet, but the relations he creates have nothing to do with Attar's.
12 See my discussion of taste in the following. Houshang Golshiri, Nader Ebrahimi were among the best examples.
13 Beyzaie, 'Cheh Mahkameh', 119–20.
14 Ibid., 120.
15 Quoted in Javanmard, *Didār*, 217, 269–70, 185–270.
16 Beyzaie, *Nodbeh*, 35, 53–4, 94–5. See also Nazarzadeh, *Tanpushi*, 69–96.
17 See Hossein (Parto) Beyzaei, *Tārikh*.
18 Beyzaie, *Namāyesh*, 84–94. See also Ashurpur, *Namāyesh-hā-ye 5*, 75–99.
19 Beyzaie, *Namāyesh*, 57–64. See also Janati, *Bonyad*, 51–7; and Matthee, 'Prostitutes, Courtesans', 121–50.
20 Shahriari, *Ketāb-e*, 80. See also Beeman, *Iranian*, 22–54.
21 See Fatemi, 'Music', 399–418; Shay, 'Bazi-ha-ye', 16–24; and Safa-Isfahani, 'Female-Centered', 33–53.
22 See Beyzaie, *Namāyesh*, 157–203; and Beeman, 'Why Do', 506–26.
23 Shahriari, *Ketāb-e*, 286.
24 Chardin, *Travels*, 201.
25 Ibid., 203. The spelling inconsistencies are in the original.
26 Beyzaie, *Namāyesh*, 107–8 for a discussion of Soltān Salim Show.
27 Ibid., 99.
28 Mew, 'Modern Persian', 904–6. Mew does not quote Chodzko, but his account is taken from *Théâtre Persan*, XV–XIX. Chodźko had already written on the subject in 'Le théâtre en Perse' in *La revue indépendante* 15, 1844, 161–208; and 'Le théâtre en Perse' in *La revue de l'Orient* 6, 1845, 119–35. See also Beyzaie, *Namāyesh*, 82–115.

29 The section on Iranian Comic and Puppet Traditions echoes aspects of my former writing on the subject in *Mythologizing*, 6–23; 'Indigenous', 498–9; and 'Reformulations', 696.
30 Scott, *Domination*, 18.
31 See my discussion of Rancière's theories in Chapter 1.
32 Goffman, *Frame Analysis*, 10–11 and 43–4.
33 For minority perspective and epistemic privilege, see Chapter 1.
34 The tale has been categorized as ATU 720 in the global system.
35 Ghaderi Sohi and Ghorbaninejad, 'Ali Nassirian' celebrate Nasiriān as the initiator of the indigenous-style modern drama in Iran. Though this is correct to some extent, and Nasiriān and Javanmard's adaptations and performances played a vital role in setting the stage, it was Beyzaie's modernist, subverting heteroglossia and his constant experimentation with indigenous forms that established them as a modern tradition.
36 For a study, see Amjad, *Tyatr-e Qarn-e*.
37 See also, Beyzaie in Qukasiyan, *Goftogu*, 20–6.
38 For an English translation, see Kapuscinski, *Modern Persian*.
39 Loloi and Pursglove, 'Translating', 65.
40 See, for instance, Rostam's song in his 'Fourth Labour'.
41 Beyzaie, 'Arusakhā', 81–2.
42 Talajooy, 'Indigenous', 516; Ensafi, *Siyāh-bāzi*; Taqiyan, *Darbareh-ye*, 138–52; and Nazarzadeh, *Tanpoush*, 110–15.
43 See Herrenschmidt and Kelllens, 'DAIVA'.
44 Safa, *Hamāseh-Sorāei*, 601.
45 For a discussion of this myth, see Beyzaie, *Hezār*, 77–9.
46 Beyzaie, 'Sunset', 109.
47 Bourdieu, *Distinctions*, 1–2. Italics are mine. Bourdieu's note to this section clarifies his idea of 'habitus': 'The word disposition seems particularly suited to express what is covered by the concept of habitus (defined as a system of dispositions) – used later in this chapter. It expresses first the result of an organizing action, with a meaning close to that of words such as structure; it also designates a way of being, a habitual state (especially of the body) and, in particular, a predisposition, tendency, propensity or inclination'. Bourdieu, *Outline*, 214, n. 1.
48 For these religious forms, see Beyzaie, *Namāyesh*, 64–7, 72–5; and Floor, *History*, 107–23.
49 Beyzaie in Qukasiyan, *Goftogu*, 12–13.
50 Ibid., 203.
51 Quoted in Miresmaeili, '82-sālegi'. See also Zandian, *Bāzkhāni*, 205–13.
52 Beyzaie and Talajooy, 'Interview'.
53 Fo, *L'operaio conosce 300 parole il padrone 1000 per questo lui è il padrone*, 107; Quoted in Scuderi, *Dario Fo*, 38.
54 Fo, *Fabulazzo*, 77; Quoted in ibid., 37.
55 Examples of the demonization of the Bahai's are so rife in Iran that I do not need to give examples. To make it more tangible for a Western reader, however, one can compare these, to the traditional demonization of Jews or Muslims in European cultures, which associated them with animal imagery or pervert sexual rituals. For a brief satiric example, see the discussion of Jews at the beginning of Woody Allen's *Love and Death* (1975).
56 For Beyzaie's creative reflection on the failures of left, see his filmscript, *Āyenehā-ye Ruberu* (1981).
57 It is said paradise is filled with the joys of being with nymphs*I say the juice of grape is fine for me//Take the one which is here and forget about the one promised*As the sound of heavy drums is only good from afar.

گویند کسان بهشت با حور خوشست*من میگویم که آب انگور خوشست/این نقد بگیر و دست از آن نسیه بدار*کاواز دهل شنیدن از دور خوشست

58 Jones, *Censorship*, 1205.
59 Wilber, *Iran*, 155.
60 Khomeini, *Sahifeh*, 78-122, 141-67, 180-99, 206-43.
61 Ibid., 261, 267-76, 285-309, 373-95, 415-24.
62 See Khomeini, *Sahifeh*, 132-47. See also Davani, *Nehzat*.
63 See Rohani, *Barresi*. See also Milani, 'Ruhollah', 350-7; Algar, 'KHOMEINI'; and Moin, *Khomeini*.
64 For nativism in Iran, see Boroujerdi, *Iranian*, particularly 52-76.
65 For the Pahlavi's royalist nationalism, see Ansari, *Politics*, 1-178. For Iranian left, see Behruz, *Rebels*, 1-47.
66 See Soyinka's perspective on Khayyam in, 'Credo of Being', 234-7; and Jeifyo, *Wole Soyinka*, 76.
67 The idea of outcasts being a source of blessing is, of course, universal, reflected, as discussed in Chapter 1 of this book, in such major legendary figures as Zāl, Philoctetes or Oedipus.
68 This walk of shame, which Beyzaie used later in his creative works, such as *Kallāt Claimed*, consisted of dressing a male convict like a woman and seating him naked and backward on a donkey. See Chapter 3 of this book.
69 Dasgupta and Rancière, 'Art is Going', 70-7.
70 See Laurence and Karim, 'Pierre Bourdieu', 189.
71 Zizek, *Violence*, 1.
72 See Talajooy, 'Intellectuals'.
73 Yarshater, 'Modern', 59.
74 See Arendt, *Eichmann*.
75 Beyzaie, 'Qesseh', 152-6.
76 The echoes of the original form of this myth can be seen in the legends of fraternal rivalry or fratricide in all cultures including the legends of Fereydun's or Oedipus's sons or Romulus and Remus.
77 Beyzaie makes this metaphor even more visual in *The Journey* (1972).
78 See Corbin, 'Mundus Imaginalis'. See my writing on *Tārā* for an extended discussion.
79 Black's reference to emerging from darkness of a box to face a world of set obsessions, echoes Khayyam's:

ما لعبتکانیم و فلک لعبت باز * از روی حقیقتی نه از روی مجاز // یک چند در این بساط بازی کردیم*رفتیم به صندوق عدم یک یک باز

80 Kapuscinski, 'Modern', 386, 38.
81 Zizek, *Violence*, 1.
82 See https://web.archive.org/web/20160307024218/http://www.dundee.ac.uk/english/joot/marionettes/
83 See the bibliography under Beyzaie.
84 Radi, 'Darbāreh', 122.
85 See Ashurpur, *Namāyesh-hā-ye 5*, 95-9.
86 Beyzaie and Rastegar, 'Dar Tāātr', quoted in *Simia*, 33.
87 Ibid., 33-4.
88 For a video recording of Beyzaie's staging which was also his directorial debut, see 'Tunel-e Zamān: Arusakhā', *Manoto TV Channel*, https://www.youtube.com/watch?v=o23x4G56aAE.

Chapter 3

1. Beyzaie, *Roshanfekr*, 114.
2. Beyzaie in Qukasiyan, *Goftogu*, 29–30.
3. Beyzaie and Soltanpur, 'Mizgerd'.
4. Sepanlu, 'Chap-hā', 46.
5. See Dolatabadi, 'Abbas Āqa', 235 and Beyzaie, 'Āzādi Mikhāstand', 133. According to Beyzaie, Soltanpur was not in Mashhad on the day, but he had visited the city three days earlier. Beyzaie and Talajooy, 'Interview'.
6. Zandian, *Bāzkhāni*, 205–13.
7. Abdi, *Gharibeh*, 18–20.
8. Beyzaie in Qukasiyan, *Goftogu*, 9–12. Abdi, *Gharibeh*, 26–8. See also Jāhed, *Az Sinemātek*, 26–30. Cine Club was later renamed *Filmkhāneh Melli-ye Iran* (Iran's National Film House).
9. See Abdi, *Gharibeh*, 34–7 for Beyzaie's meeting with the film producer Mehdi Misaqiyeh in 1966 and potential colleagues in filmmaking Ahmadreza Ahmadi and Jalal Moqaddam in 1970.
10. Beyzaie in Qukasiyan, *Goftogu*, 11.
11. *Ayyārs* were trickster warriors who lived by their wit and military skills. They could be self-serving and subservient to rulers or self-effacing and harsh with the rich and kind to the poor. The term *Javānmard* (Chivalrous young man) is also used to refer to the latter type of *ayyār*. See Ridgeon's books on *Javānmardi*.
12. See Esmaeil Kushan's *Kolāh Makhmali* (The Fedora Hat Tough Guy, 1962) or Dāvud Esmāeili's *Tanhā Mard-e Mahaleh* (The Only Man in the Neighbourhood, 1972).
13. See Siāmak Yāsemi's *Aqā-ye Qarn-e Bistom* (Twentieth Century's Gentleman, 1964) or *Ganj-e Qārun* (Qārun's Treasure, 1965).
14. See Ārāmis Aqāmālian's *Gol Āqā* (1967), Masoud Kimiaei's *Qeysar* (1969). One subcategory, which included Kimiaei's *Reza Motori* (Reza Motorcyclist, 1971) or Naderi's *Khodāhāfez Refiq* (Goodbye Friend, 1971) was less Romantic and displayed a thief or gambler losing his life in a dog-eat-dog, cruel society. Another, which included Nasser Taghvai's *Sadeq Kordeh* (Sadeq the Kurd, 1972) and Amir Naderi's *Tangsir* (Tight Corner, 1973), worked like alternative Westerns to display the rebellion of a villager against the corruption of city elites or scoundrels.
15. See Chapter 5; and Talajooy, 'Afrā', my critical analysis of the play in my translation of the play.
16. See Chapter 4; and Talajooy, 'Continuity'.
17. See Talajooy, 'Beyzaie va Jang', 147–8; and Beyzaie's remarks in Beyzaie and Bassan, 'Nomādi', 125.
18. See Talajooy, 'Uncle Moustache', 234–5.
19. Alizadeh, 'Aks', 134–5.
20. See, for instance, Zāl in *The Shahnameh* and the wise sages found in *Samak-e Ayyār*. The idea is echoed in the concept of *Pir-e Tariqat* (Spiritual guide) in post-Islamic mysticism. See also Porushani and Pujavadi, 'Pir'.
21. Beyzaie, *Amu*, 1'.40"–3'.40", 12'.44"–12'.47" and 13'.17"–13'.20".
22. Ibid., 15'.25"–15'.50", 18'.42"–18'.50" and 19'–19'.30".
23. Ibid., 0'–11'33".
24. Ibid., 5'.40"–6'.05".
25. Ibid., 5'–11'.33".
26. Herodotus, *Histories*, 238.

27 Beyzaie uses the account of Surena's procession to create a similar scene in his (Kallāt Claimed (1982).
28 Plutarch, *Lives*, 417–19.
29 Frazer, *Golden Bow*, 364–70 and 390–4.
30 Abrahams, *Book of Delight*, 266–7. Frazer, *Golden Bow*, 394. In Iranian iconography such a ring may also suggest authority. This is represented, for instance, in *Naqsh-e Rostam* in the image of the seventh Sasanian king, Narseh (R.293–303AD) receiving a ring from a female figure, who is assumed to be Ānāhitā.
31 Al-Biruni, *Chronology*, 273–5.
32 Ibid., 212. See also Beyzaie, *Namāyesh*, 37–42, 52–5; Talajooy, 'Intellectuals', 382–3; and Āshurpur, *Namāyesh*, Vol. 1, 111–18, 219–85, Vol. 3, 23–114, Vol. 5, 189–99.
33 Beyzaie, *Amu*, 14'.28"–14'.31".
34 Bakhtin, *Rabelais*, 49.
35 Beyzaie, *Amu*, 7'.18"–7'.32".
36 Rancière, *Politics*, 12–13.
37 Beyzaie, *Amu*, 13'.17"–13'.30", 14'.15"–15'.06".
38 Beyzaie in Qukasiyan, *Goftogu*, 32.
39 Ibid., 41.
40 Bakhtin, *Dialogic*, 81.
41 Beyzaie in Qukasiyan, *Goftogu*, 83.
42 Beyzaie, *Amu*, 15'.50"–19'.25".
43 Ibid., 19'.12"–19'.25" & Kimiaei, *Qeysar*, https://www.youtube.com/watch?v=QEiRurPRUo4, 97'.40"–97'.50' (Accessed 27 January 2021).
44 Beyzaie, *Amu*, 19'.30"–21'.05".
45 Hitchcock, *Rear Window*, 102'–106'.
46 Qukasiyan, *Majmu'eh*, 204–5.
47 Davaei, 'Ragbār', 216–17.
48 Tahbaz, 'Khub o Bad', 20.
49 Beyzaie in Qukasiyan, *Goftogu*, 252.
50 Ebrahimi, 'Amu Sibilu', 201–4.

Chapter 4

1 For social impacts of cinema, see also Naficy, *Social 1 & 2*; and Rekabtalaei, *Iranian Cosmopolitanism*.
2 Kupers, 'Toxic Masculinity', 713–24.
3 Bridges and Pasco, 'Hybrid Masculinities', 246–58.
4 Pardo, 'Iranian Cinema', 36–7.
5 For toxic femininity, see McCann, 'Is there'.
6 I have written on this subject in a forthcoming book on the history of manliness in Iranian cultural products.
7 Kimiaei, *Bigāneh*, 83'–83'.30" & 88'–89'.
8 Davāei, 'Bigāneh', 430.
9 Azimpur, 'Interview', (1968). See *Bigāneh*, 42', 51', 89'–91' for Farangis or Ahmad's philosophical speeches.
10 See, for instance, Davaei, 'Ragbār', 215–26, which is, at least, well-written.
11 Naficy, *Social History*, 340.

12 Ibid., 340.
13 See also Ghorbankarimi, *Colourful*, 42.
14 Heidegger, *Being*, 123–49 and 172–212.
15 Beyzaie, *Ragbār*, 15'.12C–15'.40".
16 *It's a Wonderful Life*, 24'–29.40'.
17 Mithraic orders are echoed in *zurkhāneh* hierarchies: (1) *nocheh* (novice, a trainee who has just joined *zurkhāneh*), (2) *nokhāsteh* (a rising treasure, a novice of good wrestling ability ready for initiation), (3) *pahlevān* (hero/champion, a young man who has been initiated due to his character and skills in all *zurkhāneh* exercises), (4) *kohneh-savār* (an established *pahlevān* with unique wrestling skills), (5) *pishkesvat* (a senior *pahlevān* with a established reputation as a trainer and guide), (6) *sāheb zang* (a senior *pahlevān* for whom the bells are sounded whenever he arrives at the Zurkhāneh), (7) *sāheb zarb* (a senior *pahlevān* who acts as a consultant in all matters and for whom the bell and the drum are sounded whenever he enters the *zurkhāneh*). Afshari, *Āyin*, 47–9; and Beyzaei Kashani, *Tārikh*, 40–2. In the past, women, children and non-Muslims were not allowed into *zurkhāneh*, but this prohibition decreased from the 1950s when Shaban Jafari hosted the Shah's foreign guests for special performances. See Chehabi, 'ZUR-ḴĀNA'; Vermaseren's *Āyin-e Mitrā* and Beck, 'MITHRAISM'.
18 See also Pak-Shiraz's reading of the scene, 'Construction', 314–15.
19 Lacan, *Écrits*, 1–6, Evans, *Dictionary*, 128–9 and Bowie, *Lacan*, 165–78.
20 Lacan, *Écrits*, 1–6 and Evans, *Dictionary*, 117–19.
21 Evans, *Dictionary*, 6–7 and 108–9; and Lacan, *Écrits*, 7–22.
22 Mohseni, *Lāt-e Javānmard*, 27'.30"–29'.00" & 37'.40"–38'.30".
23 Interestingly, the film's director, Moqaddam (1929–96) and the poet Ahmadreza Ahmadi (1940–) had earlier suggested that Beyzaie work with the same comic actors (Sepehrnia, Garsha and Motevasseāni) for his first film, and Beyzaie had considered making his *Cheh Kesi Raiys rā Kosht* (Who Killed the Boss, 1969), which came to nothing as the comedians found it great but too 'heavy' for the public. Abdi, *Gharibeh*, 37.
24 For a comparison between the two works, see also Tahami-Nezhad, 'Ragbār', 236–44.
25 Beyzaie, 'Kārnāmeh', 54–5.
26 Beyzaie in Qukasiyan, *Goftogu*, 91 and 187.
27 See also Ghorbankarimi, *Colourful*, 44.
28 Donen, *Singin' in the Rain*, 64'.20"–69'.
29 Naficy, *Social 2*, 363–5.
30 Bakhtin, *Problems*, 160–1, and 158–181.
31 Qazvini, 'Mir-e Noruzi', 14. See also Qazvini, 'Shāhedi Digar'; and Āshurpur, *Namāyesh*, 23–114.
32 For Beyzaie's use of *Mir-e Noruzi* for tragic purposes, see also Talajooy, 'Intellectuals'.
33 For more, see Talajooy, 'So Dies'. For Takhti, see Chehabi, 'TAḴTI'.
34 Ophüls, *Letter*, 15'–17'.
35 For an analysis of the use of light and shadow in the scene, see also Ghorbankarimi, *Colourful*, 42–3.
36 Naficy, *Social 2*, 363–5.
37 Davaei, 'Ragbār', 225.
38 Tehranian, 'Power', 198.
39 Pardo, 'Iranian', 36–7.
40 For the accounts of these assassinations, see Amanat, *Pivot*.

41 Beyzaie in Qukasiyan, *Goftogu*, 47–9.
42 See the articles on *Ragbār* in Qukasiyan, *Majmu'eh*, 213–52.
43 For interesting comments on the film, see the film's page on Persian Wikipedia. shorturl.at/emA28.

Chapter 5

1 Bakhtin, *Problems*, 166.
2 Ibid., 166–7.
3 Beyzaie in Qukasiyan, *Goftogu*, 252.
4 Ibid., 117.
5 Bourdieu, *Practical*, 40.
6 Mojabi, *Negāh*, 135.
7 Beyzaie in Qukasiyan, *Goftogu*, 193.
8 For Beyzaie's use of architecture to comment on modernization, see also Pak-Shiraz, 'Exploring'.
9 Heidegger, *Being*, 123–49 and 172–212 or Chapter 4 of the current book.
10 Alizadeh, 'Aks', 140.
11 Beyzaie in Qukasiyan, *Goftogu*, 85–8.
12 Dubbed in the culturally appropriating style of the era with all the songs performed in Persian, *Mary Poppins* and Robert Wise's *The Sound of Music* (1965) were the most celebrated child-friendly films of the era in Iran.
13 Hafez, *Divān*, 114. به کوی عشق منه بی دلیل راه قدم ** که من نمودم به خویش صد اهتمام و نشد.
14 Beyzaie, *Journey*, 5'.50"-6'.08".
15 See, for instance, Kiarostami's *Where Is the Friend's House* (1990), 36'–40'.
16 Molavi, 'Pāsokh-e Hamzeh', *Masnavi: Daftar-e Seh*.
گر بمخاری خسته‌ای خود کشتهای ** ور حریر و قزدری خود رشته‌ای
17 The earliest reference to the practice is in Ghazali, *Kimiā*, Vol. 1, 155, who says it is a religiously unacceptable hairstyle practised by some soldiers. In Ghazali's time (1058-1111), however, most soldiers serving the Seljuks or the Ghaznavids were Turkic, and its prevalence among some *ayyārs* was a post-Mongol phenomenon.
18 As Sa'di states in the tale of gluttonous worshipper in *Golestan*, 70.
اندرون از طعام خالی دار ** تا در آن نور کبریا بینی
19 See also Pak-Shiraz, 'Exploring', 817.
20 Ebrahimi, 'Amu Sibilu', 201–2, states that in 1961 Beyzaie used his first chance to work with a camera to record images of the city that were unique, including a minute reel of labourers sleeping in Tehran's alleys.
21 See, for instance, Nima Yushij's poem 'Mitarāvad Mahtāb' in which the voice expresses an intellectual concern about people being asleep: The Moonlight rises**The glow worm shines**Their sleep does not break even for a second** But my worry for these sleeping people**Breaks the sleep in my wet eyes.
می‌تراود مهتاب ** می‌درخشد شبتاب ** نیست یک دم شکند خواب به چشم کس و لیک ** غم این خفته چند ** خواب در چشم ترم می‌شکند.
22 Nateqi, 'Dar Jostoju', 266.
23 The latter may refer to the astrological belief that things go wrong when the moon is in the constellation of scorpion, but it may also refer to the tale about the death of Mohammad ibn-e Ash'ath due to being stung by a scorpion on Ashura. The idea of

animals helping Shi'i Saints echoes ancient cultic beliefs and has been used as a device to suggest that even fierce animals were better than the villains and the indifferent people.
24. For Ānāhitā, see Pourdavoud (ed.), *Avestā: Yasht-hā*, 292–353 and 149–242; and Gaviri, *Ānāhitā*. For Mehr/ Mithra, see Bahar, *Az Ostureh*, 27–41; and Schmidt et al., 'MITHRA'. For the beloved person as a blend of men and women, see Najmabadi, 'Reading' and 'Chapter 2' of *Women*, where she argues that male and female attributes were mixed in early Qajar paintings to suggest an indeterminate figure she calls 'neuter'.
25. For more, see also Issa, *Iranian*; and Pākbāz, *Naqqāshi*.
26. Such films, at one level, were intended to create modern role models for such people to gradually uproot distorted practices such as paedophilic pederasty, which Iran and other countries had inherited from the ancient eras. However, the emphasis on sex and depicting street tough guys as heroes defeated this general intention.
27. Lodge, *Modes*, 84. The italics are mine. See also Jakobson, 'Metaphoric', 56–60.
28. Beyzaie, *Safar*, 31'-32'.18".
29. Beyzaie in Qukasiyan, *Goftogu*, 75.
30. Sasan, 'Safar', 268.
31. Qukasiyan, *Majmueh*, 265–71.

Chapter 6

1. Mojabi, 'Gharibeh', 286.
2. For a study of the evolution of women in these three films, see also Khansalar, 'Space'.
3. Naficy, *Social 2*, 366.
4. Ibid., 225, 213, 222–9. Dabashi, *Close-up*, 93.
5. Sheibani, 'Film', 225.
6. As Raminfar, 'Bahram', podcast 113, states, they had probably not visited Iran's distant villages at the time.
7. Naficy, *Social*, 367.
8. In such expressions as: تن بلوری، تنی همچون بلور، سینۀ همچون بلور
9. Mehrjui and Sa'edi, *Gav*, 10'–10'.40" and 98'–101'.25".
10. Naficy, *Social 2*, 367.
11. Ibid.
12. Naficy, 'Stranger', 2954–5.
13. Eshqi, 'About Stranger', 288, 291 and 293.
14. Beyzaie in Omid, *Tārikh*, 749. See also Beyzaie in Qukasiyan, *Goftogu*, 54–8.
15. *Nobān* is a ritual of exorcism like *zār*, see Sae'di, *Ahl-e*, 83–94. For the song, see Hamidi, *Hasht*, CD1, no.2.
16. Qukasiyan, *Goftogu*, 97–8.
17. Boyce, *History 1*, 206; Skjærvø, 'Ahura Mazdā', 404–9; and Biruni, *Al-Āthār*, 216.
18. Frazer, *Golden*, 331. See also the whole discussion in 'Book II: Killing the God', 223–556.
19. Ibid., 338, 274 and 273–99.
20. Beyzaie, *Namāyesh*, 56; Beyzaie in Amjad, 'From the Land', 728–36; and Yarshater, 'Ta'ziyeh', 88–95.
21. For images of such cemeteries in Iran, see https://click.ir/1397/07/21/weird-cemeteries-in-iran/.

22 See, for instance, Naficy, 'Stranger'; Mojabi, 'Gharibeh'; Sheibani, 'Film', 211, 213, 222–9.
23 Beyzaie, *Stranger*, 14′.58″–16′.30″.
24 Beyzaie in Qukasiyan, *Goftogu*, 100.
25 Heidegger, *Being*, 123–49 and 172–212. See also my chapter on *Downpour*.
26 Beyzaie in Qukasiyan, *Goftogu*, 109–10.
27 See my Chapter on *Bashu* in Volume 2.
28 Beyzaie in Qukasiyan, *Goftogu*, 96–9 and 111.
29 Beyzaie, *Tarabnameh*, 43′–48′.40″. Bahar, *Adyān*, 125–6 also links the black to Siyāvush as a vegetation god.
30 See the chapter on *Downpour*; Lacan, *Écrits*, 1–22; and Evans, *Dictionary*, 108–9, 117–19, and 128–9.
31 See, for instance, Warren and Wells-Howe, *Ecological Feminism*, 1–28; Or Lenson and Seager, *Companion*.
32 See Biruni, *Al-Āthār*, 334–5.
33 For rationality in feminism, see Lloyd, 'Man of Reason'; Alcoff & Potter's *Feminist Epistemologies*, Chapters 8, 10 and 11; and Manes, 'Nature and Silence', 15–29.
34 Beyzaie in Qukasiyan, *Goftogu*, 96 and 99. See also Khansalar, 'Space'.
35 Beyzaie, *Namāyesh*, 56; and Beyzaie, in Amjad, 'Land', 728–36.
36 For Shakespeare's use of fools, see Bate, 'Shakespeare's Foolosophy', 17–33. Kott, *Shakespeare*, 132–4.
37 Fry, 'Third Essay', 131–239.
38 Sotudeh, 'Arusi', 41–3.
39 Beyzaie in Qukasiyan, *Goftogu*, 97, 177–8, 313; and *Namāyesh*, 37–8.
40 Beyzaie, *Hezār Afsān*, 185–6.
41 Jung, *Psychology*, 131.
42 Freud, *Interpretation*, 147–58, 159–86, and 295–362.
43 For Kafka's works as 'metaphysical' and 'ontological' magic realism, see Spindler, 'Magic', 79.
44 Beyzaie in Qukasiyan, *Goftogu*, 98.
45 Dabashi, *Close Up*, 93.
46 Dönmez, *Cinemas*, 37.
47 Jafarinejhad, *Bahram*, 12–13.
48 Mir-Hosseini, 'Negotiating', 614; Najmabadi, 'Reading', 76–89.
49 Biruni, *Al-Āthār*, 216 (Persian Text, 355); and Gardizi, *Zein-ol-Akhbār*, 237.
50 Khayyam, *Rubaiyat*, 15.

از آمدنم نبود گردون را سود** وز رفتن من جلال و جاهش نفزود// وز هیچکسی نیز دو گوشم نشنود**کاین آمدن و رفتنم از بهر چه بود.

51 Beyzaie in Qukasiyan, *Goftogu*, 98–9 and 110–11.
52 Jackson, 'Catharsis', 474 and 479–89.
53 For more, see Rachel Bowlby's introduction to Freud and Breuer, *Studies*, vii–xxxv.
54 Beyzaie in Qukasiyan, *Goftogu*, 106. In Attar's *Biographies* (*Tazkerat*, 143–4), Bāyazid's sentence is 'Glory be to me, how sublime is my dignity?'. After the disciples's failure to hurt him, Bāyazid shrinks to his normal size, which is compared to the size of a 'sparrow', and tells his confused disciples, 'Bāyazid is what you see now, that was not Bāyazid. [. . .] The Almighty Himself sprinkled the tongue of his Servant.'
55 For mystic examples, see Ibid. For folktale examples, see Behrangi, *Sargozasht-e Domrol-e Divāneh Sar*.
56 Robinson, 'Tehran's', 14.

57 Cowie, 'Tehran', 84. See also, Qukasiyan, *Majmu'eh*, 296–305.
58 Gillett in Omid, *Tārikh*, 688–9.
59 Mojabi, 'Gharibeh', 285–7.
60 Cowie, 'Tehran', 84.

Chapter 7

1 Farid, 'Ayyār'.
2 Kathleen Barry's 1979 'Victims and Survivors' was one of the earliest examples of such discourses.
3 Hooks, 'Choosing', 150–1.
4 Farmanara in Dorostkar, *Bahman*, 155–6.
5 See, for instance, Sarshar, 'Barkhi Nāgofteh-hā'; or Naficy, *Social*, 367.
6 Beyzaie and Talajooy, 'Interviews'.
7 Sadr, *Iranian*, 156.
8 Naficy, *Social 2*, 426; and Omid, *Tārikh*, 747.
9 See Talajooy, 'Khāneh'; and Sheibani, 'Outcry'; Pak-Shiraz, 'Exploring'.
10 Avelar, *Untimely*, 1–2, 51.
11 Brunner, *Cultura Autoritaria*, 29 and 53, quoted in Avelar, *Untimely*, 55.
12 Avelar, *Untimely*, 3.
13 Reati, *Nombrar*, discussed in Avelar, *Untimely*, 52.
14 Avelar, *Untimely*, 52–4.
15 I was inspired to construct this argument by reading Irzık's use of Avelar's views in 'Yaşar Kemal's'.
16 The historical analysis offered previously is my own, but for relevant discussions of Iran's contemporary history, please see, Keddie, *Modern*; Amanat, *Iran*; Ansari, *Politics*; Arjomand, *Turban*; Abrahamian, *History*.
17 Loxley, *Performativity*, 88–166.
18 Beyzaie in Qukasiyan, *Goftogu*, 176–9.
19 See also Khorsand, 'Kalāgh', 59–60.
20 See also Talajooy, 'Khāneh' and 'Bahram Beyzaie va Jang-e'.
21 This section contains revised versions of some of my arguments about *The Crow* in Talajooy, 'Khāneh'.
22 The name in Persian suggests being carefree and letting things be as they are.
23 Beyzaie, *Kalāgh*, 8'.30"–11'.45".
24 Amjad, 'Afrā', 351.
25 See, for instance, *Ārash*, *Afrā*, *Parchment of Master Sharzin* or *The New Preface to the Shahnameh*.
26 Beyzaie in Omid, *Tārikh*, 749.
27 Rancière, *Politics*, 13.
28 Lipp, 'Writing History', 66–100.
29 Beyzaie, *Kalāgh*, 28'–30', 47'–48', 72'.30"–75'.30".
30 Deleuze, *Cinema 2*, 81.
31 Golestan, *Brick and Mirror*, 5'.30"–11'.
32 Katouzian, 'Short-term'. Despite its overgeneralizations, Katouzian's analogy offers excellent perspectives about the negative impacts of such historical breaches on economic, political and cultural development.

33 Gross, 'Bergson, Proust', 369–80.
34 Beyzaie in Qukasiyan, *Goftogu*, 139.
35 Rancière, *Future*, 33–67.
36 Goffman, *Frame Analysis*, 10–11 and 43–4. See also Chapter 2.
37 See, for instance, Jahed, 'Crime'.
38 See Sepehri, 'Sedā-ye', 179; and Robinson, 'Mr Flood's', 1060–1.
39 See also Talajooy, 'Khāneh'; and Pak-Shiraz, 'Exploring'.
40 Sheibani, 'Outcry', 98–9.
41 Massoumi, *Zibāei* (Podcast), 70'-72'.
42 Daryoush, 'Iran', 201.
43 Molaei in Omid, *Tārikh*, 748.
44 Bakideh in Omid, *Tārikh*, 748.

Chapter 8

1 See the theoretical sections in Chapter 1 of this book.
2 See my introduction to Chapter 3 of this book.
3 I have written six because if it had not been for the revolution, he could have completed his *Ballad of Tārā* in 1979, but the revolution postponed the production stage by a year and the film was completed in 1980.
4 Beyzaie, 'Bahram Beyzaie Discusses', 58'.30"–62'.20".

Bibliography

Abdi, Mohammad, Ed. *Gharibeh-ye Bozorg: Zendegi va cinemā-ye Bahram Beyzaie*. Tehran: Sales Publication, 2004.
Abrahamian, Ervand. *A History of Modern Iran*. Cambridge: Cambridge University Press, 2008.
Abrahams, Israel. *The Book of Delight and Other Papers*. Philadelphia: The Jewish Publication Society of America, 1912.
Afshari, Āyin. *Āyin-e Javānmardi*. Tehran: Pazhuhesh-hā-ye Farhangi, 2005.
Alam, Asadollah. *Yāddāsht-hā-ye Amir Asadollah Alam*. Vol. 1. Tehran: Maziyar, 2006.
Alcoff, Linda and Elizabeth Potter, Ed. *Feminist Epistemologies*. London and New York: Routledge, 1993.
Al-e Ahmad, Jalal. "'Kārnāmeh-ye Taātr-e Hokumati-ye Sanglaj" and "Darbāreh-ye Pahlevān Akbar Mimirad va Ghorub dar Diyāri Gharib va Qesseh-ye Māh-e Penhān'" (1966). In *Adab va Honar Emruz-e Iran: Majmueh Maqālāt Jalal Al-e Ahmad*. Vol. 4. Edited by Mostafa Zamaninia, 1959–64 and 1973–79. Tehran: Mitra, 1994.
Algar, Hamid. 'KHOMEINI'. In *Encyclopaedia Iranica*. Trustees of Columbia University. http://dx.doi.org/10.1163/2330-4804_EIRO_COM_12401 (accessed 1 December 2021).
Aliabadi, Homayun. 'Ghorub dar Diyār-e Gharib'. *Honar*, no. 547–50.
Alizadeh, Ghazaleh. 'Aks va Āyeneh' (Photos and Mirrors). In *Majmu'eh Maqālāt dar Naqd va Mo'arrefi Āsār-e Bahram Beyzaie*. Edited by Zaven Qukasiyan, 129–96. Tehran: Āgāh, 1999.
Amanat, Abbas. *Pivot of the Universe: Nasir Al-Din Shah Qajar and the Iranian Monarchy, 1831–96*. London: I. B. Tauris, 1997.
Amanat, Abbas. *Iran a Modern History*. New Haven: Yale University Press, 2017.
Amir Arjomand, Said. *The Turban for the Crown: The Islamic Revolution in Iran*. Oxford: Oxford University Press, 1988.
Amjad, Hamid. *Tyatr-e Qarn-e Sizdahom*. Tehran: Nilā, 2008.
Amjad, Hamid. 'Afrā ya Ruz Migozarad'. *Simia*. Edited by Hamid Amjad. 2 (Winter 2008): 337–63.
Amjad, Hamid, Ed. *Simia: Vijheh-ye Bahram Beyzaie va Theatre*. Series 2, no. 2. (Winter 2008).
Ansari, Ali. *Iran under Ahmadinejad: The Politics of Confrontation*. London and New York: Routledge, 2007.
Ansari, Ali. *Crisis of Authority: Iran's 2009 Presidential Election*. London: Brookings Institution Publication, 2010.
Ansari, Ali. *The Politics of Nationalism in Modern Iran*. Cambridge: Cambridge University Press, 2012.
Ansari, Ali, Ed. *Perceptions of Iran: History, Myths and Nationalism from Medieval Persia to the Islamic Republic*. London: Bloomsbury, 2013.
Anvar, Manuchehr. *Death of Yazdegerd*. Tehran: Roshangarān, 1989.
Ardent, Hannah. *Eichmann in Jerusalem: A Report on the Banality of Evil*. New York: Viking Press, 1963.

Arjomand, Jamshid. 'Talāsh-e Nābasandeh barā-ye Shenākht-e Jahān-e Beyzaie'. In *Majmu'eh Maqālāt dar Naqd va Mo'arrefi Āsār-e Bahram Beyzaie*. Edited by Zaven Qukasiyan, 105–12. Tehran: Āgāh, 1999.

Ashoori, Dariush and Hamed Sarrafizadeh. 'Bahram Beyzaie beh Revāyat-e Dariush Ashoori'. In *Haqiqat va Mard Dānā Series. Abadiyat va Yek Ruz*. Podcast 90 (January 2019). https://telegram.me/EternityAndADay.

Ashurpur, Sadeq. *Namāyesh-hā-ye Irāni 5: Namāyesh-hā-ye Qabl va Ba'd az Eslām* [Iranian Plays 5: Other Plays from Before and After Islam]. Tehran: Sureh Mehr, 2011.

Attar, Farideddin. *Tazkerat al-Oliya* [Biographies of the Saints] (ca.1205). Edited by Mohammad Este'lāmi. Tehran: Zavvār, 2012.

Avelar, Idelber. *The Untimely Present: Postdictatorial Latin American Fiction and the Task of Mourning*. Durham: Duke University Press, 1999.

Azadivar, Hooshang. 'Bahram Beyzaie dar Jostoju-ye Hoviyat'. In *Majmu'eh Maqālāt dar Naqd va Mo'arrefi Āsār-e Bahram Beyzaie*. Edited by Zaven Qukasiyan, 85–105. Tehran: Āgāh, 1999.

Azimpur, Ismaeil. 'Interview with Kimaei'. *Film va Honar* 191 (19 June 1968).

Bahar, Mehrdad. *Az Ostureh tā Tārikh*. Tehran: Cheshmeh, 1997.

Bahar, Mehrdad. *Adyān-e Āsiyāei*. Tehran: Cheshmeh, 2008.

Bakhtin, Mikhail. *The Dialogic Imagination: Four Essays*. Austin: Texas University Press, 1981.

Bakhtin, Mikhail. *Rabelais and His World*. Translated by Helene Iswolski. Bloomington: Indiana University Press, 1984.

Bakhtin, Mikhail. *Problems of Dostoevsky's Poetics*. Edited and Translated by Caryl Emerson. Minneapolis and London: Minnesota University Press, 1999.

Bar On, Bat-Ami. 'Marginality and Epistemic Privilege'. In *Feminist Epistemologies*. Edited by Linda Alcoff and Elizabeth Potter, 83–100. London and New York: Routledge, 1993.

Barry, Kathleen. 'Victims and Survivors'. In *Female Sexual Slavery*. Edited by Kathleen Barry, 33–42. Englewood Cliffs, NJ: Prentice Hall, 1979.

Bassan, Raphaël. 'Sinemāgari keh Bāyad Kashf Shavad'. Translated by Ahmad and Anvar Miralāei. In *Majmu'eh Maqālāt dar Naqd va Mo'arrefi Āsār-e Bahram Beyzaie*. Edited by Zaven Qukasiyan, 113–22. Tehran: Āgāh, 1999.

Bate, Alexander. 'Shakespeare's Foolosophy'. In *Shakespeare Performed: Essays in Honor of R. A. Foakes*. Edited by Grace Ioppolo, 17–33. Newark, NJ: Delaware University Press, 2000.

Beck, Roger. 'MITHRAISM'. In *Encyclopaedia Iranica*. General Editor Ehsan Yarshater. https://iranicaonline.org/articles/mithraism.

Beeman, William O. 'Why Do They Laugh? An Interactional Approach to Humor in Traditional Iranian Improvisatory Theater Performance and Its Effects'. *The Journal of American Folklore* 94, no. 374, *Folk Drama* (October–December 1981): 506–26.

Beeman, William O. *Iranian Performance Traditions*. Costa Mesa, CA: Mazda, 2011.

Behrangi, Samad. *Sargozasht-e Domrol-e Divāneh Sar*. http://samadbehrangi.com/books/Domrol(www.samadbehrangi.com).pdf (accessed 5 December 2020).

Behrooz, Maziar. *Rebels with a Cause: The Failure of the Left in Iran*. London: I.B. Tauris, 1999.

Benjamin, Walter. 'Theses on the Philosophy of History'. In *Illuminations*. Edited and introduced by Hannah Arendt. Translated by Harry Zohn, 253–64. New York: Schocken, 1969.

Beyza'i, Bahram. '"The Puppets," "Evening in a Strange Land", "The Story of the Hidden Moon" (Abridged)'. In *Modern Persian Drama: An Anthology*. Translated and introduced by Gisèle Kapuscinski, 3–100. Lanham: University Press of America, 1987.

Beyza'i, Bahram. 'Marionettes'. Translated by Sujata Bhatt, Jacqueline Hoats, Imran Nyazee and Kamiar Oskouee. In *Iranian Drama: An Anthology*. Compiled and edited by M. R. Ghanoonparvar and John Green, 153–78. Costa Mesa, CA: Mazda Publishers, 1989.

Beyza'i, Bahram. *The Marionettes*. Translated and edited by Jodi-Anne George, Parvin Loloi and Glyn Pursglove. Salzburg: Poetry Salzburg, 2005.

Beyzaie, Bahram. 'Kārnāmeh-ye Film-e Golestan'. *Arash* 5 (December 1962): 51–6.

Beyzaie, Bahram. 'Namāyesh dar Zhāpon'. *Musiqi* 3, no. 94 (December 1964): 34–70.

Beyzaie, Bahram. *Āyeheneh-hā-ye Ruberu* (1980). Tehran: Damāvand, 1984.

Beyzaie, Bahram. 'Har Kas dar Iran yek Film-e Khub Sākhteh Bāshad, Mo'allem Man Ast'. *Film* 93. (Mordād 1369/August 1990): 20–1.

Beyzaie, Bahram. 'Interview with National TV' (1979). Quoted in Parham. In *Majmu'eh Maqālāt dar Naqd va Mo'arrefi Āsār-e Bahram Beyzaie*. Edited by Zaven Qukasiyan, 85–105. Tehran: Āgāh, 1999.

Beyzaie, Bahram. *Dibācheh-ye Novin-e Shahnameh*. Tehran: Roshangaran, 2001.

Beyzaie, Bahram. *Namāyesh dar Iran* (1965). Tehran: Roshangarān, 2001.

Beyzaie, Bahram. '"Āzhdahāk", "Ārash", "Kārnāmeh-ye Bondār-e Bidakhsh", "[Puppet Trilogy: "Arusakhā", "Ghorub dar Diāri Gharib", "Qesseh-ye Māh-e Penhān"]", "Pahlevān Akbar Mimirad", "Hashtomin Safar-e Sandbād", and "Soltān-e Mār"'. In *Divān-e Namāyesh 1*. Tehran: Roshangaran, 2002.

Beyzaie, Bahram. '"Chāhār Sanduq" and "Rāh-e Tufāni-e Farmān Pesar-e Farmān az miān-e Tāriki"'. In *Divān-e Namāyesh 2*. Tehran: Roshangaran, 2002.

Beyzaie, Bahram. *Marg-e Yazdgerd: Majles-e Shāh Koshi*, Sixth edition. Tehran: Roshangaran, 2002.

Beyzaie, Bahram. *Nodbeh*. Tehran: Roshangarān, 2003.

Beyzaie, Bahram. 'Roshanfekr-e Tamām Vaqt'. *Andisheh-ye Puyā* 33 (March 2016): 114–15.

'Beyzaie on Siyavush-Khani (Siyāvush Recitation) and its Mythological and Literary Roots'. Translated by Ghazal Bozorgmehr. *Iranian Studies: Special Issue: Bahram Beyzaie's Cinema and Theater*. Edited by Saeed Talajooy. 46, no. 5 (Autumn 2013): 721–36.

Beyzaie, Bahram. 'Sāyehbāzi Namordeh Ast'. *Āzmā* 102 (Khordad 1393/June 2014): 24–6.

Beyzaie, Bahram. 'Āzādi Mikhāstand barā-ye Sānsur Digarān: Goftegu bā Bahram Beyzaie keh dar Shab-hā-ye She'r-e Goethe be Jā-ye Hokumat Roshanfekrān rā beh Naqd Gereft'. *Andisheh-ye Puyā* 39 (December 2016): 133.

Beyzaie, Bahram. *Tarabnameh: A Modern Interpretation of a Traditional Play*. Stanford University. https://www.youtube.com/watch?v=nPvOYLx5ykE. (Dated 14 March 2016) (accessed 24 September 2021).

Beyzaie, Bahram. 'Bahram Beyzaie Discusses Crossroads'. Video Recording. *Stanford University: Bahram Beyzaie*. https://beyzaie.sites.stanford.edu/lectures-conferences-and-discussions (Dated 23 April 2018) (accessed 24 June 2022).

Beyzaie, Bahram. *Mahi*. Los Angeles: Bisheh, 2020.

Beyzaie, Bahram and Hamid Amjad. 'From the Land of the Pure, in Search of the Lost Origin: An Interview with Bahram Beyzaie on Siyavush-Khani (Siyavush Recitation) and its Mythological and Literary Roots'. Translated by Ghazal Bozorgmehr. *Iranian Studies: Special Issue on Bahram Beyzaie's Cinema and Theater*. Edited by Saeed Talajooy. 46, no. 5 (Autumn 2013): 737–52.

Beyzaie, Bahram and Raphaël Bessan. 'Nomādi az Moqāvemat'. Translated by Ahmad & Anvar Miralāei. In *Majmu'eh Maqālāt dar Naqd va Mo'arrefi Āsār-e Bahram Beyzaie*. Edited by Zaven Qukasiyan, 122–7. Tehran: Āgāh, 1999.

Beyzaie, Bahram and Hagir Daryoush. 'Tark-e Ghoghā-ye Dokkān-dārān'. *Cinema 6* (September–October 1977). Quoted in *Simia 2: Special Issue on Bahram Beyzaie*. Edited by Hamid Amjad. February 2008: 36–42.

Beyzaie, Bahram and Alireza Kaveh. 'Goftogu-ye Alireza Kaveh bā Bahram Beyzaie'. In *Bahram Beyzaie va Vaqti Hameh Khābim*. Edited by Alireza Kaveh, 201–24, 248–320. Tehran: Nielā, 2019.

Beyzaie, Bahram and Andisheh Puyā. 'Cheh Mahkameh-hā-ye Roshanfekri keh Nagozarāndam'. *Andisheh Puyā*. No. 12. (Jan. 2014). 119–20.

Beyzaie, Bahram and Kaveh Rastegar. 'Dar Tāātr Hameh Kar Kardeh-am'. *Rudaki Monthly Periodical* (1972). In *Simia 2: Special Issue on Bahram Beyzaie*. Edited by Hamid Amjad. Feb 2008. 33–4.

Beyzaie, Bahram and Hoda Saber. 'Shir-e Del Khun'. *Cheshm-andāz-e Iran: Vizheh-nāmeh Jahān Pahlevān Takhti (Jā-ye Khāli, Jā-ye Sabz)* (Winter 1388/2010): 122–4.

Beyzaie, Bahram and Saeed Soltanpur. 'Mizgerd-e Teātr: darbāreh-ye *Mirās* va *Ziyāfat*'. *Simia 2: Special Issue on Bahram Beyzaie*. Edited by Hamid Amjad. (Autumn 1967): 165–88.

Beyzaie, Bahram and Saeed Talajooy. 'Interviews'. *Multiple*. Conducted between December 2020 and November 2021.

Beyzaei Kashani, Hossein Parto. *Tārikh-e Varzesh-e Bāstani dar Iran, Zurkhāneh*. Tehran: Heidari, 1958.

Biruni (Al-Biruni), Mohammad (Abu Reihān). *Al-Āthār Al-Bāqiyah En Al-Qorun Al-Khāliyah* (The Chronology Of Ancient Nations). Translated by Eduard Sachau. London: W.H.Allen and CO, 1879.

Biruni (Al-Biruni), Mohammad (Abu Reihān). *Al-Āthār Al-Bāqiyah En Al-Qorun Al-Khāliyah*. Translated by Akbar Danaseresht. Tehran: Amir Kabir, 2007.

Boroujerdi, Mehrzad. *Iranian Intellectuals and the West: The Tormented Triumph of Nativism*. Syracuse: SUP, 1996.

Bourdieu, Pierre. *Practical Reason: On the Theory of Action*. Stanford, CA: Stanford University Press, 1998.

Bourdieu, Pierre. *Distinction: A Social Critique of the Judgement of Taste*. (1989) Translated by Richard Nice. Cambridge, MA: Harvard University Press, 2005.

Bourdieu, Pierre. *Outline of a Theory of Practice*. Translated by Richard Nice. Cambridge: Cambridge University Press, 2013.

Bowie, Malcolm. *Lacan*. Cambridge, MA: Harvard University Press, 1991.

Boyce, Mary. *A History of Zoroastrianism*, Vol. 2. Leiden and Köln: Brill, 1982.

Boyce, Mary. *A History of Zoroastrianism*, Vol. 1. Leiden, New York and Köln: E. J. Brill, 1996.

Bridges, Tristan and Cheri Jo Pascoe. 'Hybrid Masculinities: New Directions in the Sociology of Men and Masculinities'. *Sociology Compass* 8, no. 3 (March 2014): 246–58.

Brunner, Jose Joaquin. *La cultura autoritari en Chile*. Santiago: FLACSO, 1981.

Chardin, John (Sir). *Travels in Persia*. London: London Argonaut Press, 1927.

Chehabi, Houchang E. 'ZUR-ḴĀNA'. In *Encyclopaedia Iranica Online*, © Trustees of Columbia University in the City of New York. Consulted online on 25 February 2021 http://dx.doi.org/10.1163/2330-4804_EIRO_COM_273.

Chehabi, Houchang E. 'TAḴTI, Ḡolām-Reżā'. In *Encyclopaedia Iranica Online*, © Trustees of Columbia University in the City of New York. Consulted online on 25 February 2021 http://dx.doi.org/10.1163/2330-4804_EIRO_COM_1555.

Chodzko, Alexandre. *Théâtre Persan: Choix de Téa'ziés*. Paris: Ernest Leroux, 1878.
Chodzko, Alexandre. 'Mundus Imaginalis or the Imaginary and the Imaginal'. 1964. In *H. C. Corbin*. Last consulted online on 30 June 2021 https://www.amiscorbin.com/bibliographie/mundus-imaginalis-or-the-imaginary-and-the-imaginal/.
Cowie, Peter. '"Tehran". "In the Picture"'. *Sight and Sound* (Spring 1975): 83–4.
Dabashi, Hamid. *Close Up: Iranian Cinema, Past, Present, and Future*. London: Verso, 2001.
Darmesteter, James. '"Aban Yasht" and "Mehr Yasht"'. *Sacred Texts*. http://www.sacred-texts.com/zor/sbe23/index.htm> (accessed 5 February 2011).
Daryoush, Hagir. 'Iran'. In *International Film Guide 1978*. Edited by Peter Cowie, 199–202. New York: International Film Exchange LTD, 1978.
Dasgupta, Sudeep. 'Art is Going Elsewhere, and Politics Has to Catch It: An Interview with Jacques Rancière'. *Krisis* 1 (2008): 70–7.
Davāei, Parviz. 'Bigāneh Biā'. In *Tārikh-e Cinema-ye Iran 1279–1357*. Edited by Jamal Omid, 429–31. Tehran: Rozaneh, 1374/1995.
Davāei, Parviz. '*Ragbār*: Mā Ham Hastim' (*Downpour*: We're Also Here). Republished in *Majmu'eh Maqālāt dar Naqd va Mo'arrefi Āsār-e Bahram Beyzaie*. Edited by Zaven Qukasiyan, 215–26. Tehran: Āgāh, 1999.
Davani, Ali. *Nehzat-e Rohāniyun-e Iran*, Vols 5 and 6. Tehran: Markaz-e Asnād-e Enqelāb Eslāmi, 1998.
Deleuze, Gilles. *Cinema 2: The Time-Image*. Translated by Hugh Tomlinson and Robert Galeta. London: Athlone Press, 1989, 2–3.
Dolatabadi, Mahmud. 'Abbās Āqā to Kehili Shabih-e Hedayat Hasti'. In *Digarān-e Abbas Na'lbandiyan*. Edited by Javad Atefeh, 231–6. Tehran: Melikan, 2015.
Dönmez-Colin, Gönül. *Cinemas of the Other: A Personal Journey with Film-makers from the Middle East and Central Asia*. Bristol: Intellect Books, 2006.
Dorostkar, Reza, Ed. *Bahman Farmanara: Zendegi va Āsār; and the Full Script of Khāneh-ei Ru-ye Āb*. Tehran: Qatreh, 2002.
Eagleton, Terry. *Culture*. New Haven: Yale University Press, 2016.
Ebrahimi, Nader. 'Amu Sibilu az Didgāh-e yek Binandeh Ma'muli'. In *Majmu'eh Maqālāt dar Naqd va Mo'arrefi Āsār-e Bahram Beyzaie*. Edited by Zaven Qukasiyan, 201–4. Tehran: Āgāh, 1999.
Ensafi, Javad. *Siyāh-bāzi az Negāh Yek Siyāh*. Isfahan: Hojjat, 1999.
Eshqi, Behzad. 'Darbāreh "Gharibeh O Meh"'. In *Majmu'eh Maqālāt dar Naqd va Mo'arrefi Āsār-e Bahram Beyzaie*. Edited by Zaven Qukasiyan, 288–94. Tehran: Āgāh, 1999.
Evans, Dylan. *An Introductory Dictionary of Lacanian Psychoanalysis*. London and New York: Routledge, 1996.
Farhang, Dariush. *Nāgofteh-hā-ye* Cherikeh-ye Tārā. Video Clip Interview. Available through Āpārāt. shorturl.at/adD04 (accessed 2 February 2021).
Farid, Manuchehr, 'Ayyār-e Tanhā'. (Interview by Mehdi Tahbaz). *Rādio Fardā*. https://www.radiofarda.com/a/f7-manouchehr-farid-interview-part2/26598215.html (accessed 12 February 2021).
Fatemi, Sasan. 'Music, Festivity, and Gender in Iran from the Qajar to the Early Pahlavi Period'. *Iranian Studies* 38, no. 3 (September 2005): 399–418.
Fischer, Michael. *Iran: From Religious Dispute to Revolution*. Cambridge, MA and London: Harvard University Press, 1980.
Floor, Willem. *History of Theater in Iran*. Odenton, MD: Mage, 2005.
Fo, Dario. *L'operaio conosce 300 parole il padrone 1000 per questo lui è il padrone* (1975). In *Fo, 1966–98 Le Commedie di Dario Fo*, Vol. 3. Turin: Einaudi.

Fo, Dario. *Fabulazzo*. Edited by Lorenzo Rugierro and Walter Valeri. Milan: Kaos, 1992.
Forgeard, Marie. 'Perceiving Benefits after Adversity: The Relationship between Self-reported Posttraumatic Growth and Creativity'. *Psychology of Aesthetics, Creativity, and the Arts* 7, no. 3 (2013): 245–64.
Forgeard, Marie. 'Creativity and Healing'. In *The Cambridge Handbook of Creativity*. Edited by Kaufman, James and Robert Sternberg, 319–32. Cambridge: Cambridge University Press, 2019.
Foucault, Michel. 'Truth and Power'. In *Power/Knowledge: Selected Interviews and Other Writings 1972-77*. Edited by Colin Gordon. Translated by Coli Gordon, Leo Marshall, John Mepham and Kate Soper, 109–32. New York: Pantheon Books, 1980.
Frazer, James George. *The Golden Bough, V. VI, The Scapegoat*. London: MacMillan, 1919.
Freud, Sigmund and Joseph Breuer. *Studies in Hysteria*. (1893). Translated by Nicola Luckhurst. London: Penguin Books, 2004.
Freud, Sigmund. *The Interpretation of Dreams*. Translated by James Strachey. New York: Basic Books, 2010.
Fry, Northrop. 'Third Essay- Archetypal Criticism: Theory of Myths'. In *Anatomy of Criticism: Four Essays* (1957), 131–239. Princeton: Princeton University Press, 2000.
Gardizi, Abdolhay. *Zein-ol-Akhbār*. Edited by Abdolhay Habibi. Tehran: Bonyād-e Farhang, 1969.
Gaviri, Susan. *Ānāhitā dar Asātir-e Irāni*. Tehran: Qoqnus, 1997.
Ghaderi Sohi, Behzad and Masoud Ghorbaninejad. 'Ali Nassirian and a Modern Iranian "National" Theatre'. *Asian Theatre Journal* 29, no. 2 (Fall 2012): 495–527.
Ghaffary, Farrokh. 'Iranian Secular Theatre'. In *McGraw-Hill Encyclopaedia of World Drama*, Vol. 3. Edited by Stanley Hochman, 58–65. New York: McGraw-Hill.
Ghanoonparvar, Mohammad Reza. 'Four Boxes'. In *An Anthology of Iranian Drama*. Edited by M. R. Ghanoonparvar and John Green. Costa Mesa: Mazda, 1989.
Ghanoonparvar, Mohammad Reza. *Memoirs of the Actor in a Supporting Role*. Costa Mesa: Mazda, 2010.
Ghanoonparvar, Mohammad Reza. 'Collective Identity and Despotism: Lessons in Two Plays by Bahram Beyzaie'. Special Issue: *Bahram Beyzaie's Cinema and Theater*. Edited by Saeed Talajooy. 46, no. 5 (Autumn 2013): 753–64.
Ghazali, Mohammad. *Kimiā-ye Sa'ādat* (The Alchemy of Happiness/Salvation). 2 Vols. Edited by Hosein Khadivjam. Tehran: Elmi va Farhangi, 1985.
Ghorbankarimi, Maryam. *A Colourful Presence: The Evolution of Women's Representation in Iranian Cinema*. Cambridge: Cambridge Scholars Publishing, 2015.
Goffman, Erving. *Frame Analysis: An Essay on the Organization of Experience*. Boston: Northeastern University Press, 1986.
Gross, David. 'Bergson, Proust, and the Revaluation of Memory'. *International Philosophical Quarterly* 25, no. 4 (1985): 369–80.
Hall, Stuart. 'Cultural Studies and its Theoretical Legacies'. In *Cultural Studies*. Edited by Lawrence Grossberg, Cary Nelson and Paula Treichler, 277–94. New York and London: Routledge, 1992.
Hamidi, Hossein. Col. & Ed. *Hasht Behesht* (Eight Paradises). 4 Cds. Tehran: Mahoor, 2005.
Hanaway, William L. Jr. 'Anāhitā and Alexander'. *Journal of the American Oriental Society* 102, no. 2 (April–June 1982): 285–95.
Hashemi, Afshin. 'Chāhār Sanduq dar Partov-e Roydadhā-ye Tārikhi-ye Iran (Daheh-hā-ye Bist tā Chehel'. *Simia 2: Special Issue on Bahram Beyzaie*. Edited by Hamid Amjad. (February 2008): 99–118.

Hashemi, Mehdi. 'Marg-e Yazdgerd'. In *Chelcheragh*. shorturl.at/uK124 (accessed 26 May 2020).

Hashemi, Mehdi and Hamed Sarrafizadeh. 'Bahram Beyzaie beh Revāyat-e Mehdi Hashemi va Afshin Hashemi'. In Haqiqat va Mard Dānā Series. *Abadiyat va Yek Ruz*. podcast 171 (December 2021). https://telegram.me/EternityAndADay.

Heidegger, Martin, *Being and Time: A Translation of Sein und Seit*. Translated by Joan Stambaugh. New York: State University of New York Press, 1996.

Herodotus. *The Histories*. Translated by Aubrey de Selicourt. London: Penguin, 1954.

Herrenschmidt, Clarisse and Jean Kelllens. 'DAIVA'. In *Encyclopaedia Iranica Online*, © Trustees of Columbia University in the City of New York. Consulted online on 18 November 2021 http://dx.doi.org/10.1163/2330-4804_EIRO_COM_7971.

Hooks, Bell. 'Choosing the Margin as a Space of Radical Openness'. In *Yearning: Race, Gender, and Cultural Politics*, 145–54. Boston: South End, 1990.

Irzık, Sıbel. 'Yaşar Kemal's Island of Resistance'. In *Resistance in Contemporary Middle Eastern Cultures: Literature, Cinema and Music*. Edited by Saeed Talajooy and Karima Laachir, 49–63. New York: Routledge, 2012.

Issa, Rose. *Iranian Contemporary Art*. London: Booth-Clibborn, 2001.

Jackson, Stanley. 'Catharsis and Abreaction in the History of Psychological Healing'. *Psychiatric Clinics of North America* 17, no. 3 (September 1994): 471–91.

Jafarinejhad, Shahram. *Bahram Beyzaie*. Tehran: Nashr-e Qesseh, 2000.

Jahed, Parviz. *Az Sinemātek Paris tā Kānun-e Film-e Tehran*. Tehran: Ney, 2014.

Jahed, Parviz. 'Crime Thriller Elements in Bahram Beyzaie's Films'. In *Origins, Forms and Functions inBahram Beyzaie's Cinema and Theatre*. Edited by Saeed Talajooy. London: Gingko, Forthcoming 2023.

Jakobson, Roman. 'The Metaphoric and Metonymic Poles' (1956). In *Modern Criticism and Theory: A Reader*. Edited by David Lodge. Ex. Nigel Wood, 56–60. Harlow: Longman, 2000.

Janack, Marianne. 'Standpoint Epistemology Without the "Standpoint"? An Examination of Epistemic Privilege and Epistemic Authority'. *Hypatia* 12, no. 2 (1997): 125–39.

Jannati Attaei, Abolqasem. *Bonyād-e Namāyesh dar Iran*. Tehran: Mihan, 1333/1954.

Javanmard, Abbas. *Didār bā Khiesh*. Tehran: Farhang-e Nashr-e No, 1396/2017.

Jones, Derek. 'History of Censorship in Iran: Since 1941'. In *Censorship: An International Encyclopaedia*. Edited by Derek Jones, 1202–12. London: Fitzroy Dearborn Publishers, 2001.

Jung, Carl Gustav. *Psychology and Religion: West and East: Collected Works of C. G. Jung, Volume 11*. Translated by R. F. C. Hull. Princeton: Princeton University Press, 1969.

Kapuscinski, Gisèle, 'Modern Persian Drama'. In *Critical Perspectives on Modern Persian Literature*. Edited by Thomas M. Ricks, 381–404. Washington, DC: Three Continents Press, 1984.

Katouzian, Homa. 'The Short-Term Society: A Study in the Problems of Long-Term Political and Economic Development in Iran'. *Middle Eastern Studies* 40, no. 1 (January 2004): 1–22.

Kaufman, James C. and Robert J. Sternberg, Eds. *The Cambridge Handbook of Creativity*. Cambridge: Cambridge University Press, 2019.

Keddie, Nikki R. *Modern Iran: Roots and Results of Revolution*. New Haven and London: Yale University Press, 2003.

Khansalar, Fatemeh Mehr. 'Space and Nature in Relationship with Women in Bahram Beyzaie's Village Trilogy'. In *Origins, Forms and Functions in Bahram Beyzaie's Cinema and Theatre*. Edited by Saeed Talajooy. London: Gingko, Forthcoming 2023.

Khayyam, Omar, *Rubaiyat*. Edited by Sadeq Hedayat. Tehran: Tākh, 1998.

Khomeini, Ruhollah. *Sahifeh-ye Emām*. Vol. 1. Tehran: Mo'assesseh-ye Nashr va Tanzim, 1999.

Khorsand, Bijhan. 'Kalāgh'. In *Negahi beh Sinemā-ye Siāsi*, 54–62. Tehran: Azad, 1980.

Kott, Jan. *Shakespeare Our Contemporary*. London: Methuen and Co., 1964.

Kuban, Sima. 'Zamān, Zan, va Jāzebeh-hā-ye Basari dar Āsār-e Beyzaie'. In *Majmu'eh Maqālāt dar Naqd va Mo'arrefi Āsār-e Bahram Beyzaie*. Edited by Zaven Qukasiyan, 45–84. Tehran: Āgāh, 1999.

Kupers, Terry A. 'Toxic Masculinity as a Barrier to Mental Health Treatment in Prison'. *Journal of Clinical Psychology* 61, no. 6 (June 2005): 713–24.

Lacan, Jacques. *Écrits*. Translated by Bruce Fink. New York and London: W.W. Norton, 2006.

Lawrence, Bruce Bennet and Aisha Karim. 'Pierre Bourdieu'. In *On Violence: A Reader*, 188–98. Durham: Duke University Press, 2007.

Leiter, Samuel. *A Kabuki Reader: History and Performance* (Japan in the Modern World). London: Routledge, 2001.

Lenson, Lise and Joni Seager, Eds. *A Companion to Feminist Geography*. Oxford: Blackwell, 2005.

Lipp, Carol. 'Writing History as Political Culture. Social History versus "Alltagsgeschichte": A German Debate'. *Storia della storiografia: rivista internazionale= Histoire de l'historiographie: revue internationale= History of historiography: International Review= Geschichte der Geschichtsschreibung: internationale Zeitschrift* 17 (1990): 66–100.

Lloyd, Genevieve. 'The Man of Reason'. *Metaphilosophy* 10, no. 1 (January 1979): 18–37.

Lodge, David. *The Modes of Modern Writing: Metaphor, Metonymy and the Typology of Modern Literature*. New York: Cornell University Press, 1977.

Loloi, Parvin and Glynn Pursglove. 'Translating Persian Drama: Problems (and Solutions?)'. In *Drama Translation and Theatre Practice*. Edited by Sabine Coelsch-Foisner and Holger Klein, 61–72. Frankfurt Am Mein: Peter Lang, 2004.

Loxley, James. *Performativity (The New Critical Idiom)*. New York: Routledge, 2007.

Macfie, Alexander Lyon, Ed. *Orientalism: A Reader*. Edinburgh: Edinburgh University Press, 2000.

Manes, Christopher. 'Nature and Silence'. In *The Ecocriticism Reader*. Edited by Cheryll Glotfelty and Harold Fromm, 15–29. Athene and London: University of Georgia Press, 1995.

Massoumi, Parvanh. 'Zibāei, Sabr va Ghorur: Bā Parvaneh Massoumi'. (Podcast) In *Abadiyat va Yek Ruz*, No. 146.

Matthee, Rudi. 'Prostitutes, Courtesans, and Dancing Girls: Women Entertainers in Safavid Iran'. In *Iran and Beyond: Essays in Middle Eastern History in Honor of Nikki R. Keddie*. Edited by Rudi Matthee and Beth Baron, 121–50. Costa Mesa, CA: Mazda, 2000.

McAdams, Dan P. and Regina L. Logan. 'Creative Work, Love, and the Dialectic in Selected Life Stories of Academics'. In *Identity and Story: Creating Self in Narrative*. Edited by Dan P. McAdams, Ruthellen Josselson, and Amia Lieblich, 89–108. Washington, DC: American Psychological Association, 2006.

McAdams, Dan P. and Regina L. Logan. 'Narrative Identity'. In *Handbook of Identity Theory and Research: Volume 1 Structures and Processes*. Edited by Seth J. Schwartz, Koen Luyckx, and Vivian L. Vignoles, 99–116. New York: Springer, 2011.

McCann, Hannah. 'Is There Anything "toxic" about Femininity? The Rigid Femininities that Keep us Locked in'. *Psychology & Sexuality* (June 2020). doi:10.1080/19419899.2020.1785534.

Mettinger, Tryggve N. D. 'The "Dying and Rising God": A Survey of Research from Frazer to the Present Day'. In *David and Zion: Biblical Studies in Honor of J. J. M. Roberts Batto*. Edited by Bernard F. Batto and Kathryn L. Roberts, 373–86. Indiana: Eisenbrauns, 2004.

Mew, James. 'The Modern Persian Stage'. *The Fortnightly Review* LIX (June 1896): 902–18.

Milani, Abbas. 'Ruhollah Khomeini'. *Eminent Persians: The Men and Women Who Made Modern Iran, 1941–79*, Vol. 1, 350–7. Syracuse, New York: Syracuse University Press, 2008.

Miresmaeili, Amir Hossein. '82-sālegi-ye Bahram Beyzaie: Honarmandi keh Moqābel-e Nezām-e Hazf o Sānsur Kornesh Nakard'. *Iran Wire*, 25 December 2020. https://iranwire.com/fa/jinac/44482 (accessed 30 January 2021).

Mir-Hosseini, Ziba. 'Negotiating the Forbidden: On Women and Sexual Love in Iranian Cinema'. *Comparative Studies of South Asia, Africa and the Middle East* 27, no. 3 (2007): 673–9.

Moin, Baqer. *Khomeini: Life of the Ayatollah*. London: Bloomsbury, 1999.

Mojabi, Javad. 'Gharibeh va Meh Jashnvāreh rā Nejāt Dād' (Stranger and the Fog Saved the Festival). *Etellāāt*, No. 14577, 14 Āzar 1353 (24 November 1974). In *Majmu'eh Maqālāt dar Naqd va Mo'arrefi Āsār-e Bahram Beyzaie*. Edited by Zaven Qukasiyan, 285–7. Tehran: Āgāh, 1999.

Mojabi, Javad. *Negāh-e Kāshef-e Gostākh*. Tehran: Ofoq, 2004.

Molavi (Rumi), Mohammad Jalāleddin. 'Pāsokh-e Hamzeh'. In *Masnav-ye Ma'navi Daftar-e 3*. (1273). Tehra\n: Tolu', 1987.

Naficy, Hamid. 'The Stranger and the Fog'. In *Magill's Survey of Cinema: Foreign Language Films*. Edited by Frank Magill, 2949–55. Englewood Cliffs, NJ: Salem, 1985.

Naficy, Hamid. 'Veiled Vision/Powerful Presences: Women in Post-Revolutionary Iranian Cinema'. In *Life and Art: The New Iranian Cinema*. Edited by Rose Issa and Sheila Whitaker, 43–65. London: National Film Theatre, 1999.

Naficy, Hamid. *A Social History of Iranian Cinema, Volume 2: The Industrializing Years 1941–78*. Durham: Duke University Press, 2011.

Najmabadi, Afsaneh. 'Reading for Gender through Qajar Paintings'. In *Royal Persian Paintings: The Qajar Epoch, 1785–1925*. Edited by Layla Diba, 76–89. London: I. B. Tauris, 1999.

Nateqi, Behnam. 'Dar Jostoju-ye Hovi-yati Mafqud'. In *Majmu'eh Maqālāt dar Naqd va Mo'arrefi Āsār-e Bahram Beyzaie*. Edited by Zaven Qukasiyan, 265–72. Tehran: Āgāh, 1999.

Nazarzadeh, Rasul. *Tanpushi az Āyeneh*. Tehran: Roshangarān, 2005.

Nezam, al-Mulk. *The Book of Government or Rules for Kings: The Siyar al-Muluk or Siyasat-nama of Nizam al-Mulk*. Translated by Hubert Darke. New York and London: Routledge, 1960.

Omid, Jamal. *Tārikh-e Cinema-ye Iran 1279–1357*. Tehran: Rozaneh, 1374/1995.

Pakbāz, Ruein. *Naqqāshi-ye Iran az Dirbāz tā Emruz*. Tehran: Nārestān, 2000.

Pak-Shiraz. 'Exploring the City in the Cinema of Bahram Beyzaie'. *Iranian Studies: Special Issue on Bahram Beyzaie*. Edited by Saeed Talajooy. 46, no. 5 (2013): 811–28.

Pak-Shiraz. 'Constructing Masculinities through the Javanmards in Pre-Revolutionary Iranian Cinema'. In *Javanmardi: The Ethics and Practice of Persianate Perfection*. Edited by Lloyd Ridgeon, 297–318. London: Gingko, 2018.

Pardo, Eldad J.. 'Iranian Cinema, 1968–78: Female Characters and Social Dilemmas on the Eve of the Revolution'. *Middle Eastern Studies* 40, no. 3 (2004): 29–54.

Parham, Baqer. 'Kudak, Zan, Gharibeh va Taqdir-e Tarikhi'. In *Majmu'eh Maqālāt dar Naqd va Mo'arrefi Āsār-e Bahram Beyzaie*. Edited by Zaven Qukasiyan, 12–43. Tehran: Āgāh, 1999.

Parsa, Soheil with Peter Farbridge and Brian Quirt. '"Aurash" and "Death of the King"'. In *Stories from the Rains of Love and Death: Four Plays from Iran*. Toronto: Playwrights Canada Press, 2007.

Plutarch. 'Life of Crassus'. In *Plutarch's Lives: Pericles and Fabius Maximus. Nicias and Crassus*. Translated by Bernadotte Perrin, 313–423. London: William Heinemann, 1932.

Porushani, Iraj and Nasrollah Pujavadi, 'Pir'. *Dāneshnāmeh-ye Jahān-e Eslām*. https://rch.ac.ir/article/Details/13277. (accessed 10 March 2021).

Pourdavoud, Ebrahim. *Yasht-hā*. Tehran: Negāh, 1973.

Qazvini, Mohammad. 'Mir-e Noruzi' [New Year Ruler]. *Yādegār* 1, no. 3 (Ābān 1323/ November 1944): 13–16.

Qazvini, Mohammad. 'Shāhedi Digar Barāye Mir- Noruzi' [Another Evidence for New Year Ruler]. *Yādegār* 2, no. 10 (Khordad 1324/June 1945): 58–66.

Qukasiyan, Zaven. *Goftogu bā Bahram Beyzaie*. Tehran: Āgāh, 1992.

Qukasiyan, Zaven. *Majmu'eh Maqālāt dar Naqd va Mo'arrefi Āsār-e Bahram Beyzaie*. Tehran: Āgāh, 1992.

Radi, Akbar, 'Darbāreh-ye *Matarsak-hā dar Shab* va *Arusakhā*'. *Ārash* 6 (1963): 118–24.

Rafi Jam, Asghar. 'Bahram Beyzaie Khodash yek Daneshgāh Bud'. *Sinemā Sinemā* (2019). shorturl.at/wxETZ (accessed 5 November 2020).

Raminfar, Iraj and Shadmehr Rastin. 'Bahram Beyzaie beh Revāyat-e Iraj Raminfar'. In *Haqiqat va Mard Dānā Series. Abadiyat va Yek Ruz*. Podcasts 113, 114, 115, 116, 117 (November–December 2019). https://telegram.me/EternityAndADay.

Rancière, Jacques. *The Politics of Aesthetics: The Distribution of the Sensible*. Translated by Gabriel Rockhill. London: Continuum, 2004.

Rancière, Jacques. *Film Fables*. Translated by Emiliano Battista. Oxford and New York: Oberg, 2006.

Rancière, Jacques. *The Future of the Image*. Translated by Gregory Elliott. London: Verso Books, 2009.

Rancière, Jacques. *The Emancipated Spectator*. Translated by Gregory Elliott. London: Verso, 2009.

Rayani Makhsus, Mehrdad and Rahman Seif Azad. 'Yek Pazhuheshgar-e Teātri beh Sinema Miravad'. *Sinemā Teātr* Year 4, no. 24 (Mehr 1376/ October 1997): 56–60.

Reati, Fernando. *Nomberar lo innombrable violencia politica y novela argentina, 1975–85*. Buenos Aires: Legasa, 1992.

Rezaeian Attar, Masoud. *Roju'-e Hamzād*. Tehran: Adabestan, 1998.

Rich, Adrienne, 'Twenty-One Love Poems'. In *The Dream of a Common Language: Poems 1974–77*, 24–36. New York: W. W. Norton and Company, 1978.

Robinson, David, 'Tehran's Film Festival: Best of a Respectable Year'. *The Times*, 11 December 1974.

Robinson, Edgar Arlington. 'Mr Flood's Party'. In *Perrine's Literature: Structure, Sound and Sense*. Edited by Greg Johnson and Thomas R. Arp, 721–22. Boston: Kennesaw State University, 2018.

Rockhill, Gabriel. '"Introduction" and "Glossary of Technical Terms"'. In *The Politics of Aesthetics: The Distribution of the Sensible*. Edited by Jacques Rancière, 1–8, 80–93. London: Continuum, 2004.

Rohani, Hamid. *Barresi va Tahlili az Nehzat-e Emam Khomeini*. (AKA *Nehzat-e Emam Khomeini*) (1977–2011). Tehran: (Vol. 1, 2, 3) Moassesseh-ye Tanzim va Nashr Āsār-

Emam Khomeini, 1991 & 1997. (Vol. 4) Pazhuhesgāh-e Farhang va Andisheh-ye Eslāmi, 1991.

Sa'di, Mosleheddin. *Golestān*. (1258). Edited by M. J. Mashkur. Tehran: Eqbāl, 1963.

Sadr, Hamid Reza. *Iranian Cinema: A Political History*. New York: Palgrave Macmillan, 2006.

Sa'edi, Gholam-hussein. *Ahl-e Havā*. Tehran: Tehran University Press, 1966.

Safa, Zabihollah. *Hamāseh-Sorāei dar Iran*. Tehran, Piruz, 1954.

Safa-Isfahani, Kaveh. 'Female-Centered World Views in Iranian Culture: Symbolic Representations of Sexuality in Dramatic Games'. *Signs* 6, no. 1, *Women: Sex and Sexuality, Part 2* (Autumn, 1980): 33–53.

Said, Edward W.. 'Professionals and Amateurs'. In *Representation of Intellectuals, The 1993 Reith Lectures*, 65–84. New York: Vintage Book, 1997.

Sarshār, Mohammad Reza. 'Barkhi Nāgofteh-hā Darbāreh-ye Bahrām Beyzāie'. *Pāygāh-e Rasmi Sarshār*. http://www.sarshar.org/archives/notes/post_1391.html (accessed 14 June 2021).

Sasan, Babak. 'Safar'. In *Majmu'eh Maqālāt dar Naqd va Mo'arrefi Āsār-e Bahram Beyzaie*. Edited by Zaven Qukasiyan, 268. Tehran: Āgāh, 1999.

Scorsese, Martin. Downpour/Ragbar. *The Film Foundation: World Cinema Project*. https://www.film-foundation.org/world-cinema?sortBy=title&sortOrder=1&page=2 (accessed 13/11/2021).

Scott, James C. *Domination and the Arts of Resistance: Hidden Transcripts*. New Haven: Yale UP, 1990.

Scuderi, Antonio. *Dario Fo: Framing, Festival, and the Folklore Imagination*. Plymouth: Lexington Books, 2011.

Sepanlu, Mohamad Ali. 'Chap-hā Dah Sāl Ru-ye Āb Mineveshtand'. *Tehran Mosavvar* 39, no. 23 (8 Tir 1358 [29 June 1979]): 23–30 and 46.

Sepehri, Sohrab. 'Sedā-ye Pā-ye Āb'. In *Hasht Ketāb*. Tehran: Tahuri, 1977.

Shahriari, Khosro. *Ketāb-e Namāyesh*. Tehran: Amir Kabir, 1986.

Shamlou, Ahmad. *Negarāni-hā-ye Man*. New Jersey: CIRA, 1990.

Shay, Anthony. 'Bazi-ha-ye Namayeshi: Iranian Women's Theatrical Plays'. *Dance Research Journal* 27, no. 2 (Autumn 1995): 16–24.

Sheibani, Khatereh. 'The Outcry of The Crow: Localizing Modernity In Iran'. *Canadian Journal of Film Studies* (Revue Canadienne D'études Cinématographiques) 20, no. 2 (Fall 2011): 95–110.

Sheibani, Khatereh. 'Film as Alternative History: The Aesthetics of Bahram Beizai'. In *Familiar and Foreign: Identity in Iranian Film and Literature*. Edited by Manijeh Mannani and Veronica Thompson, 211–32. Edmonton: AU Press, 2015.

Simonton, Dean. *Greatness: Who Makes History and Why*. New York: Guilford Press, 1994.

Skjærvø, Prods Oktor. 'Ahura Mazdā and Ārmaiti, Heaven and Earth, in the Old Avesta'. *Journal of the American Oriental Society* 122, no. 2 (2002): 399–410.

Sophocles. 'Philoctetes'. Translated by Thomas Franklin. In *The Complete Greek Drama*, Vol. 1. Edited by Whitney Oates and Eugene O'Neill Jr, 555–612. New York: Random House, 1938.

Sotudeh, Manuchehr. 'Arusi dar Jangal' (Wedding in the Forest). *Yādgār* Year 1, no. 8 (Far. 1324 [March–April 1945]): 41–3.

Soyinka, Wole. 'Credo of Being and Nothingness'. In *Art, Dialogue and Outrage*. Written by Wole Soyinka 234–7. New York: Pantheon, 1994.

Spindler, William. 'Magic Realism: A Typology'. *Forum for Modern Language Studies* 39, no. 1 (1993): 75–85.

Tahāmi-Nezhad. 'Ragbāar va Notfeh-hā-ye Nomādin-e Āgāhi'. In *Majmu'eh Maqālāt dar Naqd va Mo'arrefi Āsār-e Bahram Beyzaie*. Edited by Zaven Qukasiyan, 236–44. Tehran: Āgāh, 1999.
Tahbaz, Sirus. 'Khub o Bad-e Panjomin Festival-e Film Kudakān'. *Negin* 66 (Ābān 1349/ November 1970): 18–21 and 55.
Talajooy, Saeed. *Mythologizing the Transition: A Comparative Study of Bahram Beyzaie and Wole Soyinka*. PhD Thesis. University of Leeds, January 2008. https://etheses.whiterose.ac.uk/406/.
Talajooy, Saeed. 'Indigenous Performing Traditions in Post-Revolutionary Iranian Theatre'. *Iranian Studies* 44, no. 4 (July 2011): 497–519.
Talajooy, Saeed. 'Khāneh, Khānevādeh va Shahr: Revāyat-e Tajadod dar Kalāgh va Shāyad Vaghti Digar-e Bahram Beyzaie'. *Iran Nameh* 27, no. 1 (March 2012): 142–61.
Talajooy, Saeed. 'Bahram Beyzaie va Jang-e Jahāni-e Dovvom: Revāyat-e Eshghāl va Degardisi-e Mafhum-e Mellat'. *Iran Nameh* 28, no. 1 (March 2013): 128–50.
Talajooy, Saeed. 'Beyzaie's Formation, Forms and Themes'. *Iranian Studies* 46, no. 5 (Autumn 2013): 689–93.
Talajooy, Saeed. 'Reformulation of Shahnameh Legends in Bahram Beyzaie's Plays'. *Iranian Studies* 46, no. 5 (Autumn 2013): 695–719.
Talajooy, Saeed. 'Uncle Moustache'. In *Directory of World Cinema*. Edited by Parviz Jahed, 234–5. Bristol: Intellect, 2012.
Talajooy, Saeed. 'Intellectuals as Sacrificial Heroes: A Comparative Study of Bahram Beyzaie and Wole Soyinka'. *Comparative Literature Studies* 52, no. 2 (2015): 379–408.
Talajooy, Saeed. 'Afrā Or the Day Is Passing: A Cultural Diagnosis'. In *Afrā Or the Day Is Passing: A Play by Bahram Beyzaie with Critical Material by Saeed Talajooy*. Translated and Analysed by Saeed Talajooy. San Francisco: Bisheh Publishing, 2022.
Talajooy, Saeed. 'Continuity and Resistance through Emancipatory Speech: The Story of a Book'. In *In One Thousand and First Night: A PLay by Bahram Beyzaie with Critical Material by Saeed Talajooy*. Translated and Analysed by Saeed Talajooy. San Francisco: Bisheh Publishing, 2022.
Talajooy, Saeed. 'So Dies Pahlevān Akbar (1963): Reconfiguration of the Ideals of Heroism'. In *Origins, Forms and Functions in Bahram Beyzaie's Cinema and Theatre*. Edited by Saeed Talajooy. London: Gingko, Forthcoming 2023.
Taqiyan, Laleh. *Darbāreh-ye Ta'ziyeh va Tāātr*. Tehran: Nashr-e Markaz, 1995.
Tehranian, Majid. 'Power and Purity: Iranian Political Culture, Communication, and Identity'. In *Iran: Between Tradition and Modernity*. Edited by Ramin Jahanbegloo, 185–207. Lanham: Lexington Books, 2004.
Vermaseren, Martin. *Āyin-e Mitrā*. Persian. Translated from French by Bozorg Naderzadeh. Tehran: Nashr-e Cheshmeh, 1996.
Warren, Karen and Barbara Wells-Howe. *Ecological Feminism*, 8–28. London: Routledge, 1994.
Wilber, Donald N. *Iran: Past and Present*. Princeton: Princeton University Press, 1975.
Williams, Raymond. *Culture and Society 1780–1950*. London: Chatto & Windus, 1958.
Williams, Raymond. *Keywords: A Vocabulary of Culture and Society*. Revised edition. London: Fontana, 1983.
Yarshater, Ehsan. 'Ta'ziyeh and Pre-Islamic Mourning Rites in Iran'. In *Ta'ziyeh: Ritual and Drama in Iran*. Edited by Peter Chelkowski, 88–94. New York: New York University Press, 1979.

Yarshater, Ehsan. 'The Modern Literary Idiom'. In *Critical Perspectives on Modern Persian Literature*. Edited by Thomas M. Ricks, 42–62. Washington, DC: Three Continents Press, 1984.

Zandian, Mandana. *Bāzkhāni-ye Dah Shab*. Hamburg: Dariush Homayun Publication, 2014.

Zizek, Slavoj, *Violence: Six: Sideways Glances*. London: Profile Books, 2009.

Films and play recordings

Beyzaie, Bahram. Director/Writer. *Arusak-hā* (The Marionettes) (Play) Video Recording. (1965) *Manoto TV Channel*. https://www.youtube.com/watch?v=o23x4G56aAE (accessed 18 September 2021).

Beyzaie, Bahram. Director/Writer. *Amu Sibilu* (Uncle Moustache). (1970). https://www.youtube.com/watch?v=kAM-90ido58 (accessed 28 September 2021).

Beyzaie, Bahram. Director/Writer. *Ragbār* (Downpour). (1972). DVD (Gift of World Cinema Project).

Beyzaie, Bahram. Director/Writer. *Safar* (The Journey). (1972). Personal Collection.

Beyzaie, Bahram. Director/Writer. *Gharibeh va Meh* (Stranger and the Fog). 1974. Personal Collection.

Beyzaie, Bahram. Director/Writer. *Kalāgh* (The Crow). (1977). Personal Collection.

Capra, Frank. Director. *It's a Wonderful Life* (1946). https://learningonscreen.ac.uk/ondemand/index.php/prog/001E92AA?bcast=123438253 (accessed 11 August 2019).

Donen, Stanley and Gene Kelly. Directors. *Singin' in the Rain* (1952). https://learningonscreen.ac.uk/ondemand/index.php/prog/0018C80D?bcast=135908764 (Accessed 14 September 2020).

Golestan, Ebrahim. Director/Writer. *Khesht O Āyeneh* (Brick and Mirror). (1965). Personal Collection.

Hitchcock, Alfred. Director. *Rear Window*. Paramount Pictures, 1954. DVD.

Kiarostami, Abbas. *Where is the Friend's House* (1990). DVD.

Kimiaei, Masoud. Director. *Bigāneh Biā* (1968). https://www.youtube.com/watch?v=0GsqUeQ1tHk (accessed 20 October 2021).

Kimiaei, Masoud. Director. *Qeysar* (1969) https://www.youtube.com/watch?v=QEiRurPRUo4 (Accessed 27 January 2021).

Mehrju'i, Dariush. Director. *Gāv*. (1969) https://www.youtube.com/watch?v=4Kcp6oXqOX0 (Accessed 26 February 2021).

Mohseni, Majid. Director. *Lāt-e Javānmard* (1958). https://www.youtube.com/watch?v=nV_KVUjaX5k (accessed 11 February 2020).

Ophüls, Max. Director. *Letter from an Unknown Woman* (1948). https://learningonscreen.ac.uk/ondemand/index.php/prog/000043E3?bcast=122939623 (accessed 15 November 2018).

Rogers, Charley Gus Meins. Director. *The March of the Wooden Soldiers (Laurel and Hardy: Babes in Toyland)* (1934). https://www.youtube.com/watch?v=giABfnfy9R0.

Index

Adonis (god/festival)   159
aesthetics/aesthetic   3, 9–11, 33, 35, 44, 53, 114, 120, 128, 155, 172–3, 175–6, 193, 194, 218, 237–9, 243
Ahmadi, Ahmadreza   248, 250
Akhundzadeh, Fathali   46
amateur gaze   16, 20–1, 23, 243, 244
Amjad, Hamid   59, 69, 207, 244, 246, 252–4
Ānāhitā/Anahita   146, 170, 249, 252
Arab/Arabic   6, 24, 41, 104, 137, 148, 158, 241
Arusi dar Jangal (Wedding in the Forest)   170–3, 178, 191
Ashoori, Dariush   4, 39
Ashura/Karbala   140, 146, 159, 180, 251
Attar, Farideddin   55, 167, 187, 245, 253
    Biographies of the Saints (Tazkerat al-Oliyā)   167, 187, 253
    Manteq-ot-Tair (Conference of the Brids)   55
    Oshtornāmeh (Book of Camels)   245
authoritarian/authoritarianism   22, 81, 85, 92, 99, 196–9, 202, 204, 221–3, 229. See also capitalist/capitalism
Ayyār, Ayyāri   28, 29, 43, 73, 75, 77, 167, 175, 193, 194, 248, 251, 254

Bahaism/Bahai   22, 157, 171, 190, 195, 246
Bahar, Mehrdad   252, 253
Bahar, Shamim   4
Bakhtin, Mikhail   78, 80–1, 83, 120, 133, 203, 249–51
Banietemad, Rakhshan   14
Behrangi, Samad   253
belonging   9–20, 23, 34–5, 46, 47, 49, 51, 60, 62, 64, 74, 75, 94, 96, 113, 119, 123, 126, 127, 133, 135, 137, 140, 141, 144, 151–5, 157, 162–3, 171, 173, 183,
186, 191, 199, 202, 205, 217, 222, 227, 238, 239. See also recognition
Benjamin, Walter   6, 9, 243
Bergman, Ingmar   72, 177, 201
    The Seventh Seal   177
Beyzaie's Works
    Account of Bondār, the Premier (Kārnāmeh-ye Bondār-e Bidaksh)   2, 28, 75
    Afrā, or the Day Is Passing   30, 75, 166, 207, 239, 248, 254
    Ārash   24, 28, 87, 166, 200, 238, 241, 254
    Ardāvirāf's Report   24, 30
    Azhdāhāk   24, 28, 60
    Ballad of Tārā (Cherikeh-ye Tārā)   28, 96, 137, 155, 195, 200, 239, 255
    Bashu, the Little Stranger   29, 137, 155, 156, 163, 239, 253
    Battle of Slaves (Jangnāmeh-ye Gholāmān)   29, 40
    Congregation for (performing) the Sacrifice of Sennemār (Majles-e Qorbāni-ye Sennemār)   25, 30, 32
    Court of Bactria (Divān-e Balkh)   28, 31, 75
    Crow (Kalāgh)   28, 31, 34, 35, 96, 163, 193–237, 239, 254
    Death of Yazdgerd (Marg-e Yazdgerd)   2, 29, 52, 96, 135, 180
    Downpour (Ragbār)   28, 31, 34, 74, 75, 89, 91–137, 152, 163, 164, 167, 170, 171, 183, 194, 201, 202, 206, 218, 224–6, 229, 238, 239, 253
    Feast (Ziyāfat)   28, 31, 71, 229
    Four Boxes (Chāhār Sanduq)   28, 32, 39, 40, 69, 244

Index

Journalistic World of Mr Asrāri 28, 75
Journey (Safar) 2, 28, 34, 73–7, 125, 133–55, 162, 163, 167, 180, 183, 184, 189, 190, 200, 201, 211, 215, 218, 224, 226, 238, 239, 247
Kallāt Claimed (Fathnāmeh-ye Kallāt) 28, 163, 239, 247, 249
Killing Rabid Dogs (Sagkoshi) 29, 33, 167, 201
Lonely Warrior (Ayyār-e Tanhā) 29, 75, 193–4
Mahi 23, 30
Marionettes (Arusakhā) 28, 38, 46–50, 52, 53, 69, 247
Maybe Some other Time 29, 96, 180, 200, 201, 234
Memoirs of the Actor in a Supporting Role 29, 44, 244
Mourning Wail (Nodbeh) 29, 40, 245
New Preface to the Shahnameh 29, 239, 254
Parchment of Master Sharzin (Tumār-e Sheikh-e Sharzin) 25, 29, 143, 239, 254
Puppet Trilogy (Seh-Gāneh-ye Arusaki) 33, 37, 46, 74, 97, 103, 238
Reciting Siyāvush (Siyāvushkhāni) 24, 29, 32
Reed Panel (Pardeh-ye Ne-ei) 29, 239
Sable's Night (Shab-e Samur) 29, 33
Snake King (Soltān Mar) 28, 71
So Dies Akbar the Hero (Pahlevān Akbar Mimirad) 28, 69–71, 74, 87, 97, 115, 121, 163, 171, 215, 238, 253
Stormy Path of Farmān the Son of Farmān (Rāh-e Tufāni-ye Farmān Pesar-e Farmān) 28
Stranger and the Fog (Gharibeh va Meh) 28, 34, 96, 137, 155–92, 201, 202, 206, 214, 226, 229, 235, 239, 252, 253
Sufferings of Professor Navid-e Makan and Architect Rokhshid-e Farzin (Majles-e Shabih dar Zekr-e Masāyeb-e Ostād Navid-e Mākān and Mohandes Rokhshid-e Farzin) 30, 32
Sunset in a Strange Land (Ghorub dar Diyāri Gharib) 28, 38–40, 50–62, 70
Tale of the Hidden Moon (Qesseh-ye Māh-e Penhān) 28, 38, 40, 62–8, 70
Travellers (Mosāferān) 29, 32, 180
Truths about Leila the Daughter of Edris 28, 193–6
Uncle Moustache (Amu Sibilu) 2, 28, 34, 71–89, 91, 95, 97, 111, 133, 137, 200, 238, 239, 248

Biruni (Al-Biruni), Mohamamd (Abu Reihān) 80, 175–6, 249, 252, 253
Boroujerdi, Hossein (Ayatollah) 56
Bourdieu, Pierre 9, 10, 15–16, 51–3, 61–2, 134, 243, 246, 247, 251. *See also* cultural capital
 Disposition and taste 10, 51, 246
 Habitus 9–10, 16, 51–2, 61–2, 246
Brecht, Bertolt 20, 49

capitalist/capitalism 8, 27, 53, 54, 141, 196–9, 202, 204, 222, 240
carnival/carnivalesque 8, 23, 25, 34, 43–5, 48–9, 71, 77–81, 87, 88, 119–22, 126, 130, 131, 133, 143, 159, 166–7, 170, 180
catharsis 45, 180–1, 253
children 2, 26, 34, 35, 39, 50, 71–131, 133–54, 156, 161, 166–7, 170, 185–6, 194, 199–200, 205–7, 215, 217, 222, 225, 227, 234, 238–40, 250
China/Chinese Theatre 7, 25, 72, 160, 198
Cine Club (Kānun-e Film) 40, 72
citizenship/citizen 11, 31, 35, 50, 57, 66, 73, 119, 121, 125, 143, 173, 179, 186, 192, 196, 201, 203–4, 208–9, 221, 229, 234, 239
 Women and Ideal citizenship 193–236
comedy/Comic 7, 25, 34, 40–4, 46, 56, 63, 71–90, 100–2, 106, 107, 111,

Index

117, 125, 130, 131, 133, 161, 164, 170, 218, 219, 225, 246, 250
tragicomedy 131
comic relief 107–61, 218, 225
Comic Relief in Shakespeare and Hitchcock 225
constitutionalists 111, 197–8. *See also* Mosaddeq, Mohamad
consumerism/consumerist 34, 114, 140, 141, 196–7, 199, 201, 203, 208, 215, 218, 221, 222, 234
cosmopolitanism/cosmopolitan 6, 41, 92, 223, 249
creativity 1, 4, 5, 8–10, 13–22, 25, 26, 32, 33, 35, 48, 119, 207, 221, 237, 241, 243, 244. *See also* marginalized/marginalized perspectives/marginalization; recognition; trauma
cultural capital 19, 23, 28
cultural production 3, 9, 33, 35, 71, 91, 196–9, 237
culture 1, 3, 4, 6–8, 14–17, 19–23, 27, 32–5, 38–40, 46, 50–6, 62, 63, 67, 70, 73–7, 79, 81, 83, 86, 89, 91, 98, 100, 101, 103, 104, 106, 109, 111, 112, 121, 122, 135, 140, 143, 144, 148, 151–3, 155, 157, 158, 160, 164, 175, 190, 194–6, 201, 202, 204, 208, 223, 239–41, 243

Dabashi, Hamid 6, 156, 174, 243, 252, 253
Dandy (fokoli) 94–5, 126, 225
Dārābnāmeh 175
Daryoush, Hagir 5, 72, 235, 255
death 26, 47, 49, 50, 64, 66–8, 80, 87–8, 101, 113, 115, 118, 120, 121, 125, 127–8, 137, 139, 145, 155, 158–63, 167, 171, 177, 179, 182, 186–7, 189, 191, 207, 211, 212, 214, 224–5, 231, 234, 239
Deleuze, Giles/Time-Image.13, 82–3, 211, 254
Dey-beh-Mehr 80
Diachronic 8, 228–33
Diba (Pahlavi), Farah 53, 170, 215

dominant (cultural, political, social, economic) discourses 1, 7, 8, 20, 21, 23, 27, 33, 34, 38–9, 44, 46, 50, 53, 54, 88, 127, 164, 167, 200, 208, 215, 221, 228, 233, 234, 237–8, 240
Dying God 163, 164, 179, 192. *See also* sacrificial hero/sacrifice; fertility/agent of fertility/fertility rituals

Ebtehaj, Houshang 57
emancipatory/emancipation/ emancipate 3, 8–21, 27, 32–5, 38, 39, 41, 44, 46, 52–4, 61, 68, 74–7, 81–3, 88, 91–6, 98, 101, 114, 115, 126, 128, 134, 136, 155, 166, 167, 169, 172, 175, 176, 179, 183–4, 192–201, 208, 209, 218, 223, 227, 237–9, 241, 243, 244
epic 24, 60, 67, 115, 137, 156, 164, 175
epistemic privilege/epistemic authority 16–21, 23, 34, 35, 46, 52, 73, 75, 113, 115, 116, 133, 180, 194, 207, 228, 233, 237, 243, 244, 246
Esfandārmaz/Spandārmaz 158, 170, 175–6
Esfandiyār (*Shahnameh*) 139
exclusionism/exclusionist 27, 35, 39, 40, 44, 46, 103, 112, 118, 126, 129, 134, 152, 155, 158, 160, 164, 174, 177, 180, 183, 191, 192, 195, 196, 201, 210, 239, 240
expressionism/expressionistic 10, 140, 144, 151, 196, 200, 211, 212, 222

Farhadi, Asghar 96, 235
Farhang, Dariush 3
Farid, Manouchehr 124, 193, 254
Farrokhzad, Forough 14, 20, 41, 201
  Ali Kuchulu (Little Ali) 41
femininity 93, 94, 106, 114, 158, 192, 195, 212, 249
feminist/feminism 166, 194–5, 253
Ferdowsi, Abulqasem 15, 25, 48, 106, 175. *See also Shahnameh* (Ferdowsi)

fertility/agent of fertility/fertility
    rituals   26, 34, 47, 49, 137, 146,
    155–92, 211, 214, 217, 227, 239
Fo, Dario   53–4, 246, 248
folk (culture, art forms, drama, lore,
    tales)   6, 7, 23, 26, 37–8, 40–3,
    45, 48, 50, 53, 55, 60, 62, 64, 65,
    67, 73, 76, 92, 107, 110, 114, 137,
    146, 153, 155, 167, 172, 184,
    189, 201, 237, 253
Foucault, Michel/Foucauldian   9–11, 17,
    20, 21, 61, 103, 243
framing/reframing   35, 38, 40, 44–5, 97,
    98, 104, 122, 136, 158, 163, 164,
    175, 179, 189, 197, 200, 218–19,
    227, 231, 233, 237, 241
Frazer, J. G.   79–80, 159, 249
Freud, Sigmund   20, 253
Fry, Northrop   169, 253

Gardizi, Abdolhay   175, 253
Ghaffary, Farrokh   37, 40, 72, 87, 96, 245
    Cine Club (Kānun-e Film)   40, 72
    *Night of the Hunchback (Shab-e
        Quzi)*   4, 87, 96
    South of the City (Jonub-e Shahr)   4
Golestan, Ebrahim   4, 77, 87, 94–6, 115,
    212, 224, 254
    Brick and Mirror (Khesht o Āyeneh)   4,
        77, 87, 94–6, 212, 254
    *Secrets of the Treasure of the Jennie
        Valley (Asrār-e Ganj-e Darreh-ye
        Jenni)*   96
    *Wave, Coral and Rock (Moj, Marjān,
        Khārā)*   115
Golshiri, Houshang   71, 245
Gorgani, Fakhreddin/*Veis o Rāmin*   175
Greek   5, 6, 14–15, 66, 159, 180
Grotesque   34, 78, 80, 133, 143, 148, 167

Hāmān (Haman)/Hāmān Suz   79–80,
    120
Hedayat, Sadeq   14, 20, 30, 41, 125, 195
Heidegger, Martin   100–1, 107, 126, 136,
    162, 250, 251, 253
    disposition (Befindlichkeit)   100, 107,
        126, 136, 162, 246
    thrownness (Geworfenheit)   100–1,
        136, 162, 190

Hercules/Heracles   14, 54, 66, 182
Herodotus   78, 248
Heteroglossia   46, 120, 246
Hitchcock, Alfred/86, 201, 215, 218–19,
    225, 231, 249
    The Man Who Knew Too Much   215
    Rear Window   86
Hossein (Imam)   84, 191
humour   43, 48

Ibsen, Henrik   2, 20, 72
identity   8, 17, 20, 24–6, 28–32, 34, 35,
    51, 81, 96, 97, 100, 107, 111, 113,
    124, 130, 135, 144, 149, 155,
    157, 176, 191, 193, 199–202,
    207–8, 212, 217, 225, 233, 235,
    237–9, 244, 245
imitative/borrowed modernity   114,
    146, 194, 203, 204, 233. *See also*
    Westernized/Westernization,
    Westoxicated/West-obsessed
imitative religion/traditionalism   144,
    203
India/Indian and Indonesian Theatre   4,
    7, 25, 63, 72–3, 180
indigenous/indigeneity   4, 5, 14, 17, 35,
    40, 41, 46, 77, 92, 93, 113, 135,
    155, 175, 190, 195, 200, 237,
    244–6
initiation   33, 34, 166, 170–1, 187, 189,
    191, 233, 250
intellectual/intellectuality   2, 3, 19,
    20, 22–5, 32, 34–5, 39, 48–9,
    51–3, 63, 65, 67, 72, 74, 75, 83,
    91–132, 134, 135, 143, 149, 160,
    163, 167, 176, 190, 193–236,
    238, 240, 241, 244, 247, 249–51
Islam/Islamic   1, 22–4, 27, 31, 39, 43,
    44, 56–8, 71, 73, 80, 104, 146,
    159, 171, 175, 186, 212, 240,
    243, 248
Islamist   2, 6, 8, 22, 27, 52, 58, 71, 129,
    134, 190, 195–6, 198
It's a Wonderful Life (dir. Frank
    Capra)   102, 250

Jamalzadeh, Mohamad-Ali   41
Japan/Japanese Theatre/Cinema   4, 7, 25,
    38–9, 72–3, 156, 160, 201

Javanmard, Abbas   37, 38, 40, 52, 69, 70, 245, 246
Javānmard/Javānmardi   94, 248

Kafka, Frantz/Kafkaesque   82, 111, 123, 135, 144, 178, 180, 185, 186, 203
Kānun-e Nevisandegān (Writers' Association)   71
Kānun-e Parvaresh-e Fekri-ye kudakān va Nojavānān (Kānun) (Centre for the Intellectual Development of Children and Young Adults)   2, 72, 75, 83, 88, 153
Katouzian, Homa   212, 254
Kavousi, Houshang   37, 72
Khayyam, Omar   55, 56, 58, 65, 178, 247, 253
Kheymeh-Shab-Bāzi   26, 33, 37–70. See also puppet
Khomeini, Ruhollah   57–8, 139, 197–8, 247
Kiarostami, Abbas   14, 77, 96, 201, 235, 240, 251
   The Bread and Alley (Nān va Kucheh)   77
   Break Time (Zang-e Tafrih)   77
   Close-Up   96
   Where Is the Friend's House (Khāneh-ye Dust Kojāst)   251
Kimiaei, Masoud   73, 78, 84, 94–5, 125, 137, 248, 249
   Come Stranger (Bigāneh Biā)   94–5, 249
   Dāsh Ākol   125
   Qeysar   73, 78, 84, 137, 248, 249
   Reza Motori (Reza Motorcyclist)   248
Kurosawa, Akira   72, 179, 201
   Seven Samurai   72
Kuseh bar Neshin (Ride of the Beardless One)   80, 120
Kushan, Esmāeil   97, 248
   Kolāh Makhmali   97, 248

Lacan, Jacques/Lacanian   109–10, 250, 253–5
Lang, Fritz   201
language (Persian)   1, 2, 10, 11, 20, 22, 24–5, 53–4, 71, 114, 125, 175, 210
   pure Persian   24

leadership/leader   23, 29, 31–2, 35, 39, 46, 56, 75, 110, 116, 121, 127, 137, 138, 143, 144, 239
left/leftist   2, 22, 40, 52–4, 56, 58, 71, 83, 129, 153, 190, 195–8, 201, 209, 217, 246, 247
Lodge, David   158–9, 252
lout/lāt   75, 94, 110, 125–6. See also Tough Guy Films/Culture; luti (chivalrous man)
Love   15, 16, 26, 31, 34, 43, 44, 46–7, 49–50, 54–6, 61, 64–8, 72, 74, 91–131, 133, 137, 139, 152, 155–91, 199, 202, 203, 205, 206, 209, 214, 215, 222–7, 229, 231, 234, 238, 243, 246, 252
luti (chivalrous man)   74–5, 78, 94, 110, 125–6. See also Tough Guy Films/Culture; lout/lāt

Makhmalbaf, Mohsen   14
March of the Wooden Soldiers, The (Laurel and Hardy: Babes in Toyland)   38
marginalized/marginalized perspectives/marginalization   5, 7, 8, 10, 15–21, 23, 34, 35, 38, 39, 41, 44, 45, 56, 60, 64, 69, 72, 74, 81, 82, 91, 93, 94, 103, 111, 121, 129, 130, 136, 137, 142, 144, 146, 148, 152, 156–8, 160, 162–4, 172, 173, 180, 184, 191, 192, 194–6, 199, 200, 207, 215, 225–7, 233, 234, 237, 238, 240, 244
Marxist   12, 20, 27, 71, 81, 129, 134, 198, 240
masculinity/hegemonic/toxic   23, 34–5, 71–153, 211, 215, 221, 225, 238, 239, 249
   ideal masculinity   74, 85, 93
Massoumi, Parvaneh   195, 234
master-slave binary   108–10, 124, 128, 134, 136, 144
Medieval   40, 76, 82, 83, 107, 118, 134, 137, 143, 149, 196, 211, 212, 239
Mehrjui, Dariush   4, 77, 201, 252
   The Cow (Gāv)   4, 77
meta-cinematic/meta-filmic   34, 74, 91, 93–4, 96–7, 102, 105–7, 110,

117, 124, 137, 146–7, 149, 218, 238. *See also* self-reflexive
metamorphosis 37, 156–8, 187, 204, 231
metaphor/metaphorical 15, 16, 18, 27, 35, 50, 63–5, 67, 74, 77, 81, 106, 118, 142, 150–2, 194, 201, 205, 211–12, 214, 221, 228, 232, 238, 247, 252
metatheatrical 37–70, 97, 135, 159. *See also* self-reflexive
metonymy/metonymic 13, 97, 101, 150–1
minority perspective/minority 18–21, 23, 39, 244, 246
Mir-e Noruzi (Temporary King) (Lord of Misrule) 80, 119–21, 177, 250
Mir-Hosseini, Ziba 175, 253
misogyny 93, 105–7, 160
Mithra/Mithraism 104, 146, 164, 250, 252
modern/modernity 1–8, 10, 12, 14, 20, 22, 24–7, 31, 34–5, 38, 40–2, 45–6, 53, 57, 73, 75, 76, 78, 81, 85, 92, 95, 97, 103, 111, 112, 114, 117–19, 126, 128, 137, 139, 141–2, 146, 149, 151, 158, 159, 166, 175, 176, 180, 192–237, 239, 244–7, 252, 254
modernist/modernism 10, 13, 56, 69, 246
   postmodernist/postmodernism 10, 13
modernization/modernizing/modernized 2, 6, 22–3, 31, 35, 53, 57–8, 92, 94, 112, 129, 135, 145, 157, 193–236, 239, 251
Mofid, Bahman 147, 148
Mofid, Bijhan (Bijan) 14, 20, 26, 41, 201
Moghkoshi (Magophonia) 120
Mohseni, Majid and *Lāt-e Javānmard* 94, 250
Monfaredzadeh, Esfandiyar 78
monologue 13, 60, 65, 107, 110, 111, 125
   interior monologue 13
Moqaddam, Hasan 20, 41
Moqaddam, Jalal 111, 248, 250
Mosaddeq, Mohamad 57, 112, 197
mourning rituals/mourning rites 78, 118, 179, 180

music/musician/film music 3, 37, 38, 40–2, 51, 52, 76–9, 84, 95–8, 100, 104, 110, 116–17, 125, 127, 135, 137, 141, 147–8, 151, 152, 158, 164, 170, 174, 175, 177, 189–90, 203–5, 212, 218, 222–3, 228, 245, 251

Naderi, Amir 146, 201, 248
   Davandeh (Runner) 146
   Khodāhāfez Rafiq (Goodbye My Friend) and *Tangsir (Tight Corner)* 248
Naficy, Hamid 96, 125, 156–7, 243, 249–50, 252–4
Najmabadi, Afsaneh 175, 252, 253
Na'lbandiyan, Abbas 26, 128
Narrative Identity 17–19, 96, 244
Nasirian (Nasiriān), Ali 37, 38, 41, 45, 46, 246
   Bolbol-e Sargashteh (Wandering Nightingale) 37, 45
nation 18, 22, 23, 68, 81, 94, 111, 115, 119, 152, 166
national 7, 16, 22, 29, 31, 32, 37, 38, 52, 56, 62, 70, 155, 156, 207–9, 222, 243, 248
nationalism/nationalist/nationalistic 6, 22, 32, 39, 58, 200, 238, 244, 247
nativism 41, 56, 58, 129, 146, 247.
   See also Return-to-the-root Discourses/movements/ideas
new wave/alternative films 4, 25, 73, 74, 87, 95, 96, 146, 153, 157, 193, 240
Nezami Ganjavi
   Khamseh 175

Objet petit a 109, 125, 165, 181
Omar Koshān (Killing Omar) 80
O'Neill 2, 215, 231
   Long Day's Journey into Night 215, 231
One Thousand and One Night 12, 172, 241
Ophüls, Max 122, 201, 231, 250
   Letter from an Unknown Woman 122
Outsider gaze 16, 21, 23, 35, 91, 126, 133, 157, 160, 163, 215, 224, 237

Panahi, Jafar/*The Mirror (Āyeneh)* 96, 146
Parody 84, 97, 107, 120, 124, 125, 218
patriarchy/patriarch 29, 30, 32, 35, 49, 78, 86, 92–3, 100, 143, 152, 192
performative 84, 174–5, 204, 217–20
Persian (language, litertaure, culture) 1, 18, 24–5, 31, 37–8, 42–3, 71, 78, 79, 101, 104, 123, 131, 153, 156, 175, 186, 187, 202, 245, 246, 251, 253, 254. *See also* language (Persian)
Plutarch 79, 249
post-revolutionary 26, 32, 139, 157, 195–7, 239–41
pre-revolutionary 92, 120, 196, 234, 238, 240–1
Proust, Marcel 223, 235, 255
puppet 26, 32–4, 37–70, 72, 74, 97, 103, 184, 238, 244–6
puppeteer/narrator as the embodiment of dominant discourses 37–70
purification/purgation/cleansing 80, 113, 120, 121, 137, 166, 169, 173, 180, 181, 187, 190, 212, 239

Radi, Akbar 69, 201, 247
Rancière, Jacques 7, 9–14, 21–2, 61, 81, 115, 120, 173, 209, 218, 239, 243, 244, 246, 247, 249, 254, 255
rebirth 32, 76–7, 113, 127, 137, 151–2, 156–7, 159–61, 164, 176, 212
recognition 16, 19, 34, 35, 46, 68, 74, 94, 96, 101, 109–10, 113, 119, 120, 124–6, 130, 136, 149, 165, 171, 179, 190, 191, 202, 217, 234, 238. *See also* belonging
redemption 14–19, 133, 180, 199. *See also* Narrative Identity; trauma
Reformulation (culture, artistic forms, rituals) 5, 7, 8, 14, 17, 19–20, 22, 23, 34, 35, 38, 41, 44, 45, 53, 54, 58, 67, 73, 92–4, 97, 113, 121, 125, 129, 137, 158, 166, 173, 192, 199, 201, 218, 223, 237–9, 246
Regimes of Art 9–14, 22
Regimes of Taste 52
Regimes of Truth 10, 18, 23, 33

resistance 28–31, 33, 44, 50, 51, 75, 81, 85, 87, 107, 187, 194–7, 202, 231, 234
Return-to-the-roots Discourses/movements/ideas 41, 53, 56. *See also* nativism
revolution/revolutionary 1, 2, 6, 7, 12, 14, 18, 22, 23, 25–7, 29, 31–3, 35, 40, 53, 56–8, 62, 71, 77, 92, 120, 129, 130, 134, 139, 157, 195–6, 198–9, 201, 213, 234, 237–41, 243, 255
revolution (constitutional) 40
Rich, Adrian 15, 243
ritual/ritualization/ritualize 2, 15, 23, 25, 26, 32, 34, 44–6, 53, 55, 67, 76–81, 87, 89, 97, 98, 101, 104, 113, 114, 118, 120, 127, 133–53, 155–92, 201, 218, 221, 223, 239, 246, 248, 252
romantic/romanticism 10, 12, 53, 54, 77, 94, 103, 108, 111, 114, 116–17, 125, 175, 248
romance 92, 175
Rostam 15, 139, 249

Sacred Marriage 32, 159, 166, 170–7, 192
sacrificial hero/sacrifice 22, 23, 25, 30–2, 34, 62, 66–7, 94, 97, 113, 121, 126–9, 143, 155–93, 199, 205, 238
Saʻdi, Mosleheddin 251
Saʻedi, Gholamhossein 2, 20, 26, 77, 156, 157, 252
  The Cow (Gāv) 4, 77
  Māh-e Asal (Honeymoon) 2
Said, Edward 16, 20, 21, 243, 244
Samak-e Ayyār 175, 248
Samini, Naghmeh 235
Satire/Satirical 26, 42–6, 87, 117, 125, 131, 133, 146, 148, 174, 219, 222, 225, 246
SAVAK 22, 27, 57, 78, 118, 125, 134, 198
self-reflexive (cinema and theatre) 34, 68, 74, 94, 96, 117, 124, 200, 202, 205, 208, 210, 218, 223, 238. *See also* metatheatrical; meta-cinematic/meta-filmic

Sepehri, Sohrab   223, 255
sex/sexual/sexuality   21, 95, 106, 134, 142, 147–8, 174–5, 181, 191, 193, 194, 217, 235, 246, 252
Shah (Mohammad Reza Pahlavi), Pahlavi, Pahlavi State and Pahlavi Era   2, 27, 31, 57, 58, 78, 92, 94, 111, 129, 135, 197, 198, 200, 209, 215, 222, 231
Shah (Reza Shah Pahlavi) and Early Pahlavi   57, 78, 231
Shahnameh (Ferdowsi)   15, 29, 41, 47, 48, 83, 104, 106, 111, 138, 175, 239, 248, 254
Shahrnāz and Arnavāz (*Shahnameh*) as Earth Goddess Spandārmaz (Esfandārmaz) and Water Goddess Ānāhitā   170
Shahrzād and Dināzād *(One Thousand and One Night [Hezār Afsān])*   241
Shakespeare, William   5, 20, 24–5, 37, 72, 167, 215, 223, 225, 253
Shamlou, Ahmad   14, 40, 57, 195
  Pariā (The Fairies)   40
  Qesseh-ye Dokhtarā-ye Naneh Daryā (The Daughters of Nanny Sea)   41
  Shabāneh: Yeh Shab-e Mahtāb (Nightly: One Moonlit Night)   40
Sheibani, Khatereh   156, 196, 231, 252–5
Shi'i/Shiite   25, 39, 66, 104, 114, 146, 157, 195, 252
Singin' in the Rain (Stanley Donen and Gene Kelly)   117, 250
Siyāvush (*Shahnameh*)   24, 25, 29, 32, 34, 121, 139, 159, 164, 191, 233, 253
Soltanpur, Saeed   71, 248
Sophocles   14–15, 243
  Philoctetes   14–15, 243
stranger (concept)   26, 91, 100, 122, 143, 156, 157, 159–61, 164, 173, 177, 179, 222, 223
Surena/Surenā   79, 120, 249
  Dasteh-ye Surenā (Surena's Procession)   120
surreal/surrealistic/surrealism   4, 10, 13, 34, 35, 83, 96, 123, 125, 127, 136, 142, 145, 149, 153, 155, 186, 189, 195, 200, 214
Surveillance   10, 34–5, 56, 62, 74, 78, 81, 100, 103, 107, 115, 134–6, 200, 204, 212, 225, 239
  and panopticon   103
synchronic   8, 228
synecdochic   136, 139, 142, 150–1, 204

Tabrizi, Mirza Aqa   41
Taqlid/Ruhozi (Improvisatory comedy)   25, 26, 40–2, 46, 48, 125, 244
Ta'ziyeh (Passion Plays)   5, 7, 22, 25, 26, 32, 52, 78, 84, 87, 97, 136, 137, 153, 156, 159, 160, 175, 191, 200, 244, 252
thriller/mystery/detective   34, 192–235
time (Concept)   9, 13, 65, 82–6, 88, 123, 130, 139, 150, 156, 178, 184, 193–235
Tough Guy Films/Culture   34, 73–5, 77, 78, 84, 92–8, 103–4, 106, 107, 110–13, 121–6, 129–30, 143, 146–8, 174, 193, 211, 238, 248, 252
tragedy/tragic   13, 14, 25, 40, 46, 53, 62, 68, 107, 117, 121, 131, 133, 140, 180, 184, 191, 215, 225, 250
tragicomedy   130
trauma   4, 14–20, 33, 35, 83, 108, 180–1, 193, 199, 214, 217, 229, 237, 244. *See also* marginalized/ marginalized perspectives/ marginalization; redemption
Turcoman   135, 137, 141, 152, 184
Turkish   24, 43, 73

Utopia/Utopian   8, 31, 33, 54, 56, 58, 61, 129, 141, 149, 201, 240

violence   10, 34, 37, 56, 58, 61–2, 67, 78, 84, 86–8, 91, 94–5, 97, 106–7, 111, 113, 117, 133–7, 142–3, 146, 153, 157, 162, 186, 193, 196–8, 200–1, 210, 215, 217, 220, 224, 233, 238, 247
voice/voice and noise   5, 6, 13, 15, 23, 32, 43, 48, 50, 67, 74, 77, 78, 81–2,

95, 114, 121, 167, 171, 173, 177, 178, 203, 204, 208, 210, 221–3, 233–4, 237, 239, 251
voyeurism/voyeuristic 95, 107, 123, 174

war 2, 23, 27, 29, 32, 50, 64, 66–8, 78, 102, 111, 114, 129, 155, 170, 186, 189, 199, 201, 209, 214–15, 221–2, 227, 233–4
   Greek-Troy 14–15
   Iran-Iraq 2, 27, 29, 32, 199, 201, 234
   WWII 214–15, 221–33
Wells, Orson 72
Westernized/Westernization 6, 23, 42, 95, 107

Westoxicated/West-obsessed 125, 129
White Revolution/Shah-People Revolution 23, 26, 31, 56–8, 240
Woolf, Virginia 224

Yushij, Nima 14, 41, 57, 64, 251
   Moonlight Rises (Mitarāvad Mahtāb) 251

Zahhāk 15, 24, 104, 107, 118, 170, 241
Zāl 15, 16, 138, 247, 248
Zizek, Slavoj 61–2, 247
Zurkhāneh/ZUR-ḴĀNA 63, 92, 111, 144, 250

www.ingramcontent.com/pod-product-compliance
Lightning Source LLC
Chambersburg PA
CBHW052217300426
44115CB00011B/1730